STRANGE
JUSTICE

STRANGE JUSTICE

The Selling of Clarence Thomas

---❖---

JANE MAYER
AND
JILL ABRAMSON

Houghton Mifflin Company

BOSTON   NEW YORK

For information about permission to reproduce selections from this
book, write to Permissions, Houghton Mifflin Company,
215 Park Avenue South, New York, New York 10003.

Library of Congress Cataloging-in-Publication Data
Mayer, Jane.
Strange justice : the selling of Clarence Thomas /
Jane Mayer and Jill Abramson.
p.   cm.
Includes index.
ISBN 0-395-63318-4
1. Thomas, Clarence, 1948– . 2. Hill, Anita.   3. United States.
Supreme Court — Officials and employees — Selection and appointment —
History.   4. Judges — Selection and appointments — United States —
History.   I. Abramson, Jill, 1954– .   II. Title.
KF8745.T48M39 1994
347.73'2634 — dc20
94-23355   [347.3073534]   CIP

Book design by Anne Chalmers

Printed in the United States of America

AGM 10 9 8 7 6 5 4 3 2

FOR

KATE, CORNELIA, AND WILL

Contents

STRANGE
JUSTICE

Prologue

❖

IN A SMALL HOTEL SUITE with the curtains drawn against the summer sun, flanked by two lawyers, Anita Hill at last began to answer some questions. It was August 1993. For almost two years, she had refused all inquiries from the news media concerning her part in the Senate confirmation hearings of Supreme Court Justice Clarence Thomas. During those electrifying hearings, Hill had accused Thomas of sexually harassing her, describing his behavior in the most graphic of terms. Thomas had categorically denied her story then and ever since.

Hill's insistence upon remaining nearly silent about the events that brought her to national attention had, if anything, only deepened the mystery about her credibility. Her unwillingness to speak about one of the most disputed and least resolved political confrontations of the decade seemed inexplicable. In a culture that expects even presidents to answer questions about their most intimate habits, to some, it also seemed faintly incriminating.

But although she had been courted by the media with long-stemmed roses and cash, and although her friends, her distant acquaintances, and even her elderly parents had been beseeched for help in changing her mind, Hill had resolutely declined to revisit the highly charged ground she had covered during the final days of Thomas's confirmation fight in October 1991. Instead, she had largely retreated from the public eye, getting an unlisted phone number at her modest ranch house in Norman, Oklahoma, installing a security system sensitive to movement, and, when she did go out in public, sometimes rebuking autograph-seekers for violating her privacy.

Nonetheless, the debate over whether she had told the truth about the behavior of a man now sitting for life on the country's highest court raged on without her. She had become a symbol, a touchstone for political causes not necessarily her own, canonized by the left and demonized by the right. Although opinions about her were vehement, most were based more on speculation than on hard information. The public record, after all, was slim. Remarkably, given the legendary role she had assumed in the national consciousness, Hill had testified for only part of one day — October 11, 1991.

Since then, she had given several speeches, a few for lucrative fees, and had even sat for photo sessions and media interviews on rare occasions. But while she had occasionally commented on what she saw as the ramifications of her testimony, she had deflected all further inquiry into the details of her charges. Her silence was particularly conspicuous in light of revisionist interpretations of her behavior, such as the best-selling book that appeared in the spring of 1993 entitled *The Real Anita Hill*. The book's author, David Brock, provided a wealth of what he presented as evidence that Hill was chronically unbalanced, sexually aberrant, and both personally and politically motivated to lie about how Clarence Thomas had treated her.

It was in large part because of these attacks that Hill agreed to break her silence. But she was still enormously reluctant. She had not answered either of two letters she received requesting an interview. And when she did finally agree to take questions, she stipulated that the topics of discussion be screened in advance and that her lawyers, Charles Ogletree and Emma Jordan, be present. Hill also insisted that no material from the interview be quoted for attribution until she first cleared it. Without a doubt, these were rules of engagement set by a woman who felt bitter, embattled, distrustful, and deeply weary of the fight.

Now, sitting stiffly behind a desk, looking polished but uncomfortable in a tailored suit as neutral as the hotel room's decor, Hill tried to explain how pointless it seemed to her to discuss her famous allegations. The truth, as she saw it, stood little chance of triumphing in such a politically polarized atmosphere. Meanwhile, the cost to herself had been huge. "My life," she said, weighing each word cautiously, "has changed incredibly."

Hill shifted uneasily in her chair. "When the hearings were over, it was a terrible experience. I tried to continue, to go back to the classroom, but it just wouldn't die. It didn't go away. I was told this would die down by journalists and others, but it didn't." Instead, she said, as sides were taken across the country, the political controversy over her role in Thomas's confirmation battle only grew more intense. "It has become," she said with evident despair, "bigger than Thomas — it's a crusade . . . It just causes you to wonder if there is any integrity in this whole context."

During the next two and a half hours, in an effort to restore what she saw as the integrity of her own life, Hill tried to rebut, one by one, what she regarded as the false characterizations of her own actions. Slowly, haltingly, and often begrudgingly, she addressed some of the dozens of contradictions and misunderstandings that had fed her critics. There were moments of revelation — even occasionally of humor — but for the most part Hill exuded a kind of angry, edgy distrust. She refused to criticize Thomas and avoided personal attacks of the sort that had been launched against herself. She also refused to speculate on what had motivated these attacks, sticking instead to what she knew. She offered new information about her charges only with the most tortured caution, hesitantly confirming previously unknown facts even when they supported her case. Clearly these were not events she wanted to relive.

One measure of Hill's alienation was a passage she read at a colloquy at Georgetown University's Law Center a year after the hearings. Hill explained that she had taken particular comfort in the writings of Nora Zeale Hurston, whose novel *Their Eyes Were Watching God* tells the story of a black woman who is falsely accused of murdering her husband. Hill read aloud Hurston's description of the protagonist seeing "all of the colored people standing up in the back of the courtroom . . . They were all against her, she could see. So many were against her that a light slap from each would have beat her to death." She evidently saw herself reflected in this portrait of a woman falsely accused, racially ostracized, and utterly unprotected.

To be sure, she acknowledged some positive outcomes of her testimony, both in the national political sphere and in her own life. Public consciousness of sexual harassment, for instance, had risen dramatically since the hearings. And in May 1994 she would sign a million-dollar book contract, which would allow her to take a leave of absence from her teaching job and move to Los Angeles to be closer to

several of her sisters, who live there. But in this first extended interview, the adjective Hill used to describe her personal situation was
"dismal."

"I try to continue," she said. Indeed, she noted that after trying to
resist becoming further drawn into the political maelstrom her testimony had caused, she had given up and let it devour what was left of
her life. "I had to make a decision . . . whether I could spend all of
my energy trying to disengage myself, which didn't work, or try to
make something positive of this dismal situation. Basically, that's what
I have done."

But both the impact and the outcome of the hearings continued to
amaze her. "I could never have predicted at the time what was going
to happen. I can't say that I knew all along," she said, the anger rising
in her voice. "Could you?"

———◆———

Like his accuser, Clarence Thomas also let a good deal of time pass
before speaking out.

On May 1, 1993, more than a year and a half after he assumed his
seat on the Supreme Court, Thomas delivered his first major public
address. He was preceded by a bomb-sniffing dog — a security precaution more commonly associated with heads of state than Supreme
Court justices but befitting a man who also regarded himself as out-
rageously embattled, unfairly portrayed, and politically persecuted.

Thomas had hoped to make an earlier appearance at the Seton Hall
University School of Law in Newark, New Jersey, but he had been
forced to cancel it because protesters had planned a candlelight vigil.
Almost everywhere he went, his presence provoked controversy. He
had been confronted so consistently with gawkers, hecklers, and even
a giant graffito painted on the pavement across from his office —
"Anita Told The Truth" — that he told friends that his wife had suggested he wear a disguise.

But now Thomas had accepted an offer to speak from an institution
that could be counted on to be as safe as any venue could be for him,
the Walter F. George School of Law. A small southern school known
for its conservative leanings, it was affiliated with Mercer University
in Macon, Georgia. Even here, however, the justice took no chances.
Before his lunchtime address in a nearby hotel ballroom, more than a
dozen police officers and U.S. marshals — some of them wearing uni-

forms emblazoned with "Sheriff's Special Forces Special Weapons Assaults Tactics, Bibbs County, Ga." — joined the bomb-sniffing dog and combed the lobby and ballroom like Secret Service agents expecting the worst.

Thomas's speech that day left no doubt about why he saw such precautions as necessary. Since his confirmation, Thomas, like Hill, had become a target, a symbol not of justice but of injustice. To his supporters on the right, he was a victim of political correctness run amok; to his detractors on the left, he was a liar whose very presence undermined the legitimacy of the Court.

Although Thomas had, by objective standards, won the fight with Hill and now occupied one of the most prestigious and powerful posts in the country, for him the battle had not ended either. In his own eyes, he continued to be a victim — one whose reputation had been deliberately besmirched by his political enemies. Thomas had broken his silence that day to give a new name to this cabal — purveyors of the New Intolerance, he called them. His ordeal, he said, was not a result of his own actions, not a function of his treatment of Anita Hill or anyone else, but a political, racist vendetta directed toward black conservatives like himself.

"Who are the targets?" he asked. "Those who dare to question current social and cultural gimmicks . . . those who dare to disagree with the latest ideological fad . . . The purveyors of the New Intolerance spout popular buzzwords. [But] it is no different than the racial prejudice and bigotry of years past."

Thomas noted that he had first encountered this New Intolerance in his college years, when "often I heard it said that you weren't really black unless you wore your hair in an Afro . . . As a black person, straying from this [liberal] orthodoxy meant that you were a traitor to your race, you were not a real black. You would be forced to pay for your ideological trespasses, often through systematic character assassination."

And so, with an ersatz Secret Service on guard as he spoke, it was not so much assassination as character assassination that Thomas feared. As a result, he too had gone into a kind of self-imposed exile after the hearings. He rarely spoke from the bench and was hardly ever seen at establishment social gatherings in Washington. Shortly after the hearings, he and his wife sold their townhouse in suburban Virginia and purchased an isolated home almost an hour's drive from the capital. Thomas liked to boast that the house was not even visible from the road. His wife got him two large dogs, and he, like Hill, kept his phone number unlisted. Further, he made a point of telling people that he did not read the mainstream newspapers; he canceled his subscription to the *Washington Post* and instead relied largely on his wife's reports about the contents of the city's conservative alternative, the *Washington Times,* an openly ideological newspaper owned by the Reverend Sun Myung Moon. Thomas was so determinedly out of touch that associates occasionally had to tell him about important current events.

Publicly Thomas took a defiant stance. He hoped he could stay on the Court until he was a hundred and two, he told one audience, just so that he could "outlive my critics." He was called "bitter" so often that he made a joke of it in one speech, saying he had begun to badger his wife at home, asking, "Do I look bitter?" He claimed she had replied, "Nope. Weird maybe, but not bitter."

But privately, according to friends, Thomas still felt deeply hurt by his public humiliation. Indeed, although Thomas had never again spoken the name of Anita Hill in public after the hearings, those who saw him regularly said he talked about her incessantly. He granted almost no interviews but was described by associates as a man full of rage; he frequently said the job was not worth what he had had to endure in order to get it. In fact, he told Senator Orrin Hatch's biographer that he had never even wanted to be a judge in the first place. "Ideally," Justice Thomas said, "I'd like to be a truck driver or have a small business."

❖

The spectacle of these two famous combatants — retreating bitterly into their privacy, proclaiming outraged innocence and unfair victimization, and dismissing their critics as politically motivated — is only one indication of how unresolved the conflict between them remains. Rather than dying down, their clash has become part an active battlefront in America's culture wars. The fight has gone well beyond the individuals — who have been reduced to symbols and caricatures — to strike at the heart of American politics.

Three years after the confirmation hearings, opinion is more divided than ever about who was telling the truth. Yet little more has been added to the record than it was possible to glean in that single weekend of televised hearings. The proceedings had the look and feel of a comprehensive trial, but they were only one scene of a much larger drama that had been playing out for at least a decade and, some might argue, two whole lifetimes. Moreover, what was visible to the camera was just a sliver of the real story taking place outside the public's view.

Since two people with such completely contradictory accounts cannot possibly both be telling the truth, it is clear that one of them not only lied under oath but is continuing to lie. Meanwhile, the debate about which of them lied goes on: politicians, professional commentators, and ordinary citizens across the country have taken sides, often using their opinions to support a host of ancillary political arguments. But since so few new facts in this case have actually emerged, a number of fair-minded observers of American politics have concluded that the conflict will never be resolved. For instance, Professor Stephen Carter of Yale Law School has written in his book, *The Confirmation Mess:* "Among members of the generations that came of political age over the last decade, Clarence Thomas and Anita Hill are, and probably will always be, figures of similar defining magnitude [as Whittaker Chambers and Alger Hiss]. For there is no middle ground today, and for true believers of our era, there will be no middle ground thirty or forty years from now."

Certainly it is true that many of the facts in this case are open to different interpretations, leaving difficult judgment calls about whom to believe when accounts conflict, as many in this matter do. It is probably also true that unless an eyewitness to these private events emerges, no one will ever know with absolute certainty whether Hill or Thomas — if either of them — was telling the whole truth.

But after researching the history of the Thomas nomination for more than two years, after conducting hundreds of interviews, most of them on the record, and after reading thousands of pages of documents — a great many of which were never previously shared with the public — it is now possible to offer a much fuller account than might be imagined.

When judging the narrow question of who lied, Hill or Thomas, it is worth considering whether either of them ever displayed patterns of behavior that lend support to one side or the other. As Thomas argued during the hearings when questioned about his alleged harassment, "If I had used this kind of grotesque language with one person, it would seem to me that there would be . . . other individuals who heard bits and pieces of it, or various levels of it." And since no evidence to the contrary emerged during the hearings, the public was left with the impression that Hill was alone in describing this perhaps unlawful behavior on the part of a potential Supreme Court justice. But, in fact, it is possible to document a great number of "bits and pieces" of related behavior scattered throughout Thomas's life and virtually none in Hill's. It has also been possible to locate and interview a number of additional witnesses who corroborate Hill's account, suggesting that the truth in this matter favors her much more than was apparent at the time of the hearings.

But the importance of this dispute goes far beyond who was deceiving whom. If Thomas did lie under oath, as the preponderance of evidence suggests, then his performance, and that of the Senate in confirming him, raises fundamental questions about the political process that placed him on the Court. Thomas himself has acknowledged that in the first round of hearings, for reasons of political expedience, he and the White House purposefully deceived the public about who he really was and what he really believed in order to help his confirmation chances. In a recent book, Thomas's mentor, Senator John Danforth, quotes the justice as saying, "In the hearing, I played by the rules. And playing by those rules, the country has never seen the real person. There is an inherent dishonesty in the system."

As such an admission suggests, the falsehoods and distortions involved in the selling of Clarence Thomas to the American people neither started nor ended with the treatment of Anita Hill's accusations. From the beginning, the placement of Thomas on the high court was seen as a political end justifying almost any means. The full story of his confirmation thus raises questions not only about who lied and why, but, more important, about what happens when politics becomes total war and the truth — and those who tell it — are merely unfortunate sacrifices on the way to winning.

PART ONE

1

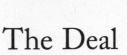

The Deal

ON OCTOBER 8, 1990, some nine months before President George Bush nominated Clarence Thomas to the U.S. Supreme Court, a private promise was made to Thomas's conservative backers: the next justice to join the high court would first and foremost be one of them.

This unusual IOU was quietly transacted at a White House reception for Bush's first choice for the high court, David Souter. The celebration was intentionally austere, in deference to the congressional budget impasse that had plunged all but the most essential government services into limbo. Under these circumstances, the two hundred justices, cabinet officers, administration officials, and personal guests at the East Room swearing-in were not even offered refreshments by a bare-bones White House staff.

Later, after Thomas was nominated, administration officials such as Attorney General Richard Thornburgh would publicly insist that ideological "litmus tests" had no place in a process as sacrosanct as the picking of a Supreme Court justice. And President Bush, too, would pay lip service to the high court's tradition of independence from political pressures, declaring that his only consideration in choosing Thomas had been to pick "the best man for the job on the merits." But on that autumn afternoon in 1990, as the Court's ideological composition teetered in the balance and the newly confirmed justice stood in the receiving line flanked by George and Barbara Bush, the next Court vacancy was being brokered in a deal that had more to do with George Bush's political ambitions than with concern for the quality of jurisprudence at the pinnacle of American law.

As he posed, smiling, for photographs with his new justice, Presi-

dent Bush was faced with an increasingly pressing problem. The right
wing of the Republican party, whose support he had inherited from
his predecessor, Ronald Reagan, and whose continued support was
essential to his hoped-for reelection, was dangerously disenchanted
with him. Even before Bush picked Souter, many conservatives were
on the brink of mutiny against his administration. They were incensed
that Bush had so cavalierly reneged on his campaign pledge "Read my
lips; no new taxes" — a promise broken the previous spring when the
White House had begun negotiating tax increases as part of the 1990
budget agreement.

Since then, Bush's relationship with conservatives had grown worse,
and Souter's appointment only exacerbated it. The Harvard alumnus
and former Rhodes Scholar, by then a member of the U.S. Court of
Appeals in Boston, was expected to be conservative, but he was also
something of a maverick, too independent to commit to any single
ideological agenda. Not even his views on abortion rights were certain. As a result, he was a severe disappointment to self-described
movement conservatives, many of them cadres of the religious right
who, having given up on passing their social agenda through the
Democratic Congress, had pinned their fondest hopes on recasting the
Supreme Court.

When Souter's nomination had been announced, Bush's chief of
staff, John Sununu, had convinced the activists not to oppose the
nominee by assuring them that, despite their doubts, he would be "a
home run" for their team. And they had dutifully cooperated, setting
aside their acute disappointment that the president had passed over
other, more ideological candidates.

But after watching Souter's confirmation hearings, many of these
activists were no longer buying the chief of staff's "home run" line.
Souter had artfully navigated his way through the hearings by refusing
to reveal his positions on any of the controversial issues facing the
Court. His so-called stealth performance, which had been coached by
the White House, had been both legally and politically dexterous. But
it had left conservative ideologues, who were still furious over the
defeat of jurist Robert Bork in 1987, feeling shortchanged and spoil-
ing for revenge. In their eyes Souter was less of a home run than, as
the conservative activist Patrick McGuigan cracked, a "bloop single."

So as the president's top aides worked their way through Souter's
swearing-in party, Sununu in particular was on the defensive. As he

entered the elegant foyer of the White House, he found himself cornered by a young, ruddy-faced conservative activist named Thomas Jipping.

Jipping was the point man on legal issues for one of the most powerful conservative organizations in the country, the Free Congress Foundation. Its leader, Paul Weyrich, was the man who first coined the phrase Moral Majority for the Reverend Jerry Falwell's organization. A charter member of the New Right, he was a leading force in the effort to promote cultural conservatism in America, an agenda including the reestablishment of school prayer and opposition to abortion and sexual promiscuity.

Weyrich wielded enormous clout in Washington; he had also founded the Heritage Foundation, a conservative think tank that supplied both policy and personnel to the Reagan Revolution. Bush and his aides found it worrisome that with its growing membership and mighty fund-raising operations, the Free Congress Foundation had by 1990 proven its ability to target and defeat candidates it found disappointing. Recently, for instance, Weyrich had led the successful campaign to kill Bush's choice for defense secretary, Senator John Tower, because Weyrich was offended by the Texan's alleged indulgences in alcohol and women. The Free Congress Foundation was not a group that the Bush White House wanted to upset, but on the afternoon of Souter's swearing-in, Jipping was upset indeed.

Sununu began the conversation by trying to rationalize the choice of Souter. He pleaded political pragmatism, pointing out that for his first Supreme Court nominee, Bush had felt that he needed someone who "wasn't a lightning rod," because at that point he couldn't afford to lose a fight over a controversial nominee. Evidently realizing how inadequate this sounded, Sununu then went a step further. "The next one," he promised, would be a true conservative. They had his word. Bush's chief of staff guaranteed that "it will be a knock-down, drag-out, bloody-knuckles, grass-roots fight."

Just nine months later, Sununu made good on his IOU. On June 27, 1991, the day that the legendary civil rights figure and only African-American Supreme Court justice in the country's history, Thurgood Marshall, surprised Washington by tendering his resignation, Sununu was on the phone to Jipping, asking for his advice on a replacement. That same evening, Jipping faxed back a detailed reply.

"From the conservative movement's perspective," he wrote, "it is crucial for President Bush to nominate a committed and recognizable conservative to succeed Justice Marshall." Jipping already had just the man, saying, "The entire conservative movement not only supports him but believes in him . . . The movement will need little energizing and will be willing to fight for him."

Jipping's candidate was a forty-three-year-old appeals court judge named Clarence Thomas.

As Jipping was arguing the obvious political advantages of appointing a black conservative to fill Marshall's seat, the aging justice himself was fretting over just this likelihood. Days shy of his eighty-third birthday, obese and wheezing, Marshall had often vowed to remain on the Court as long as the White House was occupied by a conservative president. But his mounting health problems and increasing isolation as the Court's last true liberal led him to renege. Now his worst fear was that a Republican White House, in a political move designed to disarm its liberal opponents, would replace him with a black nominee who shunned the very civil rights agenda for which Marshall had spent his life fighting.

Marshall had often ridiculed Clarence Thomas and his fellow conservatives as "the goddamn black sellouts" who directly benefited from legal remedies such as affirmative action and then denounced them. "Marshall would shake his head in wonderment that a black man who grew up in Jim Crow Georgia, and who had benefited from a thousand affirmative actions by nuns and others, and who had attended Yale Law School on a racial quota, could suddenly find affirmative action so destructive of the character of black people," observed Carl Rowan, one of the few journalists to whom Marshall granted interviews.

Marshall had bridled at Thomas's criticism of a speech he had delivered in Hawaii in 1987, when the nation was celebrating the bicentennial of the Constitution. Marshall had said that he found it hard to join in the jubilation because the honored document had excluded slaves from its enumeration of freedoms and rights. Thomas vehemently disagreed, reassuring a conservative audience that he was "wild about the Constitution."

During his final year on the bench, Marshall had grown increasingly restless and angry. His best friend and ideological soulmate, Justice

William Brennan, had retired in 1990. Brennan's replacement by Souter left Marshall as the Court's only consistently liberal voice and often as the lone dissenter on an array of critical issues — most notably the death penalty, which he passionately and consistently opposed. His dissenting opinions took on an increasingly defiant tone, though some of his legendary fighting spirit had ebbed with his health.

As a lawyer for the NAACP Legal Defense and Education Fund, Marshall had won the landmark *Brown v. Board of Education of Topeka, Kansas* decision, forcing the desegregation of America's public schools; he had also argued more than a dozen other groundbreaking civil rights cases before the Supreme Court. But now he was delegating more and more of the Court's work to his clerks. He spent some afternoons watching soap operas on the television in his chambers. During the secret conferences in which the justices discussed pending cases, Marshall was less inclined to share anecdotes about his life growing up in a segregated America, stories that had once helped to persuade his colleagues to remedy legal and social wrongs toward women and minorities.

The 1990–91 Court term had been particularly difficult and contentious. Late in the term Marshall and his clerks realized that the Rehnquist Court was about to strengthen the death penalty. For Marshall, this was the final straw. The last week in June, after confiding in a few friends, including Brennan, he informed the other justices at their final conference of the term that he intended to retire.

Two hours before he announced his resignation on June 27, Marshall released a concluding, blistering dissent. "Power, not reason, is the new currency of this court's decision-making," he wrote. "Neither the law nor the facts [in the death penalty case] underwent any change in the last four years, only the personnel of this court did." He then sent a terse letter to the White House. "The strenuous demands of Court work and its related duties required or expected of a Justice appear at this time to be incompatible with my advancing age and medical condition," he wrote to President Bush. "I, therefore, retire as an Associate Justice of the Supreme Court of the United States when my successor is qualified."

The announcement came as a thunderbolt, an unanticipated gift for conservatives and a terrible setback for liberals. Its symbolic meaning seemed clear to almost everyone: Marshall's departure would give Bush the opportunity the Reaganites had dreamed of but never realized — the creation of a solidly conservative Supreme Court majority. "All lingering doubt has been erased," noted Stephen Wermiel of the *Wall Street Journal.* "Conservatives have locked up control of the U.S. Supreme Court." Marshall's departure, Wermiel and other legal sages quickly computed, meant that liberal hopes of carving out 5–4 majorities in key cases were all but dashed. In time, a centrist coalition would change this calculation somewhat. But the enormous significance of the change virtually guaranteed a bruising political fight.

His pants hiked up, his white socks gleaming at the television cameras, Marshall faced the media the next day. A reporter asked whether he thought Bush had an obligation to appoint another minority justice in his place. "I don't think that should be a ploy," Marshall responded, "and I don't think it should be an excuse, one way or the other." The reporter immediately followed up, inquiring, "An excuse for what?" Marshall's acid response left no room for misunderstanding. Without ever uttering a name, the justice explained, "Doing wrong. I mean for picking the wrong kind of Negro . . . My dad told me way back . . . that there's no difference between a white snake and a black snake. They'll both bite."

❖

When Thomas was put forward as a possible nominee, Bush was more than receptive. He didn't actually know Thomas much better than the American public did, having talked with him privately on only a few occasions. But with no articulated judicial philosophy and no background in the law himself, Bush was so impressed by Thomas's life story that the substance of his record scarcely mattered.

First, Thomas had a compelling biography. His rise from the depths of rural poverty was an inspiring affirmation of the classic American dream. Moreover, Thomas's hard upbringing could not have been further from Bush's privileged childhood. The chance to elevate this native of humble Pin Point, Georgia, to the apex of American power was an exercise in the kind of noblesse oblige that defined Bush's concept of public service. On these emotional grounds alone, Thomas had immediately appealed to Bush when their paths had first crossed several years earlier.

Equally important, Thomas had political strengths precisely where Bush was weak. As Jipping's support indicated, the conservative judge had endeared himself to the increasingly forceful elements of the religious right then moving to assert control over many local Republican organizations around the country. This wing of the party had never entirely trusted George Herbert Walker Bush, an Episcopalian educated at Andover and Yale. Despite his insistence that he loved eating pork rinds and pitching horseshoes, Bush's country club Republicanism seemed to create an unbridgeable class and cultural divide between himself and the grass-roots social conservatives whose votes he needed. Such conservatives would never forgive or forget, for instance, that as a young Texas congressman Bush had been such an avid member of Planned Parenthood that he was nicknamed "Rubbers."

In contrast, Thomas belonged to a charismatic church in Virginia whose fundamentalist brethren at times believed they were directly possessed by holy spirits, entering trancelike states in which they talked in tongues. Although during his confirmation hearings Thomas would admit to no position on abortion, the pastor of this church once likened abortion to a holocaust. Moreover, in an effort to encourage alternatives, church donations had funded a shelter for unwed mothers next to the parsonage. Not surprisingly, Thomas's attendance at the church was viewed favorably by the religious right.

Thomas's stormy tenure as the head of the Equal Employment Opportunity Commission (EEOC) also won him points with conservatives. Not only had he opposed affirmative action as belittling to minorities, he had gone so far as to castigate members of the black civil rights establishment in harsh language no white opponent would have dared to use, accusing them of "watching the destruction of our race" as they "bitch, bitch, bitch, moan and moan, whine and whine."

With this unique résumé, Clarence Thomas was a precious political commodity. His race and background could protect George Bush and the Republican party against complaints that theirs was the party of privilege, one particularly insensitive to blacks. It would plunge liberals and black civil rights leaders — the forces most likely to oppose a Bush nominee — into a quandary based on race. And Thomas's ideological credentials could provide cover for Bush from those conservative critics who never fully trusted him. By the time Marshall resigned, this issue was even more critical than it had been when Sununu first made his promise to Jipping. In fact, it had lately become clear that if Bush couldn't placate his critics on the far right, they might mount their own presidential campaign against him, a political scenario that eventually materialized in the fratricidal challenge of the conservative candidate Patrick Buchanan in the 1992 Republican primaries.

As a consequence, Clarence Thomas was a star in a very small galaxy of black Republicans who were extraordinarily useful to the Reagan-Bush political operatives. "You knew who your friendly minorities were," explained Leigh Ann Metzger, the White House aide who served as Bush's liaison to grass-roots conservative and evangelical groups. "There weren't that many, and Clarence Thomas was one of the most prominent."

❖

This good reputation was not entirely accidental. Far more than most people realized, Thomas was himself an ambitious political networker. Indeed, he had long been planning for the day he would stand in front of the cameras and accept a Supreme Court nomination. During his fiery confirmation hearings, he would angrily declare that "I did not ask to be nominated, I did not lobby for it, I did not beg for it, I did not aspire to it." But as early as 1981 — ten years before he was appointed, when he was scarcely thirty — a number of colleagues recalled him setting his sights on Marshall's seat.

"The first day I met him in 1981, he told me he was going to be on the Supreme Court," said Michael Middleton, who was Thomas's principal deputy at the Department of Education and went on to be Thomas's associate general counsel at the EEOC. "He'd point out that Marshall wouldn't last forever, and that he [Thomas] was the highest-ranking black lawyer in government, that he had a Yale Law degree, and he had Senator Danforth behind him. No one else, he'd say, was in as good a position."

Despite his eagerness, Thomas had been passed over when President Reagan filled several vacancies on the U.S. Court of Appeals in Washington, which was viewed as a likely steppingstone to the Supreme Court. Some in the Meese Justice Department had disparaged Thomas's legal scholarship. Others doubted his loyalty, in part because of a 1987 speech in which Thomas complained that in order to win acceptance in conservative ranks, "a black was required to become a caricature of sorts, providing sideshows of anti-black quips and attacks."

So as the Reagan years drew to a close, Thomas shrewdly began to build his own bridges to Bush. He had a mutual friend introduce him to Edward Lawson, a strategically placed Oklahoma oilman who was one of Bush's top money men. Impressed by the articulate and earnest black conservative, Lawson arranged for Thomas to have what is believed to be his only private session with Bush before his nomination. This, in turn, led to assignments for Thomas in Bush's presidential quest.

Bush was anxious to include blacks in his 1988 campaign, according to political aides, and he quickly saw the advantage of working with Thomas. And Thomas proved adept at making himself useful. That summer he helped Bush write a speech for the annual convention of the NAACP. Bush wanted to convey a spirit of inclusion to minorities, part of the "kinder and gentler" America he would evoke at the Republican National Convention in New Orleans later that summer. In the speech, Bush clearly distanced himself from the Reagan administration's controversial civil rights record, promising, in words the EEOC chairman helped provide, that he would have "a positive civil rights agenda" if elected president. "I guarantee you I will be personally involved in protecting the civil rights of all Americans," Bush pledged, drawing an ovation.

After the NAACP meeting, Thomas attended the Republican convention as a member of one of Bush's caucus teams. Other blacks were not much in evidence. Of the 2,277 delegates, fewer than 100 were black. At a reception for black Reagan-Bush appointees — of which there were not many to begin with — Clarence Thomas was one of three minority appointees in attendance. Even so, he gamely gave a short speech on behalf of "all the Reagan administration minority appointments" present.

Such loyalty paid off. When Bush ascended to the presidency, one of his first important judicial decisions was to put Thomas on the prestigious D.C. Circuit. Special precautions were taken during the nomination process, including the highly unusual step of having Thomas go through "murder boards," the legal cram sessions run by administration lawyers that were usually reserved for Supreme Court nominees. This attentiveness caused at least one of the lawyers who worked on Thomas's nomination to figure that the black conservative was surely being groomed for the Supreme Court.

In fact, when Justice Brennan's seat opened up in 1990, George Bush expressed serious interest in the notion of putting Thomas, instead of Souter, on the Supreme Court. But the president's legal advisers convinced him that Thomas was so inexperienced that he would be unsalable. The president's advisers warned Bush that the American Bar Association (ABA), which rated the qualifications of federal judges, would almost certainly find Thomas unqualified, perhaps dooming his chances for the Supreme Court forever.

Less than a year later, under growing pressure from conservatives, any such reservations were overlooked.

❖

On Monday, July 1, 1991, just before the Fourth of July weekend, President Bush summoned Thomas to his oceanside home in Kenne-bunkport, Maine. In an upstairs bedroom of the seaside "cottage," as the Bush family modestly referred to their sprawling estate, the president offered Thomas the chance to become the second African-American in history to serve on the Supreme Court. Then, in an outdoor ceremony before a battery of television cameras, Thomas was introduced to the American people.

"Only in America could this have been possible," said Thomas in his acceptance speech. "As a child I could not dare dream that I would ever see the Supreme Court, not to mention be nominated to it." Tears welled up in his eyes as he thanked his grandparents and the Catholic nuns who he said had instilled in him the faith and discipline necessary to survive and triumph in the South of Jim Crow. Bush too shed a few tears; later, he confided in Wyoming's Senator Alan Simpson that he had never been more moved by a speech. Dignified, eloquent, and the virtual embodiment of American egalitarianism, Thomas seemed a shoo-in no matter how controversial his views. As Senator Orrin Hatch of Utah, a Republican supporter, warned, "Anyone who takes him on on the subject of civil rights is taking on the grandson of a sharecropper."

Bush was apparently so carried away that, when he stepped up to the microphones, he fumbled what should have been a political touchdown by garbling his message. His written speech carefully described Thomas as "the best man" for the position, a broad commendation that covered Thomas's whole remarkable life. But while responding to reporters' questions, Bush instead blurted out that Thomas was "the best qualified" person for the job — focusing attention on more conventional professional criteria, which Thomas might not meet. By substituting the wrong words, the president inadvertently raised the bar for Thomas's appearance before the Judiciary Committee.

In many ways Thomas was inspirational and impressive, but clearly he was not, as Bush insisted, the "best qualified" lawyer in the nation to sit on its highest court. Thomas had been on the bench for less than two years. It had been more than a decade since he had practiced law, and then only briefly at entry-level jobs. In contrast to Marshall, who had been a legendary litigator as well as a federal judge and U.S. solicitor general before his appointment to the Court by Lyndon Johnson, Thomas had never litigated a case before a jury. Nor, during his brief stint as a judge, had he issued a single substantive constitutional opinion. Yet on the Supreme Court, he would be one of nine ultimate arbiters of the Constitution's interpretation.

Moreover, Bush's assertion that "the fact that he is black and a minority had nothing to do with this" was so disingenuous as to be embarrassing. While ostensibly opposing racial quotas and other forms of affirmative action, the White House's only serious candidates to replace Marshall had been other minorities. Conceding the obvious, Senator Joseph Biden, the chairman of the Senate Judiciary Committee, later acknowledged, "Had Thomas been white, he never would have been nominated. The only reason he is on the Court is because he is black."

❖

In Whittier, California, far from the center of political action, the news of Clarence Thomas's nomination set off a chain of events that would prove no less historic than the public ceremony in Kennebunkport.

Forty-seven-year-old Susan Jane Hoerchner and her husband, Frederick Bray, had just returned home to their condominium from a day of dealing with routine administrative cases as workers' compensation judges for the state in nearby Norwalk. As Hoerchner turned on the television to listen to the news, her husband stood at the side of the room.

Hoerchner, a graduate of Yale Law School, had long before mentioned to her husband that she knew of a top government official in Washington who had sexually harassed one of her closest friends from law school. She had said that the transgression was all the more shocking because the official was charged with enforcing federal laws against sexual harassment. But because of a decade-old pledge of confidentiality, she had never revealed the name of the official or her friend.

Now, as the newscaster showed clips of the cheerful ceremony in Kennebunkport and the name Clarence Thomas was announced, Hoerchner was horrified. "The main thing I remember is hearing the name," she later recalled. "Then they gave his background," with the newscaster reciting the details of Thomas's illustrious résumé. As she listened, Hoerchner cried out to her husband, "He's the one!"

A sensitive, bespectacled woman with a thatch of strawberry blond hair and a blotchy complexion that often colored with emotion, Hoerchner was easily flustered. She thought of her old friend, Anita Hill, whom Hoerchner assumed must be terribly upset by the news. She recalled how "devastated" her friend had been by the behavior of the boss she admired. Swearing her to secrecy, Hill had confided in Hoerchner during a wrenching telephone conversation that "her boss, Clarence," had repeatedly pressed her to date him and had sexually harassed her at work. The conversation was unforgettable, not only because of the disturbing revelation but because it was the first time Hoerchner had ever heard anyone she knew use the term "sexual harassment."

Although Hoerchner had last seen Hill at a professional conference at the Hilton Hotel in Washington in late 1984, she still considered the Oklahoma lawyer a close friend. They had met in 1978 when Hoerchner was Hill's editor on a Yale Legislative Services project. Hoerchner was one of the oldest students in the class, having entered law school at the age of thirty-three after earning a doctorate in American studies at Emory University in Atlanta. On the surface, the bookish Hoerchner, who was shy, had little in common with the popular Hill, but they had both had more personal difficulties than the average Yale law student. Hill had grown up in poverty, on a farm without indoor plumbing, the youngest of thirteen children. Hoerchner had also lacked many of life's amenities, as the daughter of a surveyor in Chico, California. She and her family had lived in log cabins and moved constantly. By the time she reached college, she had attended eleven different schools.

At Yale, despite an age difference of more than ten years, Hoerchner and Hill became close. Hill was eclectic in her friendships. She was at the center of a tight group of black women, including Sonia Jarvis, Ivy McKinney, Kim Taylor, and Wandra Mitchell. But she also coached a coed basketball squad that included white men like Gary Phillips, who was also one of her best friends. When she arrived at Yale, she was engaged to a blond and blue-eyed man from Oklahoma. The interracial aspect of the relationship upset her parents, but even after the engagement was broken, Hill continued the friendship. At Hill's law school graduation party, Hoerchner and Hill's boyfriend joked to each other that they were the only "palefaces" invited.

Hoerchner recalled Hill as one of those people who like to please everyone, very social, not political. One of Hill's best female friends from Yale remembered teasing her when they went grocery shopping for a dinner party and Hill picked a pallid frozen quiche. "That's so bland!" her friend complained. "That's right," Hill responded. "I don't want to offend any sensibilities." Hoerchner wasn't fond of controversy, either, nor was she much of a joiner. The most political thing she had ever done was to attend Martin Luther King Jr.'s funeral in Atlanta in 1968, while she was at Emory.

Neither of them liked to offend, but Hoerchner wondered whether Hill might now feel compelled to reveal her secret. Hoerchner was intensely curious about Hill's reaction and felt she had to at least try to reach her friend. "When anything really shocking happens in public life, many people's first reaction is to start calling their relatives," Hoerchner later explained. "In my case it was shock, a desire to get in touch with the one person I knew would be affected, to see how she took it."

Getting in touch with Hill might not be easy, Hoerchner realized. Once, when she was traveling through Tulsa, she had tried but failed to obtain Hill's telephone number. At her tenth Yale reunion, in 1990, Hoerchner had asked their mutual friend Ron Allen, the class reunion coordinator, for Hill's current whereabouts. Although Hill missed the reunion because she was in Germany, Hoerchner remembered Allen's saying that Hill now had a permanent teaching position at the state law school in Norman, Oklahoma. Hoerchner picked up the phone and got Hill's telephone number from information.

Hill, also home from work, answered on Hoerchner's first try.

"Well, have you heard the news?" Hoerchner asked.

Indeed, she had, Hill replied. Her nephew Gary Lee was a reporter for the *Washington Post*. Knowing that she had worked for Thomas but not knowing many of the details, he had called to discuss the nomination. He had also asked permission to pass her name on to a colleague covering the story, who might want to hear her observations on the former EEOC chairman. Ever since this troubling call, Hill had thought of little else.

"Are you going to say anything?" Hoerchner asked.

For years, as Thomas had risen meteorically in public life, Hill had kept virtually silent about her problems with him. When he was appointed to the court of appeals, she hadn't felt the slightest urge to come forward. Now that he was about to be elevated to the most prestigious court in the country, she felt personally and professionally dismayed, but she had long before decided, for reasons that would become plain, not to get involved.

Hoerchner was somewhat puzzled by Hill's explanation of why she had chosen to keep her problems with Thomas to herself. Hill told Hoerchner that she had been "appalled" by the treatment their old Yale professor Robert Bork had received during his abortive confirmation hearings for the Supreme Court in 1987. She didn't want to see another nominee ripped apart on the basis of his personal character. "Bork and Thomas should stand or fall on their ideas," Hill told her friend.

Then Hoerchner asked to be released from the secrecy pledge she had sworn to Hill years before. "I took my promise quite seriously," Hoerchner later explained. But she was eager to tell her husband about the entire episode, including Hill's identity. Beyond that, she had no intention of sharing the news about Thomas. She would take her cues from Hill, who granted her request but clearly wanted the episode kept confidential.

The conversation moved to other topics; Hoerchner was glad to hear that Hill's parents were both still alive and active. Then they hung up. That was that, Hoerchner thought.

❖

In Washington, Kenneth Duberstein, the outside lobbyist whom Bush and Sununu had asked to serve as chief salesman in the Thomas confirmation, was watching the Kennebunkport ceremony on television. He was worried by Bush's description of Thomas as the best-qualified candidate in the country. Duberstein would be reenacting the role he had played in the flawless confirmation of David Souter: a veteran of the Reagan White House, he had fashioned the "stealth" strategy that had worked so well for Souter. But given Clarence Thomas's paper trail of controversial conservative political speeches and writings, the job would be harder this time. And with the bungled "best qualified" line, Thomas would not only have to smooth the contours of his ideology, he would have to come off as a dazzling legal thinker as well. It was enough to give the pretzel-loving lobbyist heartburn.

Only days after his nomination, Thomas walked into Duberstein's well-appointed lobbying firm in the heart of downtown Washington for the first of several critical strategy sessions. The office, in a modern luxury high-rise, was dark, quiet, and coolly anonymous, but the services rendered were highly personal. Deputizing an unelected, private lobbyist such as Duberstein to commandeer one of the administration's most sensitive political battles simply reflected the reality of power in Washington in 1991. By the end of the 1980s, many of the paid consultants who had become fixtures in political campaigns a decade earlier had realized that there was even better money to be made in the corporate sector, advising businesses that needed to know which levers to pull in Washington. And a lucky few of these consultants, like Duberstein, managed to cross-fertilize their clients, representing both business people and politicians at the same time. It was a natural symbiosis, since in the capital, businesses needed campaigns to win favorable legislation, and campaigns required so much money they had become businesses.

The Duberstein Group charged blue-chip clients, including General Motors and Aetna Insurance, annual retainers of $250,000 or more for using its political contacts to secure legislative favors. However, for its best advice, Duberstein charged the White House nothing at all. But the pro bono practice had obvious advantages. The corporate clients were impressed by the lobbyist's political clout, which helped them gain access to the top levels of the Bush administration.

Although the White House had its own staff dedicated to handling congressional issues such as confirmations, Duberstein had a lot more influence inside the Senate. He had begun his career in government working for Senator Jacob Javits of New York and ended it rehabilitating the battered image of Ronald Reagan after the Iran-Contra affair, serving as his last chief of staff. A jocular, roly-poly charmer, Duberstein had even managed to win over the notoriously prickly Nancy Reagan. Although he could seem as huggable as a teddy bear, occasionally his bemused brown eyes narrowed to an intense glare, revealing a touch of grizzly underneath.

It was clearly a difficult and awkward circumstance that brought the lobbyist from Brooklyn and the nominee raised in Georgia together that July. Duberstein needed to vet every aspect of Clarence Thomas's life. Any skeletons, he knew, were probably well buried. Thomas had, after all, been through four Senate confirmation hearings since 1981. But Duberstein knew all too well that the level of scrutiny directed at a Supreme Court nominee was of an altogether different order of magnitude. The Court had become such an ideological battleground that interest groups on all sides would be culling Thomas's record for ammunition. The lobbyist also knew that when hundreds of reporters and interest group investigators dug for dirt at the same time, they would likely come up with a few surprises. He wanted to know about those surprises ahead of time.

His forte was in defusing negative rumors before they ever exploded into news accounts that could reach the public. During the Souter confirmation, for instance, Duberstein had spent weeks quietly trying to convince reporters that the judge, a bachelor who lived near his mother in New Hampshire, was neither a stand-in for Anthony Perkins in *Psycho* nor a homosexual. Although the public never got wind of his machinations, Duberstein had deftly extinguished the latter rumor by circulating to newspaper reporters — completely off the record, so not for publication or attribution to the White House — the name of a woman whom, it seemed, Souter had once dated seriously.

Such early defensive maneuvers were the lesson learned both from recent presidential campaigns and from the 1987 battle over Robert Bork, which Duberstein had experienced as a senior White House official. The Reagan White House had allowed Bork's opponents to caricature him, without a swift rebuttal, as a hardhearted, fringe conservative far outside the mainstream of constitutional legal thinking. Bork's poorly defended nomination had haunted all subsequent confirmation efforts. Thus, with Souter, Duberstein had mobilized early, making sure he left no charge unanswered — preferably before it reached the newspapers.

Already, one such poisonous rumor about Thomas — that he had physically abused his first wife, Kathy Ambush Thomas — had begun to circulate around town. But administration officials had interviewed

Thomas's former in-laws and the former Mrs. Thomas herself before naming him, and they had been assured that the Thomases' divorce had been routine. Moreover, Thomas had been granted custody of their son, Jamal, which would have been improbable if there had been physical abuse in the marriage. Still, the rumor was a warning flag. Thomas himself was so nervous about what might be dug up about him that almost as soon as he was nominated, he felt as though "you're waiting in the wilderness for someone with guns to find and kill you." His sense of impending doom became so great, he found himself literally peering through the windows of his suburban town-house, looking for assassins.

But on that day in early July, it was Duberstein who was stalking his past. He stared Thomas in the eye and asked him if there was anything that could come back to haunt him. The nominee assured him that beyond some provocative speeches and writings, there was nothing. Or almost.

Despite his active participation in college athletics and an ability even now to bench-press 250 pounds, Thomas, it turned out, had managed to get a draft deferment for "curvature of the spine," which enabled him to avoid military service in Vietnam. He also admitted that, as he had previously told the FBI, he had taken "a few puffs" of marijuana as a student. The illegal use of marijuana had been enough to torpedo another Supreme Court nominee, Douglas Ginsburg. But in Duberstein's capable hands, both of these potential problems would be contained brushfires, portrayed carefully to sympathetic reporters as youthful indiscretions of the kind that would bar the entire baby boom generation from holding office. Under his supervision, the White House itself would leak the marijuana story, which Duberstein portrayed to a reporter as nothing more than a one-time experiment.

Duberstein even saw a way to play another potential scandal in his client's favor. Someone told the *New York Times* that Thomas had kept a Confederate flag in his office — an insult to the civil rights community in particular and African-Americans in general. When Duberstein and a Justice Department official checked the story with Thomas, they discovered that in fact it was the Georgia state flag, which incorporates the Stars and Bars motif. Recognizing that the mistake was, as the Justice Department official later put it, "a gift," they decided to fax the stories about the misidentification immediately to the office of Georgia's Senator Sam Nunn, whose support of

Thomas they very much wanted. Nunn, they calculated, would be drawn to a native son so loyal that he displayed the state's flag in his office — even as he would be annoyed at the unfairness of the liberal media, which, as usual, did not understand how to portray the South.

Deft though these early maneuvers were, Duberstein knew they were merely the opening skirmishes in what promised to be an extraordinarily difficult fight. Already, he was acutely aware of one fundamental problem: although the nominee was in many ways personally impressive, in Duberstein's view Thomas did not have a legal mind of the same caliber as Souter's.

◆

The week after the July Fourth holiday, Thomas went to the White House to meet the legal coaches and squads of other political foot soldiers whom Duberstein would deploy on his behalf. The guards didn't recognize him when he arrived at the White House's wrought-iron gate. Only after presenting his Virginia driver's license could the stocky, bespectacled judge gain entrance to the office of Chief of Staff Sununu, where a meeting was being held for his benefit.

There, following an enthusiastic ovation, Thomas was formally introduced to the nearly twenty White House and Justice Department "handlers" whose job would be to join Duberstein's efforts to sell him over the next two months. Each had his area of specialization, including one person assigned to ghost-write op-ed newspaper pieces endorsing Thomas.

As this ploy suggested, the White House realized it would not be enough for Duberstein to wage a brilliant defense. A vigorous offense and a clear message would also be needed. As an administration official told the *Washington Post,* "Think of it like a presidential campaign. We have a compressed period of time in which we will make the case that our candidate is decent, honest, qualified, intelligent and fair. They [the opposition] will try to make the case that he is ultra-conservative, against women and minorities, unqualified and a little strange. Our job, as it is in any campaign, is to block their message or at least dilute it and get ours out."

In essence, the campaign wouldn't be unlike that of a Madison Avenue advertising firm pitching a new product. But a certain delicacy was required. Much of the lobbying and politicking would have to be done without any visible connection to the administration, since the White House had to maintain the appearance that the Supreme Court and Clarence Thomas himself were above politics. For now, he would have to be completely sequestered from the press and the public, maintaining a decorous distance from his own campaign. And so, after the greetings were over, Thomas was escorted out of Sununu's office before the political talk began.

Sununu then took command. A gruff, imperious man, he peered out at the group and demanded, "So what's our game plan?"

The handful of young conservative lawyers from the White House counsel's office who had pushed hard for Thomas were tempted to present him as a hard-edged ideologue of their own ilk. The confirmation battle would be a brave and exciting holy war.

But Attorney General Richard Thornburgh, who was preparing to run for the Senate from Pennsylvania, had serious doubts about whether Thomas would be, as he put it, confirmable if the extremism of his views was fully revealed to the public. Thomas's beliefs, according to this calculation, were certain to ignite a storm of opposition among women's groups, which were ready to fight any nominee who could endanger the legality of abortion. And as a conservative who bucked the orthodoxy of the liberal establishment and stood with Ronald Reagan against affirmative action, Thomas could also easily inflame the civil rights groups that had served as the linchpin of the coalition that had defeated Bork. Thomas may have been chosen in order to appease the right wing, but from this point on, in order to get through the Democratic Senate, he would have to appease everyone else. A campaign of ideas wouldn't do.

Thornburgh nudged his aide, a tall, silver-haired, little-known Justice Department lobbyist named John Mackey, and urged him, "You talk."

Mackey had come to know Thomas and his record by working on his nomination to the appeals court. Thomas had proven to be a skillful politician, in Mackey's estimation. He had softened his ideological edges, even reaching out to civil rights leaders, and he had courted moderate Democratic senators when necessary. What had impressed Mackey most was that once Thomas started talking about his deprived childhood, opponents usually melted. Mackey had been astonished by the power of his life story. "From the outhouse to the courthouse — everybody loved that," he later observed. Unlike everyone else in the room, he had been through this before with Thomas, and he knew that the safest and best strategy was to bury ideology and sell biography.

"Just keep getting his personal story out," Mackey told the group. "Tell the Pin Point story."

2

❖

The Pin Point
Reality

WELL BEFORE the White House handlers seized on the Pin Point strategy as the best way to sell him to the outside world, Clarence Thomas had demonstrated a canny sense that his future lay in mythologizing his past. Like Abraham Lincoln, who has been called both "the first author and the greatest dramatist" of his own log cabin legend, Thomas understood early in his career that the story of his rise from poverty would resonate deeply in a country that prizes self-sufficiency and hard-won success.

By the mid-1980s, when he was still a relatively unknown official in the Reagan administration, Thomas had begun to give a series of moving autobiographical speeches and interviews describing the searing pain he had suffered growing up poor and black in the South. Although he could appear formal and awkward in official settings, he seemed to lose his inhibitions when recounting the stinging slights and the backbreaking work he, his young mother, and his grandparents had endured — the sweltering rides they were forced to take in the back of segregated buses, and the long hours he himself had worked, rising before dawn and studying at the kitchen table late into the night, accompanied only by the early tunes of the Supremes on the radio.

In the two administrations Thomas served, both of which were clubs composed largely of white and privileged men of means, his emphasis on his deprived background gained him attention and set him apart. This was true even among the handful of other black officials working for Reagan and Bush, most of whom were well connected and well born, scions of black Republican families some of whose political antecedents could be traced back to the days of Lincoln. Only Ronald Reagan, the son of an alcoholic shoe salesman, surpassed Thomas in his knack for transforming heartrending personal anecdote into high political art.

Thus, well before his character was championed by George Bush as "a model for all Americans" or challenged by Anita Hill as less than suitable for the Supreme Court, Clarence Thomas had already defined his political qualifications less in terms of his work than of his life. His emphasis was not on how he had acted to right the world's wrongs but, rather, on how he had advanced despite them. In his speeches, his success served as his best argument for political conservatism. Thomas described his solitary climb with no outside help from origins far worse than Lincoln's log cabin as his ultimate credential, more meaningful, he told graduates of Savannah State College in a typical commencement address, than all of his other degrees from "elite" schools combined.

As he explained in another speech, on the occasion of his son's high school graduation, "Honesty, hard work, discipline, and I would throw in chastity, obedience and humility" were the only means of his survival. "These are the things my grandparents and the nuns pushed and which I hated, but which worked. But for them, God knows where I would be. Probably dead."

His success, he emphasized, owed nothing to the government — a point he used to buttress his opposition to the welfare state. Having made it on his own, he believed other disadvantaged Americans should too. As he told a gathering of the Chamber of Commerce in Palm Beach, Florida, in 1988, "We [blacks in the South] learned to fend for ourselves in a hostile environment . . . not only without the active assistance of government, but with its opposition."

Like all myths, however, Thomas's telling of his life story was trimmed for drama and emphasis. The reality was both more complicated and more interesting. In the end, what he edited out may be as important as what he left in.

Thomas was born to a woman whose life was, without a doubt, as hard as almost any in America. Leola Williams (as she was later known) was born illegitimate, and her mother died in childbirth when Leola was only three. Her father, Myers Anderson, wanted little to do with his daughter, so after her mother's death Leola was sent to Pin

Point, Georgia, fifteen miles southeast of Savannah, where she was brought up by a strict, illiterate maternal aunt. Aunt Annie, as she was called, kept Leola from playing with other children, forced her to keep house, and in other ways, as Leola put it, "was real hard on me." Leola said she "never got over" the loss of her parents. She longed so badly for the things other children had, she resorted to making baby dolls out of clumps of weeds, washing the roots for hair. At the age of twelve, she finally got her first real doll, only to have it taken away as punishment by her aunt. Four years later she became pregnant, dropped out of school, and soon was cradling a real child in her arms, Clarence's older sister, Emma Mae.

On June 23, 1948, Leola — still a teenager — gave birth to her second child and first son. Clarence was born in a rough wooden shack on the edge of a lush and humid tidal marsh. The walls were insulated only with newspapers and caulked with library paste mixed from flour and water. Instead of electricity there were kerosene lamps, and instead of plumbing, an outhouse. Thomas's mother was attended by a midwife, of whom she later said, "They stuck by you, but oh, did you feel the pain."

A little more than a year after Clarence's birth, Leola's third child, a boy named Myers, was born. And when the children were still what Leola called "hand babies" — requiring constant care — their father, M. C. Thomas, a maintenance man at a local dairy, deserted them. The reason, Leola learned, was that he had impregnated another woman, whose father threatened to shoot him if he didn't marry her. Some years later, Leola would hear from the children's grandfather that her children's father had spawned a third family as well.

It was unclear to neighbors and friends whether any of M. C. Thomas's unions were legal. What was clear was that, at least in Leola's case, the marriage involved an unplanned pregnancy and never seemed meant to last. "We didn't know anything about birth control or where babies came from," she later explained. And "when you got pregnant, you just had it." Once pregnant, though, she recalled telling the aunt who took care of her, "You can make me marry [the father], but you can't make me stay with him."

It was a humiliating situation for Leola and her children in the tiny, Baptist, churchgoing community of Pin Point, a settlement of a few dozen black families founded by freed slaves shortly after the Civil War. Most of them eked out a marginal living beneath the moss-covered oak trees by fishing for oysters and crabs. Despite the poverty, the community's social mores were traditional, making desertion and illegitimacy unusual. "It certainly wasn't usual so far as I was concerned" is how one former neighbor from Pin Point, Thad Harris, put it.

Throughout Clarence's childhood, the boy's father was a painful absence, gone without explanation, as far as the children knew. After he departed, Leola was forced to leave Clarence and his siblings with the same Aunt Annie who had made her own childhood such a misery while she went into Savannah to work for a white family as a servant, earning $14 a day. Their father never visited, called, or wrote, and Leola rarely spoke of him. But, she recalled, the children never stopped asking her, "Why'd he do it? Why'd he leave?" The awkwardness must have been compounded by the fact that their father's father still lived in their tiny hamlet and drove the school bus.

In later life, Clarence Thomas launched a successful search for his lost father, who had settled in Philadelphia. And, to Leola's chagrin, the Bush White House arranged for the now white-haired old man to attend its gala celebration on the South Lawn after Thomas was confirmed to the Supreme Court. Earlier, however, Thomas rarely spoke of his father other than in brief, bitter terms. One colleague in Washington recalls that after a twenty-minute conversation, Thomas turned to him and interjected, "You know, I've just spent more time talking with you than I have talked with my own father in my whole lifetime."

"What whites don't realize," said a black journalist who came to know Thomas fairly well, "is that [he] is not just a black guy alienated in a white world. He starts out as a little black boy not accepted in the black world. He has no money, no family . . . This puts him at the bottom of the pecking order among southern blacks, a community that is far more close-minded and rigid than many whites imagine. As soon as he was born, he was just out there, a floater."

Indeed, abandonment had been a recurring theme in generations of Thomas's family. His great-great-grandmother had been born a slave in nearby Liberty County and emancipated at the age of nine. In time, she had a son who abandoned his young children, leaving them in her care. One of these children was Myers Anderson, Thomas's grandfather, who found his own father's desertion so painful, relatives say, that he refused ever to speak of him. And although Myers Anderson eventually became a respected member of the community and a role model so powerful that Thomas would later refer to him in speeches as "the strongest man in the world," at a young age he too sired and then abandoned an illegitimate child, Leola, who became Thomas's mother.

As an adult, Thomas would sermonize on the ostensibly strict "family values" and old-fashioned morality that helped him survive poverty, even suggesting in one speech that "when I grew up, there was more a feeling of responsibility for kids that you brought into the world . . . These were values you learned . . . the government didn't have a damn thing to do about it." Yet given his family history, this self-portrait seems more wishful than factual.

It was this world of hardship and exclusion that Thomas so movingly recalled in his later speeches. Pin Point was best captured by a South Georgia saying that one worked "from can't to can't," meaning from the time one can't see in the morning until the time one can't see at night. In all directions, its horizons were limited. The labor was manual and hard, the hours long, and the pay pitiful. Thomas's mother, like most of the women in Pin Point, began her working life picking the meat out of crab shells and heading shrimp at the A. S. Varn processing plant, a collection of rusty shacks at the water's edge. Leola started working there at the age of nine; although there were child labor laws, she said the plant's owner paid little attention to them, hiding the young children on the rare occasion that inspectors came by. Education at the segregated public school was a luxury enjoyed between work shifts; health care, child care, social security, and other government programs designed to ease the burdens of poverty, infirmity, and old age were scarcely heard of.

The world beyond Pin Point was essentially off-limits — a white world of "can'ts." It was racially segregated by Jim Crow laws, under which African-Americans were legally excluded from almost all the privileges of citizenship they had won after the Civil War. They were barred from such civic amenities as public beaches, libraries, and parks. They were effectively, if not explicitly, deprived of the vote by white primaries, poll taxes, and literacy tests. And their relegation to second-class citizenry was so regimented, they not only had to enter separate doors and attend separate schools, they were required to swear to tell the truth using separate Bibles when appearing in court.

Chatham County, in which Savannah was located, had a history of slightly more enlightened racial attitudes than the rest of Georgia, stemming from its days as a busy port through which a number of Caribbean and other free blacks had passed. For instance, no lynching had ever been recorded in the county. Even so, Savannah's few timid nods to its black population were undermined by crude racism. In 1947, for example, the year before Thomas was born, the city became the first in the Deep South to allow black men on the police force. But the "colored" officers were barred from carrying firearms — and from arresting white suspects.

"The white and the black were two separate worlds," recalled W. W. Law, a prominent leader of the NAACP in Savannah when Thomas was a boy. "Blacks had no participation in city hall and very little participation in public life — they were only allowed in as messengers, custodians," domestics, and in similar roles. "When a black had to go into the white world, he knew how to conduct himself — he'd have to be careful when going into a bank or a store not even to brush up against a white person. More important, a black man could not be found in a situation where a white woman could claim rape, because a white person's word would be taken at face value, and a black person would be assumed to be lying." It was, in short, the incarnation of Chief Justice Roger Taney's infamous 1857 ruling in the Dred Scott case: "A Negro has no rights which a white man need respect."

But if Thomas's prospects during his early childhood were bleak, they improved dramatically in 1955, when he was six. Oddly, a family tragedy proved to be his salvation. On a cold morning when his mother had left for her domestic job in Savannah, he and his brother accidentally set the house on fire, apparently igniting the curtains in the wood stove. Within minutes the shack had burned to the ground, leaving the family destitute. Thad Harris, the neighbor who was a carpenter, helped borrow the money to build a new home for the family. But Clarence Thomas never lived there or anywhere else in Pin Point again.

In the following months, Thomas's mother took the boys to live with her in a squalid tenement in one of the black neighborhoods that ring Savannah's historic mansions. There they lived in a one-room apartment with a shared outdoor toilet. Ultimately, as she told it, she found conditions too much to bear and begged her father to help.

Thomas's recollection of how Myers Anderson came to intercede is somewhat different. He has told a number of people over the years that at about that time his mother became romantically involved with a man who had no interest in taking on her children. As his friend Michael Middleton remembers it, Thomas "told me his mother dumped him and his brother on the grandfather because she'd met some man." So by the age of seven, Clarence Thomas had been abandoned by both parents.

Thomas's grandfather, according to Leola Williams, did not step in happily. "I asked Daddy if he'd help me with the kids," she recalled. "He said 'NO!' I just went off crying." Myers Anderson was a stern and forbidding presence, so disapproving of her, she said, "all he had to do was look at me and I'd cry." But according to Leola, Anderson's wife, Christine, threatened to leave him if he didn't help with the grandchildren, and finally he agreed.

The hardships preceding this adoption were undoubtedly seared deeply into Thomas and may partially explain the sense of victimization he later exhibited. In particular, the abandonment by his mother upset him deeply, according to many who knew him over the years. Indeed, a frequent observation of women who encountered Thomas as an adult was that he still seemed very angry at his mother.

❖

At the moment that Myers Anderson took the first-grader and his brother in, Clarence Thomas entered an entirely different world, one far more middle class than what he publicly portrayed in his later speeches and writings.

If life in Pin Point was defined by the phrase "from can't to can't," life with Anderson was equally defined by his own favorite saying, "Old Man Can't is dead; I just helped bury him." Where passivity and poverty had characterized Leola's world, iron-willed determination in the face of endless obstacles characterized that of Myers Anderson, whom Thomas would later cite as the single greatest influence in his life.

Anderson had never gone beyond third grade, but he was an intelligent and driven man. In 1929 he moved from rural Liberty County, where he had inherited the family's plot of farmland, to Savannah, there turning a pushcart he built and pulled himself through the cobblestone streets into a small but successful coal, oil, and ice delivery business. His work habits were legendary, and his success, given his limited means, was remarkable. In addition to running the delivery business and the small farm, he built and managed several rental houses. He wanted to expand into the building business, but the city denied him a permit to make cement, he believed because of his race.

Raised a Baptist, Myers Anderson converted to Catholicism, partly because it entitled his grandsons to attend parochial schools at a reduced tuition. He told them again and again that he had been unable to get any further, so he was counting on them to do better. He was so intent on their getting a good education, he said that if they died, he'd drag them to class anyway for three days, just to make sure they weren't faking. A favorite saying of his was "Hard times make monkey eat cayenne pepper," and it seems that, in his demanding hands, both boys learned to swallow quite a lot.

By all accounts, Thomas's grandfather was an exceedingly stern taskmaster, determined to teach his grandsons the value of hard work but uncomfortable when it came to providing affection or even conversation. Although Thomas later praised his grandfather fondly, acquaintances said that in his early years he sometimes complained of the tough treatment in his home. He told several colleagues at the EEOC that his grandfather rarely spoke to him as a boy other than to order him to do some chore. And a Yale Law School colleague said that he was surprised by Thomas's exaltation of his grandfather during the confirmation hearings; in school he had talked about how hard his grandfather had been on him, physically and otherwise, specifically mentioning that if he and his brother so much as overslept, "they'd have the shit beaten out of them."

Myers Anderson's rationale was that in order to survive in a racially hostile world, his grandsons would have to work twice as hard as anyone else. So Thomas and his brother were made to rise before dawn to help their grandfather deliver coal and oil and spent their holidays and weekends doing heavy farmwork for him. There seemed to be a tinge of cruelty in some of Anderson's actions. Thomas, for instance, recalled that his grandfather had removed the heater from the fuel delivery truck because he felt that, even on freezing winter mornings, heat was not conducive to good work habits.

In the old-fashioned way of many such families, challenges to authority were met with frequent and humiliating corporal punishment. A particular torture was the front hall coat closet, where, according to Leola Williams, Anderson used to lock the boys when they misbehaved. "My daddy was hard, the kids couldn't get away with nothing," she recalled. Sometimes when her father was too tired or busy to beat the boys himself, Leola said, he would call her to whip them for him. But the little boys soon got too fast for her to catch, so instead, she said, "I would have to throw my shoes at their heads to catch them at all." So harsh was the physical punishment, according to Armstrong Williams, later Thomas's aide at the EEOC, that Thomas still bears a thin scar from a whipping his grandfather administered with an electrical cord. Allen Moore, who became a friend of Thomas's in Senator Danforth's office, said to *U.S. News and World Report,* "Clarence told me that he tasted the belt regularly."

The school that Myers Anderson chose for his grandsons apparently provided little respite, since the nuns also enforced strict discipline with the rod, occasionally drawing blood, according to some of Thomas's colleagues. "The entire education was about being submissive to authority," recalled Carol Delaney, who attended Catholic elementary school in Savannah around the same time as Thomas before going on to become an anthropologist. The simple act of questioning a biblical story, she said, could result in severe punishment. "We were physically punished — slapped and hit by the nuns, who also threw erasers at us." As Leola put it, "Those nuns and them, they would paddle your tail."

The tight discipline made Thomas behave, but the harsh treatment apparently had serious repercussions. From an early age Thomas was, according to his mother, stubborn and argumentative. Unable to vent his anger at his grandfather, she said, he would try to bully her. "You don't question Clarence," as she put it, echoing a line many subordinates at the EEOC would later use in describing him. When she tried, "he'd sit in a big chair, boasting and telling me, 'You don't know what you're talking about.'" It made her so mad, she said, "I'd kick the chair over and tell him, 'You don't talk to me like that.'" But, Leola continued, "that's Clarence. If you told him no, don't do something, he'll keep doing it. He wouldn't listen." She also noted that, like her father, Clarence could sometimes just look at her and make her cry.

But if Thomas and young Myers were literally whipped into shape by their grandfather, at least their physical surroundings were markedly improved. The boys now lived in the tidy bungalow with electricity and indoor plumbing that their grandfather had built a stone's throw from the railroad tracks on the city's east side — the house that Thomas's mother later inherited and still lives in. Meanwhile, their older sister was excluded from the more middle-class household. Emma Mae was left behind in Pin Point with Aunt Annie. In contrast to her brothers, who attended parochial school in Savannah, Emma Mae went to Pin Point's segregated public school. While her brothers were made to do their homework, she picked crab meat before and after school. Later, when she reached eighth grade, her grandfather tried to place her in parochial school too, but by that time she was already hopelessly behind academically, and she begged to return to her familiar life in Pin Point.

Later, when Emma Mae's life deteriorated to the point where she went on welfare, Thomas publicly singled her out as a case study of the kind of dependence that public assistance breeds. (Privately, colleagues said, he was more disparaging, sometimes belittling his sister and mother. One EEOC worker recalled his describing them as "trifling and lazy.") Yet the two siblings' lives diverged long before welfare was an issue. Emma Mae's lack of success might more logically be seen as a lack of opportunity — the sort of opportunity that Thomas was given and she was not. While she stayed behind in poverty, living her life as it had been led by generations of women in their family, Thomas was lifted into the middle class by good fortune in the shape of a determined grandfather who took his future seriously.

The subsequent portrait of Thomas as a self-made man, single-handedly escaping the depths of deprivation, would therefore rankle some of those who knew him earlier. "It's a myth to say those boys were poor," said Roy Allen, a Georgia state senator and a supporter of Thomas who was a classmate of his at St. Benedict the Moor, a black parochial grammar school. Allen pointed out that "Boy" and "Peanut," as Thomas and his younger brother were respectively known, "always had pocket money and never went without anything." He acknowledged that their grandfather made them work so hard that he used to joke with Clarence that he had personally lived through slavery. But in Allen's eyes they were not poor. "I mean, how many kids' fathers ran a coal and oil business?"

Similarly, his grandfather's best friend, Sam Williams, said, "He likes to talk so much about pulling yourself up by your bootstraps. But how are you going to do that if you've got no boots? He forgets to say that first someone had to give him boots — and that person was his grandfather." And Floyd Adams, another boyhood friend of

Thomas's, who went on to run Savannah's black newspaper, commented, "Everyone is emphasizing that he grew up in Pin Point in poverty. But when his grandfather took over, Clarence moved into what would be considered a fairly successful black middle-class family."

To some observers, such as W. W. Law, the Savannah civil rights activist whom Thomas once called "a childhood hero of mine," the distinction is crucial in trying to understand what he saw as Thomas's lack of empathy. Law, whose views on civil rights put him at odds with Thomas's later politics, knew the family well and watched Clarence grow up. "Thomas's was a select, pampered development that wasn't the experience of the vast majority of blacks," said Law. "Except for his earliest exposures, all of his experience was in white groups. He was in a very elite and ideal situation."

❖

The main difference between young Clarence Thomas and most blacks growing up in Savannah was his superior education. From the early days of slavery in Georgia, the education of African-Americans had been considered subversive and, for many years, illegal. After Nat Turner's rebellion in Virginia in 1832, slaveowners became so afraid of the blacks they were enslaving that Georgia imposed a steep fine and up to thirty-nine whiplashes on anyone who dared teach an African-American, whether slave or free man, to read or write.

Thus Savannah's first public school for black children was built by the victorious Yankees in 1867; although it was far too small to accommodate the city's black population, it remained the only such facility until 1915. After that, black children were also taught in makeshift classrooms carved from spare bedrooms and other rooms. Conditions were so overcrowded that there were often fifty pupils in a class. The school year was divided into half-day sessions; even in the 1950s, their teachers earned only half the salaries paid in the white schools. The segregated public school system was therefore guaranteed to perpetuate inequality, which is why it was such an early and obvious target of the civil rights movement.

Later, in his speeches, Thomas cited this poor education as one of the many disadvantages he overcame, for instance telling an audience in 1988 that "I don't understand how it is that people today are getting worse educations than I received in the segregated schools of

Savannah." But with the exception of first grade, which Thomas attended near Pin Point, he was spared this second-rate education. His segregated parochial school, founded in 1878, was staffed by a rare group of determined white Franciscan nuns who believed that the black children of the South were worth both converting and educating. Taunted as "nigger nuns" by some whites, the sisters devoted themselves to their pupils, drilling into them a sense of purpose and academic rigor rarely found in the segregated black public schools.

Although the school was neither wealthy nor expensive compared with other private schools, its $20 tuition nonetheless put it beyond the reach of most black families in Savannah. "The majority of our people were just too poor to pay its fees," confirmed Law. He contends that "all those Catholic school kids had superiority complexes," a theory buttressed by a schoolmate of Thomas's, Lester Johnson, who noted that "we were taught we were smarter than the other blacks."

The result, Law suggested, was that Thomas never shared the plight of more ordinary blacks. Interestingly, Thomas later found fault with the Supreme Court's seminal school desegregation ruling, *Brown v. Board of Education,* because he believed it was wrong to assume that all-black institutions were necessarily inferior. He explained this and other defenses of black educational facilities as a question of respecting black separatism, although his point of view was rarely shared by blacks who had actually experienced the segregated school system in the South. But it seems possible that his views about the ineffectiveness of government interference were partly shaped by his exemption from the central political drama of his own time: federally forced school desegregation.

Thomas's later characterization of having "fended for himself," not only without government assistance but with its "active opposition," thus seems oddly oblivious of the fact that all around him, beginning in the 1950s, the federal government was implementing policies without which most "black people might still be riding in the back of the bus," as William E. Nelson, professor of political science and black studies at Ohio State, put it.

Indeed, it's hard to overstate the intensity of the battle swirling just outside Thomas's own classroom doors — or the effect that the seismic shifts in federal policy had on the lives of many other blacks and whites. In Thomas's first year of life, President Harry Truman, in a controversial State of the Union address, called for more extensive civil rights laws, including the establishment of some sort of fair employment practices program — the bud of the idea that eventually grew into the EEOC. The speech touched off such furious opposition in Georgia that Senator Richard B. Russell proposed exporting the state's black population to the North. Leading the fight against such racial progress was the staunch segregationist J. Strom Thurmond — the same man who would champion Thomas's nomination to the Supreme Court some four decades later.

On May 17, 1954, when Thomas was five, the Supreme Court handed down its unanimous decision ordering the end of public school segregation. The lead attorney was Thurgood Marshall, then head of the NAACP's Legal Defense Fund. Georgia's governor, Herman Talmadge, vowed to block integration even if he had to defy federal troops. Three years later the Georgia House of Representatives sent a resolution to the governor asking for the impeachment of six U.S. Supreme Court justices. As Thomas later recalled of the "Impeach Earl Warren" billboards dotting the highways of his childhood, "I didn't quite understand who this Earl Warren fellow was, but I knew he was in some kind of trouble."

But in distant Pin Point, the Supreme Court seemed so remote that Thomas's mother later said, "If anyone had told me I'd birth a son to sit on the Supreme Court, I wouldn't have believed it." In fact, she recalled, "an old woman told me Clarence was going to be someone when he became a man. I just laughed."   •

Thomas was certainly aware of the struggle for racial progress taking place all around him. His grandfather was an active member of the NAACP; at one point he was dubbed a "sharpshooter" for the effectiveness of the boycotts he led against white businesses that wouldn't hire blacks. W. W. Law recalled that Anderson attended meetings regularly and provided the organization with free heating fuel. Sometimes Thomas's grandfather would bring the boy along to meetings. "But most of the time he was in boarding school," recalled Law, "where he was surrounded by whites."

According to Sam Williams, Thomas's lack of gratitude for what his grandfather and the civil rights movement had done for him formed the beginning of an estrangement that became so irreparable, the two were barely on speaking terms at the time of Anderson's death in the spring of 1983. What made his grandfather's bitterness particularly sharp was the sense that Thomas had betrayed him, according to

Williams, who said that, early on, "Thomas used to tell his grandfather he was going to be a civil rights lawyer and come back here and help his people. Instead, Thomas just helped Thomas. He saw [that] the money and career opportunities were on the other side. His grandfather was so disappointed, he hardly spoke of Thomas in the later years."

Yet in his public speeches, including his Supreme Court confirmation hearings, Thomas spoke often about how much he loved and admired his grandfather. It is likely that his sense of gratitude grew in the years after his grandfather's death; he did, after all, keep a photograph of his grandfather on his desk at the EEOC. But both Sam Williams and W. W. Law also charged Thomas with distorting the truth about his upbringing for political effect. In an interview, Law said, "I don't like talking about this because Thomas is local, and that makes it very hard." He then shut his eyes and in an agitated voice added, "Thomas just said those things to make him seem black. But all along he's been making choices to benefit Thomas and no one else."

A measure of the extent to which Thomas appears to have been willing to revise his personal history when politically useful arose in a speech he wrote in 1984 on behalf of President Reagan's reelection campaign. In the speech Thomas described eloquently his reasons for becoming a Republican, suggesting that it was the only party that truly represented his grandparents' values of hard work and self-reliance. He said he lectured his grandparents on this so persuasively in 1982, the year before they both died, that although they had been lifelong Democrats, "needless to say, they voted Republican."

But according to Julie Martin, the chief registrar in Hinesville, Georgia, the seat of Liberty County, where Thomas's grandparents had retired, Myers Anderson registered as a Democrat in 1977, and in both 1980 and 1982 he voted in the Democratic primaries — the only part of the election cycle requiring a public avowal of party affiliation. In addition, the county registrar has no record that Thomas's grandmother, Christine Anderson, was registered to vote at all.

❖

Despite the relatively middle-class comfort of his elementary and high school years, Thomas continued to feel inwardly deprived. Without a warm relationship with his mother, father, grandfather, or even with his younger brother, his early years were emotionally austere. Thomas might have turned to surrogates or friends. But, by his own account, he frequently found himself a solitary, excluded outsider, "a nerd," as he put it in one of his speeches, who decided by the age of sixteen that it was "better to be respected than liked." His popular and outgoing schoolmate Roy Allen confirmed the self-portrait, noting that "he is about the very last person you would invite to a party."

Although smart, hard-working, and full of determination, physically Thomas was at a disadvantage. Not only was he short, and in his teen years slight, but he also had exceptionally dark skin and African features years before the Black Is Beautiful movement made them desirable. "He was darker than most kids, and in that generation, people were cruel," recalled Sara Wright, a librarian for the *Savannah Morning News* who attended elementary and junior high school with Thomas. "He was teased a lot, they'd call him 'Nigger Naps'" for his tightly curled hair. "A lot of girls wouldn't want to go out with him."

Thomas himself remembered being called "ABC," or "America's Blackest Child." Even friends recollect taunting him that "if he were any blacker, he'd be blue." As Lester Johnson, who is now a lawyer in Savannah, recalled, "Clarence had big lips, nappy hair, and he was almost literally black. Those folks were at the bottom of the pole. You just didn't want to hang with those kids."

The blacks in Savannah, like most of the South's black society, observed a rigid caste system, a relic of slavery in which the closer one was to white, the higher one's social standing was. The most prominent black families in town since before the Civil War were for the most part what a local history of African-Americans calls "high yellow," or mulatto. At the same time, many of those with purer African bloodlines, like Thomas, were made to feel inferior.

Later, Thomas would speak of the self-hatred he felt and the way it strengthened his determination to prove his tormentors wrong. Even as an adult, he was acutely sensitive to color differences, according to colleagues. At Yale he talked bitterly about the "light-skinned elite" blacks who he thought had it easier than the darker ones. His closest friends at Yale, such as Harry Singleton and Frank Washington, recalled how the three of them would spend hours around Singleton's kitchen table discussing the advantages that lighter, better-connected blacks in the school enjoyed.

Some remembered Thomas's opinion that the civil rights establishment, too, was simply a privileged, light-skinned cartel bent on excluding people like himself — which became part of his rationale for opposing it. "He really hated the light-skinned leaders like Benjamin Hooks and [former HEW secretary] Patricia Harris," recalled Michael Middleton, Thomas's trusted, liberal colleague in Washington. "He thought they were 'bourgeois Negroes' who thought they were white."

At the same time, a number of EEOC colleagues believed that once in power, Thomas treated light-skinned women in particular with more deference than those with darker skin, showing a kind of contempt toward those more like himself. "He had more respect for light women, and he was definitely different around white people," asserted a former employee at the EEOC whom he eventually fired, Angela Wright. Wright, who was willing to testify that Thomas had made crude and unwanted sexual comments to her in the office, thought it unlikely that he would have behaved so disrespectfully had she had lighter skin.

When Anita Hill surfaced with her allegations, Thomas offhandedly confirmed this prejudice by telling his mother that there was no way he could have been seriously interested in Hill, because she was too dark for his taste. As his mother recalled the conversation, Thomas asked her, "Mamma, what kind of women do I like?"

Leola Williams, who is as dark as her son, said she hadn't thought much about it.

"Well, what color was Kathy?" he persisted, referring to his first wife, Kathy Ambush, who was three quarters black and one quarter Japanese.

"She was brown," Leola said she answered.

"And the others?" inquired Thomas.

"They've all been light-skinned too," his mother said.

"Right," she says Thomas answered. "So what would I want with a woman as black as Anita Hill?"

If anything, Thomas's Catholic education seems to have only intensified his sense of social exclusion. "It made you a double minority," said his schoolmate Lester Johnson, who also went on to college at Holy Cross. "You'd go to a party on a Friday night where everyone else was eating fried chicken, and since you had to have fish, people would ask, 'Man — what is wrong with you?'"

At least Thomas had the company of other black Catholics well into high school. But in 1964, after finishing tenth grade at St. Pious X, the segregated parochial high school on the east side of Savannah, Thomas enrolled as one of only two blacks in a vigorous course of study for the priesthood in the previously all-white St. John Vianney Junior Seminary. Thomas was, in the eyes of one of his stern early teachers, Sister Mary Virgilius, "not a genius," but he showed a level of self-discipline and determination that was extraordinary. Thus, when he embraced his grandfather's dream that he enter the priesthood, he applied himself with unusual seriousness for someone his age.

Thomas later recalled that the other kids on his block called the seminary the "cemetery"; indeed, it was almost as remote and peaceful as the grave. St. John Vianney's was a simple collection of low concrete buildings, like barracks, housing sixty candidates for the priesthood on a beautiful, marshy island some thirty minutes' drive from Savannah. The seminary was lucky enough to have a rector, William Coleman, who was known for his progressive views on questions of race. And so, as the civil rights bill was being debated in Washington, the seminary opened its doors to Thomas and one other black student, offering scholarships as needed. Although Thomas had to repeat tenth grade, he was given a coveted place. Such special help allowed later opponents to argue, as Alvin Golub of the EEOC did, that "Thomas was helped by the kinds of affirmative action programs he opposed from the day his grandfather first got him placed in white Catholic schools."

Even for the white students, St. John's was a lonely place. As a former classmate, Mike Dillon, recalled, "It was really isolated, and giving up girls — well, it was just terrible." On weekends, Dillon recalled, most boys' families would visit. But although Leola Williams believed her father used to visit, Dillon said he couldn't remember ever seeing anyone from Thomas's family at the school.

No one recalled Thomas so much as flirting with a girl, let alone dating one. As a potential priest, he was admonished by his teachers to resist the charms of the opposite sex on weekends and holidays. Thomas's old schoolmate Lester Johnson recalled Thomas's trying to convince him to join the seminary too, at the request of the nuns, who used Thomas as a black recruiter. But Johnson was concerned about how Thomas survived without girls. Thomas answered, "It's not so bad — you know we come home sometimes." "Sometimes!" Johnson recalled exclaiming. "How you gonna get a girl if you're not there every weekend?" He concluded that Thomas must not know much about girls.

If Thomas was unsophisticated about girls, certainly the nuns had done little to change that. The only sex education the youngsters at St. Benedict's and St. Pious X received, recalled Johnson, was from their own parents — which Thomas lacked. After sixth grade, boys and girls were separated in class and, Johnson recalled, "we were lectured about sin all the time." The nuns' view of women at that time, according to Carol Delaney, who was taught by them in Savannah, "was that we should become wives and mothers and submit completely to male authority. The husband was the head of the wife, as Christ was the head of the church. Women were associated with sin through Eve."

With few distractions, Thomas thrived in the disciplined environment of the seminary, excelling in Latin, a subject he hadn't been exposed to earlier, unlike many of the other boys. He also tackled English with enthusiasm; it was his toughest subject, and so, with typical determination, he later majored in it in college. The caption for his senior yearbook photograph perfectly summarized both his outstanding scholastic record and his immense drive to prove himself: "Blew that test: Only a 98."

Socially, however, Thomas's progress took a different path. For many of his sixteen years, he had been in one way or another an outsider, but during his three years at St. John's and an additional year at Immaculate Conception Seminary College in Conception Junction, Missouri — again as one of a handful of blacks pioneering in a white institution — his sense of racial alienation intensified. Dillon, like other white students at St. John's, recalled Thomas as a "cheerful" kid with a wonderful laugh who was also "the best athlete I ever saw." Moreover, Dillon suggested there was no racial tension in the seminary because "we were all one big family." Yet Thomas's memories of his years there are unrelentingly bitter. "Not a day passed that I was not pricked by prejudice," he told an audience in 1985. What Thomas specifically recalled, he said, was that when the lights were turned out, a classmate would taunt, "Smile, Clarence, so we can see you."

What bothered him more than the joke itself was that among all his fellow Christians, lying on cots side by side, no one ever came to his defense.

At Immaculate Conception, where he was one of only three blacks in a much larger institution, he said the racism was so offensive that it eventually drove him not just from the school but also from Catholicism itself. The white seminarians there would cross the street, he said, when they saw him coming. Once, when Thomas first entered his room, a roommate drew a knife in a crude, joking welcome. The breaking point, he often said, came in the spring of 1968 when Martin Luther King Jr. was assassinated. Thomas, who revered King, was heartsick to hear a fellow seminarian respond to the news of the shooting by saying, "Good — I hope the SOB dies." Soon afterward, he said, he packed his bags and left.

Colleagues who were also black pioneers in white Catholic schools suggest that it is hard to convey the awful disillusionment they experienced on learning that their fellow Catholics were just as bigoted as the rest of the white world. "It was such a shock," recalled Roy Allen, who entered a white Catholic high school in 1964. "It made you question the church." In Thomas's case, the racism at the seminary was so deeply upsetting that it was, as Russell Frisby, a friend from law school, later noted, "the first thing [Thomas] told you about himself." Indeed, in 1984 it dominated an interview he gave the Holy Cross alumni paper, in which he described himself as "a black spot on the white horse" during his seminary years and charged that the seminaries had even temporarily discontinued awards, "like Athlete of the Year, that I was likely to win." It's difficult to know whether some of the slights Thomas recalled were magnified by his own disposition to feel excluded. His white classmates and teachers sounded surprised to hear of the racism Thomas described; they noted, for instance, that he was named Class Superjock at Conception, despite his recollection of having been denied athletic honors.

After he left the seminary, Thomas never told his mother the Martin Luther King story. "I just had felt he didn't want to go, but Daddy had pushed him into being a priest," she recalled. Nor did other classmates remember it exactly as Thomas told it. A close friend at Conception, Tom O'Brien, recalled that, a month or two before the end of the term, Thomas came to him teary-eyed and simply said he was leaving because he had run into "too many rednecks." But while the details varied — possibly depending on how comfortable he felt with his audience — the underlying theme did not. Well before Anita Hill testified against him, his sense of being treated unfairly by the world had become the leitmotif of his life story.

❖

The decision to abandon his grandfather's dream that he become a priest had traumatic consequences at home. Myers Anderson was so angry that he told his grandson that if he believed he could think for himself, then he could also feed, clothe, and shelter himself. A few weeks short of his twentieth birthday, Thomas was thrown out on his own.

He turned to one of the nuns who had taught him as a child, and she suggested he apply to Holy Cross, an excellent Jesuit college in Worcester, Massachusetts. Like many white colleges that felt an awakened sense of social conscience after the King assassination, in 1968 Holy Cross decided to pursue black students more aggressively, setting up a King scholarship fund and recruiting across the country. Thomas received one of these special scholarships, and according to John E. Brooks, who became the president of Holy Cross, he "certainly" benefited from affirmative action.

Thomas's journey into higher education in the North opened up a world to him that no one in his family had ever entered. His grandmother's homespun advice, humorously recalled by Thomas in a speech, suggests the cultural divide he was crossing: change your clothes, she admonished him, and don't eat anyone else's chitterlings. Thomas was able to poke fun at his own naiveté as a stranger in the North, recalling how he had returned in bewilderment to the newsstand after purchasing his first copy of the Sunday *New York Times,* asking to know why the funny papers had been left out.

At Holy Cross, which Thomas entered as a sophomore (having received credit for his year at Conception), he soon made himself more at home than he had been anywhere else. There were enough other black students to form a clique, and Thomas, who also had white friends, found himself relatively popular; he was nicknamed "Cooz," after the Boston Celtics' star Bob Cousy, whose basketball prowess he liked to imitate. Thomas played intramural football and basketball and ran as a sprinter. He supplemented his financial aid by waiting tables in the dining hall. But his friends remembered him most for reminding them that they were in college not to play but to learn, so that they could get ahead in the real world.

The liberal arts education at Holy Cross exposed Thomas for the first time to the writings of many of the nation's best black minds. The works of Richard Wright, in particular, "really woke me up," Thomas later said. His favorites were *Native Son* and *Black Boy* because, as he put it, these novels of trapped and violent racial rage "capture[d] a lot of the feelings that I had inside that you learn to repress." *Native Son,* the story of Bigger Thomas, who accidentally suffocates his wealthy white employer's daughter and is falsely accused of raping and murdering her, struck a particularly deep chord in Thomas. Twenty-five years later, Thomas would echo some of these powerful themes during his Supreme Court hearings.

As his appetite for Wright suggests, he was already examining the issue of race in America, beginning a thoughtful, iconoclastic search for answers that would occupy much of his life. As a habitual outsider, Thomas rejected many of the orthodoxies concerning racial remedies well before many of his peers; he questioned, for instance, the benefits of affirmative action and welfare long before it was fashionable to do so — almost, it sometimes seemed to his friends, because doing so was unfashionable.

At the time of his nomination to the Supreme Court, much was made of Thomas's radicalism at Holy Cross. In notes Thomas made for a speech at Emory University in 1988, he described this period as his "days of rage." He flirted with black separatism and with the Black Muslim religion, and, like many of his generation in the angry days after the slaying of King, he was attracted to the militant "black power" message of the Student Nonviolent Coordinating Committee (SNCC) leader Stokely Carmichael rather than the more pacifist, traditional civil rights remedies that his grandfather and the NAACP championed. His friends recalled that he helped draft the charter of the Black Student Union, hung a Malcolm X poster in his dorm room, wore a goatee and combat boots, volunteered at a breakfast program for poor and mostly black children, and participated in a number of campus protests.

But in an era when Malcolm X's autobiography was on the school's freshman reading list and torn fatigues and berets were the fashion, it was easy to confuse style with substance. A more accurate portrait of Thomas during that period, gained from interviews with fellow students, suggests that in comparison with many others he was a moderate, notable less for his radicalism than for his outspoken and often argumentative independence of thought. Already he was seeking out isolated, idiosyncratic positions where, characteristically, he could be alone.

As one classmate, Jaffe Dickerson, recalled, there were always four views on any issue: the left, the right, the center, and Thomas's. Thus, when the black students on campus voted to live together in a separate dorm, Thomas was the sole person against it. He argued, according to his later recollection, that if blacks wanted to segregate themselves, they might as well attend a black school like Howard University. Another argument Thomas made seemed designed to put everyone on edge: he didn't want to live among blacks because he didn't want to make it so easy for whites to avoid him, recalled a former friend.

The other black students nonetheless went ahead with their separatist dorm. Thomas moved in too — but he brought along his white roommate from the year before. Much later, after becoming an ardent conservative, he would lament that his views so isolated him that "I don't fit in with whites and I don't fit in with blacks." He suggested that his experience at the forefront of integration had contributed to this alienation. But as his behavior at college suggests, Thomas sought out isolated positions well before he had a coherent political philosophy.

Socially, as well, Thomas was frequently a solitary figure. To be sure, he had friends, many of whom remember him for the heartiness of his laugh. But much of his time was spent alone, usually studying. His classmates recalled that when they went to dances at nearby schools on Saturday nights, Thomas often preferred to stay in the basement of the college library. When the school threatened to shorten the Saturday night library hours, he petitioned the authorities to keep the facility open. And when others went away during holidays, he stayed in the otherwise empty school, explaining later that he viewed such breaks as a valuable opportunity to get ahead of the other students.

Academically, his efforts paid off. He wrote to a friend that he had managed to maintain a 3.7 grade point average, and he graduated in 1971 with honors, ranking ninth in his class. Succeeding was a point of political and racial pride, recalled Lester Johnson, who by then had followed Thomas to Holy Cross. In its effort to recruit black students,

Johnson explained, Holy Cross had admitted a number who, as he put it, "were just jokes. The rest of us knew that the white students were looking at us, suspecting there's another dummy who doesn't deserve to be here. It was the kind of affirmative action that came from guilt, and which really hurt a lot of America." The upshot, suggested Johnson, was that "we all carried a lot of anger inside — and it pushed us to excel."

The experience apparently stung Thomas quite deeply, since he later cited it as his chief cause for turning against affirmative action. He saw himself as stigmatized rather than helped by race-conscious aid, an analysis that no doubt reflected the emotional pain he felt but that again overlooked the advantages he had enjoyed — such as his admission to St. John Vianney, Immaculate Conception, and Holy Cross in the first place. The resentment Thomas felt toward the helping hand he grasped set him apart from a number of other minority students at the time — both at Holy Cross and at Yale Law School — many of whom didn't care as much about others' perception of how they had gotten there. At Yale, which Thomas attended as an affirmative action student, he felt, he said later, that his presence was so resented by the white professors and students that it was as if a monkey had jumped from the carved arches of the Gothic law school building onto his back. He never seemed to believe he had enough acceptance, which caused some friends to wonder if the problem wasn't more internal than external.

"I was an affirmative action student at Yale Law, and I never felt looked down upon," said one classmate, Tony Califa. "But [Thomas has] written that he felt under attack. If so, it was in his head." Lester Johnson, Thomas's friend since childhood, saw the problem as deep-seated. "It's hard to say whether Clarence ever truly had any real self-esteem — I'd have to say no," suggested Johnson. "Mine came from my parents. But in his case, I think his grandfather taught him ethics and discipline, but nothing beyond that. I always knew I would be successful before I was. But Clarence was the other way around. He always had to prove it, and even then, I'm not sure he believed it."

At Holy Cross, just as in the seminary, the burden at times seemed too much, and Thomas again flirted with dropping out. He later told the alumni magazine that in the fall of 1969, the beginning of his second year there, "I had my trunk all packed. I had decided that it was true, what the other blacks had been saying: that Holy Cross was a crusher, that it would break your spirit." John Brooks, then the vice president, helped persuade Thomas to stay. But the following spring he was just as fragile. At that point, he told friends, he would have dropped out if he hadn't been afraid of losing his student deferment and being drafted into the Vietnam War.

❖

Although Thomas adopted the political liberalism of the day, registering as a Democrat as soon as he turned eighteen, voting for George McGovern for president in 1972, and smoking marijuana on occasion, his views on the role of women were distinctly old-fashioned. In part, they may have reflected his strict Catholic upbringing. And he may have been influenced by the role of women in his own family, since his mother and sister were left far behind educationally and professionally while he and his brother, who would become an accountant, pursued careers.

But his view of women also mirrored the current antipathy between many militant black males and predominantly white feminists. At a time when some women were beginning to make political demands, most black activists considered sexual equality far less important than racial equality, and some were actively hostile to feminism. This attitude was captured memorably by Stokely Carmichael's famous rebuttal to complaints about male chauvinism within SNCC: "The only position for women in SNCC is prone."

Russell Frisby confirmed Thomas's conservative view of women's roles: "He felt that women should be at home, and that women's groups were benefiting at the expense of minorities." A female graduate student at Yale who knew Thomas at law school added, "At that time, I didn't know the word 'male chauvinist,' but now, in looking back, I can say he defined the term. He barely spoke to women; he was so condescending and accustomed to them being subservient that when I'd offer an opinion in a conversation, it irritated him. When I talked, he'd just ignore me, he'd only talk to the men. He thought women belonged in the kitchen."

Fortunately, at about the time he seemed most dispirited about Holy Cross, Thomas met a woman who fit his feminine ideal. Her name was Kathy Ambush, and she was a student at a neighboring women's college. Short, quiet, and a touch heavy, with long dark hair that reflected the heritage of her Japanese grandmother, she was the daughter of a dental technician in Worcester. Her family, a friend says, "must have seemed to Thomas like the black version of *Leave It to Beaver*. She had a big, warm, middle-class family that was as comfortable as Thomas's was not." Moreover, she was, as Frisby recalled, "a fifties kind of woman — very traditional."

Within only days of their meeting, recalled Thomas's friend Eddie Jenkins, Thomas said he was in love. Soon Ambush could be spotted on campus; one classmate, Edward P. Jones, remembered seeing her dragging an enormous duffel bag of Thomas's laundry up the stairs to his room. Some friends of Thomas's wondered if the match would last. "She was so quiet, and so shy. Well, I just didn't know if she was up to him," recalled Lester Johnson. "They were from completely different worlds." But on June 5, 1971, the day after Thomas's graduation, they were married at All Saints Episcopal Church in Worcester.

Old-fashioned though Thomas's views of women appear to have been, as far back as Holy Cross there was evidence of another pattern of behavior, in some ways equally Victorian. While Thomas argued against premarital sex and adultery, telling one friend that he would leave a wife on the spot if she was unfaithful to him, he also showed an unusual interest in talking about sex in gross and explicitly anatomical language, according to several college classmates. By the time he reached Yale Law School, Thomas was known not only for the extreme crudity of his sexual banter, but also for avidly watching pornographic films and reading pornographic magazines, which he would describe to friends in lurid detail.

An interest in pornography might ordinarily be considered a private matter. But colleagues recall that Thomas was notable for the unusually public nature of his enthusiasm for pornographic materials — his detailed descriptions of the movies and magazines he had seen were an open form of socializing during these years that seemed funny to some, offensive to others, and odd to many. It is for this reason that when Anita Hill accused Thomas of talking crudely to her about sexual matters, which she found strange, a number of otherwise impartial schoolmates of Thomas's were struck by the familiarity of the behavior she described. And because of their vivid memories of Thomas's way of talking, they did not believe his professions of "horror" at "this kind of grotesque language" during the hearings.

For instance, a friend from Holy Cross, Gordon Davis, now an engineer in Worcester, Massachusetts, recalled of Thomas that "ninety-nine percent of the time he was a perfect gentleman. But one percent of the time he would go off the deep end. He'd say stuff I can't possibly repeat, stuff that would turn your ears red, things having to do with a person's anatomy. He'd say things like 'Suck out of my ass with a straw' all the time, but this was different — it was a lot worse, and I don't feel comfortable talking about it."

Another classmate, Edward P. Jones, the author of a book of short stories, *Lost in the City,* had very much the same recollection. At Holy Cross he roomed with Thomas's best friend there, Gilbert "Gil" Hardy, and so spent hours in long conversations with the two in their dorm. As Jones saw it, Thomas was memorable for the crude sexual language he used. He and Hardy used to call each other "bitch" routinely in a kind of rough, affectionate banter that would degenerate into gross excess as they tried to one-up each other in their insults. While some might see such joking as typical of college students, in Thomas's case, according to Jones, it reached unusual proportions. "It got so vicious, it would have reduced other people to tears," he said. Perhaps, Jones speculated, Thomas's extreme language reflected the sexual preoccupations and awkwardness of "a man who was used to all-male institutions and didn't really know how to relate to women, and maybe didn't know how to show affection."

Thomas's fellow students at Yale had similar memories. A black female graduate student with whom Thomas and his wife socialized recalled that he was set apart by his interest in not just seeing but also talking about pornography. "He would carry this pornographic tabloid-type publication, some magazine with sexually explicit color photographs, around in the back pocket of the overalls he always wore, and show it to some of the men in our group, talking and laughing about the pictures. Then the men would come and tell us about it."

At the time, Yale Law School was showing pornographic films previously banned from public consumption. The films, mainstream X-rated productions like *Deep Throat* and *Behind the Green Door,* with explicit sex scenes and full nudity, were widely attended on campus and considered something of a joke, complete with hooting coed audiences. But Thomas, she recalled, went beyond these mainstream pornographic movies and attended the more hard-core ones then being shown at one of the city's downtown movie houses, the Crown Theater. "All of us knew that Clarence was into these real kinky movies, not just regular pornography," she said. "Everybody who knew Clarence knew he was into pornography."

After seeing these films, she and a number of other graduate students recalled, Thomas would come back and regale his friends with detailed descriptions. At the time he was married and had, in 1973, fathered a son, Jamal. But Kathy, like most of the other women in their set, was excluded from these pornographic forays.

Henry Terry, a black law student a year behind Thomas who is now an attorney in Boston, also recalled that Thomas and a good friend, Frank Washington, went to the Crown Theater to see pornographic movies almost every week. Thomas would come in the next day "roaring with laughter and having animated discussions" about what he'd seen. "I knew him well," said Terry. "It was a thing with him. Everyone knew it. That's just what he did." Asked about Terry's recollection, Washington declined to comment.

Later, when judging who was telling the truth during the hearings, Terry thought that Thomas's regular attendance at pornographic films was less important than the kind of language he used. Like his Holy Cross classmates, Terry remembered Thomas as "one of the crudest people I have ever met. He was one of those people who can sound dignified in a courtroom or whatever when he needs to. But when you get him with friends, he's crude — I mean really crude — profane, scatological, and graphic. A lot of us black males growing up in the fifties were crude, but Clarence was more so.

"So," Terry concluded, "when Anita Hill started talking, I knew the man was guilty. 'That's my boy,' I said. 'That's him talking.' I'm certain she was telling the truth, because the examples she gave sounded too much like him for it not to have been Clarence."

Clarence Martin, a lawyer in Savannah who befriended Thomas during a summer job after his second year of law school, also remembered his interest in seeing and talking about pornography. "We were all into pornography," he said. "It was just part of the way we grew up. With Clarence, it was just a way for him to have a good time. He liked to talk about it. I guess he enjoyed it."

After Thomas entered the more appearance-conscious world of Washington politics, he was more discreet, but the pattern evidently remained much the same. As the wife of a fellow black congressional aide who declined to be named recalled, Thomas often went out with her husband and a third black male friend to watch what she termed "porno flicks. It was a guy thing," she maintained. "They'd come home and talk and laugh about it, saying, 'You wouldn't believe the strange things these people do.'"

Later, during the confirmation hearings, she said she and her husband had "a shared sense of disbelief. We couldn't get over Clarence wrapping himself in his innocence, expressing horror at the mention of body parts, and being so vehement in his denial. He's a friend, so we wouldn't want to hurt him, but we had a good laugh over it, thinking how folks are really buying this!"

Interestingly, all the people who recalled this side of Thomas are black. In front of whites, suggested some of those who know him well, his behavior was different, more guarded, particularly as he moved on in his career. "There definitely was a difference in the way Clarence was among blacks and whites," confirmed Judith Winston, a former colleague of Thomas's at the Department of Education who is now the agency's general counsel. "He was more relaxed around blacks, as most of us are."

While this observation is hardly surprising, it may explain how white friends of Thomas's such as Senator John Danforth of Missouri and Dean Charles Kothe of Oral Roberts Law School could have a completely different impression of him. During the confirmation hearings, when asked about the likelihood of Thomas's making crude remarks to Anita Hill, Kothe said that in their several years of professional association he had never heard Thomas "utter a profane word" or "make a coarse remark . . . I can't believe this man would even think in terms of pornographic movies — I just can't!" To believe otherwise, Kothe testified, Thomas "would have to be the greatest actor of all time." If Hill's charges "were true," he said, "it is the greatest Jekyll and Hyde story in the history of mankind."

❖

Thomas entered Yale Law School in the fall of 1971, just as it had begun an ambitious affirmative action program aimed at making minorities at least 10 percent of each class. In Thomas's first year, even with the aggressive recruitment program, the school still had been able to enroll only 12 blacks in a class of 170 students — some 7 percent. Thomas accepted the financial aid offered but later discounted any benefit he'd gotten from the affirmative action. In an interview in the

Atlantic Monthly in 1987, he commented, "This thing about how they let me into Yale — that kind of stuff offends me. All they did was stop stopping us."

Thomas nevertheless arrived at Yale filled with idealism. As he later put it, "At that age, you actually think you can go out and change the world. I wanted to right some wrongs that I saw in Savannah, some specific wrongs with respect to my grandfather and what he was able to do with his life, as well as the overall wrongs that I saw as a child there." He continued to share many of the liberal views of most of his classmates. He opposed the war in Vietnam, and he devoted time to fighting discrimination and poverty by working at New Haven's Legal Assistance Association. At one point, he planned to work on a study of racial discrimination in the grading of southern bar exams along with Lani Guinier, a fellow law student.

During the summer of his second year, however, Thomas seemed to reach a turning point in both his ideology and his ambition. Sponsored by the NAACP, he became a summer associate in Savannah's first integrated law firm, Hill, Jones and Farrington, which was known for championing civil rights cases. The summer fellowship, earmarked for those working on racial issues, particularly minority law students, was another form of affirmative action that benefited Thomas.

In the friendly milieu of the law firm, Thomas appeared some-what aloof, going his own way in small ways and large. Colleagues recall him working alone and with great intensity in the firm's law library, sometimes drumming his feet on the floor so noisily he had to be asked to stop. While other lawyers in the firm used a form book to file motions — a universally accepted shortcut — Thomas insisted on writing every word of each motion himself. And unlike the other young associates, Thomas eschewed the two-martini expense account lunches in Savannah's best restaurants to which the partners regularly treated them.

A former partner, Bobby Hill, who became a mentor to Thomas that summer and whom Thomas later named in a speech as one of the great role models in his life, believed that Thomas boycotted the lunches because he resented his white and lighter-skinned black colleagues, most of whom were better off than he. "He had a disdain for rich black kids and for the white lawyers in the firm," said Hill, who is black. "We had two [whites] in the firm at the time, and they often came to the lunches with us. I think that's why he went off on his own." Instead, he said, Thomas brought his own lunch, usually Spam. "I gave him a hard time about that Spam," recalled Hill.

Evidently Thomas had less and less sympathy with his colleagues' civil rights goals as well. According to his best friend at the firm, Clarence Martin, "He thought the South would never change and we were just whistling in the wind. He was very disillusioned, and he had great disdain for the system." Martin recalled that Thomas fixed his sights on new goals that summer. Thomas told him that what he really wanted was to go into private practice, become a great trial lawyer, and make a lot of money. "We used to love to dream about what we would do with the money," Martin remembered.

These goals proved elusive. Inhibiting Thomas was his less than exceptional performance at Yale. His academic records remain, with his consent, sealed. But professors and administrators from his era recall him as an average student, hard-working but not particularly brilliant. There is only one professor — Thomas I. Emerson — whose records have been made public. Thomas elected to take Emerson's first-year course on politics and civil rights in 1972, and Emerson's notes show that he finished the class near the bottom, with a 69 for the semester. One of only two students who scored lower was Thomas's friend and later a witness against Hill, John Doggett.

During his last year at Yale, Thomas applied to a number of blue-chip law firms, but they completely shut him out. To some extent this reflected the still bigoted employment practices of many of the larger firms. In 1974, integration may have reached the elite schools of the Ivy League, but it had yet to penetrate the inner sanctums of the legal profession, especially the leading firms of Georgia where Thomas most wanted to work.

"It was a funny time," recalled Frank Washington, Thomas's friend and classmate. "It was the beginning of many blacks just coming out of all the elite schools, and certainly it was harder for those of us with no connections. I applied to forty law firms and got only one job offer. Clarence had none. It was terribly disillusioning."

Thomas was very bitter about being turned down; years later, he told Emory Law School students that he had saved every single one of the rejection letters. "No one would hire me after law school," his notes for another speech show. "I felt beaten." And in a commencement address to Syracuse University College of Law in 1991 he said,

"Since my reason for going to law school in the first place was to return to Savannah to assist in righting the wrongs which I felt existed there throughout my childhood, I can't say this was a high point. In fact, if anything, I was steeped in frustration."

What Thomas failed to mention, however, was that he could have returned home to "right the wrongs of his childhood" if he had wanted. Although rejected by Georgia's best-paying law firms, Thomas had been offered a job by the Savannah firm at which he'd spent the previous summer, practicing exactly the kind of idealistic law he described in his speech at Syracuse. According to Bobby Hill, Clarence Martin, and a third partner, Fletcher Farrington, who supported Thomas's nomination to the high court, Thomas was invited to come and work for Hill, Jones and Farrington as soon as he finished law school.

The choice was Thomas's, Farrington recalled, and Thomas turned the firm down. Farrington said the reason Thomas gave him was that his wife didn't like Savannah. Martin, his best friend in the firm, recalled other misgivings. He thought Thomas felt the pay at the fledgling firm was too low. Regardless, by the time Thomas had the chance to "right the wrongs" of his Pin Point boyhood, his ambition lay elsewhere.

3

❖

Joining the Club

AT A TIME when the country's top corporate law firms were still hiring very few blacks, opportunity arrived on the Yale campus in the form of John C. "Jack" Danforth, Missouri's Republican attorney general. A Yale Law School graduate, a member of the school's board, and a man committed to advancing the cause of civil rights, Danforth came to New Haven expressly to recruit a black lawyer for his office. Professor Guido Calabresi, later the law school's dean, recalled Danforth's asking "for the names of very able black students. He was concerned with diversity very early on." Calabresi recommended Thomas's friend Frank Washington and one other recent graduate, Rufus Cormier. However, both already had solid job offers. But Washington, in turn, suggested that Danforth talk to Thomas.

"Saint Jack," as John Clagett Danforth would later be dubbed by his Senate colleagues, was part of an increasingly endangered political species as the 1970s wore on: moderate blue-blooded Republicans in the Rockefeller mold. Gentlemanly, moral, and broadly cultured, he had an old-school style that gained him much admiration in some circles, but he seemed increasingly anachronistic at a time in national politics when both the Republican and Democratic parties were becoming polarized by narrow, single-issue interest groups. It took an independent thinker like Danforth — who could oppose both abortion and the death penalty — to reach out to an unknown, unemployed, and unconnected young black Democrat and welcome him into the overwhelmingly white Republican club.

The grandson of William H. Danforth, who had founded the Ralston Purina grain and pet food company, Jack Danforth seemed animated by a combination of respect for the capitalist system, which had made his family fortune possible, and heartfelt compassion for those less privileged. This duality had manifested itself as early as his student years, for after obtaining an undergraduate degree from Princeton, he chose to earn graduate degrees at Yale in the seemingly incompatible disciplines of law and divinity. This combining of God and Mammon, Christian rectitude and worldly ambition, was visible in his early professional days, too, when Danforth worked on Wall Street for a corporate law firm and spent his free hours ministering to dying cancer patients. Even as a senator, he could be found on Tuesday mornings delivering the sermon at the city's most establishment Episcopal church, St. Albans Chapel.

Influenced both by his grandfather's emphasis on good works and by his activist aunt, Dorothy Compton, who worked to improve race relations in America, Danforth entered politics in 1968 with the zeal of a missionary. After returning from New York to his home state of Missouri, he won the race to become its attorney general, making him the first Republican to win statewide office in a decade. The Vietnam War was raging, Robert Kennedy and Martin Luther King Jr. had just been assassinated, triggering race riots across the country, and Richard Nixon, promising to restore law and order, was about to enter the White House.

As a moderate, Danforth committed himself to providing more opportunity to those without his advantages. Lacking close ties to St. Louis's black community, he decided to search for the best and brightest young aides in the country, paying special attention to minorities and the underprivileged. It was on one such scouting trip in 1974 that he visited his alma mater, Yale Law School.

In Danforth's eyes, Clarence Thomas displayed a number of admirable traits. Although he was not ranked near the top of his class, his triumph over poverty and discrimination suggested that he was a disciplined, strong-willed person and made for an impressive life story. And although Danforth was a Republican in Missouri and Thomas was a Democrat from Georgia, Thomas's former aspiration to become a priest appealed to Danforth's deeply religious nature, especially given Thomas's statement that he had abandoned the path to the priesthood after encountering too much bigotry at the seminary in Danforth's own state. For a patrician bent on making racial amends, Thomas was in many ways the perfect recruit.

In later descriptions of this crucial first career step, Thomas emphasized that he only agreed to accept the job from Danforth after being assured that racial considerations would in no way give him any advantage. "I have never forgotten the terms of his offer to me," he said, for instance, at his confirmation hearings: "more work for less pay than anyone in the country could offer." And indeed, his starting salary of $10,800 was meager. But Thomas's point concerning race neutrality overlooked the fact that according to both Calabresi and Thomas's friend Washington, Danforth had come to Yale specifically to hire a minority lawyer.

Thomas was less than enthusiastic about the helping hand offered by Danforth. According to his friend Clarence Martin, he was upset that the only viable offer he got on graduating from Yale required him to become a public servant. "By the time he went to Missouri, he was very disillusioned," recalled Martin. "He didn't want the attorney general's job. He never wanted to be part of government, and in fact, he resented it. He'd wanted to be this great trial lawyer in private practice. But he lost his self-confidence after all the Atlanta firms turned him down."

❖

Before Thomas could assume his duties, he had to pass the Missouri bar exam. He wanted to take the summer off to study, but he had "no money, no place to live," as he later described this phase of his life. So Margaret Bush Wilson, who later became chairperson of the NAACP, allowed Thomas to live at her house in St. Louis while he studied. "She provided me not only with room and board but advice, counsel, and guidance," Thomas recalled. "As I left her house that summer, I asked her, 'How much do I owe you?' Her response was, 'Just along the way, help someone who is in your position.'" With his admission to the Missouri bar in September, Thomas moved his family to Jefferson City. He and his wife — who was working to complete the college education she had interrupted in order to follow him to law school — and their son, Jamal, lived in a small, simple apartment two blocks from the state penitentiary.

Thomas was highly sensitive about not appearing to be an affirmative action hire who might be considered less qualified than his white colleagues. During this period as well as later, Thomas made a point of avoiding any assignment that might suggest racial stereotyping, asking specifically to work on tax cases. His thinking, as he explained it in "pep talks" he gave to the students at Lincoln University, the small, predominantly black college where Kathy Ambush Thomas was studying, was that racial pigeonholing of any sort was a trap. What mattered, he warned the students, was succeeding in the white world, not as minorities but as equals. Hired for reasons of diversity, he was determined to prove that his value had nothing to do with the color of his skin.

By most accounts, Thomas served the attorney general admirably. His colleagues described him in his first few years out of law school as energetic, well disciplined, and of at least average skills, and they were impressed by his good humor and ability to fit in with the otherwise white staff. Mark Mittleman, his fellow assistant attorney general, recalled that he was an able writer and that "he had a talent for saying a great deal in a few words." Another former assistant, S. Joel Wilson, remembered that "he carried his load." And if at first he didn't fit in politically, that soon changed, for it was during this period that he left behind the McGovern wing of the Democratic party and, in a break with the traditions of his family and friends, registered as a Republican.

Looking back, Thomas and many of his admirers would explain his migration to the right as a genuine intellectual evolution resulting from long hours of reading and discussion, which persuaded him that the liberal remedies for poverty and racism were not only ineffective but harmful. Inevitably, others were less convinced by his increasingly conservative ideology and saw rank opportunism in this political transformation. They charged that Thomas's ideals seemed tailored to fit the opportunities, which, starting with the moderate Republicanism of Danforth, followed an increasingly rightward course. In all likelihood, Thomas's conversion was some combination of the two, both an iconoclast's rejection of conventional thinking and a young man's recognition of the path that offered him the best chance to get ahead.

Thomas was unabashed about the usefulness of being a black conservative. Cindi Faddis, who met him during the years he worked for Danforth, remembered that "he said that he thought he'd have an advantage as a Republican. He was up front about it. He said, 'If I belong to the Republican party, I could go further.'"

Clarence Martin, who visited Thomas in Missouri, found the trans-

formation in his formerly liberal friend — with whom he had worked
only the summer before — quite remarkable. Gone was Thomas's college dorm poster of Malcolm X, replaced by an oversize poster of a
Rolls-Royce. No longer dwelling on being shut out of private practice,
Thomas now had a new avenue for his ambitions. As a Republican,
he told Martin, he planned a big future in politics. "I remember him
sitting with his feet up on the desk, smoking a cigar," said Martin. "I
saw a change in Clarence then. He said, 'The Republicans are going
places in the next ten years, and I'm going to attach my wagon to their
star.'" Martin forgave Thomas's apparent ideological expedience. "In
many ways he was already conservative in his social views," Martin
noted. "And he really admired Danforth. I'd ask him, 'How can you
become a Republican?' And he'd say, 'Blacks need to be on both sides,
and these people are power.' It was a matter of practicality."

Similarly, Fletcher Farrington, the Savannah law partner who supported Thomas's nomination to the Supreme Court, said that Thomas
once explained his political shift as largely a question of advancing
his own ambition. "He told me that he talked to the Democrats first,
but they weren't particularly interested in him. Then he went to the
Republicans, and they embraced him. I don't want to say that Clarence was a complete opportunist, but to some extent his politics were
shaped by his opportunities." This was hardly surprising, Farrington
suggested, because from the start "his ambition was not to make a
particular change in society but to go as far as he could go."

But to some, such as Thomas's mentor of the previous summer, the
civil rights lawyer Bobby Hill, the explanation that the young lawyer
was merely hitching his wagon to a rising star had "an immoral cast,"
raising questions about what else he would do to advance himself.
"You can't tell me that it wasn't just about getting ahead, because
ideologically, from me to Danforth is a long way," said Hill. "You're
talking two extremes. I'm a liberal civil rights lawyer, and he's a Republican patrician. Thomas didn't care if he was hitching himself to
a good star or not," contended Hill. "The only thing he cared about
is the one thing that the two of us had in common: we were both
rising."

Although Thomas was increasingly outspoken in Danforth's office
about such issues as the evils of welfare — which he described to one

colleague as virtually a white conspiracy meant to maintain blacks at substandard levels — he was apparently silent about another controversial issue, abortion.

During Thomas's first year in Missouri, there was widespread talk in the office about *Roe v. Wade,* the Supreme Court's ruling that established a pregnant woman's legal right to choose whether to have an abortion before the fetus was viable. Danforth opposed the ruling, which was passed down the year before Thomas joined his staff, and was trying to challenge it in a case that became known as *Danforth v. Planned Parenthood.* But while Thomas participated freely in other political discussions, frequently offering examples drawn from his own family, no one recalled his expressing any opinion on the subject of *Roe.* Later, during his confirmation hearings, Thomas would testify that he had never debated the ruling in his life.

Although he may have kept silent in the office, some people did recall discussing abortion — though not necessarily the *Roe* ruling — with him. Thomas's mother, Leola Williams, remembered clearly that she and Thomas discussed the issue and that his opinion was based on her experience. He opposed abortion on demand, she said he told her, because "if you had had one, where would I be?"

And in or about 1974, the year he graduated from law school and the year after the *Roe* decision, Thomas participated in another family discussion on the subject. According to his sister, Emma Mae, that year she herself had an abortion, and either then or afterward she talked about it with him. Thomas, she said, was "understanding" because she had been told by a doctor that, having become pregnant despite the use of an IUD, she was in danger of dying if she carried the baby, which would have been her fifth child, to term. It was a painful predicament, but if it caused Thomas to disagree with Danforth about *Roe* that year or later, he kept it to himself.

❖

Thomas's two and a half years in Danforth's office provided him with his only real litigation experience. Early in his tenure, he would sometimes argue appeals in criminal cases before the state's three courts. But much of his time was spent in the civil division handling an array of tax cases, mostly routine appeals rather than jury trials. Indeed, when Thomas was asked in 1989 to list the most significant cases he had litigated on a questionnaire required of aspiring federal judges, he mentioned no jury trials at all. Instead, he listed a number of arcane tax cases, including an oral argument he had made before the Missouri supreme court in which he had argued, unsuccessfully, that the state should be able to levy taxes on receipts from pinball machines. His most significant victory, apparently, was an argument against the use of vanity license plates by Missouri's VIPs.

There was one jarring recollection in the generally positive picture painted by Thomas's colleagues in the attorney general's office. According to Andy Rothschild, now an attorney in St. Louis but then a friend and fellow lawyer, Thomas liked to taunt another member of the office, who was prim and painfully shy, by making outrageous, gross, and at times off-color remarks. "Clarence was loud and boisterous, kind of the office clown. He couldn't help himself but to needle the guy — he just liked to get under his skin," Rothschild recalled in an interview.

The target of Thomas's taunting was John C. Ashcroft, who would later replace Danforth as attorney general and eventually become Missouri's governor. A tightly wound, strait-laced teetotaler who was the son of a fundamentalist minister and who was himself a gospel singer and songwriter, Ashcroft was easily flustered by Thomas, according to a second colleague who also remembered such episodes. This apparently encouraged Thomas to goad him further.

Thomas parted company with the attorney general's office by January 1977, when Danforth became a U.S. senator. With Danforth's help, he got a job in the legal department of Missouri's Monsanto Chemical Corporation. Dealing with environmental and regulatory matters, Thomas doubled the salary he'd earned with Danforth. He handled the company's registration of its herbicidal products with the Environmental Protection Agency while monitoring product liability cases involving Monsanto's crop chemicals. But the big cases, in which the company was exposed to potential damage awards, were farmed out to private law firms, as is typical in such large corporations.

Thomas's experience at Monsanto enabled him to develop a useful expertise in the emerging field of environmental law. In this entry-level capacity Thomas did well, if not exceptionally so. Later, Monsanto's general counsel, Richard W. Duesenberg, said of his performance: "In a staff of extremely competent and bright lawyers, Clarence Thomas could and did hold his own."

In August 1979, after a little over two years at Monsanto, Thomas was offered a new opportunity. Once again it came from Danforth. Anxious to integrate his Senate staff, he approached Thomas about becoming one of his legislative assistants in Washington.

As before, Thomas accepted the job only after being assured that his assignments would be in areas not related to race. Drawing on his stint at Monsanto, he agreed to specialize in environmental and energy issues. "He wanted to work on those issues because they were not identified with blacks," recalled Robert Harris, another black congressional staff member who befriended Thomas at the time. He also made little effort to forge friendships with other blacks on Capitol Hill. During the late 1970s, a black congressional staff group met periodically for lunch and other occasions, but Thomas attended only rarely. Harris, who headed the group, thought Thomas avoided it because "there was an element of not wanting to be that closely connected with something so identifiably black. We discussed that."

None of the other black congressional staff members who came to know Thomas at this point remember him as especially gifted. (One called him "an okey-dokey sort of guy. He was absolutely not a standout.") But whether his colleagues knew it or not, his ambitions were extraordinary. Less than a year after arriving in Washington, over lunch with a reporter in the Washington bureau of the *St. Louis Post-Dispatch*, Thomas mentioned that he had his eye on a better job. Jon Sawyer, now the paper's Washington bureau chief, recalled being astonished when Thomas, who was an affable but completely unknown aide to a freshman senator, announced that the spot he wanted was nothing less than a seat on the U.S. Supreme Court.

To get there, however, it would be useful for Thomas to have patrons who were well to the right of Danforth. And while Thomas could sound moderate when loyalty to his patron required it, he had already embraced ideas and cultivated contacts who were considerably more extreme. By the time the power in the party shifted rightward, Thomas was uniquely well positioned.

❖

Many of the ideas that influenced Thomas during his steady evolution to the right came from a senior fellow at Stanford University's Hoover Institution named Thomas Sowell. Sowell had emerged in the 1970s as an intellectual leader of the tiny black conservative movement by taking the left-wing, separatist racial theories of Malcolm X and combining them with the purest, most right-wing economic doctrines of the Chicago school, where he had been a protégé of the conservative economist Milton Friedman. The result was a prickly laissez-faire survivalism that rejected all well-intentioned government help from whites as unwanted interference designed to coopt and corrupt its beneficiaries, be they the actual recipients of welfare programs or the bourgeois blacks who administered them.

At times Sowell sounded much like Malcolm X, who castigated integration as "a foxy Northern liberal's smokescreen" meant to seduce a few "token-integrated Negroes [to] flee from their poor, downtrodden black brothers." Similarly, Sowell opposed integration techniques such as busing and affirmative action. Echoing Malcolm X, he suggested that these schemes were designed to help a black elite widen the class gulf between itself and the black masses. Also like Malcolm X, Sowell harshly criticized the civil rights community, which he saw as a self-serving, snobby clique. "The NAACP's agenda," Sowell wrote, "reflects the priorities of the elite: equal access to white institutions and white neighborhoods allowing them to escape the black masses." Under affirmative action, he charged, "those who were already well off were made even better off — while the ostensible beneficiaries were either neglected or made worse off." But while Malcolm X believed that blacks ought to turn inward as a community and help themselves, Sowell advocated self-help with a conservative twist, arguing that each individual ought to look out for himself.

In this intellectually audacious black economist, Thomas found an inspiration and a role model. Sowell's theories allowed Thomas to connect his earlier interest in black separatism with his newfound Republicanism. It wasn't a big leap from a black militant's suspicion of white government to a conservative's suspicion of all government.

Sowell's class politics also touched a nerve in Thomas. The Stanford economist's attack on the alleged elitism of the civil rights establishment provided Thomas with an ideological outlet for his simmering anger at the lighter, more privileged blacks he had felt snubbed by, first as a child and later at Yale. Moreover, the ostracism of Sowell by more mainstream black thinkers also spoke to Thomas, who had himself been an outsider for so much of his life. Thomas first read Sowell's works in the mid-1970s, and he found them so stimulating that on one occasion he went to hear Sowell speak specifically so that he could introduce himself afterward. Sowell's doctrines prompted an intellectual breakthrough; as Thomas later said, "It was like pouring a half a glass of water on the desert. I just soaked it up."

Thomas was also quite taken with Sowell's controversial opinion of women. Acquaintances remembered Thomas's approvingly paraphrasing Sowell's view that the reason women earned substantially less than men on average was that many women wanted it that way: they took less demanding jobs so they could drop in and out to have babies. Later Thomas would echo this theory when, as chairman of the EEOC, he was forced to wrestle with the issue of pay inequity between the sexes.

Thus by 1980, as Reaganomics swept the country, Thomas already subscribed to positions well to the right of Danforth. But if Sowell had shown the way intellectually, it took an even better-connected black conservative to pave Thomas's career path into the new administration.

❖

Thomas first learned of J. A. "Jay" Parker in the late 1970s when a colleague in Danforth's Senate office tossed a copy of Parker's publication, the *Lincoln Review,* over the desk divider. A few minutes later he heard Thomas calling the magazine's editor and booming at Parker, "My name is Clarence Thomas and I like what you have to say!" In Parker, Thomas found not just a kindred political spirit — a man who courted controversy and seemed to relish his role as a provocateur — but also a valuable escort into the once obscure but by 1980 strategically important subculture of far right politics. Parker was more conservative than the Reaganites. While Reagan won election by demanding deep cuts in social programs even as he vowed to maintain a social "safety net," Parker believed the government had no responsibility whatsoever to take care of the destitute. He opposed both state and local aid, whether for food, clothing, or housing.

Parker had credentials unlike those of any other African-American. He was virtually the only black active in the Draft Goldwater campaign in 1959. In 1965 he became the first black to sit on the national board of Young Americans for Freedom, a group that supported the Vietnam War and functioned as a virtual finishing school for young Reaganites. Parker also belonged to the American chapter of the

World Anti-Communist League, a global alliance of the far right that was regularly criticized by human rights activists for its alleged inclusion of Nazis, neo-Nazis, and Central American death squad leaders in its crusade against communism.

The proud son of a short-order chef and a domestic servant from Philadelphia, Parker liked to say "I'm conservative because I was poor." Presumably he did not become conservative in order to get rich, but he seemed to have a talent for finding wealthy sponsors for his unusual views. In 1977, for instance, as opposition to apartheid grew in America, his knack for profiting from his politics raised eyebrows. Parker became a lobbyist for the South African government and helped promote the concept of restricted black homelands — as opposed to full citizenship — for the country's black majority. Particularly as the United States began to weigh economic sanctions against the racist government, Parker's visibility as a black American promoting white rule was much appreciated by the South African government. He was paid handsomely for his services by the Pretoria regime; between 1985 and 1988, for instance, the embassy paid his company more than $1 million. Some of it was spent lobbying Reagan administration officials, among them Clarence Thomas, by then chairman of the EEOC, who was on Parker's guest list for a dinner with South Africa's widely shunned ambassador to the United States.

Many blacks saw Parker as a collaborator with the enemy, an opportunist who enriched himself by providing a black cover for white racists. But Thomas saw in him a fellow individualist, a well-connected lunch companion, and a good bridge to the Reagan White House. Parker was an old ally of Reagan's first-term counselor and later attorney general, Edwin Meese III. And immediately after the 1980 election, it was Meese who directed the new president's transition team and thus controlled thousands of desirable federal jobs.

In a chain of events that proved pivotal to Thomas's career, in November 1980 Meese asked Parker to head the transition effort at the EEOC. Parker in turn invited his young protégé, Clarence Thomas, to join his transition team. Thomas's prospects were thereby dramatically improved: not only would he help draft the new administration's policies, he was also almost certain to be offered a job.

The EEOC, with its responsibility for policing racial and other forms of discrimination in the workplace, was among the agencies that the Reagan administration would have happily abolished, had

Congress allowed. Since that wasn't politically possible, it was instead marked for radical restructuring, which some believed was designed to cripple its effectiveness. Shrewdly, the administration realized that if minorities could be found to carry out its mission, they would protect the White House against allegations of racial insensitivity. Parker, who believed the government had no business playing social worker, was glad to help. And Thomas evidently was as well.

Perhaps because of Parker's controversial reputation, his link to Thomas's first job in the Reagan administration was obscured by the Bush White House when Thomas was nominated for the Supreme Court. Memos about reconstituting the EEOC that Thomas wrote to Parker in 1980 during the transition period were submitted to the Judiciary Committee with Parker's name blacked out. These memos, however, provide a valuable record of Thomas's migration to the right as he began to embrace the views of his sponsors more and more.

In one such memo, Thomas excoriated what by 1980 had become the principal tool of disadvantaged groups fighting against illegal discrimination: the class action lawsuit, or, as it was known at the EEOC, the use of "patterns and practices" cases. Instead, hewing to a line popular with both Parker and Meese as well as with employers across America, Thomas suggested that worker discrimination should be proven case by case, fought one individual at a time, rather than by whole segments of the workforce. No one needed to spell out the impact: it was like lurching backward in time and efficiency from the fastest assembly line to the slowest handmade production.

Thomas launched his other major attack on the EEOC's expansive new guidelines on sexual harassment. The transition team report, co-written by Thomas in 1980, denounced the new definition of harassment — which included unwelcome sexual attention, whether verbal or physical, if it created a hostile work environment — as too lenient. The definition was so broad, the report said, it would lead to "a barrage of trivial complaints against employers around the nation." Moreover, the report dismissed the effort to prevent such problems as completely futile. It stated, "The elimination of personal slights and sexual advances which contribute to an intimidating, hostile or offensive working environment is a goal impossible to reach."

Twelve years later, with Thomas joining the majority, the Supreme Court ruled that both this broad standard of sexual harassment and the necessity of eliminating it entirely from the workplace were, without exception, the law. But in 1980, as Thomas was poised to enter the federal bureaucracy and, for the first time in his life, to supervise the work of others, his attitude toward harassment was dramatically different.

❖

A month and a half after Ronald Reagan won the presidential election, Thomas paid his own air fare for a trip to San Francisco, where, at the invitation of Sowell, he attended a conference of black conservatives. A decade earlier, the notion of such a conference might have been dismissed as oxymoronic; now, this gathering served as an unofficial job fair for those jockeying for posts in the new administration. With Ed Meese scheduled to deliver a major address, visibility at what became known as the Fairmont Conference — named for the stately old Nob Hill hotel where the meeting took place — could vault a young aide like Thomas onto a new rung of prominence and power.

Sowell had organized the conference, hoping that by 1980 there would be enough black conservatives to populate a new organization, one that could potentially counter the influence of the NAACP. The hope turned out to be in vain, as Parker later admitted, because black conservatives were such individualists that "by definition we can't be organized. It's like pulling teeth just to get them out to lunch."

More than a hundred people attended the conference, but it was Thomas who caught the eye of a young black reporter who covered the meeting for the *Washington Post*. "You have heard of Clarence Thomas, but not by name," wrote Juan Williams. "He is one of the black people now on center stage in American politics: he is a Republican, a long-time supporter of Ronald Reagan, opposed to the minimum wage law, rent control, busing, and affirmative action."

Williams later explained that he focused on Thomas because, unlike many of the other participants, including the difficult Sowell, Thomas was accessible and open to argument. In fact, although Thomas later complained to Williams that the piece had made him a pariah among other blacks, at the time, said Williams, he seemed eager to cooperate.

It was in this interview that Thomas first publicly denounced his sister's reliance on public assistance. "She is so dependent," Thomas told the *Post*, "she gets mad when the mailman is late with her welfare check . . . What's worse," he continued, "is that now her kids feel entitled to the check too. They have no motivation for doing better or getting out of that situation."

Actually, according to Thomas's sister, she had by this time already stopped receiving any form of public assistance and was instead working double shifts for the minimum wage of $2.35 per hour at a nursing home in Savannah. It also bothered her that Thomas neglected to mention some extenuating circumstances: for at least some of the time she was on welfare, she said, she had to quit work in order to take care of their aunt Annie, who had been incapacitated by a stroke.

This public attack on Thomas's own kin breached all canons of acceptable behavior in the family-centered South, where many offered to help even distant relations. Thomas later told a personal aide that he had been so upset when his comments appeared in print, he had driven nonstop from Washington to Georgia to apologize to his sister (an event she said she has no memory of).

In any case, Thomas's harsh words reflected his thinking in 1980; they also meshed seamlessly with the bold rhetoric of the new president. Reagan had come to power in part by capitalizing on the resentment of working-class whites toward black welfare recipients, the most undeserving of whom he spotlighted in his speeches as "welfare queens." Thomas's disparaging words about his sister were thus likely to catch the eye of the Republican talent scouts, which in fact they did.

Equally dramatic was Thomas's pledge to the *Post* to reject categorically any job in the Reagan administration directly connected with matters of race. "If I ever went to work for the EEOC, or did anything directly connected with blacks," Thomas said, "my career would be irreparably ruined. The monkey would be on my back again to prove that I didn't have the job because I am black. People meeting me for the first time would automatically dismiss my thinking as second-rate."

Again, these comments were consistent with previous statements he had made and with the views of the new administration. (In his speech at the Fairmont Conference, Ed Meese promised not to limit black appointees to "black work" — an assurance that would be broken almost immediately in Thomas's case, among others.) But it is hard to ignore a double irony. First, at the time he made the statement,

Thomas had already been working on the EEOC transition team for a month and a half, a fact he failed to mention to Juan Williams. Second, a year and a half after saying that working for the EEOC would irreparably harm his career, he became its chairman.

Why Thomas singled out the EEOC in his conversations with Williams is unclear. No doubt he was expressing his true feelings about such work. He may also have been trying to warn his would-be employers that beyond the transition, he didn't want to be further stereotyped. In either case, only two months after the Fairmont Conference Thomas was forced to choose between his beliefs and getting a desirable job with the new administration. He chose the latter. According to the *Washington Post,* Thomas was first offered a job that, as he had requested, had nothing to do with race. If he accepted the position, he would be working in the White House as one of its countless low-level policy aides, and his assignment would be to analyze the environmental and energy issues he had worked on for Danforth. But Thomas rejected the offer, and soon the administration came back offering a more prominent post. This time he was asked to be assistant secretary for civil rights in the Department of Education, overseeing the enforcement of civil rights laws as they pertained to all levels of education in the country — exactly the kind of "black work" he had so publicly eschewed. And this time Thomas took the job.

Apparently he anguished over his decision quite vocally. Among others, he consulted Allen Moore, Danforth's director of legislation, and Moore recalled that "his gut instinct was not to take [the job]. He felt he would be on the minority track, the track saved for symbols." But Moore said that he argued that Thomas would be "nuts" to turn it down. As Moore remembered it, he told Thomas, "You are thirty-two years old, a legislative assistant, and you have been handed an opportunity to run an office in a federal agency with a large staff. Forget about being a stereotype. This is visibility, responsibility, a presidential appointment." Thomas's qualms about taking this step were no doubt heartfelt. But his ambition propelled him forward.

❖

Although Thomas was willing to bite his tongue about "black work" in order to get a foothold in the Reagan administration, the fit proved less than comfortable, according to some of those who worked with him during his tenure in the new Department of Education. The department had been formed only two years earlier, during the Carter administration; Thomas served for twelve months — from May 1981 until May 1982 — and it was an awkward place to be. Not only had Reagan vowed to abolish the entire department as unneeded bureaucracy, but the more conservative members of his administration were also bent on gutting many of the civil rights laws that Thomas was supposed to oversee. Having resisted a job involving race, Thomas now found himself stuck in the middle of a racial brawl.

"I felt there was even a bit of embarrassment at being in the position he was," said Judith Winston, a Carter appointee who, as assistant general counsel, oversaw issues concerning educational equity. Winston had a chance to observe Thomas closely and considered him caught in a bind: "As one of the few black conservatives, he ended up being treated by his own party in a way he said he opposed. I always felt he resented the position of having to defend these civil rights cases at all." Perhaps as a result, many found Thomas chilly, sarcastic, and short-tempered during this period. "You couldn't argue with him," recalled one colleague, his former Yale classmate and a Carter Democrat, Tony Califa. "Instead, I'd find myself having to back down, saying things like 'Oh, I didn't know that,' to which he'd reply, 'I could fill a book with what you don't know.'"

Winston, however, saw the surly exterior as a defense to cover Thomas's lack of expertise. "[Thomas] intimidated a lot of white appointees because they didn't know how to read him. He had a way of sitting quietly and glowering, giving very short yes and no answers to complicated questions," she recalled. "But I think it was a front — the fact was that he didn't know a lot about how the civil rights laws worked, and he didn't want to let on in meetings that he was less than knowledgeable."

She found him a quick study, though, and at least in the beginning, she said, Thomas seemed open-minded, eager to learn, and anxious to stake out a middle ground between the staunch civil rights critics in the Reagan administration, who wanted him to abandon completely the federal government's enforcement role, and the civil rights community, which demanded that the department continue to enforce the laws. The clash, Winston recalled, resulted in "many stormy meetings" and once again left Thomas where he so often landed, "in no-man's land. He was caught between blacks, who saw him as being used, and the whites in the administration, some of whom I remember him angrily describing as bigots who really thought blacks were inferior."

Chief among those in the administration who aggravated him was the assistant attorney general for civil rights, William Bradford Reynolds, whose interference Thomas bitterly resented. Another antagonist was Reynolds's Justice Department colleague T. Kenneth Cribb Jr., an ultraconservative from Spartanburg, South Carolina, who, among other things, suggested that citizens were under no legal obligation to comply with court-ordered busing. Thomas was not alone in suspecting that some of these officials had a racial bias. Terrel H. Bell, who was secretary of education at the time, recalled in his memoirs being "shocked at the sick humor and racist clichés" voiced by some Reagan appointees, who, for instance, referred to Martin Luther King Jr. as "Martin Lucifer Coon," called Arabs "sand niggers," and described Title IX, which prohibits sexual discrimination, as "the lesbians' bill of rights." To such hard-liners, the Civil Rights Act of 1964 and subsequent legislation outlawing racial, sexual, and other forms of discrimination in education and elsewhere were unwanted interferences in the free market and thus obstacles to be overcome.

Thomas's view of these highly charged issues was evidently of less than major importance to the administration. During his tenure, for example, the Justice Department sent shock waves through the civil rights community by backing tax-exempt status for Bob Jones University, a Christian college in South Carolina that refused to admit blacks. Thomas thought the move a terrible mistake, and in a different administration the opinion of the black titular head of civil rights enforcement in the Department of Education might have mattered. But in this case, Thomas was ignored.

In the midst of this maelstrom, Thomas struck Judith Winston as "very confused. The confusion, from my standpoint, stemmed from the fact that he was permitting himself to be used, and he knew it. Others saw him as combative, but I thought he was ill at ease with himself. He was a willing instrument, very pragmatic; he saw the opportunities for someone who would go along. But he resented some of the things that the Republican political appointees were trying to talk him into." Nonetheless, Thomas had an argument ready for those who questioned why he stayed. It was better, he told Winston and a number of others, to deal with "out-and-out racists" than the kinds who "are racist behind your back. At least," he argued grimly, "you know where you stand."

Despite such indignities, it was clear that no matter how outlandish some of his old colleagues from Yale and Georgia thought his embrace of conservatism was, it had paid off handsomely. While many of his friends were still unrecognized drones in legal offices, Thomas was already one of the highest-ranking blacks in the U.S. government.

Thomas's political career was thriving, but in other ways the early eighties were a difficult period for the young lawyer. By the time he reached the Department of Education, his marriage, already frayed, was coming apart. The couple's friends described the basic problem as "a mismatch of ambition." Thomas's classmate from Holy Cross, Gordon Davis, suggested that an additional factor was that Kathy Ambush Thomas had not shared Thomas's political odyssey to conservatism. Davis said that while she had dutifully followed Thomas to Washington, she had "hinted that their views had become so different, they couldn't stay together."

One Yale classmate who encountered Thomas on a bus ride home during the end of his stint in Danforth's Senate office was struck by his anger at both his wife and his son, who was then about eight: "He was really mad at his wife, saying that she was coddling their son too much. Jamal wasn't doing well at school. Kathy thought he had learning disabilities. But Clarence thought the boy just wasn't trying hard enough. It was like he blamed them both."

At about the same time, Thomas's wife recounted to an officemate that she had fallen asleep at the wheel while driving alone in the car, only to wake up in the hospital with Thomas berating her. His chief concern seemed to be that she had wrecked their car. As she told it, the episode crystallized for her Thomas's absence of compassion. "Her attitude," recalled the colleague, "was, 'Can you believe how cold this guy is?'"

Kaye Savage, who had met Thomas through her work as a career civil servant detailed to the Reagan White House, was struck, she later told others, by how angry he seemed about his marriage at this time. "He'd gone through a bad period, he and his wife had separated, then reconciled, then separated again. His life wasn't going the way he'd planned. His son was back and forth [between him and his wife]. He was angry because it hadn't ended up being the way he wanted. To him, it was like a flaw."

Thomas seemed to be a perfectionist, determined to exert more control over every aspect of his life. Every weekday he rose at four in the morning, lifted weights, and then went to church, skipping Sundays in order to avoid other people. He liked to say "God is all right; it's the people I don't like." Such extreme self-discipline struck acquaintances like Savage as both impressive and troubling. "I guess I felt like he had never recovered from whatever happened to him as a child," she later said, "and his marriage falling apart just reinforced that. It seemed as if he hated his mother, his grandmother was terribly fundamentalist, and like he just hated women."

During this difficult period, Thomas confided in Tony Califa, the liberal Democrat who worked with him at the Department of Education, that he just hadn't enjoyed family life. "He said that some people are not cut out for it, and he was one of them. He said he hated mowing the lawn over and over, and just being tied down by a family routine." Thomas decided never to have children again and had a vasectomy — a step his second wife would try to persuade him to reverse.

Thomas's penchant for contrary behavior occasionally bordered on the perverse during this time. In a town obsessed with its football team, the Washington Redskins, Thomas made a point of embracing their blood enemy, the Dallas Cowboys. And in conversations about the popular *Star Wars* movies, Thomas announced to Califa and others that his personal hero was Darth Vader, the movies' incarnation of evil.

After separating in January 1981, then reconciling in the early summer, Thomas and his wife parted for good in August, just a few months into his term at the Education Department. Thomas moved into the spare bedroom of Gil Hardy, his closest friend since the days when they were, as Thomas put it, "the two slowest guys on the [Holy Cross] track team." Hardy was also in the throes of a divorce, living in an apartment in the Adams Morgan section of downtown Washington. According to a girlfriend of Hardy's who encountered Thomas there, "Clarence had changed quite a lot, at least outwardly," since she had first known him at Holy Cross.

"In college he had been very square, not very attractive, the kind of guy who didn't know how to buy a suit or shoes that matched. It was like the social component of his life was missing. But by this time he seemed to have mastered the yuppie image. He knew he was going places. The impression he gave was that he was the anointed one." What she remembered most vividly, however, was the way Thomas woke up each morning. He had a theme song which he would play at high volume in his room at the start of every day, "kind of like a mantra."

"What's that?" she remembered asking Hardy when she was first rocked out of bed by it at an early hour.

"Oh, that's just Clarence," Hardy replied with a laugh. "It's his theme song." The song, "The Greatest Love of All," was a pop anthem celebrating self-love later rereleased by Whitney Houston. Its chorus went:

> The greatest love of all is happening to me —
> Learning to love yourself is the Greatest Love of All!

As his song suggested, Thomas seemed suspicious of romance and intent on embracing his new, independent status. It was, after all, something of a novelty. He had gone from the chaste life of the seminary directly to college, where he had married his first serious girlfriend only months after they met. Thus the summer of 1981 was the first time in Thomas's adult life that he was truly free and on his own.

It was precisely at this sensitive point in his personal life that Thomas began to assemble his staff at the Department of Education. He was determined not to take whatever inexperienced campaign workers the White House threw his way; even before starting the job, he asked his friend Hardy for the names of possible candidates. Hardy, who was a partner in a Washington law firm, suggested that Thomas interview a young, black, female law associate at the firm who wanted to get into government. Her name was Anita Hill.

The match was an immediate success. Hill, twenty-five years old, was eager, ambitious, smart, and attractive. Although she had no political experience — a situation that would later require Thomas's aide Phyllis Berry to reclassify Hill's job as a career civil service rather than a political position — Thomas nonetheless told Hill on the spot that he would like her to come and work for him as soon as he was confirmed.

4

◆

Talking Wild

BY THE TIME she met Clarence Thomas, Anita Faye Hill had come a long way from the barren stretch of mud-caked fields in the northeast corner of Oklahoma where her life began. It was "a part of America," as she later said, "that is getting lost in the rush of modern times and quick development." Indeed, her birthplace of Lone Tree, a settlement of dusty little clapboard houses strung together on rutted dirt roads several miles outside the small, all-white town of Morris, seems almost untouched by the modern world. If there were a single word to describe Hill's upbringing there, it would be "old-fashioned."

In time, some people would suggest that Hill and Thomas had similar backgrounds: they had both come from families that were poor, rural, and black. They did share many similar deprivations. Hill, like Thomas, attended segregated schools until ninth grade, although her schools were public, not private; and, like Thomas, her chores stretched from dawn until dusk — feeding hogs, chickens, and cattle, picking peanuts, chopping cotton, cooking sorghum, and plucking feathers from geese for sale as pillow stuffing. Hill's parents, too, were strong disciplinarians as well as traditional Democrats who revered Franklin Roosevelt and, later, Martin Luther King Jr.

In other respects, however, Hill's family was entirely different from Thomas's. The Hill family farm, like Thomas's Pin Point home, might not have indoor plumbing, but it covered some 250 acres. And while the work was backbreaking, the family had a spirit of self-sufficiency and well-being that had been passed from father to son, like the land itself, which had been allotted to them by the government shortly after the Civil War. Where abandonment and rejection marked Thomas's earliest memories, Hill's were formed in the heart of a strong, proud, and very much intact family.

Born in 1956, Anita was the youngest child in a line of thirteen. She was surrounded by doting older siblings, grandparents determined that she and the others should "be someone," and parents who fussed over her as the baby of the family, encouraging and protecting her in a way they simply hadn't had time to do for many of the others. "When she got a cold," recalled one relative, "it was a big deal. She was kept in bed for a week."

Hill revered her parents, Albert and Erma, as role models; to her they were honest, hard-working, and righteous figures, and she remained close to them in her adult life. To some extent, Thomas's grandfather had played a similar role. But by adulthood Thomas had rebelled against his grandfather's politics and religion, rejecting many of the institutions his grandfather had embraced, such as the Catholic Church and the NAACP, and instead striking angrily and questioningly into the world on his own. In contrast, Hill held fast to the people and lessons she had grown up with. When she finally entered the faraway professional world of Washington, she seemed something of a throwback — polite, strait-laced, and almost too naive to have come so far. She was the kind of young woman, recalled a friend, who returned from visits home carrying an extra suitcase filled with vegetables from her mother's garden.

Even within her family, Hill, whose relatives called her by her middle name, Faye, was seen as something of a goody two-shoes. To be sure, there were few temptations in Lone Tree. It offered a schoolhouse, a church, a creek for baptisms, and virtually nothing to do at night. Yet, said one relative, Hill seemed completely at home in that strict, small world. "Bookish" and "sheltered" were how relatives described her. "She was very much under her mother's wing, and the Bible was the main text of her mother's teachings," recalled one relative. "Moral lessons were drawn all the time." Typical, according to one family member, was Hill's disgust after seeing an episode of *Peyton Place* on television for the first time at the age of ten or eleven.

"Why do they do like that?" she asked her mother.

"It's not that they are mean-spirited," her mother, Erma, replied carefully. "It's just that they have ugly ways."

Propriety to the point of repression was a family trait. The Hills were so private that the topic of Anita's testimony was never even broached when she returned home for Thanksgiving a month after millions of Americans watched the confirmation hearings on television. "We wanted a pleasant occasion," explained one family member with characteristic reserve.

This ethic — silence was always preferable to confrontation — kept the family from discussing its one disgraced member as well. Whereas most of Hill's siblings achieved considerable success, her older brother Allen followed a downward spiral that ended in the state penitentiary. Even Allen understood this code: according to relatives, he begged the authorities not to inform his parents of his legal problems.

Sex, in particular, was a taboo subject in the Hill household. The family farmhouse, adorned with a portrait of Jesus, was "like a church," recalled one relative. "You just wouldn't say certain things in such a place." Hill's oldest sister, Elreatha Lee, recalled that the way she figured out how babies were made was by finding, when she was seven, a 4-H pamphlet entitled "Training the Child from One to Six Years," which she spirited off to the barn for serious study. The Hill daughters weren't allowed to date until they were sixteen; even then they were required to take a brother along as a chaperon. A number of boys expressed interest in Anita, who was always pretty, despite her dark, plastic-rimmed eyeglasses. But, recalled a cousin, "she never gave them the time of day. Between work and school, she was too busy."

Billy Reager, one of the handful of Hill's black high school peers, who later faulted her for embarrassing African-Americans in the hearings, recalled that in school "she was different from other kids. She wasn't weird. But she studied more. She didn't go to parties. She didn't waste time chasing boys. It was like even back then, you could sense she was going places." But despite being "a bookworm," as he put it, Hill was always popular. "If there was a perfect person, it was Faye. Everyone just loved her."

In an interview, Elreatha Lee suggested that the family's reserved social manner was passed down from its Creek Indian forebears, who had intermarried with the family's African-American slave ancestors; together they moved from North Carolina to the new territory of Oklahoma in the nineteenth century. The Hill children had been taught to be proud of their Native American traditions, some of which stretched into their own childhood. A Creek headdress worn by one of Hill's grandfathers hung on the stairs. And a Creek corn dish, sofkee, was a favorite in the family.

The mixed heritage, suggested Elreatha, added to a sense of stature already fostered by the relative erudition of the family, studded as it was with ministers and teachers. Her family was, as she put it, "maybe a little more advanced, a little more special, than other families." This attitude of slight superiority was a trait that detractors would say Hill carried with her into adult life. Some saw it as producing a commendable adherence to high standards for herself and those around her; others found her prickly and brittle, a person who liked to have things her own way. She could be petulant when she didn't get what she wanted, but she was so polite and unwilling to offend that she wouldn't always make her feelings and intentions clear. As one friend put it, "Anita's difficult. She knows what she wants but she doesn't like to reveal too much of herself. When it comes to politics and a lot of other things, she's hard to pin down — she prefers to travel under Swiss passport."

While Hill tried to appear publicly neutral, privately, her rigid mores made her anything but. The result, this friend learned in one contretemps with Hill, was that she was both quick to take offense and reluctant to give it. This combination could make her seem aloof, and her ambivalent response to difficult situations meant that she often sent mixed signals, making misunderstandings likely.

But if Hill struck some as uptight or even prissy, a person so private she could be hard to read, even her strongest detractors suggested no pattern of dishonesty or unethical behavior. Indeed, no one could recall Hill's having ever told a lie, and Thomas himself stopped short of accusing her directly of lying during the hearings. Questions can be raised, and were during the hearings, about the accuracy of her memory, the precision of her language, and even the clarity of her judgment about herself and others. But by all accounts, Hill had been scrupulous about being truthful all her life. In this, too, she was a product of her past. As her nephew Gary Lee, who grew up with her, explained, "It sounds corny, but we were brought up to tell the truth, do your best, be civic-minded, and to do your duty for your country." All but one of the Hill boys, he pointed out, served in the military. Five of the children — including Anita — became valedictorians of their high school classes, and one was a salutatorian; three graduated from college, and two from junior college. Lee himself attended Phillips Andover Academy on a full scholarship before graduating from Amherst College.

"People are cynical about these things in Washington, D.C.," he said. "But given the way [Hill] grew up on a Bible-quoting farm in rural Oklahoma, you can understand that there was a sense of mission within the clan. Until the hearings, it was expressed mostly within the family. We were taught to tell the truth, make it quick, and make it simple. The hearings were just the first time it was applied outside the family."

❖

Another quality valued by the family was ambition. Elreatha recalled that when she was growing up, there were few opportunities for young black women like herself. "There really wasn't much open for us — maybe to be a nurse or a teacher." Still, when she dropped out of college to get married, her father was sorely disappointed, suggesting that he had "always expected better from me."

But Oklahoma was a Jim Crow state in those days, and blacks were routinely barred from even low-level jobs in which money was handled, such as bank teller or cashier. Poorly paid, dead-end posts were the rule. Elreatha recalled a childhood train trip on which she crossed from Kansas, where integration was accepted, into Oklahoma, where it was not. At the state line, a curtain was dropped between the black and white passengers who had previously been sharing the car.

Two years before Anita was born, however, the *Brown* decision rendered segregated schools unconstitutional, making it only a matter of time before the educational and professional horizons for young black women would begin to widen. Hill's childhood took place against the backdrop of the struggle for civil rights. Nearby schools were forced to integrate, sometimes causing intense conflict. Even in Morris, where the school desegregation proceeded peacefully, it was understood that all the black families would live outside the town limits. The churches, which were the center of social life, were also habitually segregated, as were the town's better jobs. Given such limited horizons, a young black woman with ambition would have no choice but to leave town.

Hill realized this at an early age. "We both wanted to go to bigger, better places than Morris," confirmed Hill's best friend in high school, Susie Clark. Early on, Washington became the focus of Hill's ambition: as far back as high school she told friends that the place she dreamed of working someday was the White House.

Clark, for one, never doubted that Hill would succeed at whatever she undertook. The two girls — one black, one white — were the top students in their class. They competed for the role of valedictorian (Hill won) and between them they captured just about every other honor. "She was really one of the brightest people I've ever met," said Clark, who eventually returned to teach special education and English at Morris High School. "She could read and just remember everything. And I'd have to debate whether to study, but Faye just knew she was going to have to give things up to get where she wanted to go."

"She was one of the two smartest kids I've taught in the last thirty years," commented Hill's teacher and coach, Bill Bearden. She was, in his eyes, "a model student" who also had a lot of friends; she was in the pep club, the Future Homemakers of America, and on the student council. Bearden's son, Bill Jr., was a classmate of Hill's; he added that Hill was "easygoing and even-tempered, not overly serious or odd. She was someone who you figured would accomplish something good for herself."

By the time she graduated from the predominantly white Morris High School in 1973, Hill had been accepted by Oklahoma State University in Stillwater on a full scholarship. There, according to Bearden, she got straight A's. She majored in psychology because, said Clark, who went on from Morris with her and in the beginning was her roommate, "we both just loved discussing people." Hill made friends easily, dated a lot, and enjoyed having both male and female friends over to watch TV with her, recalled Clark. Although they decided they ought to meet new people after a year or so, their decision to room together, she said, "worked out wonderfully. She just always had a lot of poise, a lot of class, a lot of dignity. She was private — there were a lot of times she didn't speak unless she had something to say."

Hill excelled at Oklahoma State, a sleepy, sprawling school best known for its agriculture department. She was a National Merit Scholar, a Regents Scholar, and was on the dean's and the president's honor roles. She was a freshman counselor and served on the advisory board of the Women's Council — a post reflecting her burgeoning interest in women's rights. When in 1977 Hill won the full Earl War-

ren Scholarship to Yale Law School, financed by the NAACP Legal
Defense Fund, her childhood friends were impressed but not surprised. In the family, however, where Hill's generation was the first
even to attend college, it was an achievement so great, Elreatha Lee
said that "in this family, even before the hearings, she had already
made history."

At law school, according to professors who remembered her, Hill
did well but not outstandingly so. She lived by herself in an apartment
off campus and made many friends across racial and political lines.
Hill continued to date her college sweetheart, a quiet white music
student who moved east with her after college. The relationship still
troubled her parents. Said one of her relatives, "It wasn't that her
parents didn't like him, it was just that they didn't really accept him,
and maybe they were afraid of how, in the long run, it would work
out for her." The affair ended in much heartbreak, said the relative,
adding, "I fear racial considerations within the family broke them
up." As the outcome suggests, Hill may have been an adult, but she
was above all else a dutiful daughter.

As most of her siblings moved on, married, and had children, Hill
explained to one that she was "married to her career." Later, the
sibling recalled her musing sadly that she might have liked to get
married and have children, but by the time she was ready, there were
few black professional men who were both appealing and available.

After graduating from Yale and passing the District of Columbia
bar exam in 1980, Hill was finally able to pursue her dream of working in Washington. Her hope, she told friends and family, was to work
in civil rights. Although she held traditionally Democratic views on
such issues as affirmative action, she had never burned with ideological fervor. Perhaps it was simply a reflection of the politically quiescent
time, but friends at Yale recall Hill as moderate, pragmatic, and more
or less apolitical. Whereas Thomas, who attended college and law
school six years ahead of her, had volunteered in a breakfast program
for poor black children and debated racial questions into the night,
Hill had filled her free hours at law school coaching the coed basketball team. If she was noted for anything, said one schoolmate, it was
for being "religious and quiet."

Deborah Leavy, a student in the class behind Hill, said the only
thing she recalled Hill ever doing to call attention to herself was to
sing a gospel song in the student talent show. Leavy, now a liberal

Democratic activist who went to work for the Senate Judiciary Committee and later the American Civil Liberties Union, said, "I know troublemakers because I am one. And Anita definitely was not." Similarly, Mary Coombs, a lawyer who worked in the same law firm as Hill, said that later attempts to paint Hill as a closet ideologue were groundless. "The notion that she was a radical feminist is absurd," said Coombs. "She was very shy. She wasn't the sort you'd even make a dirty joke in front of."

Thus, as she headed off to Washington in the midst of the 1980 presidential campaign, Hill seemed less interested in pursuing a specific political agenda than in accomplishing what her parents and grandparents had always asked of her. After all the years of serious study, after crossing the racial barriers that had limited so many of her older siblings, she wanted finally to "be someone."

❖

Hill made a promising start in Washington. Although she had ranked only in the middle of her class at Yale, she was invited to be an associate at the prestigious Washington law firm of Wald, Harkrader & Ross, where she had already served as a summer associate. Wald, Harkrader enjoyed a liberal and scholarly reputation and was by September of 1980, when she joined it, one of the most sought-after law firms in the country, especially for those hoping to launch careers in Washington.

In the half-dozen years between Thomas's and Hill's graduations from law school, the top law firms in the country had dramatically changed their attitude toward hiring minority lawyers. By 1980, it was common for law firms to compete for the best black students much as some colleges bid for star athletes. The change came in part because groups of women and minority students had threatened to sue restrictive law firms and cause them to be banished from recruiting on campuses altogether.

Hill had been drafted to join Wald, Harkrader by Gil Hardy, Thomas's friend and classmate at Yale Law, who had become a valued partner in the firm and was responsible for minority recruitment. Hardy took Hill under his wing immediately upon her arrival, along with Elaine Robinson, another black woman who was also a first-year associate.

Hill and Hardy soon became so friendly that a few of the other partners thought he might be romantically involved with her, despite the firm's discouragement of partner-associate romances. Shortly after the 1980 election, Larry Hughes, another Wald partner, invited Hardy to join him and his wife for dinner and an evening at the Kennedy Center. Hardy asked if he could bring a friend, never mentioning that his guest would be Anita Hill, whom Hughes knew. Hughes recalled the evening as very pleasant — they heard one of Aaron Copland's symphonies — and commented that Hill, once she relaxed, was good company. "She was so serious and shy," he said. "She needed to lighten up a little and learn to laugh more." Later, he realized that Hardy had brought her along not because they were romantically involved, but because he wanted to help bring her out of her shell.

Hill's competence at Wald became a matter of sharp conflict during Thomas's confirmation hearings; some of Thomas's supporters tried to undermine Hill's credibility by suggesting that she had been asked to leave the firm because she had not met its professional standards. Hill denied the charge roundly, testifying that "it was never suggested to me at the firm that I should leave the law firm in any way." But shortly after she made this statement, an affidavit was submitted by one of the firm's partners, John Burke, suggesting that he personally had told her to start looking for work elsewhere. The contradiction, of course, raised questions about Hill's truthfulness. Later, it drew the attention of David Brock, who theorized in his book, *The Real Anita Hill,* that Hill may have invented the notion of having been sexually harassed in order to cover up her embarrassing failure at the firm — and then used the same excuse at the EEOC.

Hardy might have been able to settle this dispute, since he had introduced Hill and Thomas and was one of the few people who knew both of them well. But Hardy was killed in a freak diving accident in Aruba in 1989, leaving behind a widow, children, and many mysteries.

Although Wald, Harkrader dissolved during the legal recession of the late 1980s, its personnel records have been reviewed and finally shed light on Hill's performance at the firm and the circumstances under which she left. The records confirm that Hill worked at the firm for only eleven months; in July of 1981, she left to join Thomas at the Department of Education. It is not unusual for associates to leave after two or three years, when law firms begin giving them some indication of their chance of making partner, but leaving after less than one year is unusual. The firm's records also show that during this short tenure, Hill was seen to be making satisfactory but not outstanding progress.

Hill's performance was first evaluated in February 1981, when the partners got together at a retreat to discuss the forty or so associates. About eight of the partners filled out work evaluation sheets on Hill. Judith Hope, a partner and Republican activist who later recalled shortcomings in Hill's work, supervised her on an aviation matter and rated her as "adequate" at the time. A few rated her highly, including one notoriously difficult partner. But there were more than a few criticisms. One partner complained that she was prone to disappear into the library and had left work altogether during one emergency assignment. Her recorded billable hours — which law firms use as a measure of productivity — were among the lowest of all the associates.

When the partners on the associate development committee met to give their review to Hill herself in the spring of 1981 — about the time she talked about a job with Thomas — she was told that her work was "generally adequate" although "uneven." Bill Weissman, one of three partners on the committee, didn't recall much about Hill's reaction. "It wasn't a brilliant performance review," he said, "but it was perfectly acceptable. There was no reason for her to be upset."

The records do not indicate that Hill was in any professional trouble. Had she been on the verge of being fired, a record certainly would have been kept for legal purposes. More than a dozen former Wald partners were adamant that she was not asked to leave the firm. Even those who remembered her as less than glittering, such as Tom Schwab, who described her as "mousy and shy," agree that "Anita Hill was not asked to leave the firm."

The matter of Burke's affidavit to the Judiciary Committee, in which he swore that he had personally told Hill to seek work elsewhere during an "uncomfortable" thirty-minute performance evaluation, thus becomes rather puzzling. Schwab, for instance, sat next to Burke, a corporate lawyer who had joined the firm just a few months before Hill, and he didn't recall Burke's ever complaining or saying much of anything about Anita Hill. Another partner, Jeffrey Liss, suggested, "If Anita was having trouble, I probably would have known about it. She talked to Gil [Hardy] a lot. Gil and I shared a secretary. We were close, as co-workers go."

Odder still, Burke said in his affidavit that he was the partner in charge of assigning work for the firm's tax and business law section, and it was because Hill had done work for his group that he had been in a position to give her a negative evaluation. But the firm's employment records offer no indication that Hill ever performed assignments for Burke. Any partner who supervised an associate was expected to fill out an evaluation form, and Burke never wrote anything about Hill. Also according to the records, the firm was not broken down into departments and did not establish specialty groups with partners heading them until March 1982 — eight months after Hill departed. Only then did Burke became head of the group he thought Hill was a part of.

Finally, in her first interview on the subject since Burke filed his affidavit, Hill adamantly denied his charges and added, "I didn't work with John Burke." When the firm expanded onto another floor, she thought she may have occupied the same suite as Burke. But she added, "I didn't have any kind of interaction [with Burke] except passing interaction as you would with somebody who might be in the same suite of offices with you or nearby." Although it remains possible that Burke did have some sort of talk with Hill, there is no evidence of it.

Burke, who declined requests for an interview, did work closely with Elaine Robinson, the other black woman associate in Hill's class. Robinson was having problems at Wald, according to the firm's records; she did work for Burke and did leave the firm a bit after Hill did. Burke has denied to friends and others that he confused the two women, but several former Wald partners, including Donald Green, who said he likes and admires Burke, believed he simply got the two young women mixed up.

Although Hill was performing adequately at Wald, her goal had never been to spend her career at a law firm. She thought she'd get good legal training in private practice, but for years she had told friends and relatives that she hoped to work in the area of civil rights for some part of the government. She was encouraged by the success of some of her friends from Yale, including Susan Hoerchner, who were working in government agencies where they seemed to have both challenging and fulfilling jobs.

Evidently Hill felt comfortable confiding her ambitions to Hardy, and when Hardy learned that his friend Clarence Thomas would be assuming the top civil rights post at the Education Department, he strongly recommended Hill for a job there. When she left, most of her colleagues at Wald assumed that she had received a better offer. "I assumed Gil had gotten her this interesting job," recalled Robert Skitol, another Wald lawyer who was friendly with Hill. "The associate's life isn't for everyone. You can get stuck in the library a lot."

By contrast, working for a rising black star like Thomas promised to be an exciting challenge. Although Hill had always been a Democrat, party labels apparently meant little to her compared to the opportunity to work in civil rights. The offer from Thomas to be his single special assistant seemed like the break she had been hoping for almost her whole life.

❖

In the beginning, Thomas and Hill agree, their professional relationship was, as Hill later put it, "relaxed and open." Hill initially believed she had been hired largely because she and Thomas had such similar backgrounds. They apparently enjoyed swapping notes on their childhood years, with Thomas breaking into soliloquies about how the hardships he had overcome had shaped his philosophy. Hill's more moderate views soon became a source of some friction, however. Thomas often prodded Hill about them, requiring her to justify her position in lengthy debates. Later, conservative detractors would strive to portray Hill as politically motivated against Thomas, perhaps so much so that she would lie to stop him from reaching the Supreme Court.

But no one who knew Hill well, including Thomas, could quite imagine her as a ruthless political saboteur. When asked point-blank about this during the confirmation hearings, Thomas declined an opportunity to indulge Senator Howell Heflin's description of Hill as "a zealous civil rights supporter." "I cannot characterize her that way," Thomas demurred. Others who recall arguing politics with Hill during that period, including her far more liberal nephew Gary Lee, who was by then a reporter for the *Washington Post,* remember her as supportive of the Republican agenda.

"She felt that the old solutions hadn't worked that well, and the new ones were worth a try," recalled Lee. "She was not so much a true believer in Reagan as she was a supporter of civil rights work, but she could be very defensive about what she was doing. She made the arguments for Reagan, and she did it well." If anything, Hill was typically ambivalent, traveling under her preferred "Swiss passport," pragmatically embracing the job as her best chance of launching a civil rights career without entirely approving of the administration. "She was glad to be working in the public sector but unsure about where the administration was going. She seemed to be wrestling with it a lot," Lee said. Since at first Thomas had his own reservations about the administration, ideologically Hill and Thomas were probably not so far apart.

Although Hill recalled being upbraided for one early assignment — a speech she wrote for Thomas on minority educational institutions — for the most part he seemed pleased with her work. Later, her detractors would suggest she may have invented the harassment issue to cover a failure to thrive in the federal government. But Thomas himself testified, "She repeatedly received promotions, as scheduled, as far as I can remember. In fact she may have been promoted on an accelerated basis. Her assignments, for her age and experience at that time, I think, were fairly aggressive."

Others at the Department of Education recall Hill as being in a coveted and privileged position. As Thomas's closest aide, she was constantly in his office and eagerly claiming the seat nearest him in conferences. At meetings with Justice Department officials — the bane of Thomas's existence both at Education and the EEOC — an administration lawyer recalled, Hill reverently walked several paces behind her mentor, whom she deferred to solicitously in discussions. If either was disappointed with the other, no office colleagues said they sensed it.

But within three to five months of her arrival, Hill recalled, her career, which was at that time virtually her entire life, began to fall apart. Nothing in her brief legal career or her many years as the darling of her family and teachers had prepared her for what she said happened next.

Thomas has "categorically" denied "in the strongest terms" every one of Hill's allegations concerning the behavior over the next twenty-three months that she came to believe was sexual harassment. He agreed during the hearings that the behavior she described was degrading and humiliating; he acknowledged that in his opinion, her charges, if proven true, would have constituted sexual harassment. But he said he could not imagine a single thing he had said or done to cause any such offense. Considering that he had defined the behavior she described as unlawful, his ascension to the Supreme Court clearly hinged on the credibility of his denial. Given these stakes, it is worth taking a closer look at Thomas's and Hill's famously contradictory accounts.

Thomas began to ask her out socially three to five months after she began working for him in July 1981, according to Hill. His approach was unusual. Rather than asking her to join him for a specific date or event, like a movie or dinner, he expressed his interest as a casual command, saying, "You ought to go out with me sometime." She turned him down firmly, she recalled, explaining that she enjoyed her work and believed it "ill advised to date a supervisor." But he would not take no for an answer. Instead, she testified, "In the following weeks, he continued to ask me out on several occasions. He pressed me to justify my reasons for saying 'no' to him."

According to notes taken by a former Senate aide, James Brudney, of a private conversation he had with Hill weeks before she accused Thomas publicly, Hill acknowledged that from the beginning, and throughout Thomas's alleged harassment of her, she never took the obvious but impolitic step of telling him directly that she was not romantically interested in him. Instead of risking the chance of insulting her boss, she avoided confrontation by erecting a professional barrier; impersonal and inoffensive, her response was likely to do little damage to her career. As Brudney's notes show, Hill acknowledged that when turning Thomas down, she, "cited work, didn't cite not liking him." She blamed herself belatedly for not being more forceful: the notes also show that Hill described herself as having been "pretty naive, stupid," at the age of twenty-five.

In using the workplace as a shield, Hill was displaying her preference for privacy and polite relations. But her social niceties may have been misinterpreted by Thomas at first. He offered a very different view of events. He testified both to the Senate and in his interview with the FBI that he never once asked Hill out. Rather, he said that he thought of Hill and his other staff members as just like "my kids" — and he added emphatically, "I . . . do not commingle my personal life with my work life."

However, according to Hill, Thomas's behavior soon became almost insufferable. She told Brudney that Thomas "never said, 'Date or I'll fire you.'" But the pressure was such that before long, in her words, "I found it impossible." "Thomas," she testified, "began to use work situations to discuss sex. On these occasions he would call me into his office for reports on education issues and projects, or he might suggest that because of time pressures we go to lunch at a government cafeteria." But after a brief discussion of work, "he would turn the conversation to a discussion of sexual matters. His conversations were very vivid. He spoke of acts that he had seen in pornographic films involving such matters as women having sex with animals and films showing group sex or rape scenes. He talked about pornographic materials depicting individuals with large penises or large breasts involved in various sex acts. On various occasions, Thomas told me graphically of his own sexual prowess" — mentioning at one point that he had "measured his penis, which he said was larger than most."

These private conversations, from Hill's standpoint, were "offensive and disgusting, and degrading." Hill recalled that as they became increasingly upsetting to her in the winter of 1981 and early spring of 1982, she became slightly more aggressive toward Thomas. Although she continued to refrain from telling him that she had no interest in him, she expressly told him that she did not want to talk about what she discreetly called "these kinds of things." According to Brudney's notes, Hill tried lamely to change the subject. She also described trying to dismiss such disturbing gambits as Thomas's boast about how "all my friends say they don't do oral sex — I do — I'm into oral sex" by blandly suggesting in her best Sunday school manner that "everyone is interested in different things."

It is possible that these mild evasions failed to make Thomas understand that Hill found such talk, as she later put it, both "disturbing" and "disgusting." But Thomas never offered this argument. Instead, he denied that these conversations ever took place: he testified that he had never spoken to Hill at all of sexual matters and, furthermore, that he had no inkling whatsoever of her discomfort. Hill insisted otherwise and argued that not only was her discomfort obvious, she also sensed that it "urged him on, as though my reaction of feeling ill at ease and vulnerable was what he wanted." Hill's observation that Thomas seemed to enjoy picking on her precisely because she was so ill at ease makes her recollection reminiscent of the descriptions of

Thomas taunting the prudish John Ashcroft in Danforth's Missouri office.

To Hill, the style of Thomas's advances suggested an underlying hostility; she testified that she "never felt that he was genuinely interested in me — only in coercing me." Such a distinction would help to explain why Hill, who initially admired and defended Thomas, felt disturbed rather than flattered or elated by his interest. As Thomas's behavior caused her increasing distress, Hill confided in one of her closest friends from law school, Susan Hoerchner, who was also working for the government in Washington. Hill later explained that she had hoped Hoerchner might have some ideas on how she could get Thomas to stop.

Hoerchner confirmed this early discussion to congressional investigators, to the FBI, and in her testimony. She acknowledged that her recollection, particularly when it came to the timing of events, was hazy, but she said she distinctly remembered that at some point after Hill began working for Thomas, she had asked Hill in one of their many phone conversations how things were going. And instead of getting the usual, cheerful "Just busy," she said, Hill "sounded very depressed and spoke in a dull monotone." Hill then confessed that there was a "serious problem" at work. As Hoerchner recalled it, Hill said she was being "sexually harassed" by "her boss, Clarence." Hoerchner, who is not particularly assertive, was unable to give Hill any useful advice. Instead, she tried to provide "comfort." But even there, she felt inadequate. "At the end of the conversation," Hoerchner conceded, "she sounded more depressed than when it began."

❖

When her allegations against Thomas reached the Judiciary Committee, Hill at first told congressional investigators and the FBI that Hoerchner was the only person in whom she remembered confiding her problems with Thomas. By the time of the hearings, however, three other people had reminded her that she had also told them about it, so she expanded the list of corroborating witnesses to include John Carr, Joel Paul, and Ellen Wells. Hill explained her memory lapse by saying that the situation with Thomas had been so painful that she had "repressed" many of the details from ten years earlier, including whom she had spoken with and when.

In fact, Hill had forgotten that she had also confided in a fifth person, one whose involvement was extensive and direct. His name was Bradley Mims, and Hill had so completely forgotten about him that even in the summer of 1993, after being reminded of his cameo role in her life, she still was unable to recall his first name accurately. The two had not spoken to each other for a decade and had no contact during or after the hearings. But Mims remembered the events in question quite clearly, despite the passage of time. And once reminded of him, Hill confirmed his account.

By the time Hill surfaced publicly, Mims was working as a lobbyist in the congressional affairs office of the Smithsonian Institution. He loved working for the government, and having seen a number of political brawls like the one this confirmation battle was turning into, he had no desire to get involved in any way that might jeopardize his job. Besides, he knew Hill well enough to suspect that her story wasn't simple. Her ambition, he thought, had made her partly responsible for her problems with Thomas, because she had wanted the job so much that she had stayed on beyond the point when it was reasonable. Yet, as Mims wrestled with his conscience about whether he ought to speak up, his memories of the period when he knew Hill came flooding back.

A dozen years later, Mims still vividly remembered the night that he met Hill. It was the very beginning of 1982, and they had both enrolled in a night class — a course for federal employees interested in improving their writing skills. Coincidentally, they had spoken on the phone that day because she had been trying to reach his boss. After the members of the class introduced themselves, she sent him a note: "Hi — I'm Anita Hill, the person who called your office earlier today."

Mims was working for a Democratic congressman at the time, and he knew Hill's boss by reputation as one of the few prominent black conservatives. Mims remembered Hill as openly ambitious and proud of working for such a powerful black official. Despite the differences in their politics, he recalled, they became close for a brief time, occasionally seeing each other outside class. She was conservative — though not quite as conservative as he understood Thomas to be — a bit aloof, and even prim. But he also found her attractive, bright, and all-around good company.

One night, only a couple of weeks after they'd met, Hill came to class looking upset. Ordinarily poised and composed, this time she looked, Mims recalled, as if she might have been crying. During the break, Mims asked her what was wrong. She replied, "Clarence is doing real wild stuff. I don't want to talk about it."

But with a little goading she did anyway. She said that she and Thomas had gone to lunch earlier that day, as they had on several other recent occasions. During the meal, Thomas had begun saying "really crazy stuff to her — talking wild." Mims knew exactly what she meant by "talking wild" — in their social set, it was slang for using explicit sexual language. Mims recalled that "she was clearly out of kilter about it. She seemed withdrawn and distracted. She still seemed to like and admire Thomas, but she just didn't know how to take it, how to deal with it, and what effect it would have on her. She seemed confused about what kinds of signals he was sending. She wasn't crying, but she was very upset."

Although Mims was not an eyewitness, he did see and talk to Hill regularly as she endured what he understood to be extremely explicit and upsetting sexual comments from Thomas. Mims's recollection provides contemporaneous support for Hill's main accusation against Thomas concerning his lewd or "wild" talk. It also confirms a number of other details, large and small, that lend credence to her account.

For instance, Mims specifically recalled that Hill's first confession to him of her experiences with Thomas came as early as January of 1982, which fits the time that Thomas's offensive behavior emerged, according to Hill's testimony. Mims also specifically remembered that Hill told him that some of Thomas's sexual conversations took place over lunch — which she testified to as well. Moreover, he confirmed that she seemed deeply upset — corroborating her testimony that Thomas's talk had been unwelcome and disturbing. Mims sensed further that she was worried about "what it meant for her," which supports the fear she later described that her boss's behavior might jeopardize the work situation she so valued. Finally, Mims confirmed Hill's account that she was extremely confused about "what signals" Thomas was trying to send — an indication that she found his behavior out of the ordinary.

While sympathetic at the time, Mims nonetheless asked Hill the obvious question: if Thomas's behavior was such a problem, why not just get another job? "Hell, you're a Yale lawyer," he remembered telling her. "You can go anywhere you want."

But Hill's reaction was anguished, he said, and somewhat calculating. She was young, she liked her work, and she knew Thomas was going places. As Mims put it, "She wanted to ride his coattails." Thomas was simultaneously the best and worst thing that had ever happened to her — both offering and threatening the career she had always wanted.

"I was really upset," she later testified. "I felt my job could be taken away or at least threatened. That I wasn't going to be able to work. That this person who had some power in the new administration would make it difficult for me in terms of other positions." Equally important, Hill was not confrontational by nature. As she admitted, "It was also unpleasant, and something I didn't want to deal with."

It irked Mims, however, that not long after one of their conversations, he took Hill on an office picnic at which his own boss treated him poorly; rather than being sympathetic, she asked irately how he could stay in such a job. Mims concluded that Hill lacked a certain amount of self-awareness, not to mention empathy.

❖

In February 1982, nine months after his arrival at the Department of Education, Thomas was nominated to become the next chairman of the EEOC. As Thomas had divined, the Republicans were eager to the point of desperation for black recruits. A full year after Reagan took the oath of office, the White House had still identified so few qualified black conservatives for positions in the administration that it was having trouble filling vital posts. A particularly embarrassing hole was the chairmanship of the EEOC. Despite the administration's stance against affirmative action, it was widely understood that the White House had been looking for a black for the job in order to insulate itself against any charges of racism. A White House aide told *Newsweek* that the administration had approached ten or twelve black lawyers, but none wanted to implement Reagan's plan to dismantle well-established methods of fighting discrimination in the workplace.

In June 1981 the White House had finally nominated a little-known black businessman from Detroit for the post, William M. Bell. But the nomination quickly ran into trouble. Although Bell listed himself as head of an executive headhunting firm, the company wasn't listed in the phone book, and it turned out that Bell was in fact the firm's sole employee. Worse, he had not placed anyone in a job for more than a year. Bell's credentials were so shaky that even Dan Quayle, then a conservative Republican senator from Indiana, announced he would oppose him. In November 1981, the White House was forced to withdraw the nomination.

The administration's new candidate for the post was only thirty-three. He had served for less than a year as head of the Education Department's Office of Civil Rights. He was a novice bureaucrat who had never run a large agency or organization. Still, by the time that Clarence Thomas was named, he was the administration's best — and indeed only — candidate.

❖

To the surprise of many who learned of her complaints about Thomas, Anita Hill moved to the EEOC with him after he won confirmation that May. An important factor in her decision, Hill explained later, was that Thomas's harassment had recently subsided. In her interview with Brudney, Hill attributed this change in Thomas's behavior — which lasted for about six months, covering the end of her time at the Department of Education and the start of her work at the EEOC — to his romantic involvement with a woman named Lillian McEwen. Those who later defended Thomas — among them his secretary, Diane Holt, and his law school friend and successor in the Department of Education, Harry Singleton — said that he could not possibly have been romantically interested in Hill because he was dating McEwen during the entire time that Hill worked for him. But according to Hill and others, his relationship with McEwen was an on-and-off affair that, at least when it began, in the spring of 1982, allowed Hill to feel "relief and hope."

The temporary cessation of Thomas's harassment is central to Hill's credibility; it makes more plausible both her decision to follow him to the EEOC and also her story that during this period she allowed him to drive her home one evening and come into her apartment in order to help her hook up a new stereo. Had he been actively harassing her, both actions — each requiring her to choose to remain in close contact with him — would be difficult to fathom. But if she believed that Thomas was safely involved with another woman, she might well have felt able to resume friendlier relations.

But Hill's and Thomas's testimony on the subject of his only visit to her apartment was completely contradictory. Hill testified that she and her roommate, a fellow Yale Law graduate named Sonia Jarvis, believed that Thomas's sole visit to their Capitol Hill apartment occurred on an evening in the spring of 1982 when he helped connect the stereo. But Thomas testified that he had no recollection of having ever helped Hill with a stereo. "No," he said, "I don't remember helping her install a stereo or turntable . . . that would not be my recollection, Senator." Instead he said that on a number of occasions when they were at the Department of Education he had dropped Hill off after work, sometimes going in for a Coke or a beer to finish the conversation they had been having on the way home.

Again, Brad Mims's memory is helpful. He recalled being surprised by Hill's behavior in what he thought was April or May of 1982. Only a few months after telling Mims about Thomas's upsetting treatment of her, she mentioned that Thomas had stopped by her house over the weekend to install her new stereo. She had initially asked Mims for help, but he'd been tied up that weekend; a stereo buff, he recalled being a little surprised that she hadn't waited for him to do it. He also remembered that later he had personally inspected the installation that Hill said Thomas had done and pronounced it "a lousy job."

"I thought you didn't like the guy," Mims recalled saying to Hill after hearing that she had let Thomas into her house. But she replied, "Clarence was nice this time. He drove me home and came in and put it together." It all seemed a little peculiar, but Mims concluded there had been a change for the better in their relationship, and that Hill was no longer troubled by Thomas.

Mims's memory again weighs against Thomas's credibility. Not only did Mims provide contemporaneous corroboration of Hill's account of Thomas's help with the stereo in her apartment, he also corroborated the larger and more important piece of Hill's testimony: her assertion that during this crucial time in the spring of 1982, she no longer feared Thomas.

Much has also been made of Hill's choice to follow Thomas to the EEOC, given her reservations about his behavior. Hill testified that among the reasons she chose to follow him was her fear that without Thomas, her job at the Department of Education wasn't secure. In part, this was because she had been Thomas's special assistant — a position any new appointee would want to fill personally. Furthermore, the department itself had been earmarked for elimination by President Reagan.

Thomas's defenders have questioned the credibility of Hill by pointing out that her job was a career civil service slot, not a political one, and thus virtually impossible to eliminate. Moreover, Thomas's successor and closest friend, Harry Singleton, has said that he told Hill she could work for him as one of his "attorney advisers," so her continued employment was secure.

But when asked about this, Hill said she recalled no such discussion with Singleton. More important, she added, "No one knew what was going to happen at the Department of Education. And that's what was actually continually on my mind at the time. History is what it is. The department's still there. But I still can't say for certain what would have happened to my job if I had stayed there, and Harry Singleton can't either."

Judith Winston, who worked with both Thomas and Hill at Education, believed that Hill had reason to be concerned. While her career civil service status guaranteed her a job, there was no guarantee that Hill would remain special assistant to the head of the office of civil rights or even in that department. The smart move for an ambitious young attorney interested in civil rights was to follow her boss to a more powerful position.

And Hill was ambitious, even if she often seemed reluctant to admit it. By emphasizing her fear about what would happen if she didn't leave Education, Hill downplayed the other side of the equation: her desire for particularly rewarding work. By going with Thomas, Hill would continue to be his special assistant — now only one of many, but still a coveted position at the side of one of the most powerful black men in Washington. Clearly Hill was less interested in remaining employed than in having a challenging career — and the opportunity for upward mobility rested with Thomas. Since, according to Hill, Thomas had ceased harassing her, her ambition, as much as anything else, explains her decision to continue working with him.

In her first and least guarded conversation on the subject with an official — her private talk with Brudney — Hill named yet another factor in her decision that she chose not to mention in the hearings: a kind of naive loyalty. Brudney's notes show that she explained that at the time, she had a "strong feeling Clarence Thomas had hired me

— given me a break. But [I] felt conflicted given [the] kind of pressure he put on me." She pointed out that she "was twenty-five years old, and naive."

Hill may have "assumed that the issue of the behavior of Clarence Thomas had been laid to rest" when she chose to go with him to the EEOC in May 1982. But within three to five months, Hill testified, her assumption proved wrong. That fall, she told Brudney, Thomas's relationship with Lillian McEwen faltered and he resumed his sexual attentions. His actions were, if anything, even more bizarre than before.

His comments during this period, she testified, "were random and ranged from pressuring me about why I didn't want to go out with him to remarks about my personal appearance." In her private conversation with Brudney, she provided specific details, noting that, for instance, Thomas would say he "could see [my] slip through [my] dress." He said, "I can see your body — [that] is [a] provocative slip you're wearing." In her written statement to the Judiciary Committee, Hill stated that Thomas would "comment on what I was wearing and whether it made me more or less sexually appealing." Brudney's notes reflect that Hill told him that Thomas "leered" when she entered or left a room. This, she said, made her increasingly "self-conscious about my appearance."

One of the oddest of Hill's recollections was that one day when she and Thomas were working in his office, he got up from the table where he had been sitting with her, went over to his desk to retrieve a can of Coca-Cola, and, after staring at it, demanded to know, "Who has put pubic hair on my Coke?"

"I didn't have a clue how to interpret that," Hill testified. "I did not know. It was a strange comment for me. I thought it was inappropriate, but I did not know what he meant."

In the hearings, Thomas sounded equally baffled and offended by such language. Asked by Senator Orrin Hatch if he had ever said such a thing, Thomas replied, "No, absolutely not."

"Did you ever think of saying something like that?" Hatch asked.

"No," replied Thomas.

"That's a gross thing to say, isn't it? Whether it's said by you or somebody else?" continued Hatch.

"As far as I am concerned, Senator," Thomas said, "it is, and it is something I did not, nor would say."

But Hill, it turns out, is not the only employee of the EEOC who attributed this vivid phrase to Thomas before the hearings. Marguerite Donnelly, a senior trial attorney at the EEOC until she went into private practice in 1986, distinctly recalled being told by a co-worker in the early 1980s that Chairman Thomas "had said — and I thought it was in the presence of several people — that there was a pubic hair on his can of Coke." Donnelly said she told her husband, Allan Danoff, who was an attorney at the EEOC until 1985, about the peculiar comment. When interviewed, Danoff confirmed this. "We certainly did hear about it back then," he said.

Thomas's aide Michael Middleton also said that he heard the pubic hair story associated with Thomas before 1985, when he too left the EEOC. "I have this vision of Clarence at the EEOC picking up a Coke and saying, 'Who put this pubic hair on my Coke?'" recalled Middleton, formerly Thomas's principal deputy at the Department of Education and associate general counsel at the EEOC and now a professor of law at Missouri North Central University. Middleton also remembered telling his wife about it at the time. During the hearings, he said, he turned to her and asked if she remembered the story, and she told him that she did.

But the memory, Middleton went on, is after all this time quite hazy. For instance, he can't say for sure whether he witnessed Thomas's saying it or just had it described to him back then. He also worked with Hill, and it is possible she may have told him about it herself — although he doubted it and she had no recollection of it. "It could have been a joke I heard him tell in the office," Middleton said. But the testimony definitely sounded familiar to him. "It's vague. I just know that pubic hair in a Coke can was not new to me [during the hearings] with Clarence Thomas," he said.

Since no one actually heard Thomas utter the line to Hill — she testified that it happened when she and Thomas were alone — the independent recollection of three former EEOC attorneys that they too heard about Thomas's remark contemporaneously does not necessarily corroborate her account. No one recalled hearing that the remark was made specifically to Hill. Further, Donnelly thought the statement was made in front of a group of people; Danoff heard it from her; and Middleton thought he might have been present when

Thomas made the statement. It's possible that all are correct — that the line was somehow amusing to Thomas, who repeated it several times in different circumstances. What seems unlikely, however, is that three senior lawyers in the agency could remember the same statement coming from a man who says he never uttered it to Hill or anyone else.

Thomas's bafflement seems all the more questionable when the views of his otherwise neutral former classmates are considered. According to a number of those who attended Holy Cross and Yale with Thomas and who recalled the extreme crudity of the sexual banter he enjoyed, Thomas's asking who had put pubic hair on his Coke can was precisely the kind of statement typical of him. For this reason, Hill's testimony on the subject struck each of them independently as a turning point in weighing his credibility.

For instance, Gordon Davis, a friend at Holy Cross, said, "I didn't know what to think until I heard the Coke can story. When I heard that, I knew he'd say stuff like that. He's not a bad person, but he had strange ways of making an impression."

Another friend from Holy Cross, the writer Edward P. Jones, also lost any doubts that Hill was telling the truth at the hearings when he heard her specific charges about the kinds of language Thomas used. "The Coke can thing did it for me," said Jones. "It's like you remember some kid who always wore his hat a certain way — to me, it was 'I remember that kid, that's the way he talked, that's him.' It's the same hat, the same style, the same kid."

And remarks like that about the Coke can were why his colleague from Yale Law, Henry Terry, said, "When Anita started talking, I knew the man was guilty."

❖

Another odd recollection of Hill's was that during this period, Thomas called her into his office at the EEOC one day and proceeded to discuss a pornography star with a very large penis named Long Dong Silver. During the hearings, Thomas was asked by Senator Howell Heflin about Long Dong Silver. "Have you ever heard the name of that?" he asked.

"No, Senator," Thomas replied.

It is entirely possible that Thomas was telling the truth. But the interest in pornography that Thomas first exhibited at Yale apparently continued through the early 1980s, when Long Dong Silver was a well-known figure among fans of X-rated movies. According to Barry Maddox, the proprietor of Graffiti, a video rental and equipment store just off Dupont Circle, a few blocks from the EEOC's headquarters, the store began to rent pornographic videos in 1982. Not long afterward, Maddox recalled, Thomas became a regular customer.

Graffiti no longer carries adult films and keeps no records of its customers' rentals. (Even if it did, releasing them without a court order would be illegal.) But Maddox was taken aback by Thomas's testimony during the hearings. "Clarence Thomas was a regular customer of adult movies," said Maddox. "Not a notorious one — but he rented hundreds of movies. Some of the movies he rented were kids' films for his son. Others were X-rated. Our staff remembers him in the adult shelves."

Among the pornographic movies that Maddox stocked openly in the adult section of his shelves was the so-called Electric Blue series, starring the grossly deformed black male actor whose stage name was Long Dong Silver. The movies are not considered hard-core because they don't actually show Silver having sex. They merely simulate the activity — which was all they could do, since his physical deformity was of such grotesque proportions that it apparently incapacitated him. Said Maddox of the movies, "It was a freak-of-nature kind of thing. It was very well known at the time. The same movies were available in Maryland and Virginia too."

It was also in Graffiti that Frederick Douglass Cooke Jr., a Washington attorney and the former D.C. corporation counsel, saw Thomas at the cashier's counter in the late 1980s with another "freak-of-nature" kind of film. Cooke thought it pretty amusing to run into the chairman of the EEOC, whom he had met once or twice on a social basis, standing with a triple X videotape entitled *The Adventures of Bad Mama Jama*. The photographs on its jacket, featuring five sex scenes with the eponymous Mama, were memorable. Shown in one sequence, "Bang the Elephant," Mama — a pitifully obese black woman — was squatting naked on all fours, her pendulous breasts and midriff brushing the floor as a naked white male grabbed her from behind. The cover promised "The Hottest, Sexiest Pounds-per-square-inch woman you'll ever meet!"

It wasn't the only time Cooke encountered Thomas as he rented videos at the store, but this particular selection struck Cooke as unusual enough to mention to a colleague at work. They had a good laugh about it and thought little more of it until Anita Hill came forward, alleging that Thomas had described bizarre pornographic "materials depicting individuals with large penises or breasts involved in various sex acts."

❖

There is also reason to believe that in addition to frequenting Graffiti, Thomas was an avid consumer of sexually explicit magazines while Hill was working for him at the EEOC. Kaye Savage, the White House appointee, recalled visiting the chairman's first real bachelor pad in the summer of 1982, not long after Hill had moved to the agency and toward the end of the period that she identified as the hiatus in Thomas's attentions. It was a junior efficiency apartment in a high-rise building in southwest Washington, where he had moved after leaving Gil Hardy's spare bedroom.

Savage was friendly with both Thomas and Hill. Having learned that Savage was a jogger like himself, Thomas had offered to go shopping with her over a weekend for special running shoes designed for city pavements. Since becoming chairman of the EEOC that May, Thomas had relied on the agency's car and driver for official business, but this left him stranded on weekends. So Savage had agreed to pick him up at his apartment.

He had only recently set up housekeeping, and the place, as she recalled, was still underfurnished: there was little more than a mattress on the floor and a stereo. But one other feature made a lasting impression on Savage. Thomas had compiled and placed on the floor "a huge, compulsively organized stack of *Playboy* magazines, five years' worth of them, organized by month and year." The walls of the apartment were also memorably covered. There was only one main room, but all of its walls — as well as the walls of the little galley kitchen and even the bathroom door — were papered with centerfolds of large-breasted nude women.

Savage recalled staring awkwardly about her; the display seemed so out of character with everything else she knew about Thomas. He was a fanatic about discipline and a daily churchgoer. He was serious about his career and honest to the point of indiscretion about his ambitious plans for the future. (Thomas had told her, as he had told others, that he planned to replace Thurgood Marshall on his retirement from the Supreme Court.) But his evident enthusiasm for pornography suggested to Savage that Thomas had a private side that was very different from his public persona. To her, the contrast seemed, as she later put it, "a little crazy."

Savage couldn't contain her curiosity, so she asked Thomas why he had so many sexually explicit magazines. "I don't drink, and I don't run around," he replied, implying that the magazines were his one recreational vice. In fact, she later told a congressional investigator, Thomas said that the magazines were the only possessions he had deemed worth taking with him from his collapsing marriage.

It was a little unusual, Savage believed, for a man of Thomas's age to remain so absorbed by girlie magazines. As it happened, she thought it odd enough to mention in passing one day to Hill, with whom she occasionally went shopping in consignment stores on weekends.

"Yeah," she remembered Hill's saying wearily, without a flicker of surprise, "that's Clarence."

❖

Hill never told Savage about Thomas's disturbing behavior toward her. She also did not confide in her roommate, Sonia Jarvis, who was far more of an activist than Hill and might have pushed her to do something about it. But in the fall of 1982, as Thomas, according to Hill, began to renew his sexual pressure on her, she confided one day in another friend, Ellen Wells. During the hearings, Wells corroborated Hill's account of their conversation.

Hill met Wells at a friend's birthday party, and the two struck up an immediate friendship. Wells remembered that she admired Hill's pink Chanel-style suit. She found Hill "funny and pleasant, and we just hit it off." Wells, who came from a long line of black Republicans, was poised and quietly dignified; like Hill, she had been brought up to be unwaveringly "ladylike." She was also eminently trustworthy, the kind of person, as Wells later said of herself, "who people are always confiding in, maybe because I'm not very judgmental."

Wells also knew and liked Thomas. They had both belonged to a tiny fraternity of black Republican congressional aides when he had worked for Danforth and she for Congressman John Anderson. When Hill explained to Wells in confidence why she appeared to be, in Wells's description, "deeply troubled and very depressed," Wells said her first reaction was, "Oh my God, she's talking about one of my friends!"

During the hearings, Wells testified that neither she nor Hill was the type of person who felt comfortable using sexually explicit terms. "Professor Hill is a very private person, and I am a very private person," she noted. So she hadn't pressed Hill for details of Thomas's behavior. But it was clear to Wells that Hill felt Thomas's behavior was inappropriate, that the conduct was of a sexual nature, and that it was causing her much distress.

"One of her [Hill's] questions was, 'Why was he doing this?'" Wells said in an interview. "She wanted to know what she had done to cause this. It was like she was saying, 'This is repulsive and embarrassing — and I just don't know how to handle it.'"

"I was saying, like, 'I don't know. Do you think you need to change your perfume?'"

Wells admitted that she was "totally out of my depth. As far as I knew he was a married man, or separated maybe, but still married. And he was her boss. The issue to me was how to try to turn him off without alienating him." As she told the Senate, the advice given to every young girl who wanted to get ahead was, in her mother's words, "Leave friends behind — because you don't know who you may need later on." At the end of her talk with Hill, Wells admitted, "We came to no conclusions. I felt powerless and impotent when it came to helping my friend."

❖

By the winter of 1982, Hill was beginning to suffer from the stress she was experiencing at work. In a conversation with Brad Mims at about that time, she confided that she had been trying to pursue a long-distance relationship, mostly by phone, with a bright, up-and-coming lawyer whom she had met through a friend at Wald, Harkrader. The young man, John Carr, was finishing graduate school at Harvard, and she admitted to Mims that she was very interested in him. As Mims recalled it, Hill was upset because she had lost her composure while talking on the phone with Carr. Carr had deduced that she was distressed about something and had asked her about it.

At first, she had not volunteered any information. But he kept pressing her, and she finally admitted that her boss had been making extremely disturbing sexual advances to her at work — both at that time and before.

After telling him about her confession to Carr, Mims recalled, Hill said, "I'm so embarrassed — I started talking on the phone about the things that Clarence did, and I just started to cry." She was very worried about what Carr would think of her and whether her emotional outburst would ruin her developing relationship with him. Carr, too, recalled this phone conversation and said that it occurred in the late winter or early spring of 1983. He remembered that rather than thinking less of Hill, he decided that this proved he had been right all along about how strange Thomas was. Apparently Carr had enjoyed teasing Hill about Thomas's contrary ways; it was odd, he believed, for a black man to be so conservative, Republican, and outspoken against traditional civil rights remedies. Consequently, when Hill finally described Thomas's offensive behavior, Carr recalled, he said something like, "See — I told you that he was unnatural." The irony of Hill's predicament particularly struck Carr, who thought it was amazing that this harassment could occur at the EEOC, of all places.

Carr was concerned about Hill's obvious distress, but he said that from that point on Hill kept her thoughts about Thomas to herself. She was afraid, she later told others, that no one would believe she was being sexually harassed at work by the head of the federal agency responsible for preventing sexual harassment.

But although she rarely spoke of her unhappiness, she was apparently finding it increasingly difficult to function. In her private discussion with Brudney, his notes show, she related that by late 1982 she was feeling "chilled out in decisions" by Thomas and worried that this was not just a function of her "inexperience" at the agency "but [in the] back of [my] mind maybe my refusal to have sex" with him.

In January, Hill made a New Year's resolution: to get a new job. According to her testimony, she began making discreet inquiries about other employment. Kaye Savage confirmed this, saying that she recalled Hill's confiding that she was looking for work elsewhere and even thinking about returning to Oklahoma — a plan that to Savage, at least, seemed to make no sense, given Hill's terrific position.

By February the strain had evidently become too much. Hill was hospitalized for five days with an undiagnosed stomach problem that her doctors believed was stress-related. A number of friends — Ellen Wells, Kaye Savage, and her EEOC colleague Nancy Fitch — either visited or called, but no one knew exactly what was ailing Hill. "I knew she had huge digestive disorders," said Savage, "but she never really explained it." When Wells called Hill in the hospital, she was only slightly more forthcoming, saying that she thought her health problems were "related to stress at work."

———❖———

In March, Thomas mentioned to Hill that he would be speaking the following month in Tulsa, the big city closest to her parents' farm, and invited her to accompany him. Hill leapt at the chance to go home. But what was supposed to be a quick trip to the O. W. Coburn School of Law at Oral Roberts University, where Thomas was speaking, turned into the surprisingly abrupt end to Hill's career in Washington.

That weekend Charles Kothe, the founding dean of the new law school at Oral Roberts, asked Hill, as he later put it, "out of the blue" to come there and teach. The law school was far more fundamentalist than Hill herself; it was so extreme that it was having accreditation problems with the American Bar Association, and clearly the school was a huge step down from the kinds of institutions Hill had attended. Hill had been at the EEOC for less than a year, so short a time that leaving the job would be hard to explain to future employers. Moreover, she had never taught school in her life. But without hesitating, Hill jumped at the opportunity to get out of the EEOC.

During the hearings, Kothe suggested in language badly damaging to Hill's credibility that her belief that Thomas had harassed her sexually must have been a "fantasy." Kothe knew them both and believed no other interpretation was possible. As proof, he noted not only that Hill seemed on perfectly comfortable terms with Thomas during their trip to Oral Roberts in April 1983, but that when Thomas returned to Tulsa in April 1987 to give another speech, she seemed happy to see him. Although by then she had moved on to Oklahoma State University in Norman, she joined Thomas and Kothe for dinner and even offered to drive Thomas to the airport the following morning.

Neither Kothe nor Thomas mentioned it in the hearings, but by April 1987 Thomas was engaged to marry his second wife, Virginia

Lamp, the following month, which may have reassured Hill. Kothe was also scarcely a neutral observer. As early as 1984, Thomas had made Kothe his special assistant at the EEOC. As an outside consultant, Kothe directed ad hoc projects for Thomas, frequently working out of Thomas's own office in the building. Among his special assignments was a thirty-three-page study called "The Success Story of Clarence Thomas." Kothe also traveled with Thomas throughout the country, even touring Savannah's swamps with him — a trip that included stops at his boyhood haunts but omitted visits to his nearby relatives, including his mother. Kothe seemed to revere Thomas, inviting him to his home repeatedly and fondly recalling in a later interview Thomas's deep laugh and the soul-searching conversations the two had shared on religion and other topics.

Some of the others at the EEOC viewed Kothe as something of an aging eccentric, a kind of elderly problem case who had to be kept busy and out of the way. But evidently it was clear to Hill that Kothe was one of Thomas's best friends, and to stay on good terms with one she would have to stay on good terms with the other. Both men continued to play essential roles in her career. A glowing recommendation from Thomas had been crucial, Kothe testified, in convincing him and Oral Roberts to follow through on his initial teaching offer to Hill. Later, after the law school collapsed in 1986, it was a favorable recommendation from Kothe — who was still a consultant to Thomas — that helped secure a job for Hill in Norman.

Some wondered why Hill didn't bring sexual harassment charges against Thomas immediately after she left the EEOC, before the statute of limitations ran out. But Hill believed, as she later testified, that had she come forward, it would have ruined her career. As she put it, "I can speculate that I would have lost my job at Oral Roberts." In light of the close association between Thomas and Kothe, her judgment may have been sound.

❖

In July 1983, on the last day of her job at the EEOC, Thomas made one last and particularly memorable comment to Hill, according to her recollection. It took place at a restaurant in Georgetown, not far from the office. Thomas had not let up on his pressure tactics, pointing out that since she would no longer be working for him, she no longer had an excuse not to date him. Hill demurred, as usual, suggesting that she still didn't think it appropriate. But she had agreed to dine out with Thomas this once after he promised that it would be a professional rather than a social farewell. And for part of the evening he kept his word, using the time to review her work.

But toward the end of the evening he made what she later described as "a comment I'll never forget." She discussed the incident with Brudney; according to his notes, Thomas had said, "If you were ever to tell anyone what went on between us, you could ruin my career."

"You're probably right," Hill said she answered. "[It's] not something you'd want me to talk about."

Later, many who watched the hearings suggested that the truth lay somewhere in the middle of Thomas's and Hill's conflicting accounts and that perhaps Thomas may not have understood how objectionable his behavior was in Hill's eyes. But if Hill's account of his parting words is accurate, there was no such misunderstanding. Rather, Thomas was painfully aware that his behavior had been so offensive that it could destroy his career if word of it ever got out.

But evidently he felt that his secret was safe with Hill, and she did not indicate otherwise. Instead, Hill recalled, she told Thomas that she would rather just "forget about the unpleasant experience."

❖

A short time after she left Washington, Hill said she had one other conversation that haunted her for years to come. In the fall of 1983, after settling into her teaching job at Oral Roberts, she decided to visit her friends in Washington one weekend. In her private conversation with Brudney, Hill described a particularly painful visit to the apartment of a woman named Linda Lambert, a friend of hers who had also befriended Thomas, first while working for him at the Department of Education and later at the EEOC, where he had made her a consultant, like Dean Kothe.

Lambert, it turned out, lived in the same high-rise apartment building in Southwest where Thomas lived — the building that Kaye Savage had visited. And although Hill may not have realized it at the time, Thomas and Lambert had become close friends.

With her EEOC career now behind her, Hill mustered the courage to tell Lambert her real reason for leaving. But, according to Hill, after she had confided in Lambert and described what she viewed as

Thomas's two-year-long campaign of sexual harassment, Lambert surprised her by exclaiming, "I don't believe it!"

"What do you mean?" Hill responded, unnerved and hurt by her friend's skepticism.

"Not that I don't believe you," Lambert went on, "but [I] can't believe Clarence Thomas would do it."

At that point, Hill told Brudney, she became very upset and "started crying."

This conversation with Lambert became seminal in her thinking about whether to discuss the experience with anyone ever again. As she told Brudney, she "felt if my friend reacted this way, others on his side would react [the] same way." So, for nearly a decade, she "never brought it up again."

5

❖

The Turkey Farm

As CHAIRMAN of the EEOC, Clarence Thomas had many concerns that were more pressing than Anita Hill. When he took over the commission in the spring of 1982, he might just as well have ascended the bridge of an ocean liner destined to ground itself on the nearest sandbar against the wishes of its crew.

Ronald Reagan had been elected in part by vowing to end government's intrusions into the free market, especially those made in the name of social engineering. And if any agency epitomized all that he found objectionable, it was the EEOC. The commission's sole purpose was to enforce the statutes of legislation that, from their inception, Reagan had vigorously opposed — the 1964 Civil Rights Act, which barred racial, sexual, and other forms of discrimination in every American company of fifteen or more employees. But as Reagan soon learned, it was simpler to put an agency on ice than to do away with it completely. Funding might be cut and missions redefined, but without congressional approval — which was not forthcoming — federal departments were virtually impossible to abolish. This left unwanted offices like the EEOC in the anomalous position of functioning without a mandate.

As a result, hundreds of career federal employees were subjected to a kind of ideological whiplash. Anthony DeMarco, an attorney who had been with the EEOC since 1973, working amicably for both Democrats and Republicans, recalled the change: "When Thomas first got there in 1982, we were going gangbusters. But he put a screeching halt to that." At first many of the employees were so confused about how to proceed from day to day, said another former EEOC lawyer, that behind closed doors "people would spend all day in endless rounds of bridge games."

Complicating matters further, the EEOC became a refuge for otherwise unplaceable political appointees. "Even before Reagan, there were a lot of flaky people there," recalled Marguerite Donnelly, the former EEOC attorney, "but under Reagan it got progressively worse. It became a dumping ground." Among themselves, some employees referred to the agency in the 1980s as "the Turkey Farm."

While this situation undoubtedly proved difficult for many EEOC employees, it was even more of a challenge for Thomas. An outsider with only one year of experience in government, he was suddenly responsible for thirty-one hundred employees and charged with the task of redirecting the entire federal approach to job discrimination, an issue as polarized and painful as any in America. More difficult, Thomas and the administration he served were not necessarily in agreement about what approach to take.

Thomas's own views were still evolving. But already it was clear that, unlike his predecessors, who had been at the forefront of the push to integrate America's workplaces, Thomas didn't really embrace integration as a goal in and of itself. His own unhappy experience as a black pioneer in white educational institutions had convinced him, as he told Juan Williams — who wrote a thorough profile of him in the *Atlantic Monthly* — that "there is nothing you can do to get past black skin." He continued: "I don't care how educated you are, how good you are at what you do — you'll never have the same contacts or opportunities, you'll never be seen as equal to whites."

If Thomas believed there was no real remedy for racism, he also believed that the techniques that had been used to fight discrimination in the past, such as busing and hiring goals, were worse than useless. In his view, even the *Brown* decision, the foundation of all subsequent integration efforts, had been condescending to African-Americans by suggesting, as he read it, that minority students would do better simply by sitting next to whites. This idiosyncratic reading of the case did not square with the experience of most blacks in America, for whom separate had in fact meant unequal. Thomas, however, cast this view as a matter of black nationalism, praising Malcolm X for being "hell on integrationists" and asking, "Where does he say you should sacrifice your institutions to be next to white people?"

Affirmative action too, as Thomas saw it, was "a crutch," degrading in its implication that African-Americans needed assistance. Like his mentor Thomas Sowell, he believed that "quotas," as he put it, adopting the pejorative description of affirmative action favored by conservatives, were taken advantage of only by elites. Ignoring his own experience and the growing ranks of the self-made, newly educated black middle class, Thomas argued that "if quotas help you — fine. If they help you get a BMW or a Mercedes, say that is why you want quotas. Man, quotas are for the black middle class. Look at what's happening to the masses. They are my people. They are just where they were before any of these policies."

In voicing these opinions, Thomas was in harmony with the Reagan administration. But he had arrived at these conclusions from a completely different starting point. Where many of his colleagues believed that America had already more or less achieved a color-blind society — or at least had come close enough not to need additional government interference — Thomas was certain from his own experience that this was a fantasy. The playing field, as he saw it, would never be level, and the government could never remedy prejudice so deep and widespread. All it could do was to try to compensate individuals who could prove that they had suffered some kind of discrimination. And this, rather than changing society, became the mission of the EEOC, as Thomas narrowly defined it.

His bitter perspective on the subject of race would be a constant source of friction and pain for Thomas as one of the administration's top black officials, particularly during his first few years at the EEOC. He considered himself something of an African-American nationalist, a radical who could, in two speeches in 1983, praise the Reverend Louis Farrakhan — the vitriolic, anti-Semitic Black Muslim leader — as "a man I have admired for more than a decade." Yet Thomas was frequently the subject of attacks by civil rights leaders, many of whom considered him an Uncle Tom and a traitor to his race for abandoning the broader, more active role of his predecessors at the EEOC.

As a consequence, during his first few years at the EEOC, Thomas was, if anything, more isolated and angry than ever. His treatment as he stepped into the limelight, he said, made him "boil inside." As such a comment suggests, his increasing success had little impact on his habitual sense of victimization. While his status as a conservative black Republican opened one door after another, his speeches demonstrated an increasing preoccupation with how unfairly he had been treated, first as a poor black child and now because of his unpopular political beliefs.

"The harangues to which we [black conservatives] were subjected," Thomas said in one such speech, "were considerable. There was no place any of us who were identified as black members of the administration could go without being virtually attacked." The hazing from other African-Americans in particular was so vicious, he said, even his friends were attacked. One friend, according to Thomas, was forced to leave a party just because he was known to associate with him.

To be sure, Thomas's sense of being shunned was not without basis. At least some of the hostility, however, was generated by his own belligerence. A number of other black Republicans served the Reagan administration with far less controversy. But Thomas inflamed the bad feeling he engendered with insulting comments about civil rights leaders, such as his often-quoted statement in 1984 about their doing little more than "bitch, bitch, moan, moan, and whine."

Meanwhile, he felt that the white conservatives in the administration did not treat him much better. In an angry speech delivered in 1987 to the conservative Heritage Foundation, Thomas said, "It often seemed that to be accepted within the conservative ranks, and to be treated with some degree of acceptance, a black was required to become a caricature of sorts, providing sideshows of anti-black quips and attacks."

Indeed, Angela Wright, whom Thomas appointed in 1984 and fired a year later as head of the EEOC's communications department, said she was appalled to find him playing exactly that role in front of white officials. "When whites were around, he would make racist remarks or jokes in order to get their support," she recalled. "His attitude was that blacks are parasites, which was a way of boosting himself in their eyes, since he was the exception, a self-made man." Wright remembered one incident in particular: when a prominent white official complained to Thomas that he couldn't get a loan, Thomas suggested the problem was that the man "wasn't black" so he couldn't get special government handouts. As she recalled it, he went on to say: "Now if you wore a dashiki and grew an Afro, you would get all the government money you want."

On another occasion, when the subject of Mississippi's legacy of racism came up in a meeting attended mostly by white staff members, Wright remembered Thomas's "sitting there and rearing back in his chair with a cigar in his mouth and saying, 'I got no problem with Mississippi. You know why I like Mississippi? Because they still sell those little pickaninny dolls down there. And I bought me a few of them too.'"

At the same time, Thomas's relations with his employers were less than congenial. In his first year at the EEOC, he tried to take a principled stand in favor of keeping extant affirmative action plans on the books, only to be publicly dressed down by the White House. At issue was a plan, agreed to earlier, that would integrate the police department in New Orleans by promoting equal numbers of black and white officers until the department, like the population it served, was half black and half white. The Reagan Justice Department, however, was eager to strike down exactly this sort of regulation and wanted to overturn the New Orleans plan before a federal court of appeals.

Although in most instances Thomas opposed such statistical goals and timetables, he prepared a separate brief arguing that the Justice Department ought not to provoke new conflict by overturning plans that had already been decided. Otherwise, he argued, the department would "invalidate innumerable conciliation agreements, consent decrees, and adjudicated decrees to which the commission is a party, as well as the commission's own published guidelines regarding appropriate affirmative action."

The brief signaled that Thomas believed he, not the Justice Department, should handle matters involving employment-related racial discrimination — which in previous administrations had been very much within the chairman's purview. As the agency's deputy director, Al Golub, recalled, "He prided himself on being his own man. He had a deep dislike for [Assistant Attorney General for Civil Rights] Brad Reynolds for trying to take over the whole civil rights milieu."

But before the EEOC's dissenting brief could be filed, Thomas was summoned to the White House, where he was told explicitly that the administration would speak "with one voice." Clearly, on matters of discrimination that voice would belong to Reynolds, as had been the case during Thomas's stint at the Department of Education. To make the humiliation complete, the Justice Department spokesman fed the news of Thomas's browbeating to the press. Not surprisingly, the EEOC's separate brief in the New Orleans case was never filed in court.

Without the ability to chart his own course at the EEOC — at least insofar as it conflicted with that of the administration — Thomas became increasingly frustrated. At a lunch in the White House mess when Reynolds was ordering Thomas to push the administration line even harder, Thomas reportedly snapped back, "Don't tell me what to do, Brad. All I *have* to do is to die and stay black."

As Golub saw it, "Thomas was pretty much left to suffer in Reynolds's backwash. I take him at his word that he was his own man and had his own opinions. But if he was," suggested Golub, who watched as Thomas toed the line, "there was a high level of hypocrisy there."

❖

Soon after he marked his six-month anniversary at the commission, Thomas was also beset by a number of personal burdens. His wife left him with full custody of their ten-year-old son. His finances were strained to the point that he had trouble paying his income taxes, and a lien was placed against him. And in the spring of 1983 — as Anita Hill was planning to join him on his trip to Oklahoma — both of Thomas's grandparents died, one three weeks after the other.

These events weighed heavily on Thomas. According to many of his colleagues, he behaved like a virtual recluse during this period, staying in his office as much as possible, speaking rarely in meetings, and consistently exuding gloom. "We had a brooding chairman," Golub recalled. In contrast to earlier chairmen, who always led their meetings, "Thomas wouldn't say anything," according to Golub and several others. "It seemed he didn't like the cases, and he didn't like the issues. He wasn't happy about being there." Even one of his staunchest defenders, his congressional affairs expert, Phyllis Berry, acknowledged that she couldn't get Thomas to come out of his office. Making him socialize in the early months of his tenure, she said, was "like pulling hens' teeth."

A year after joining the EEOC, Thomas weighed quitting altogether, according to a homily he later delivered in his church. "I had been thrust into highly visible and controversial positions, and for the first time in my life, found myself embroiled in controversy. I had been asked by then-President Reagan to run a difficult agency, and found it to be much more than I had been warned about, and far more than I had bargained for. And just as the criticism poured in, and the problems of the agency overwhelmed me, my grandfather died. I had taken the criticism and faced up to the problems. But somehow when the person who fed you, and sheltered you, cared for you, raised you — somehow when that person dies, it's hard to handle."

❖

Attacked from the outside and undercut by the administration from the inside, Thomas was understandably anxious to put together a loyal staff. Dodging a steady stream of political misfits sent his way by the White House, he instead built a wall of hand-picked employees whose chief function, it seemed to many, was to promote and protect him. Golub, who had been at the EEOC since 1963 and who became quite close to Thomas for a while, put it this way: "Thomas assembled a palace guard. He built a personal staff, completely dependent on him, without any role in the agency's larger mission. Mostly," he said, "they were concerned with marketing the chairman."

Thomas was particularly loath to be tarnished by bad publicity. "Publicity was the catalyst that drove everything," said another former top official, who declined to be named. "When it was bad, it drove him nuts." The harshest reprimands seem to have been reserved for employees who might reflect poorly on Thomas's own performance. And this included whistle-blowers who went to the press or to authorities with complaints about problems within the agency.

Golub, who eventually retired because his liberal views were incompatible with Thomas's conservative ones, nonetheless respected him and took no sides in the Hill-Thomas dispute. But he did believe that Thomas required an unusual degree of submission from his staff. "Under Thomas," he said, "the levels of sycophancy reached Olympian proportions."

Especially in his first few years at the commission, Thomas recruited some staff members who didn't share his conservatism. Anita Hill was one example; also among those he brought with him from the Department of Education was Michael Middleton, a Carter Democrat who became Thomas's associate general counsel. Middleton, a well-liked moderate, viewed Thomas as pragmatic, smart, and — at least in the beginning of his tenure — willing to forge some middle ground between extremists in the Reagan administration and in the civil rights community.

But although Thomas was flexible enough to hire people with different views and to enjoy informal political debate, in the office he required a level of obedience on policy and other matters that many employees found extreme. Dozens of his colleagues say Thomas did not tolerate dissent and was apt to take any opposition personally. As Middleton put it, "He's a charming, engaging person if you're with him. But you just don't have arguments with him. Especially when he's your boss." Or as another top attorney at the commission who resigned in 1985 explained, "He had about the least judicial temperament of anyone I've ever met. As he saw it, you were either with him or against him. And if you were against him, it was a personal betrayal."

Not surprisingly, Thomas's staff seemed to be composed of deferential people who could be counted on to agree with him. (Many of these same staff members would testify for him during the hearings.) Among them was his secretary, Diane Holt, whom he brought with him from the Department of Education. Another close aide was his assistant and personal friend J. C. Alvarez, who had also previously worked for Senator Danforth.

An especially loyal member of this group, who called himself Thomas's "confidential assistant," was Armstrong Williams, who came to work for Thomas in January 1983. A suave and stylish African-American, Williams was a protégé of the former segregationist Strom Thurmond and had a flair for social networking. Williams caught Thomas's attention when, as a low-level aide at the Department of Agriculture, he managed to convince Richard Pryor to speak at a Reagan administration event commemorating Dr. Martin Luther King Jr. The bold stroke turned into a publicity coup that helped deflect attention from Reagan's opposition to making King's birthday a national holiday.

As Williams told it, the Monday after Pryor's speech, Thomas called him and said, "Young man, I think that was a very impressive affair you pulled off. It did a lot of good for this administration, particularly given the perception that we're not doing enough with civil rights. What are you doing at Agriculture? Your skills could be put to better use." From that point on, at the EEOC and afterward, Williams applied himself with similar enthusiasm to burnishing Thomas's public image.

Some of Thomas's aides were so devoted to him that their behavior raised eyebrows at the EEOC. In particular, Phyllis Berry, the director of congressional affairs, was recalled by many as admiring Thomas to an extent that others found odd. In the confirmation hearings, she described herself as "the chairman's eyes and ears." According to Angela Wright and a number of others, Berry took her responsibility quite literally, even standing on toilet seats in closed bathroom stalls in order to report back to Thomas on other employees' private conversations.

Berry, a young black Republican from North Carolina, was considered by many people, including Wright, to be politically astute and extremely bright. But her behavior became a subject of intense office gossip when she wore a black, chin-length mourning veil to work, according to three colleagues, including Armstrong Williams. She also conducted animated conversations with herself — once, according to one of these colleagues, over tea set for two. Eventually, despite her devotion, Thomas was forced to take action, limiting her duties to the point where some believed Berry was fired, though she maintains that she resigned. To some who knew her at the EEOC and later witnessed her performance at the hearings, her solemn testimony in support of Thomas was hard to take seriously. Al Golub, for instance, commented, "Seeing Phyllis Berry commenting on the strangeness of Anita Hill was reality turned on its head."

Thomas could be extraordinarily nice to the less powerful people at the commission. He joked with the maintenance men and cleaning ladies, insisted on addressing his chauffeur, James Randall, as "Mr. Randall," and swapped tales of deprivation with others who had come up the hard way. "He used to come past my desk to talk about being poor in Georgia," Jewel Mack, an EEOC secretary, recalled. "We were always laughing about how we both picked cotton."

But in the eyes of many who had worked at the agency before he arrived, Thomas changed the EEOC's culture to the point that it became hostile to independent thinkers for the first time in its history. Golub, who received glowing performance evaluations from Thomas at first, resigned in 1984 after a number of tough political discussions in which he and Thomas strongly disagreed. "I decided it was time for me to leave," Golub said. "I got political signals from him that I hadn't heard from any other directors of either party."

❖

Thomas imposed order in other ways as well. Though politically vibrant, under previous administrations the EEOC had been poorly run, and it had been regularly chastised by the General Accounting Office for squandering funds and failing to keep adequate track of personnel, caseloads, and other basic matters. When Thomas took over, for instance, there were only two computers (both malfunctioning) with which to track the agency's annual caseload of sixty thousand complaints. And according to news accounts, the corridors were stacked with cardboard cartons of moldy files.

Thomas's first act was to remove the sign "Chair" that had hung over his predecessor's door and replace it with the more traditional "Chairman," which was also the title by which he demanded to be addressed. In short order he requisitioned a new computer system and in other ways introduced the commission to a more efficient and more authoritarian management style. In fact, a number of officials at the commission believed that Thomas was an excellent and demanding administrator who frowned on anything short of perfection from his employees. For instance, when one of the married commissioners became romantically involved with a married member of his senior staff, both individuals were urged to leave, which they did.

By the time of the confirmation hearings in 1991, his defenders described Thomas's tenure at the EEOC as one of Prussian order during which impropriety of any sort, sexual or otherwise, was simply not tolerated. This high standard, his supporters asserted, made it unthinkable that Thomas himself had acted improperly toward female members of his staff and entirely implausible that someone with a grievance as serious as Hill's would have failed to bring it to the attention of authorities. Thomas testified that his intolerance for sexual harassment at the EEOC was "adamant," unwavering, and unmistakable, and aides knew that if they engaged in it or other "inappropriate conduct," as he put it, "You will be fired, simple." As Thomas's friend and successor at the agency, Evan Kemp, wrote in a letter of support following Hill's accusations, "Thomas admonished . . . against even the appearance of impropriety [and] backed up this admonition with a record of disciplining employees who engaged in sexual harassment" and other forms of inappropriate behavior. (In the same letter, Kemp noted that "Clarence finds pornography repulsive.")

Indeed, it appears that by the time he had been at the EEOC for three years or so, Thomas's sensitivity to sexual harassment had grown considerably. Whereas he had warned in the 1981 transition report that strict enforcement of sexual harassment statutes could lead to a "barrage of trivial complaints," in 1985 he was praised by several women's groups for urging the solicitor general, Charles Fried, to file a friend-of-the-court brief in the case of *Meritor Savings Bank v. Vinson*. *Meritor* contended that sexual harassment in the workplace constituted a serious form of discrimination — a position the Supreme Court ultimately upheld.

But earlier, when Hill worked for Thomas, his record regarding alleged sexual misconduct among the staff was mixed. Probably the most challenging case Thomas dealt with personally revolved around allegations that Earl Harper Jr., a regional attorney in the Baltimore field office who had been with the agency for more than twenty years, had sexually harassed a secretary named Patsy Stewart. Stewart sued the EEOC under Title VII, the provision barring sexual discrimination in the workplace. According to Stewart's complaint, Harper had on several separate occasions manhandled her, propositioned her, and rubbed his genitals in front of her. Further, Stewart alleged that when she rejected his advances, he refused to promote her. Her attorney contended that this treatment constituted sexual harassment and had resulted in Stewart's emotional collapse. Harper, who had won a number of commendations from the agency and risen to a fairly senior position, denied all of the charges both then and later.

In late 1982, a pretrial investigation was launched. A confidential report on the findings, which was circulated to Thomas, found many similar and potentially devastating allegations from other female employees against Harper. Because of this, Nestor Cruz, the agency's acting legal counsel, suggested in an internal memo that the EEOC settle Stewart's case quickly to avoid "subjecting the agency to negative public scrutiny." Consequently, a settlement was offered to Stewart, leaving Thomas with the question of how to discipline Harper.

According to Cruz's settlement recommendation of November 19, 1982 (which was never released), at least seven female employees at the EEOC in addition to Stewart had complaints, ranging from Harper's allegedly fondling himself in front of them to his allegedly forcing a secretary to have sexual relations with him in a hotel room during a business trip. A number of the women said they had felt it necessary to seek other employment.

The internal document, which names each of these women, also shows that a number of other employees, many of whom Harper had supervised, alleged that they had had consenting sexual liaisons with him, including a secretary with whom Harper denied having been sexually involved; he later amended his response, explaining that he had initially forgotten the incident. "The fact that Mr. Harper seems unable to remember with whom he has and has not had sexual relations undermines his credibility," the report noted.

Because the disposition of Harper's case occurred at about the same time that Hill was working for Thomas, the case was cited during the confirmation hearings as a contemporaneous indication of Thomas's attitudes on sexual harassment inside the EEOC. Thomas testified that he had no tolerance for such behavior; commenting on Harper's case, he said, "I felt very strongly that he should have been fired, and that was my view. I felt and continue to feel that individuals engaged in this conduct should be fired, and that's the approach I took at the EEOC."

However, the record, reconstructed from internal memos and interviews with several of the individuals involved, is more complicated. In December 1983, Thomas did indeed concur with the agency's general counsel, who wanted to fire Harper summarily. But Harper then appealed to Thomas. And Thomas subsequently took no action.

To the consternation of Stewart and her lawyer, instead of being fired, Harper was allowed to retire at the usual age, with full benefits, in October 1984. According to Middleton, who personally favored a lenient approach because he felt the agency did not have the evidence to support a tougher stance, the failure to take decisive action occurred because "Thomas wanted someone else to take responsibility for firing Harper — he didn't want to do it himself." The upshot, charges Stewart's attorney, Sue Silber, was that "when push came to shove, Clarence Thomas did not take sexual harassment seriously."

❖

Of course, in an agency of more than three thousand employees with some fifty field offices, no administrator could be held accountable for every personnel problem. But in another case that Thomas personally reviewed, questionable behavior was, if anything, rewarded while those who blew the whistle paid the price.

The case involved a nest of allegations coming from the Philadelphia field office, which was under the direction of Johnny Butler, a six-and-a-half-foot-tall former Howard University football player. According to official internal documents in the case, a white lawyer named John Lokos believed he had antagonized Butler, in part by speaking to office colleagues about Butler's personal life. In particular, Lokos told a secretary in the office, according to these documents, that he had disturbed Butler and a female EEOC employee in a compromising position on the floor of Butler's office. Butler adamantly denied Lokos's story, at the time and later, terming it "slander." And his anger at Lokos was evident. At a 1984 EEOC managers' retreat, Joseph J. Schutt, director of the agency's investigative branch, the Office of Audit, told investigators that he heard Butler say "in a very loud fashion" that he was "going to get that white motherfucker."

Thirteen months later, Lokos was told by supervisors that he was being fired. At this point, Lokos filed a formal complaint against his supervisors in the Philadelphia office, in which he made a number of serious allegations about what he regarded as wrongdoing in the office. None of these complaints were leveled at Butler, who by then had been named Thomas's acting general counsel in Washington and who also retained the title of Philadelphia district director. Instead, Lokos complained to an EEOC investigator about his belief that a half-dozen attorneys there had been engaged in the practice of private law while performing their ostensibly full-time EEOC jobs.

For Thomas, the Philadelphia case was complicated because by the time the allegations reached him, he had become friendly with Butler, whom he had promoted. The two socialized together, watching football games and, according to colleagues, copying each other's blustering style. Said one former EEOC employee who was close to Butler, "Johnny made Clarence feel like he was one of the guys."

The EEOC's Office of Audit nonetheless investigated Lokos's claims about corruption in the Philadelphia office and concluded that, during a period when the EEOC was so far behind on cases that it sometimes couldn't settle them before the statute of limitations lapsed, seven of the office's attorneys had indeed been practicing private law for several years. Two had formal stationery printed with the name of a private partnership and the EEOC's address. Some were listed as private attorneys in the Yellow Pages. And a recovered computer disk from the government office showed such outside legal work as a drunk driving case, real estate cases, and a number of divorces.

Lacking the power to subpoena these attorneys, the investigators were unable to determine whether any of these activities were unlawful. Joseph Schutt therefore suggested that the investigation be turned over to the FBI, which could deliver a subpoena. Instead, the investigation ran aground when, according to an internal document summarizing an interview with Schutt, "Butler somehow obtained a copy of . . . the Office of Legal Counsel's report to Chairman Thomas. Subsequently, Butler 'tore into' the Legal Counsel . . . ," as Schutt had put it. And Thomas soon took Butler's side, sending Schutt a copy of the investigators' findings with a note attached asking, "Is this all we have after this protracted and unfocused investigation?" Schutt believed that Thomas had not even completely read the report about the Philadelphia office.

The case was never sent on to the FBI, as Schutt had requested. Nor was any disciplinary action taken. Instead, under Thomas's chairmanship, it appears that several cases of serious and internally supported allegations of sexual and other misconduct at the EEOC were not seriously pursued. And in the Philadelphia case, those who sought to investigate were penalized. The message to potential complainants inside the commission was hardly reassuring. As Susan Dunham, a law professor at American University who worked on a number of sexual harassment cases at the EEOC, later remarked, "Within the EEOC during those years, there was an atmosphere of fear and intimidation."

To be sure, a few people still spoke out against what they saw as problems. But their forthrightness was not generally appreciated. For example, early in Thomas's tenure, Frank Quinn, the veteran head of the San Francisco office, was quoted in *Newsweek* about the backlog of cases building up under Thomas's stewardship. Quinn was months away from retirement, but after the remark, Thomas tried to have him transferred to Birmingham, Alabama, away from his family in San Francisco. Thomas argued that the transfer had been pending before Quinn's criticism. But Quinn managed to get a court injunction canceling the transfer, which was found to have at least the appearance of being capricious and vindictive.

Later, when the backlog of age discrimination complaints grew so enormous that more than ten thousand cases were on the verge of being abandoned because the statutes of limitations were expiring, the head of the St. Louis office, Lynn Bruner, also spoke out. Having failed to get the attention of the EEOC's headquarters, she told the press how dire the situation was. Alarmed, the Senate subcommittee on aging asked Bruner to testify about the problem.

The day before she was scheduled to appear in June 1988, Bruner received an unusual job performance evaluation by fax from Washington, criticizing her for presenting "the chairman in a negative light" and downgrading her previously "satisfactory" job rating to "minimally satisfactory." She was also informed that she would be demoted from head of the St. Louis office to deputy in Phoenix. Like Quinn, Bruner charged that she had been punished for speaking out; only when a special counsel set up to protect government whistle-blowers started investigating this claim did Thomas abruptly change her rating back to "fully successful" and cancel her demotion.

Five years later, Bruner remained angry about Thomas's harsh treatment. "He lied about me and about the lapsed age discrimination cases in his testimony to Congress," she said in an interview. "He lied about very specific details that he knew he was lying about. But everyone was scared to death of him. He had a reputation for being extremely retaliatory, which clearly he was with me. You stood a chance of being [ruined]. People were out to protect their asses — with good reason."

Against this backdrop, it becomes easier to comprehend why, when asked later about why she failed to file a formal complaint against Thomas, Anita Hill cited the hostile environment that she faced.

◆

During his confirmation hearings, Thomas said he found it impossible even to imagine how Hill had believed him to be pursuing her, given his strict rule about not mixing his personal life with his professional life. "I did not, and do not, commingle my personal life with my work life. Nor did I commingle their [my employees'] personal life with the work life," he testified. Further, he denounced Hill's charges as contrary to the experience of every other female employee who worked with him at the EEOC. Hill, he argued, "is the only person who has been on my staff who has ever made these sorts of allegations about me." Indeed, no one else during the hearings or since has come forward to accuse Thomas of sexual harassment.

But in the months and years after Hill left the EEOC, three other women who worked for Thomas there experienced, witnessed, or were told about behavior on his part that was strikingly similar to that which Hill described. Not one of these women ever met Hill before she came forward, and although all three agreed to testify on her behalf during the confirmation hearings, none was called. The Judiciary Committee was apparently concerned that two of the three women were fired by Thomas and the third resigned, a record that might be seen as coloring their opinions — or freeing them to speak out.

The first woman was an attractive black Republican political appointee named Angela Wright, whom Thomas hired at the age of twenty-nine to be the agency's director of public affairs, reporting directly to him. She started at the EEOC in March 1984 — about eight months after Anita Hill had moved to Oklahoma. With her dark skin, high cheekbones, and long, thick black hair, Wright could have been Hill's sister. But she was as sharp-tongued and outspoken as Hill was polite.

Wright had been fending off male advances for years and knew how to handle herself. What she had more trouble handling was a streak of impetuousness. She had worked in the office of a Democratic congressman from North Carolina, Charlie Rose, but had been fired for walking off the job after a tiff. She had also resigned flamboyantly from a job at the Agency for International Development (AID), where she had written an inflammatory letter accusing a supervisor, who was unhappy with her performance, of racism. Her jobs for the Republican National Committee and the Republican Congressional Committee ended less controversially, but at the latter job too Wright had raised some eyebrows by criticizing a dilatory Xerox repairman so severely at an out-of-town seminar that he had leapt into her lap and started to choke her. And after about a year at the EEOC, she was fired by Thomas, for reasons that would be disputed during his confirmation hearings.

Wright had a pronounced aversion to bullies — she once flung a plate in defense of a younger brother. She was bright, fearless, and brazenly candid, speaking her mind with little inhibition, regardless of the consequences. As she put it, "I'm not the kiss-up type."

Wright came from North Carolina and had switched to the Republican party at a time when, under Chairman William Brock, party leaders were making a major push to recruit black voters. Wright was already a conservative on social issues such as school prayer. And she was also pragmatic; like Thomas, she had realized that "the Republicans were the ones with the jobs."

Not long after she arrived at the EEOC, Wright's troubles with Thomas began. She later swore in an affidavit that Thomas began to "consistently pressure me to date him." His first such attempt, as she told it, happened during a retirement party for another staff member. She recalled that Thomas, who was seated next to her, turned to her and, out of everyone else's hearing, said, "You look good, and you are going to be dating me, too."

It was not, Wright said, the only such statement he made, but rather, she soon learned from experience, quite typical of him. "In general," she told congressional investigators, "given the opportunity" — by which she meant a moment when no one else could witness their conversation — "Clarence Thomas would say to me, 'You know you need to be dating me — I think I'm going to date you — You're one of the finest women I have on my staff. You know we're going to be going out eventually.'"

Wright's description of Thomas's mode of operation bore many similarities to Hill's, which is all the more notable because Wright was deposed before Hill testified. Like Hill, Wright noticed that Thomas had an odd way of ordering her to date him: rather than asking her out on a date or requesting her company for a specific activity, he would speak as if issuing a command, "like all he had to do was decree it." As Hill recalled during the hearings, Thomas would say, "You ought to go out with me."

Wright, a single woman like Hill, did not react positively to Thomas's advances or his tone. She said that although she tried to stay on friendly terms with him at the office, she was never attracted to him. She felt that "he didn't seem to particularly like women. It seemed instead, like now that he had power, he thought he was entitled to them carte blanche." His whole approach made her feel, she said, "like a piece of meat."

This attitude, Wright felt, was exemplified by a question Thomas asked her while on a trip to an EEOC seminar in the fall of 1984. Although she said she was not certain of the destination, she later told officials that she believed the trip may have been to Denver. (In fact, Thomas's records indicate that on September 12, 1984, he attended an EEOC seminar in Denver, as did Wright.) Clearer in Wright's mind than the date or venue was her memory of Thomas's question as the chairman of the EEOC and his employee walked to the conference center. According to her affidavit, he asked, "What size are your breasts?"

Wright's recollection is reminiscent of Hill's. Like Hill, Wright stated that Thomas unexpectedly initiated a discussion of breast size — though in this case the subject was her own. Also like Hill, Wright thought the smartest tack to take for the sake of her career was to try to change the subject. According to her affidavit, "I said something like 'I think you best concentrate on remembering the names of the people you are going to be sharing the panel with.'"

Wright also recalled that Thomas used the context of private business meetings to make humiliating comments about her anatomy. Although she did not volunteer it to congressional investigators because, she said, it was too embarrassing, she later confirmed a friend's account that in one such EEOC meeting Thomas told her, "I really love the hair on your legs — I think hairy legs are much sexier." Wright said, "I have no problem taking compliments from men, but there's a limit to everything. His comments weren't friendly banter, they were from the angle of 'I'm your boss, so I have the right.'" According to Wright, the reference to her legs was just part of a pattern that Thomas had of appraising both her body and the sexual appeal of her wardrobe. In this, too, her account was much like that of Hill, who would testify that in the office Thomas had made numerous "remarks about my personal appearance," commenting "on what I was wearing and whether it made me more or less sexually appealing."

Unlike Hill, though, who knew of no other women in her position, Wright said she didn't feel particularly singled out. She believed that Thomas frequently made similar comments about many of the females in the agency. "He would say," she recalled, "'I've got some fine women on my staff'" and then go on to appraise them. Or, she said, he would ridicule those who were less attractive with snide comments and nicknames. For instance, according to Wright, Thomas routinely referred to one employee, an attorney, as "Big Ass" behind her back.

Wright, like Hill, also described a single impromptu evening visit by Thomas to her apartment on Capitol Hill. One night, she told congressional investigators, she answered the doorbell and was surprised to see Thomas standing there. She invited him in, asked what he was doing in the neighborhood, and offered him a beer. He stayed and talked for so long, she had to start "yawning and becoming distracted" to get him to leave. It was after midnight when he finally went home. Asked by investigators whether she was "afraid" of Thomas that night, Wright responded with characteristic bravado, "I was never afraid of Clarence Thomas."

Unlike Hill, Wright said that in her estimation, Thomas's social pressure and commentary on her sexual appeal did not constitute sexual harassment — because she never felt harassed by it. As she put it, "I am a very strong-willed person, and at no point did I feel intimidated by him. Some other women might have," she allowed, "but these were not situations I ran home and ruminated on."

If anything, Thomas's behavior annoyed her. Wright remembered telling her friend Phyllis Berry that she was sick of Thomas's bothering her all the time at work and was thinking of going elsewhere. According to Wright's recollection, Berry, who fancied herself as Thomas's favorite female aide, assured Wright that she shouldn't feel singled out, with words to the effect that "he's a man — he hits on everyone."

Berry, with whom Wright had fallen out by the time she left the EEOC, has denied the comment, thus raising questions about the accuracy of Wright's recollections. Given that Wright had a checkered employment record and was ultimately fired by Thomas, she might be dismissed as an unreliable source. But it happens that she had a confidante at the EEOC, an older speechwriter in whom she confided her travails with Thomas.

Wright's friend, a published novelist, television screenwriter, and schoolteacher named Rose Jourdain, not only corroborated Wright's account, she expanded on it. Jourdain, who is older than Thomas, was never an object of his sexual attention. But she did get to know him well, reporting directly to him and conversing with him at length while working on many of his speeches. She told congressional investigators that she remembered Wright quite clearly: "When Ms. Wright first came in [to the EEOC] she was very enthusiastic about her job. She was happy to be there." But as time went on, "she confided to me increasingly that she was a little uneasy and grew more uneasy with the Chairman, because of comments that she told me he was making concerning her figure, her body, her breasts, her legs, and how she looked in certain suits and dresses."

Although Wright later said she had viewed Thomas's alleged inappropriate behavior as little more than an annoyance, Jourdain recalled moments that had reduced Wright to tears — suggesting that Hill was not alone in finding Thomas's conduct in the office both disruptive and upsetting. On one occasion, Jourdain remembered, Wright came into her office to cry because she had bought a new suit and Thomas had "evidently quite a bit of comment to make about it — how sexy she looked in it, and that kind of thing . . . It unnerved her a great deal."

It was Jourdain who first told investigators that Wright had stormed into her office one day, slammed the door behind her, and demanded, "Do you know what he [Thomas] said to me?" The answer, Jourdain remembered, "had something to do with 'Ooh — you have very sexy legs,' or something like 'You have hair on your legs and it turns me on,' or something like that." Jourdain also independently recalled an occasion when Wright told her that Thomas had struck up a "conversation about bra size" — an apparent reference to the Denver trip. Wright's recitation of offensive behaviors "happened so much," according to Jourdain, "it was a constant kind of 'Do you know what he did?'" from her.

According to Jourdain, Wright was "increasingly nervous about being in his [Thomas's] presence alone." The problem became particularly acute when Thomas began scheduling one-on-one meetings with her at the end of the day. Wright became so uncomfortable that she would ask Jourdain to wait for her in the building until she was able to leave.

Wright's tenure at the EEOC came to an abrupt end in April 1985. She recalled that she was stunned to arrive at work one morning to find a brief note from Thomas taped to her chair, saying in essence, "You're fired." Even though she had come to have mixed feelings about her job, she took pride in her work and felt the firing was unwarranted. She confronted Thomas in his office and asked for an explanation. According to Wright, he told her that he was dissatisfied with her work and with her failure to "wait for him outside his office after work."

"I have tried to be a loyal employee, and I have tried to be your friend," Wright said she protested.

"Well," Thomas replied, "I never cared anything about loyalty, and I don't care a whole lot about friendship."

"Well then," said Wright, "I hope you will be a very happy and successful man, but I doubt it."

Then, according to Thomas's assistant Armstrong Williams, Thomas told him that he added, "And when you go, take your friend [Jourdain] with you" — thus firing Rose Jourdain as well.

Looking back, both women believe that Thomas's behavior was motivated as much by disrespect as by attraction. Asked why Thomas would have treated her and Hill as they claim he did when so many other women who worked for him described him as personally correct and professionally supportive, Wright offered a theory. "Thomas," she suggested, "treats different types of women differently. He has more respect for light-skinned women. It's racist, but I think he definitely treats white differently than black, and among black women I have seen a real difference depending on skin color." Wright pointed out that both she and Hill are dark, while most of the women whom Thomas promoted and who testified on his behalf during the hearings were light, Hispanic, or white.

Thomas himself gave currency to this theory in his comment to his mother that Hill was too black for him; he also discussed it in the first private conversation he had with Senator Arlen Specter of Pennsylvania about Hill's charges. In trying to explain Hill's motives, Specter recalled, Thomas speculated that she might have been angry that during their time at the EEOC he had dated and promoted "women of a lighter complexion." Thomas told Specter that "there seemed to be some tension . . . and some reaction, as I recall it, to my preferring individuals of the lighter complexion."

Jourdain also felt that Thomas's sexual comments had less to do with romance than with hostility. As she saw it, "Clarence took a certain joy in making people uncomfortable, you might say harassing them. I think the only thing he was in love with was the conquest of power."

❖

A third African-American woman who worked for Thomas at the EEOC, a special assistant named Sukari Hardnett, also thought Hill's descriptions of Thomas's behavior rang true. As Hardnett recalled it, Thomas's behavior toward her was odd but certainly not egregious. He never pushed her to date him or did anything that even approached sexual harassment. But Hardnett said she too had witnessed Thomas treating women on his staff in ways she found inappropriate. In the context of Wright's and Jourdain's statements, her account lends credibility to Hill's contention that Thomas "used business meetings and discussions to talk about dating . . . and sex." And it makes it even more difficult to believe that Thomas's separation of work and play was quite as categorical as he said it was.

Hardnett joined the agency as a law clerk in the chairman's office in September 1985, about five months after Wright had been fired and two years after Hill had left. At the time, she was a thirty-five-year-old law school graduate, light-skinned, slender, and socially better connected than Thomas. Politically, she was far more liberal, but she said she did not realize at first how conservative he was. She was friendly with Gil Hardy — like herself, a Democrat — and Hardnett and Hardy were both part of a circle Thomas had hoped to join, of young, successful black professionals who vacationed together in Oak Bluffs, a seaside town on the Massachusetts resort island of Martha's Vineyard.

Before long, Hardnett said, she attracted Thomas's attention. "I saw him every day," she recalled. "Every morning he wanted me to have coffee with him. He called me at home and told me about his relationships with women. He told me he didn't know any nice women, and he would like to meet some."

Soon, she said, he began calling her into his office for business meetings; then, instead of discussing the EEOC, he would talk about his private life. He told her, for instance, that his relationship with Lillian McEwen had foundered on their political differences because she viewed him as "a puppet of the Republicans." He said he planned to "buy her [McEwen] a mink coat anyway." On another occasion, he told Hardnett that he had become involved with a woman he had met in Ohio, but he was having trouble accepting that she wore her hair in cornrows. Such conversations, Hardnett said, "made me very uncomfortable."

As Hardnett commented in a statement she prepared for the Senate, "Clarence Thomas pretends that his only behavior toward those who worked as his special assistants was as a father to children, and as a mentor to protégés. But that simply isn't true. If you were young, black, female, and reasonably attractive, you knew you were being inspected and auditioned as a female . . . Women know when there are sexual dimensions to the attention they are receiving. And there was never any doubt about that dimension in Clarence Thomas's office."

In an interview, Hardnett expanded on this statement, noting that her own experience wasn't unique. "Clarence often befriended attractive single women in the commission," she said. "Suddenly they would have coffee in the morning, lunch in the afternoon, and dinner. It wasn't like he had to ask anyone out on dates — if the chairman wants you at seven in the evening, he doesn't have to ask you out on a date."

In her opinion, in late 1985 and early 1986 Thomas was virtually "auditioning women" from the office for roles in his private life. For instance, one day Thomas spotted an attractive woman visiting Hardnett, a friend of hers who looked "almost like a twin of Anita Hill," according to Hardnett. The woman, whom Thomas knew slightly, worked in the EEOC's office of review and appeals. As Hardnett remembered it, "He asked me early the next day to invite her back to the office." When she did so, Hardnett said, Thomas sat down with the two women "and talked to us about male-female relationships and whether we wanted to have children or not. I thought it was a little strange. I thought it would be business related."

Hardnett recalled that after that meeting, Thomas frequently asked her how her friend was doing. "He told me, 'I am very attracted to her, but I have to give serious thought to her statement that she wants to have children. I don't want to have any more children, so I can't act on my feelings. But if things were different, I certainly would.'" Hardnett said she thought the whole thing "very strange" because her friend had never been the least bit interested in Thomas; in fact, her friend was at the time dating one of his friends. "He just had concocted this whole thing," she said.

Hardnett became increasingly unhappy with Thomas, but she explained that she was thirty-five when she worked for him, and by then "I knew how to handle someone like that." In contrast, she said, "Hill was ten years younger. She wasn't part of the same social circle. She had no employment history to draw on. She was unconnected and naive."

Eventually, after failing in an effort to be reassigned to another supervisor, Hardnett chose to leave the agency. But even for her there were repercussions after her attempt at reassignment. Once rebuffed, she said, Thomas became "very, very cold." He went from calling her at home to refusing even to say hello in the hallway. The impact was magnified by their colleagues; as Hardnett said, "Once you have been in the chairman's grace and fallen, then everyone else treats you as an outcast."

In this respect too Hardnett's account is reminiscent of Hill's, particularly her comment that she feared toward the end of her employment that she was being "chilled out in decisions." Another female EEOC employee who fell out of favor with Thomas put it succinctly: "With Clarence, you went from hero to zero overnight."

Of course, some women were flattered by the attention and quite clearly enjoyed Thomas's company. Phyllis Berry, for instance, testified that she had been "privy to the most intimate details of his life." Berry became acquainted with some of the women Thomas dated as well as with his first wife and his son. Similarly, when his aide J. C. Alvarez was asked during the hearings whether Thomas had discussed pornography or sex with her, she testified that "Clarence and I were . . . personal friends for many, many years. Our kids went to the same school together. I knew his wife. We were going through divorces at the same time and everything else. We had the kind of confidences, personal conversations, that close friends have, and any more than that really is not relevant."

Another EEOC employee, Linda Lambert Jackson — the woman in whom Anita Hill said she had so haplessly confided her secret about Thomas in the fall of 1983 — testified on his behalf that he had helped her through a difficult divorce. After discovering that they lived in the same building, she said, "we had numerous conversations about work, politics, and personal issues. We became very good friends in the process."

While the picture of Thomas painted by these women is far kinder than that offered by Hill, Wright, Jourdain, and Hardnett, it is worth noting that none of these accounts supported Thomas's testimony that he never mixed personal and professional matters. On the contrary, these accounts together reveal a pattern of behavior suggesting that Thomas used his political power to pursue women who worked for him — even when they evinced no interest or were made quite uncomfortable by him. If Wright, Jourdain, and Hardnett are accurate in their recollections, Thomas felt free to comment on the anatomy and sexual appeal of more than one woman who worked for him. More serious, Thomas's behavior caused Hill to leave a job she had always wanted, Wright to consider leaving, and Hardnett to choose unemployment over continuing to work for him.

❖

The years that these women worked for Thomas were not easy ones for him, either. Although he came into conflict with the Justice Department during the time Hill worked for him, by 1985 his relations with the administration were, if anything, even tenser. Rumors began circulating within the administration and the press that Thomas would not be reappointed when his term expired in 1986. Aware of his precarious situation, he quietly made it known that he was interested in returning to the private sector. But neither his experience at Monsanto nor his chairmanship of the EEOC proved much of a lure. According to colleagues, he had visions of a six-figure salary and a top corporate post, not the sort of middle management job in "human resources" typically given to affirmative action hires. But as he sought a respectable exit from the government, no lucrative offer materialized.

After Reagan's reelection in 1984, the administration began reassessing every major appointment with an eye toward consolidating its conservative gains. According to the EEOC's associate general counsel, Michael Middleton, Thomas was summoned to a meeting at the White House at the end of 1984 or early in 1985 and given an ultimatum: "They were tired of his arguments. If he wanted to stay, he had to play." The payoff, Middleton believed, was made quite explicit: if Thomas joined the team, the federal judgeship he longed for might be available.

Middleton recalled this turn of events quite clearly. The two men had worked closely together for a number of years, but not long after his meeting at the White House, Thomas told Middleton in a long conversation that he would no longer be giving credence to Middleton's more liberal views. Middleton took the hint and sought work in academia, soon accepting a job at Missouri North Central's law school.

Thomas replaced Middleton and other liberal aides with proven conservatives, many of whom were picked by the White House. "You have no idea how weird these people were," recalled Tony DeMarco, an EEOC lawyer and Vietnam veteran who had worked well for both Republicans and Democrats. DeMarco particularly cited Jeffrey

Zuckerman, a white lawyer and White House ally who became Thomas's chief of staff in late 1984. Zuckerman, whose subsequent nomination to become the agency's general counsel was rejected by the Senate in 1986, argued in EEOC staff meetings that the Equal Pay Act actually hurt blacks because it deprived them of jobs that employers would be willing to give them if they could be paid less than whites. Although he belonged to an agency entrusted with fighting job discrimination, Zuckerman, DeMarco and critics in the Senate said, believed that discrimination should be left to the marketplace.

Other senior officials in the agency recalled that Zuckerman and Thomas would prowl the halls, promising, "Heads are gonna roll." DeMarco was one whose head was on the block before long. The three other managers in his office, their supervisor, a highly respected lawyer named Constance Dupree, and a number of other career employees were, like Middleton, all removed in what DeMarco called an "ideological bloodletting."

Stricter ideological enforcement caused changes throughout the agency. In speechwriting, Rose Jourdain was replaced by Ken Masugi, a law professor at the University of California at Irvine. Masugi was a follower of the arcane conservative legal thinker Harry Jaffa, a professor at Claremont College who had risen to fame by writing Barry Goldwater's famous apologia for fanaticism: "Extremism in the defense of liberty is no vice." Jaffa and Masugi were among the cultlike followers of the German philosopher Leo Strauss. The so-called Straussians considered themselves an intellectual elite, capable of understanding higher meanings in classic texts such as Machiavelli's *Prince,* which they believed lesser minds could not truly fathom. With these credentials, Masugi and several of his conservative colleagues saw themselves as bringing needed intellectual depth to the Reagan administration.

Thomas had already demonstrated his interest in more accessible conservative thinkers, such as the popular author and proselytizer for self-interest Ayn Rand. (He had made the movie version of her novel *The Fountainhead* required viewing for his favorite aides and often praised her other works.) Now Masugi and his like-minded colleagues would take him several ideological steps further, writing some of Thomas's most controversial speeches on esoteric philosophical subjects.

One theory that seemed especially appealing to Thomas was the idea that God-given "natural law" should take precedence over man-made law. Some believers in this precept saw as illegitimate any laws that undercut absolute rights to property, including zoning laws, environmental laws, and some health regulations. At a time when Attorney General Meese was encouraging conservative politicians to disregard liberal Supreme Court rulings if they disagreed with them, this view of a higher legal authority than the written law was radical indeed. Thomas's support of the natural law theory became all the more controversial after he praised a speech in which his fellow conservative Lewis Lehrman used natural law as a basis for opposing abortion. Lehrman argued that abortion violated every being's God-given, "unalienable rights" to life — a position inconsistent with the Supreme Court's *Roe* ruling.

During these later years at the EEOC, some supporters asserted, Thomas still displayed a restless and independent intellect. Pam Talkin, a moderate Democrat who eventually replaced Zuckerman as Thomas's chief of staff, commented that despite countless hours of political discussion with Thomas, she could never predict where he would come out on an issue. "His thoughts are always evolving," she told the *Wall Street Journal* in 1991. Indeed, both his hiring of Talkin and the many unorthodox comments he made to Juan Williams, whose profile of him in the *Atlantic Monthly* appeared in early 1987, reflect an open, questioning mind.

But from 1985 on, Thomas's public stands were almost uniformly synchronized with those of the most conservative elements in the Justice Department. For instance, shortly after joining the commission, he had made a real effort to defend federal guidelines that required employers to keep their job applications, tests, and interviews from being racially or sexually biased. Civil rights leaders used these Uniform Guidelines on Employee Selection Procedure as a cudgel in their effort to force large companies to hire more women and minorities. Although the administration reviled the Uniform Guidelines, Thomas pointed out in a public forum that "we are not dealing with zoning ordinances here. Whole classes of people in this country have come to rely on the vital protection offered by measures such as these."

But just weeks after Reagan's reelection, Thomas alarmed civil rights leaders by unceremoniously reversing himself and pronouncing the Uniform Guidelines "too rigid." Similarly, whereas he had once fought for some affirmative action plans, such as the one affecting the New Orleans Police Department, now he submitted an EEOC brief that joined the Justice Department in arguing that all such plans and agreements were illegal. Affirmative action, Thomas declared without reservation, was "a fundamentally flawed approach."

In July 1986, just before Congress began hearings on Thomas's reconfirmation as head of the EEOC, the Supreme Court disagreed, rejecting the EEOC and Justice Department briefs. It ruled that affirmative action was a legal and valid remedy in the fight against discrimination. Faced with questions from the Senate Judiciary panel about his vacillation on this issue, Thomas reversed himself yet again, promising to practice affirmative action if that was what the law required.

The EEOC had long been a giant mill for processing all of America's inequities in the workplace, but under Thomas the conveyor belt was slowing. In the first half of 1986, as the issue of his reappointment to the chairmanship approached resolution, the EEOC was forcing settlements in only 13.6 percent of the cases it closed, compared with 32.1 percent in fiscal 1980. And of the cases it reviewed, it was finding "no cause" to prosecute 56.6 percent of them, a rate twice as high as in the final year of the Carter administration.

Nonetheless, on August 12, 1986, Thomas won unanimous Senate confirmation to a second term. As Al Golub, Thomas's former deputy director, explained it, "Liberals do not know how to aggressively cross-examine a black man. The Democrats were intimidated by him." A few tremors of discontent did rise to the surface. Two Democratic members of the Senate Labor and Human Resources Committee, Howard Metzenbaum of Ohio and Paul Simon of Illinois, voted in committee against recommending Thomas for a second term. Metzenbaum declared that Thomas had "not brought to the [EEOC] a vigorous determination to enforce the law." But the senator later conceded, "Most people just don't like to vote 'no' in a confirmation process. There's a disposition that unless there's something strong enough to actually convict a nominee, you should go along and get along."

By September, all harsh words had apparently been forgotten as Thomas was joined by his former nemeses — Reynolds, Meese, and South Carolina's Senator Strom Thurmond — for a gala swearing-in at the EEOC. Flanked by the men whose rigid line against affirmative action he had now so wholeheartedly embraced, Thomas visibly flinched, according to a news account, when Reynolds raised a glass and toasted a man he evidently still regarded as an outsider.

"It's a proud moment for me to stand here," Reynolds said as some of Thomas's aides stared awkwardly at their feet, "because Clarence Thomas is the epitome of the right kind of affirmative action working the right way."

Thomas's prospects soon brightened in other ways as well. In early 1987, he met Virginia "Ginni" Lamp, a sunny, trusting, blue-eyed lawyer from Nebraska. Physically and psychologically, Lamp and Thomas seemed to be complete opposites. Whereas Thomas had mocked his own sister's financial dependence, Lamp took homeless strangers out to lunch. Thomas was often moody and aloof; Lamp was invariably warm and cheerful. For her sweet naiveté as well as her color, Lamp was dubbed "Snow White" by some of Thomas's African-American colleagues at the EEOC. Politically, however, the two were a perfect match. Lamp worked for the U.S. Chamber of Commerce, where she had been the spokeswoman for the drive against family leave and "comparable worth," the movement calling for women in jobs similar to those traditionally held by men to be paid comparably. Lamp opposed the measure on the grounds that the government should not dictate wages. (For the same reason, she also opposed the national minimum wage.) And as a leading female opponent of a cause championed by many women, Lamp had experienced some amount of ostracism, just as Thomas had been spurned for opposing causes dear to many African-Americans.

Lamp was, if anything, more conservative than Thomas. Her family, well connected and well-to-do, had provided the backbone of Goldwater's support in Nebraska. Her father, a developer who had built some of the most exclusive planned communities outside Omaha, was a party activist, as was her mother. When Lamp decided to move to Washington, her parents helped her find her first job there, a staff position in the Senate office of Republican Hal Daub of Nebraska.

While in the capital, Lamp joined an assertiveness training group called Lifespring. She became deeply involved in the group but was troubled in 1985 when, during a Lifespring exercise, trainees were forced to take off all but a bikini to the tune of "The Stripper." As she described the incident, participants were pelted with questions about sex and urged to ridicule fat people's bodies. "I had intellectually and emotionally gotten myself so wrapped up with this group that I was moving away from my family and friends and the people I work with," Lamp later admitted. "My best friend came to visit me and I was preaching at her, using this tough attitude they teach you."

Lamp withdrew from the group and left Washington for a while in order to regain her balance. Not long after she returned, she met Clarence Thomas at an Anti-Defamation League colloquium on civil rights. Thomas offered her a ride home, and three months later he confided in his colleague Rosalie Gaull Silberman that he was "in love." In May 1987, Lamp and Thomas were married.

Lamp introduced Thomas to her church, Truro Episcopal, in Fairfax, Virginia. The church, as it happened, was popular with many Reagan administration ultraconservatives and served as a center of anti-abortion political activity. The rector during the 1980s, John W. Howe, was a vocal opponent of abortion, arguing, for instance, in a letter written on Truro stationery in 1984, that abortion was "nothing short of a holocaust." By the time Thomas joined the church, Howe had helped to form an affiliated group, the National Organization of Episcopalians United for Life (NOEL), which could always be counted on to supply busloads of people for anti-abortion demonstrations.

During the confirmation hearings, Thomas would successfully dodge questions about his opinions on abortion. But there was no question that both the church and Lamp were useful in giving him greater entrée to the innermost circles of conservative Republicans. As Thomas acknowledged in an article he wrote in 1987, conservatives had a way of distrusting and excluding recent converts like himself, particularly black ones. "If you were not with us in 1976," he wrote of their attitude, "do not bother to apply." Virginia Lamp would be perceived by even the best-connected conservatives as a born insider. To Thomas she provided not only a measure of personal happiness and stability, but also, in the waning days of the Reagan administration, even stronger Republican credentials.

6

❖

Benched

THE WASHINGTON that Anita Hill left behind in 1983 was a Republican town, dominated by the outsize figure of Ronald Reagan. But Hill, who registered as a Democrat upon her return to Oklahoma, soon found herself in even more conservative country. The campus of Tulsa's Oral Roberts University was referred to as the City of God; its sweeping front lawn was dominated by a sculpture of praying hands that reached several stories into the sky. And just as these hands dominated the landscape, the Christian faith in its most fundamentalist form dominated the institution.

Founded by the aging evangelist for whom it was named, the school espoused a rigid religiosity. Two years before Hill's arrival, the American Bar Association had refused to accredit the new law school because its students and faculty were required to recognize Jesus Christ as their personal savior. The certification was vital to the school's survival; without it, graduates would be unable to practice law in most places. Although in 1981 the school won a lawsuit protecting its religious requirement, it still had only provisional ABA accreditation when Hill arrived, making its future extremely uncertain.

In addition to recognizing Christ, students were required to sign an honor code, promising, among other pledges, to attend religious services faithfully, not to drink, and not to engage in sex until marriage. The subcutaneous body fat of each student had to remain at or below a certain maximum percentage, the level of which was decreed by Oral Roberts himself. If a student exceeded this percentage, he was forced to lose weight or leave. Talking in tongues was as common on this campus as second languages were at most others. And the range of political thought was so conservative that Reagan's supporters were considered the campus liberals; many more were those philosophically aligned with Patrick Buchanan, Reagan's fiery communications director.

Women and blacks were scarce in the student body and scarcer still on the faculty. The law school's dean, Charles Kothe, made no secret of Anita Hill's appeal as a double minority at a time when the school was desperate to become fully accredited: he believed that minority hires were essential to prove its otherwise suspect diversity. As Kothe put it later, "Here we had a chance to hire the first black woman Yale Law graduate in the Southwest — it was a coup whether she could teach or not."

Hill had never taught before, and in an institution where most students and faculty opposed affirmative action, the perception that she simply filled a quota made her position even more challenging. Despite her limited expertise, she was now expected to deal with such exacting areas of the law as the uniform commercial code. And having just turned twenty-seven that summer, she was the same age as or younger than many of her students.

From the start, Hill was baited by a number of self-described "rednecks," a loose pack of loudmouthed white male students who enjoyed playing crude pranks. Calling themselves the Fringe Riders — the name referred to the fringe of a golf course — they made a sport of disobeying Hill. Whistling, catcalling, and refusing to stand up or sit down when Hill asked them to, the Fringe Riders took great delight in disrupting her classes. As one of them, Lawrence Shiles, later said, "She commanded no respect from the students — her class was like a kindergarten class." He believed she deserved no respect since, in his view, she was "just there as window dressing. The school was having constant accreditation problems, and you hire someone like Anita Hill just to fill a double position, female and black."

Shiles in particular had a difficult time handling the academic material in Hill's class and received a C in the course. He was still angry about the grade a decade later, calling Hill "a totally incompetent teacher." In the end, Shiles got through law school "by the skin of his teeth," according to Dean Kothe.

Lurking beneath much of this behavior was racial bias, according to Ken Ferguson, one of Hill's few black students, who now teaches law at the University of Missouri. Looking back, he believed that Hill "did a very good job, especially given her lack of experience." But he said that some of the students were "extremely nasty." Referring specifically to Shiles, he said, "It went far beyond ordinary razzing. People made noises in her classes and went out of their way to trip her up. It was out of the ordinary." He believed that many of the Fringe Riders "were particularly vocal and negative because they just assumed that white people were better, and that blacks didn't meet the standard."

Asked about this hazing years later, Hill declined to comment, suggesting only that it was impossible for her to know what had motivated it. The collapse of Oral Roberts's law school in 1986 allowed her to leave the Fringe Riders behind, she thought for good, and thanks to Dean Kothe's recommendation, to take a far better teaching position at the state university's law school in Norman. There she moved into a small ranch house and settled into a peaceful routine, teaching contract and commercial law as well as a slightly less starchy seminar on civil rights. She seemed to thrive: she won tenure in four years and was elected by her colleagues to the law school's Committee A, a small executive committee that dealt with such sensitive issues as hiring, tenure, and salary matters.

In the summer of 1987, Hill had an opportunity to leave Oklahoma and return to Washington. Joel Paul, a young international law professor who had met Hill at various professional gatherings, had invited her to do a summer research project at American University's Washington College of Law, where he taught. The two became friendly that summer, and Paul urged Hill to think about transferring there permanently. But although she was tempted to live in a more cosmopolitan environment, where she would be less isolated as an African-American, she decided against moving because "she thought the school was a bit too progressive for her." In particular, Paul remembered, she was put off when some other law professors attacked her for defending Robert Bork during a lunchtime conversation. Hill had taken a typically complicated stance, suggesting that while she did not necessarily share all of Bork's views, she disapproved of the way his beliefs had been distorted by his opponents in their effort to kill his nomination. Her ideological neutrality had so infuriated some of the other faculty members, Paul said, "she thought she would be more at home in the more traditional milieu of the Middle West."

As her potential sponsor at AU, however, Paul had been troubled by one aspect of Hill's résumé. He had noted that after doing well at Yale Law School and working briefly at one of the most prestigious law firms in Washington, she had worked for less than a year at the Department of Education and then taken a promising position at the EEOC, only to leave abruptly to teach at the unaccredited and now defunct law school at Oral Roberts University. This progression made no sense to him. He was especially puzzled by the rapidity of her decision to teach at Oral Roberts: the American Association of Law Schools had set up a formal method of applying for teaching jobs — applicants were screened in a pool — but evidently Hill had just grasped at her first offer. He didn't want to sound condescending, and as an East Coast Jew educated in the Ivy League, he was concerned about seeming insensitive to her religion. But if he was going to champion her to the law school's hiring committee, he had to be sure that she had nothing to hide.

Over a picnic lunch on the last day of Hill's stay that summer, Paul asked directly about the move to Oral Roberts. Hill answered just as plainly, telling him that she had had to leave the EEOC because she was being sexually harassed by her supervisor. She didn't go into much more detail that Paul could later recall, in part because it was clear that they both found the subject embarrassing. Looking back, he wasn't even positive she had named the supervisor, and since at that time he had never heard of Clarence Thomas, the name would have meant nothing to him if she had. The rest of the conversation about the harassment was very awkward. "What are you supposed to ask when someone tells you this?" he later wondered. "I asked if she'd filed a complaint. She said I didn't understand — it was a very hostile environment."

Paul was amazed by the notion that a senior official at the EEOC, of all agencies, had harassed someone he knew and admired to the extent that she had abandoned a promising career. "It was so hard to believe," he later said, "I decided to discuss it with a colleague of mine who had represented a number of women employees who had brought cases against the EEOC during that period." The response of his colleague, Susan Dunham, who was then in charge of the law school's

Legal Methods Program, was also memorable to Paul: "She said that it was her observation that the EEOC was a case of the fox guarding the henhouse."

❖

The same summer that Hill was defending aspects of Robert Bork, Clarence Thomas was eying Bork's vacated seat on the prestigious U.S. Court of Appeals for the District of Columbia Circuit. The D.C. Circuit, as the court was known, presented the ideal opportunity for Thomas. But although he had served loyally in the Reagan Revolution and proved his strength as a team player to the president's men — most notably those in Meese's Justice Department — he was still languishing at the EEOC. He had served for more than six years in the executive branch; he had watched federal judgeships come and go, but never seemed to make the cut. He was no closer to his ultimate ambition of a seat on the Supreme Court than when he started the decade.

In Ronald Reagan's Justice Department, filling the federal courts with able conservatives was a top political priority undertaken with the utmost seriousness. And according to a former Justice official who worked closely with the lawyers involved in judicial selection, Thomas was not seen as qualified, especially for a slot as powerful as the one Bork had occupied. "You just wouldn't appoint a token to a judgeship as important as the D.C. Circuit. It was never seriously considered," said the official. After years of fighting racial preferences as demeaning while taking advantage of openings earmarked for minorities, Thomas was evidently still in the impossible position of being viewed as an underqualified token himself.

Reagan's nominee for Bork's seat turned out to be a widely respected, mainstream Republican named Judith Hope. She had been, coincidentally, a partner in the law firm for which Anita Hill had worked (and would play an inconspicuous part during the hearings as one of Hill's detractors). But Hope was never confirmed. Instead, on the outside chance that Michael Dukakis would be elected president in 1988 and then appoint a Democrat to fill the seat, the Democrats on the Senate Judiciary Committee delayed confirming Hope — until time ran out.

When George Bush was elected, he earned the right to pick his own nominee, thus providing Thomas with another chance at the seat. But

George Bush insisted that Clarence Thomas was "the best-qualified" man for a seat on the Supreme Court when he announced the nomination in Kennebunkport, Maine, on July 1, 1991.

AP/Wide World Photos

Thomas, shown here in a picture from his high school yearbook, excelled at the private religious schools he attended but felt intense racial isolation.

Reuters/Bettmann

Thomas's relationships with both his mother and his sister were often severely strained, but past troubles were set aside after he was nominated for the Court. He is shown here on the first day of the hearings with his wife, Virginia Lamp Thomas; his mother, Leola Williams; and his sister, Emma Mae Martin.

Top: Armstrong Williams, who worked as Thomas's aide at the EEOC, helped his mentor throughout the confirmation process, first by giving him public relations advice, then by trying to debunk Anita Hill's story.

Middle: Angela Wright worked for Thomas at the EEOC and later said he had made inappropriate sexual comments to her. Although she was subpoenaed and traveled to Washington, the Republicans on the Judiciary Committee fought to keep her on the sidelines, and she never testified.

Bottom: J. C. Alvarez, Nancy Fitch, Diane Holt, and Phyllis Berry all worked for Clarence Thomas at the EEOC and testified that the behavior Anita Hill described did not in any way fit the man they knew.

Hill had planned to spend the Columbus Day weekend of 1991 in Oklahoma, celebrating her mother's eightieth birthday. Instead, most of the family flew to Washington to be by her side during the hearings. Here, Hill's parents, Albert and Erma, hold up their daughter's high school graduation picture.

At first, Hill remembered telling only her Yale Law School friend Susan Hoerchner (*left*) about being harassed. But she had also told other friends—Ellen Wells, John Carr, and Joel Paul—who appeared as witnesses on her behalf.

Above: Charles Ogletree, a professor at Harvard Law School and an experienced trial lawyer, was initially reluctant to serve as Hill's lead counsel. Not until the morning of Hill's appearance did he agree to take on the role.

Left: James Brudney, an aide to Senator Howard Metzenbaum, had the most frequent contact with Anita Hill before her story was leaked to the press. His contemporaneous notes of an early conversation with Hill matched her Senate testimony almost exactly.

Top left: Thomas talks with Senator John Danforth of Missouri (*right*), his patron in the Senate, and Senator Orrin Hatch of Utah, another stalwart supporter.

Top right: Kenneth Duberstein, a Washington lobbyist, helped to moderate the effect of Thomas's controversial positions in order to sell him to Democrats in the Senate.

Bottom: Stanley Grayson, Carlton Stewart, John Doggett, and Charles Kothe appeared as witnesses for Clarence Thomas. Their testimony helped damage Anita Hill's credibility, although even Thomas's most zealous supporters worried that Doggett had gone too far in suggesting that Hill had fantasized about having a romantic relationship with him.

AP/Wide World Photos

Top left: The Judiciary Committee chairman, Senator Joseph Biden, was most concerned with being perceived as fair by both sides. Senator Edward Kennedy might have been expected to question Thomas aggressively, but his own indiscretions made him reluctant to play an active role in the hearings.

Top right: The Reverend Louis Sheldon, the guiding spirit behind the Traditional Values Commission, organized a group of African-American pastors to help create the appearance of grass-roots support for Clarence Thomas.

Bottom: Senator Hatch used an allusion to pubic hair in the 1971 bestseller *The Exorcist* to suggest that Hill had fabricated her testimony against Thomas.

Jose R. Lopez/NYT Pictures

In the final hours of the hearings, on October 13, Anita Hill posed in her hotel suite with her advisers and lawyers. From left to right: (*standing*) Sonia Jarvis, Warner Gardner, John Frank, Charles Ogletree, Kim Taylor, Shirley Wiegand; (*seated*) Kim Crenshaw, Janet Napolitano, Emma Jordan, Hill, Susan Deller Ross.

The date of Thomas's official swearing-in as the nation's 106th Supreme Court justice was pushed up because the White House was worried that reporters might uncover new stories about his private life. Here, he is shown with the other justices in an official photograph.

when the White House counsel Boyden Gray first drew up a list of top candidates, Thomas's name was not on it. Although Thomas had tried to make himself useful to Bush throughout the 1988 presidential campaign — helping with the speech to the NAACP and serving on one of Bush's caucus teams at the convention — the hard truth was that he was still relatively unknown in Washington. It often seemed that the biggest impression he had made was on his critics: he was despised by liberal Democrats and disowned even by many black Republicans.

A painful reminder of Thomas's low profile had come at a dinner honoring black officials in the Reagan administration that was sponsored by the Council of One Hundred, a group of establishment black Republicans. Thomas wasn't even seated on the dais with the other politicians. Armstrong Williams, who attended the dinner, remembered scanning the hotel ballroom and finding his friend and mentor seated in the hinterlands, "practically out the door." To help soothe Thomas's hurt pride, Williams escorted his guest and former boss, Senator Strom Thurmond, over to greet the EEOC chairman.

More surprising, perhaps, was that despite his years of service to Reagan, Thomas was still relatively unknown to his fellow conservatives as Bush took power. "No one in the conservative community knew Clarence Thomas," acknowledged Clint Bolick, a supporter who had worked for Reynolds at the Justice Department and for Thomas at the EEOC.

Underscoring this situation, a month after the election a conservative coalition met to review possible names for the Supreme Court during the Bush years. The only black candidate considered was Samuel Pierce, the outgoing housing and urban development secretary and a Rockefeller moderate. Thomas wasn't even seriously discussed.

Clearly, if Thomas wanted a seat on any court, his political profile needed to change dramatically. Later, during his Supreme Court confirmation hearings, Thomas would protest that he had never lobbied for or purposely positioned himself for a top judicial nomination. But, beginning in 1988, what Thomas did do was to launch an aggressive, canny, and in the end very effective campaign for the Court.

His first move was to take Bork's seat, and this required three distinct steps. First, in order to attract President Bush's attention, Thomas needed ardent supporters, preferably from the right. Since he still wasn't well known among this group, he needed a well-placed and enthusiastic ideological patron. Second, he had to minimize the opposition, which meant defusing his tense relationship with the black civil rights establishment — a tricky balancing act, given his first goal of impressing the right. Last, Thomas had to work around the Democratic majority in the Senate and piece together enough votes to assure his confirmation.

The task wasn't easy, but Thomas was undaunted. In all, his campaign for the appeals court lasted eighteen months — from the summer of 1988 until he took his seat on March 12, 1990.

❖

A warning bell sounded in that same summer, 1988, when Justice William Brennan was hospitalized with pneumonia. Justice Marshall, the Supreme Court's other liberal octogenarian, had also recently been hospitalized for blood clots and other ailments. For years Thomas had been telling his black colleagues that he would occupy Marshall's seat someday. If true, he was going to have to move quickly.

About that time, Thomas agreed to have dinner with Patrick McGuigan, then the legal director in charge of judicial matters for Paul Weyrich's powerful conservative group, the Free Congress Foundation. McGuigan, an irrepressible ideological warrior whose intense eyes and unkempt hair were reminiscent of the young Edgar Allan Poe, was a huge fan of Thomas's, though he had never met him. He admired Thomas's opposition to affirmative action, which he took quite personally since he believed his own white male cousins in Detroit were denied jobs in favor of minorities. He already knew Virginia Lamp Thomas from Chamber of Commerce events. But now he felt it was finally time to sit down with Thomas and get to know him.

During their dinner — held at the Monocle, a restaurant on Capitol Hill favored by insiders and lobbyists — McGuigan made one point clear. He thought Thomas had a very good shot at a federal judgeship, and he was willing to mobilize the right behind him. But the lesson of Bork's defeat was that judgeships were now political campaigns. In order to win, Thomas would virtually have to run for office. "You know, you're a very smart guy," he told Thomas, "and eventually you're going to be nominated to the federal bench." But when it happened, he warned, Thomas could expect five minutes of the president's time. If he was lucky, he might get fifteen minutes of the attorney general's time. And if the assistant for legislative affairs at the

Justice Department thought the nomination was one of its most important, then perhaps Thomas would get a full 2 or 3 percent of his
time. Although McGuigan himself was committed to, as he put it,
"credentialing a black conservative," Thomas could expect at most
10 percent of McGuigan's and other conservative activists' time.

"Do you know what that means?" McGuigan asked Thomas.

"Yeah," Thomas replied. "I'll have to do it myself."

"Son," said McGuigan, "go to the head of the class."

Whatever else the two talked about that night remains private, but
it seemed clear from the enthusiasm McGuigan demonstrated regarding Thomas's candidacy for the court that no disagreements arose
about McGuigan's ongoing crusades: the outlawing of abortion, the
abolition of affirmative action, and the restoration of what he considered "family values" — including a war on pornography.

Thomas also needed to become better known around the White
House counsel's office. Bush had sent a reassuring signal to hardliners
such as McGuigan by placing two prominent conservatives, Boyden
Gray and Lee Liberman, in that office, where they could oversee judicial selections. Thomas knew both of them casually through his
efforts to participate in the Federalist Society, a conservative legal
group, some of whose members championed the notion that legal
authority on such issues as the minimum wage and safety laws at work
should not be determined by the federal government. During the early
Reagan years, Federalist Society chapters had sprung up at law schools
across the country in reaction to what the society's members considered the left-wing orthodoxy dominating many law faculties. By the
end of his tenure at the EEOC, Thomas had spoken to several of
these chapters; no doubt they were favorite audiences because he both
shared their views and realized their growing power in the Republican
party over judicial appointments.

Liberman, a small, bespectacled young woman with enormous intellectual energy, had been one of the group's founders, helping it grow
into a spawning ground for many of the young lawyers now in the
upper echelons of the Justice Department. Gray, a tobacco heir from
North Carolina whose father had been a golfing companion of Bush's
father, was also a Federalist Society regular in Washington, viewing
its events as "intellectual feasts." Given to eccentric passions — he
was once seen walking his pet potbellied pig outside his Georgetown
mansion and sometimes drove a battered jalopy fueled by ethanol —

he found the ideas of the Federalists well suited to his conservative, patrician tastes.

By giving Gray and Liberman the decisive voice in judicial selection, Bush made it clear that when it came to the courts, he intended to keep conservatives happy. Lacking an articulated judicial philosophy, Bush viewed the courts in political terms. His policy was essentially a continuation of the Reagan effort to move the judiciary to the right, but in the hope of putting his "kinder, gentler" face on the courts, Bush placed a greater premium on finding qualified women and minorities, albeit conservative ones, to fill judicial vacancies. Bush's former campaign manager and the current chairman of the Republican National Committee, Lee Atwater, insisted that if the party's support was to grow, it needed to present a more inclusive, tolerant image, or as Atwater put it, be a "big tent." With the memory of the Willie Horton ads still fresh in both Bush's and Atwater's minds, it was time to make amends, and visible court appointments were one way to do so.

This shift in emphasis at last presented Thomas with the opportunity he had been waiting for. As he had long reckoned, the list of well-connected, conservative African-American officials with law degrees was very short, and his name belonged at or near the top. The White House just needed to be reminded of this.

His friend and former EEOC employee Clint Bolick was the eager messenger. Bolick described Thomas's many attractive qualities to Lee Liberman, underscoring Thomas's devotion to the philosophy of Ayn Rand. Good to his word, McGuigan helped Thomas's cause by calling in a favor. Earlier, when Richard Thornburgh had been nominated for attorney general, McGuigan had denounced him as too moderate. Asked by the White House to keep quiet, however, he had agreed to hold his fire. As soon as Thornburgh was confirmed, he invited McGuigan to have breakfast — and McGuigan's first order of business was to lobby for Thomas's appointment to the appeals court.

Others pitched in as well, among them Thomas's friend and successor at the EEOC, Evan Kemp, who was also a close friend of Gray's. And it didn't hurt that Ricky Silberman, Thomas's close friend and vice-chair at the EEOC, was married to Judge Laurence Silberman of the D.C. Circuit. Silberman was a respected Reagan appointee, and he and his wife boosted Thomas's profile in influential Republican circles.

The campaign to make Thomas judicial timber was successful. Soon he occupied a solid position on the short list of candidates. And one year after the campaign was launched, his name rose to the top: with Gray's and Liberman's final blessings, President Bush nominated Thomas to the D.C. Circuit on July 11, 1989.

❖

The news of Thomas's nomination nonetheless surprised many in Washington's legal circles. Even some of the conservatives who had worked with him were taken aback. "When I heard he'd been picked for the appeals court I started calling my friends from Justice," said a former administration lawyer. "We all said, 'What are they doing?' We were amazed."

Perhaps sensing the shaky nature of the appointment, the White House treated the Thomas nomination with particular care. Eddie Mahe, a GOP consultant with strong ties to the new administration, called Murray Dickman, the attorney general's top lieutenant, and convinced him that Justice needed to hire a full-time consultant to help Thomas prepare for his confirmation hearings — an unusual precaution for an appointment other than to the Supreme Court. "He wasn't getting the right help," Mahe explained. "The Bush administration was sloppy in its confirmation prep."

Mahe, who had started the GOP's black voter outreach programs in the 1970s, knew Phyllis Berry from her days at the Republican National Committee. He thought she might be of some help, and as it happened, she had not taken a new position since leaving the EEOC. Despite a reputation for odd behavior, Berry would bring a number of assets to the task of preparing Thomas: she was familiar with his record, knew his friends and enemies, and had acute political instincts. But given the strained circumstances of her departure from the EEOC, she told Mahe she wouldn't take the job unless Thomas himself asked for her help. He called, and Berry signed on.

Berry became Thomas's de facto political manager. She would be responsible for executing the second phase of his campaign for the court — the taming of the opposition. "I ran this like a campaign," she explained later. "We needed a strategy. I made a plan. I looked at the opposition, who had spoken against him at EEOC reconfirmation. I had Clarence make courtesy visits to civil rights leaders. I thought about disgruntled EEOC workers, feminists — anywhere opposition was likely to come from."

One potential land mine lay in Winston-Salem, North Carolina, where Angela Wright, the outspoken young woman whom Thomas had so humiliatingly fired from the EEOC, was now a journalist. She had tried to reach Thomas on several occasions, once to see if the EEOC might be interested in hiring an entrepreneur she knew in the telephone business. But the chairman had never returned her calls.

Now, shortly before the announcement of Thomas's appointment to the court, his longtime personal aide, Armstrong Williams, dropped by Wright's office and offered to take her out to lunch. The visit came as a surprise, and while they chatted about other matters, Wright was drawn into a long conversation about Thomas. "You know he's on his way to the appeals court," she recalled Williams saying, fishing for a response. "What do you think of that?"

Wright could not recall her exact response but said, "I'm sure it wasn't particularly nice. I probably told him, 'I don't care what Clarence Thomas does with his life.'" Wright did remember that Williams tried to soothe any raw feelings, saying, "The chairman feels really bad about you."

Later Williams claimed that during lunch, Wright "swore revenge" on Thomas — a vow he said she fulfilled by providing damaging information about him at the time of his Supreme Court confirmation hearings. But Wright's memory was quite different.

"Armstrong knows I didn't swear revenge," she said. "Clarence Thomas did me a favor. He was wrong to fire me — I didn't deserve that — but the truth is that I don't belong in the political arena. I'm not the most diplomatic type."

It was not the last time Thomas and his supporters would try to keep Wright happy. But as Berry scanned the horizon for other hidden dangers, one person she never thought of, she said, was Anita Hill.

❖

Thomas also had institutional enemies to worry about. Berry realized that if he was going to make it to the appeals court, he would have to try to reach a détente with the major civil rights organizations and black professional groups. By the end of his tenure at the EEOC, most mainstream black leaders refused even to meet with him. Their predictable rejection of Thomas and his views had only succeeded in isolating him further, creating a downward spiral of mutual distrust.

In the weeks before his appointment, Thomas launched a calculated charm offensive. "Suddenly, in like June of 1989, Clarence Thomas changes," recalled Barbara Arnwine, the executive director of the Lawyer's Committee for Civil Rights, a liberal group. Thomas was still at the EEOC, but the news of his appointment to the court was imminent. "He's suddenly dripping honey to everyone. It occurs to me that he wants something."

Judith Winston, who by then had left the Department of Education for the Women's Legal Defense Fund, agreed with Arnwine, whom she happened to talk with about that time. "There's been a personality transformation overnight," she told Arnwine. For months Winston had been trying to meet with Thomas about his abrupt rejection of the Uniform Hiring Guidelines, an important issue for her group, but she hadn't been able even to get an appointment. "Suddenly Clarence was accessible and amenable," she recalled. "At first I thought he was being nice because he'd worked with me at Education." But when Thomas was appointed to the court the following month, she said, "I realized he was being nice because he didn't want any extra opposition."

The critical group that Thomas needed to win over was the NAACP, long the bellwether of the civil rights establishment. If the NAACP mounted a united opposition, it would trigger an avalanche of opposition by other groups. Berry worked relentlessly to set up a meeting with Althea Simmons, a legendary figure who was then the group's director in Washington. But Simmons was in the hospital, recovering from serious surgery. Finally, however, she agreed to a bedside meeting after Thomas's office began calling daily, begging for an audience.

On the day of the scheduled visit, in early 1990, George Kassouf, an official of the Alliance for Justice, a liberal interest group and a critic of Thomas, happened to call Simmons to ask where the NAACP stood on his nomination. "Funny you ask," she told Kassouf, according to his recollection, "because guess who's coming over today to see me." When Kassouf asked if he could attend the meeting too, Simmons told him to leave for the hospital immediately; Thomas was expected any minute.

On his arrival, Kassouf found Simmons's room at Howard University Hospital set up like an office, complete with a fax machine. A few minutes later, Thomas came in with two colleagues. The EEOC chairman, according to Kassouf, was extremely respectful of Simmons. He told her, "You can't know the troubles I've seen," and then described his conflicts with Reynolds and Meese, blaming them for undercutting his attempts to uphold civil rights.

Kassouf felt that Thomas was overstating his differences with the Reaganites and interjected, "With all due respect, his rendition of his record is different from the facts." But at this point Johnny Butler, the former football player and controversial friend of Thomas's, who was one of the EEOC deputies at the meeting, raised his voice. Soon the argument between Kassouf, a bantamweight intellectual, and the towering Butler raged so hotly across her bed that Simmons had to quiet everyone down. The visit, which lasted an hour and a half, ended more cordially.

Simmons asked Kassouf to stay when the others left. He recalled her seeming very torn. "I wanted you here because I feel there are two Clarence Thomases," Kassouf said she told him. "There is the one who says nice things about civil rights, and the other, whose harsh statements I hear and writings I read. After the debate today, I'm still confused." Now that Thomas was positioning himself for wider acceptance, she said, "I don't know who the real Clarence Thomas is."

Nonetheless, Thomas's bedside visit had its desired effect. A few days later, Simmons told *Jet* magazine that she found her long chat with Thomas reassuring. "He had not forgotten his roots or Black folk," she said. On her recommendation, the NAACP took no position on the nomination, thereby signaling that civil rights groups would not attempt to block it. Barbara Arnwine's organization followed suit, also taking no position. None of these groups believed they would gain political mileage in fighting the nomination of another black.

The courting of Simmons — who died before Thomas took his oath of office — demonstrated the power of Thomas's personal story. What later came to be called the Pin Point strategy — the emphasis on his autobiography, particularly his struggle to rise from the poverty and segregation that marked his early life — could bridge the gulf between him and his black opponents despite their political differences. For those on the right seeking a foolproof nominee, the power of Thomas's life story was also evident. Patrick McGuigan, among others, emphasized the biographical aspect in his advocacy of Thomas, writing a profile of Thomas's difficult early years in his conservative newsletter, "The Family Law and Democracy Report." Not long afterward, the conservative *Washington Times* ran a similar article. There, for the first time in print, Thomas told the horrifying story about how his fellow seminarian had cheered the death of Martin Luther King Jr.

In the months after his nomination, Thomas made private overtures to other important members of the black leadership. He flew to Detroit for a four-hour meeting with Damon J. Keith, a federal appeals court judge and well-known civil rights lawyer. Keith was a liberal Democrat who had been appointed to the federal bench by President Carter; a man with precisely the opposite view of life to Thomas's, he had a reputation for being sympathetic toward civil rights plaintiffs and criminal defendants. But Keith was also a savvy politician at the pinnacle of Detroit's power elite, and he felt a racial bond with Thomas, no matter how antithetical their philosophies. Keith, too, agreed to help and contacted other leading black legal professionals on Thomas's behalf, including William Coleman, a prominent black Republican and trusted associate of Justice Marshall's. Prodded by Keith and Coleman's daughter Lovida, a Yale Law School friend of Thomas's, the senior Coleman wrote a letter endorsing Thomas.

"I think this is a fine appointment," he wrote to President Bush in October 1989, "and that Mr. Thomas will add further luster and judicial ability to the Court." Coleman also nodded to Thomas's biography, noting, "His starts and advantages in life at the beginning were in no way equal to that of my children's."

Coleman would have regrets when Thomas was nominated to the Supreme Court.

❖

The third phase of Thomas's campaign required lining up the necessary Senate votes. Here John Mackey, a Justice Department lobbyist, took over. Mackey, a charming and resourceful political operative who had once been an FBI agent, had just been through a bruising battle with the NAACP and had come away wiser. The NAACP had fought and defeated another black conservative Bush appointee, William Lucas, on the grounds that he lacked sufficient legal experience to be assistant attorney general for civil rights. When civil rights groups and other liberal organizations launched their assault, Lucas had no one in the Senate to stand up for him. Mackey realized that Thomas, too, would be eaten alive unless he could find some Senate patrons.

Like a football coach tutoring his star quarterback, Mackey spent many hours dissecting the Lucas defeat in conversations with Thomas. Thomas even talked directly to Lucas to prepare himself for the ordeal. Mackey impressed on Thomas that Jack Danforth, his old boss, was a good patron, but that he needed bipartisan support. The ideal target, Mackey thought, was Sam Nunn; a shrewd politician from Thomas's native state of Georgia, Nunn was one of the Senate's most influential Democrats. As chairman of the powerful Armed Services Committee, Nunn was a respected moderate. When he decided how to vote on an important matter, he almost always carried other senators with him, Republicans as well as Democrats.

Mackey was impressed to find that Thomas had already found a circuitous route to Nunn through his old friend Larry Thompson, a lawyer who had worked with him at Monsanto. Thompson had served as U.S. attorney in Atlanta during the Reagan administration, and from there accepted a lucrative partnership at the firm of King & Spalding, a pillar of the southern establishment in Atlanta. He was now surrounded by Nunn's political supporters and contributors, including Griffin Bell, the former attorney general in the Carter administration and the firm's senior partner. Judge Bell, as he preferred to be called (from his days on the federal bench), was still one of the most important men in Georgia politics. With the help of Larry Thompson, Thomas arranged to pay the judge a courtesy call.

As Bell remembered it, Thomas didn't ask outright for him to help influence Nunn but confided that he was "embarrassed" that he did not have the support of either of Georgia's senators. "He gave me his life history," Bell said, chuckling. "He's pretty good at that."

Even though Bell recognized Thomas's ploy, he found the Pin Point story compelling and felt Thomas was deserving. "I can't believe Sam Nunn won't help you," he recalled saying. The judge promptly wrote a letter to Nunn, asking him to meet Thomas. Nunn proved accommodating, and the encounter went well. By the time Thomas was introduced to the Senate Judiciary Committee, Sam Nunn was at his side, and Nunn's support had the desired ripple effect among other moderate Democrats.

Also standing by Thomas before the Judiciary Committee was his Missouri patron, Danforth, who had cemented Thomas's support with moderate Republicans, just as Mackey had hoped. Further, Mackey and Thomas had worked hard to win the support of both of Thomas's current home-state senators, Virginia's Charles Robb, a moderate Democrat, and John Warner, another moderate Republican. When they came on board, Mackey knew he didn't have to worry about the ghost of Bill Lucas haunting his nominee.

The Democrats on the Judiciary Committee were still nervous about the nomination. They, too, were weary after the Lucas fight. But they were also concerned about rumors that Thomas's D.C. Circuit nomination was a prelude to bigger things, especially if Thurgood Marshall should ever resign or die. Joseph Biden, the Judiciary Committee's chairman, got in touch with the White House. If Thomas was auditioning for the Supreme Court, Biden said, he could expect rough questioning. The Justice Department sent word back that there was no intention of pushing Thomas that high. If Biden gave his support now, he could rest assured that the Supreme Court was not in the picture.

The hearings began in February 1990. Thomas struck just the right note, sounding like a reasoned supporter of judicial restraint, not a conservative ideologue. "I think my obligation . . . is to follow the Supreme Court precedent, not to establish law on my own," he testified. All the careful political preparation paid off. While there was a smattering of opposition from a few women's and civil rights organizations, the hearings were relatively smooth.

The only thorny issue that arose was the EEOC's handling of the lapsed age discrimination complaints. Among other things, the threatened demotion of Lynn Bruner, who had sparked the congressional hearings into the issue, raised troubling questions about Thomas. David Pryor, the Arkansas Democrat who had investigated Bruner's claims of retaliation, was still so angry about the case that he gave a speech denouncing Thomas on the Senate floor. But the jeremiad had little effect, in part because it was delivered just after the Judiciary Committee, on February 22, 1990, voted to confirm Thomas, 12–1.

The lone holdout was Thomas's longtime critic Howard Metzenbaum. Even Paul Simon, the Illinois Democrat who had voted against Thomas's reconfirmation as EEOC chairman, believed that Bush had the right to select his own man for the appeals court. But Simon, like Biden, made it clear that he would oppose Thomas for the Supreme Court. And Biden made sure to remind the White House of their agreement: in his opening remarks, he stressed that "the standard for the district court and the circuit court is different from the standard for the Supreme Court."

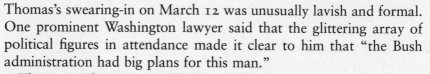

Thomas's swearing-in on March 12 was unusually lavish and formal. One prominent Washington lawyer said that the glittering array of political figures in attendance made it clear to him that "the Bush administration had big plans for this man."

The court Thomas joined had an illustrious history. Until Reagan's presidency, the twelve-member D.C. Circuit court was a progressive bastion known for liberal legal warriors such as David Bazelon and J. Skelly Wright. Since the court had jurisdiction over the home of the federal government, its judicial activism spilled into numerous policy areas; in earlier days, the court had championed the rights of the mentally ill, broadened the rights of criminal defendants, and allowed consumer and environmental groups to sue federal agencies successfully. Because it was often called on to mediate disputes between the executive and legislative branches and because it ruled on the constitutionality of federal laws and administrative regulations, the D.C. Circuit was considered the second most important court in the nation.

But by the end of the Reagan years, Bazelon and Wright had both died and the court became ideologically divided. Abner Mikva, a former Democratic congressman, Ruth Bader Ginsburg, and Patricia Wald remained energetic Democratic holdovers. Equally influential, however, were two conservative former law professors, Antonin Scalia and Robert Bork, who in the 1980s radically shifted the panel's direction toward judicial restraint. Joined later by another forceful conservative, Kenneth Starr, the Reagan appointees moved to limit the scope and source of suits against the government as well as the panel's powers of judicial review, which had been used during the Bazelon era to override Congress and the executive branch.

By the time Clarence Thomas arrived, Scalia and Bork were gone — Scalia to the Supreme Court, Bork to private practice. But their conservative replacements enjoyed a decisive majority on the court, and Thomas developed an unusually close friendship with — some would say reliance on — his fellow jurist Laurence Silberman.

Unlike his speeches and writings at the EEOC, Thomas's D.C. Circuit opinions read as if they had been stripped of controversy. As an appeals judge, Thomas would not leave a problematical paper trail when, and if, he was nominated to the Supreme Court. He also rarely expounded opinions from the bench. During the twenty months that Thomas served on the court, he was generally quiet during oral arguments, according to most clerks there. And in a departure from the normal practice, the administration took an active role in helping Thomas pick his clerks. Most were carefully culled from the best law schools, and many of them were Federalist Society alumni; their draft opinions needed little embellishment. According to clerks from other chambers, Thomas leaned especially heavily on them.

During his time on the D.C. Circuit, Thomas heard more than a hundred and fifty cases and wrote twenty-five opinions. Several clerks remember that he was a very slow writer. His votes showed him to be generally tough on criminal defendants, and in affirming a number of convictions, he rejected defenses of entrapment, inadmissible evidence, and inadequate legal representation. In keeping with his philosophy of judicial conservatism, Thomas was inclined to defer to the decisions of administrative agencies. (In one case, *Tennessee Gas Pipeline v. Federal Energy Regulatory Commission,* he was highly critical of the federal agency but could not bring himself to override its prerogative to decide rates.) This conservative approach was important, because the court's three-judge panels subsist on a steady flow of appeals of decisions and actions made by executive agencies.

Thomas's performance in two other cases left some observers unhappy. Although Danforth was his single most important supporter, Thomas participated in the appeal of a case filed against Ralston Purina, the foundation of the Danforth family fortune, by Alpo, a rival pet food conglomerate. The companies sued each other over alleged false advertising for their respective dog foods. In his ruling, Thomas vacated a $10.4 million judgment against Ralston, but sent the matter to the district court for recalculation of the award. (Ironically, the lower court ended up increasing the damages against Ralston, to $12.1 million.) Given Thomas's connection with Danforth and that Danforth's personal holdings in Ralston were valued at $7.5 million or more, a few legal ethics experts and liberal legal groups questioned whether Thomas should have taken part in the case. Federal judges are required to withdraw from cases in which their "impartiality might reasonably be questioned," yet they are given considerable latitude in interpreting this proscription. But after Thomas was nominated for the Supreme Court, a law professor retained by the White House said that his participation had been proper.

Thomas also incurred criticism for participating in the opinion that freed Lieutenant Colonel Oliver North. North had been convicted for lying to Congress about the Iran-Contra affair, but his conviction had been overturned because the jury was considered tainted by information from the congressional hearings. The opinion in which Thomas participated, issued by the full circuit court, denied the special prosecutor's request for a rehearing, marking the end of North's legal troubles. Thomas voted with the majority after having twice praised North in public for standing up to Congress, which Thomas said was "out of control."

Thomas seemed to enjoy the relative isolation of court life, confiding in one colleague how relieved he was to be out of the socially demanding world of politics. In contrast to his embattled tenure at the EEOC, the biggest office controversies he now faced involved the annoyance his cigar smoke caused the clerks on the other side of his chamber's air vent and the delay in getting his new furniture.

There was a flurry of excitement in Thomas's chambers when Justice Brennan retired after the 1990 Court term. Thomas's name appeared on a few of the shortlists in the media, and for several days there was a reasonably good chance that he would be picked. Despite Biden's warnings, President Bush liked the idea of nominating Thomas. It would be healthy, some of Bush's aides argued, to have a black on the Court to balance Justice Marshall, and waiting for Marshall's retirement meant leaving the White House open to charges of tokenism if Thomas were given his seat.

But Bush's advisers, having just helped Thomas get through one set of hearings, were leery of pushing the new judge too far too fast. He might fit politically, but Bush's top legal advisers warned him that because of his short tenure on the bench, Thomas's legal qualifications would be assailed. They pointed out that the American Bar Association would almost assuredly rate Thomas unqualified for the Supreme Court, which would probably torpedo future plans to elevate him altogether.

So in July 1990 Bush nominated David Souter. But the message sent to Thomas's chambers from Gray's office was heartening: just wait.

❖

During this period of mounting anticipation, Angela Wright again heard from Thomas's former aide Armstrong Williams. Although now in private practice in public relations, he continued to promote Thomas, with whom he consulted regularly.

Seven months after Thomas was nominated to the appeals court, Wright had applied for a new job at a bigger newspaper, the *Charlotte Observer*, and had unexpectedly received a highly favorable recommendation from Thomas, who made no mention of the fact that he had summarily fired her. Instead, according to the personnel records of the paper, which hired Wright in February 1990 as an assistant metropolitan editor, Thomas offered a new version of the circumstances of her departure in which he implied that it had been her idea, not his. According to the paper's executive editor, Jane Shoemaker, who reviewed Wright's personnel file, Thomas told the paper that Wright had left the EEOC because she was young and had wanted to try something else. He described her as talented and bright.

Wright later said that, at the time, she "couldn't figure out why he would lie for me." Her puzzlement had remained until the call from Armstrong Williams.

"I hear the chairman told your employer that you walk on water," Williams said, according to Wright.

"Yeah," acknowledged Wright. "Why'd he do it?"

"Well, you wouldn't believe it," Williams said, "but the chairman is a changed man! Besides," he noted, "he expects to be nominated to the Supreme Court. What do you think of that?"

Recalling the conversation, Wright said the word she believed she chose to express her opinion was "ridiculous."

PART TWO

7

Marshall's Heir

GEORGE BUSH had promised to set a "kinder, gentler" tone than his predecessor on the corrosive issue of race in America. So when the unexpected news of Thurgood Marshall's resignation reached him by hand-delivered letter at noon on June 27, 1991, it was clear to his staff, despite the president's stated opposition to the use of quotas in promoting minority hiring, that they must find a black, a Hispanic, or a female replacement. The shortlist of contenders they drew up included no white men.

The choice of another minority to replace Marshall reflected in part Bush's image of himself. Casting himself as a progressive on racial issues, the president often cited the fund-raising he had done for the United Negro College Fund as a Yale undergraduate and the record of his father, Prescott, who supported civil rights legislation as a senator from Connecticut. As vice president, Bush had lobbied Reagan to sign the bill making Martin Luther King Jr.'s birthday a national holiday and to extend the Voting Rights Act. At the 1988 Republican convention, he had conspicuously invited Dr. King's widow, Coretta, into the Bush family box. And as president, his record of appointing blacks to government posts far surpassed that of previous Republican presidents — and of many Democrats too.

But, as on many other important domestic issues, there were two George Bushes when it came to civil rights. In 1964, in his first, unsuccessful Senate race, Bush ran as a Goldwater Republican, railing against the civil rights bill that eventually became the foundation of the EEOC. After his defeat he confessed to the Reverend John Stevens, an Episcopal minister, that he regretted having taken "some of the far right positions I thought I needed to get elected," but later Bush's footprints continued to lead in every direction. As vice president, he stood by silently while President Reagan initially fought to protect the privileged tax status of all-white private colleges such as Bob Jones University. And in the 1988 campaign the racist Willie Horton ads, created by consultants with links to Bush, left both the new president and his top political strategist, Lee Atwater, open to charges of race-baiting. Thus, rather than following any consistent set of principles, Bush's record on race reflected a struggle between the forces of enlightenment and expediency. And by the time Marshall resigned, political pressures from the right again dominated, overshadowing Bush's more progressive impulses.

In Clarence Thomas, Bush found a nominee whose personal contradictions perfectly matched his own political ones. Thomas was a black conservative who could symbolize diversity while denouncing the very concept of affirmative action. His considerable personal and political appeal was instantly apparent, not only to such conservatives as Thomas Jipping (the author of the fax sent to Sununu on the evening of Marshall's resignation), but also to Bush's White House counsel Boyden Gray, who called Thomas in to meet with him at 4:30 P.M. that same day.

Bush charged Sununu, Gray, and Thornburgh with the task of making a final recommendation. Thomas was the only African-American under serious consideration, but Sununu, keeping an eye on the 1992 reelection campaign, briefly considered the political advantages of appointing a Hispanic instead, since such important states as California, Texas, and Florida had large populations of Hispanic voters. But the ideal Hispanic candidate proved elusive. After learning of the right's enthusiasm for Thomas and realizing what a paralyzing predicament a conservative black nominee would present to liberal Democrats, Sununu soon agreed with Gray that Thomas more than satisfied their requirements. Thus, within forty-eight hours of Marshall's resignation and after minimal discussion, Thomas became the front-runner for the nomination.

Only two major concerns lingered. The first was whether Thomas was too extreme to be confirmed by the Senate. The deciding factor was whether he could rely on his mentor, John Danforth, to squire him through a potentially difficult fight. With his reputation for high-minded moderation, particularly on civil rights, Danforth was the ideal shield for Thomas against charges that his views on race were far outside the mainstream. Danforth could help, not only with moderate Republican senators like John Chafee of Rhode Island, David Durenberger of Minnesota, and William Cohen of Maine, but also with the Democrats, who held the majority.

But relations between the White House and Danforth were at a nadir. The senator had been lobbying Sununu and Gray about strengthening the 1964 Civil Rights Act; the same week that Marshall resigned, negotiations had broken down acrimoniously over the White House's immovable opposition. Worried about whether this might affect Danforth's enthusiasm for helping Thomas, Vice President Dan Quayle placed an urgent call to the senator just hours after receiving the news about Marshall. During his tenure as a senator from Indiana, Quayle had befriended Danforth and so felt comfortable asking whether he would "go to the mat" for Thomas.

Danforth believed that modern judicial confirmation battles had become as "vicious as political campaigns." He had been deeply troubled by the campaign against Bork, who had been one of his professors at Yale, and he was determined to protect his protégé from a similar fate. Despite his current dispute with the White House, he would, he promised Quayle, "do anything I can to ensure the confirmation." Also reassuring to the vice president was Danforth's assessment that Thomas was "confirmable"; the Missouri Republican felt confident that he could put together a strong coalition of Republicans and southern Democrats. Quayle rushed over to the Oval Office with the encouraging news.

The White House's other major concern about Thomas was harder to assuage. It was clear, regardless of later protestations to the contrary, that the politics of race would decide this nomination. But serious questions remained about whether Thomas — who had criticized the *Brown* decision — could get past the civil rights community, let alone be popularly accepted as a fit heir to the legendary figure who had won so many critical civil rights victories.

African-American politics was not familiar terrain to the Bush White House. But from the start, the administration realized that broad black support was essential to getting Thomas confirmed. If blacks could be enticed into identifying with Thomas's inspiring life story, the groundswell of popular support would probably silence the civil rights establishment, which otherwise would cut down a candidate with such conservative views. But if Thomas failed to win the hearts and minds of ordinary African-Americans, civil rights leaders would be emboldened to oppose him as well, and nervous white voters in the Senate would quickly follow. Stripped of race, Thomas would fare no better than Robert Bork.

As a consequence, Thomas would now need what he had never before valued, popularity among African-Americans — or, failing that, at least the appearance of it. This issue was of such concern to the White House that before naming Thomas publicly, Bush privately sounded out the Sullivan Group, an elite association of black Republicans. Asked if Thomas was someone they could support, the group's members were not sure how to respond and so gathered for an emergency meeting the weekend after Marshall's resignation.

The group, unknown even in Washington's political circles but tremendously influential in the White House, was led by Health and Human Services Secretary Louis Sullivan, a distinguished academic who was the highest-ranking African-American in the Bush administration and a family friend of the president's. Another important member was Constance Newman, a top campaign worker who had served as Bush's principal liaison to the black community and now headed the Office of Personnel Management. Another member of the group, William Coleman, a former transportation secretary and a distinguished Republican lawyer who was Thurgood Marshall's closest friend, didn't attend the meeting but was consulted separately by Bush before Thomas was named.

Just as Bush had feared, several members of the group expressed reservations about Thomas's qualifications and ideology. Some felt that Coleman deserved the seat. But he was already past seventy, so despite his credentials as a moderate and his reputation as a civil rights crusader, he was not, the group realized, a viable candidate. Some members also liked Amalia Kearse, a black appeals court judge in New York. But she would be too moderate for the conservatives whom Bush needed to satisfy with this nomination.

The member most sympathetic to Thomas was, unexpectedly, Constance Newman. A moderate in the mold of the former senator Edward Brooke of Massachusetts, she was friendly with the leaders of many liberal civil rights organizations. But she also knew and liked Thomas, who had befriended her while working in the Bush campaign. As the discussion went on, the apparent gradually became the inevitable: everyone agreed that Marshall's seat should remain in black hands, and Thomas was, for better or worse, the only black on the president's shortlist.

After the meeting broke up, word filtered north to Kennebunkport that these essential Republicans would give their blessings, however tepid, to Thomas. A few of them, including Sullivan, promised to lobby for him at the conventions of major black organizations during the summer. But such lukewarm support, particularly from blacks in the nominee's own party, sent a strong message: if Thomas needed African-American solidarity to secure his nomination, the White House would have to generate it. With only two months until the confirmation hearings, this would take quick and deft work.

❖

As these early machinations suggest, Bush's naming of Thomas on July 1 was the beginning rather than the end of the White House's involvement. And if Thomas had long been frustrated by his status as an outsider, he would now receive altogether different treatment, for the vast powers of the federal government were about to be deployed on his behalf.

The White House's strategy had two parts. Inside the Beltway, Bush's top political, legal, and congressional liaison aides would conduct an aggressive campaign to win the necessary fifty-one votes in the Senate. This would entail a courtesy call to every senator who would see Thomas and frenetic horse-trading for votes as the confirmation battle drew near. During his visits to Capitol Hill, the nominee was expected to hew closely to the Pin Point plan, telling and retelling the stories of his early deprivation and steering clear of his controversial record.

Except for these excursions, the strategy called for Thomas to keep the low profile befitting a Supreme Court nominee. For most of the summer, he would remain in seclusion as he studied with Justice Department experts for the hearings. He did emerge occasionally, such as when reporters raised questions in July about two 1983 speeches in which he had praised the Black Muslim leader Louis Farrakhan. Thomas himself issued a statement denying that he had ever embraced Farrakhan's anti-Semitic rantings. But for the most part, others spoke

for him during this period of intense scrutiny — among them his former EEOC aides Clint Bolick and Armstrong Williams. (The former
was now working at a conservative legal group allied with the New
Right leader Paul Weyrich, the Landmark Center for Civil Rights; the
latter was a public relations executive, the partner of Oprah Winfrey's
boyfriend, Steadman Graham.)

While this plan more or less resembled other recent Supreme Court
nomination strategies, the White House came up with an unusual
outside-the-Beltway strategy too, designed to impress upon the Senate
that Thomas, unlike Bork, enjoyed widespread popularity among ordinary citizens, particularly blacks, and so was a safe vote for the
swing Democrats from the South. If successful, this campaign would
deflect attention from Thomas's record and qualifications, showing
him as nothing less than the people's choice.

This undertaking resulted in what seemed to be a spontaneous outpouring of ostensible grass-roots support for Thomas throughout the
summer. But beginning immediately after his nomination, this support
was almost wholly orchestrated and generated by professional politicians and special interest groups — some of them forming new front
organizations only for this purpose, many of them based in Washington and tied directly or indirectly to the White House. To a great
extent, this strategy reflected the lessons learned by conservatives from
the debacle of Robert Bork. But in that fight, outside interest groups
stopped a White House nominee. This time the White House used
outside interest groups to sell one.

❖

As with any modern campaign, the first phase of this effort was to
assess the candidate's standing in public opinion polls. Shortly after
the announcement from Kennebunkport, a small group of aides in the
White House — who, during the next two months, would meet on
the Thomas confirmation as often as daily — began by taking a hard
look at their nominee's numbers.

Leading this group, beneath Sununu, was Fred McClure. As head
of congressional liaison, he was the highest-ranking African-American
on Bush's White House staff. Joining him was Mark Paoletta, a young,
conservative aide to Boyden Gray. An especially important member
of the group was Leigh Ann Metzger. At thirty, Metzger was already
a prominent force in the New Right; she had been a political strategist

in Phyllis Schlafly's Eagle Forum and now served as Bush's deputy assistant for veterans, law enforcement, and, crucially, religious groups. Having grown up in Georgia and attended Atlanta's huge First Baptist Church — popularly known as the "buckle of the Bible Belt" — Metzger wisely recognized an enormous and largely overlooked potential base of support for Thomas in the nascent alliance between politically conservative white evangelicals and socially conservative black pastors. She sensed that these pastors and their generally apolitical flocks were natural conscripts into the fight for Thomas. They just needed to be mobilized.

As they pored over the first poll results on the nomination, McClure and the others were jubilant. According to *USA Today,* 54 percent of black Americans already supported the nominee, an impressive number considering Thomas's record of hostility to the beliefs many black Americans held sacred. Thomas enjoyed the same level of support among blacks and whites. The Pin Point story he told during the nomination ceremony, they figured, must have begun a racial bonding process. Painting these numbers in the most positive light, the White House quickly declared that Thomas enjoyed broad support in the black community, taking the first step toward portraying him to the Senate, the media, and the citizenry as Marshall's rightful heir.

In fact, other surveys soon showed that blacks were conflicted about the nominee, and most of those polled, like the rest of America, knew so little about Thomas that their impressions were malleable. The national polls, many of them based on minuscule samplings of black voters (who are routinely underrepresented in most political surveys), suggested that the White House had a long way to go. In July, for instance, a Time Magazine/CNN poll found black support for Thomas at slightly lower levels than among whites, with 49 percent of white respondents favoring his nomination, and only 45 percent of blacks. Moreover, the roughly one hundred blacks called by Yankelovich Clancy Shulman, which conducted the poll, expressed deep ambivalence about Thomas; a majority agreed that he "understood the black experience," but fully 30 percent branded him an Uncle Tom.

By immediately declaring victory, however, "the White House made it feel that southern blacks were strongly for Thomas," commented John Gomperts, one of the lobbyists for People for the American Way, a liberal interest group opposed to Thomas from the outset. David Bositus, a senior research analyst at the Joint Center for Political and

Economic Studies, a black think tank in Washington, agreed. "I do think making strong statements about overwhelming support helped persuade southern senators," he said, looking back on the fight. But in reality, he noted, "there never was a groundswell."

Nor was there immediate resistance. What all the polls showed most clearly, including one taken in July by the *Wall Street Journal* and NBC News, was that a large majority of blacks — in the July poll the number was 63 percent — said they needed to know more about Clarence Thomas to form an opinion. Such ambivalence and ignorance created a natural political vacuum in the black community, a vacuum the White House was eager to fill.

But as they planned their strategy, Bush's aides were confronted by one apparent obstacle: an arcane law, known as the federal anti-lobbying act, that prohibited the use of taxpayer funds to spread domestic propaganda or to organize outside lobbying campaigns to pressure Congress. If followed to the letter, it would prevent the White House staff from directing anyone outside the government to lobby any particular senator on behalf of Thomas. But the law had plenty of loopholes and gray areas.

David Demarest, a White House communications adviser who was involved in the confirmation campaign, later couched the ethics of the situation this way: "We have to walk a fine line . . . We can lobby Congress on behalf of our own programs, but we cannot solicit groups to engage in lobbying campaigns on the Hill. The law is easily circumvented. For instance, I can say to a group, 'These are our priorities, and I hope you support us.' But I can't give them a list of target legislators to go lobby."

The Republicans had proven imaginative at orchestrating such grass-roots public opinion campaigns before. The Reagan administration, for example, had set up an elaborate network of outside groups to conduct a "public diplomacy" campaign in support of the president's efforts to aid the Nicaraguan Contras. And during the Persian Gulf War, Bush operatives had encouraged the creation of an array of pro-war "citizens" groups that helped sway public opinion sharply in favor of U.S. military intervention. But the White House had never tried to use this approach for a judicial nomination, and because of the anti-lobbying act's prohibitions, such an initiative could prove tricky.

One way around the law was to use people outside the government. Just as the intelligence agencies often used "cut-outs" — nonagency personnel — to direct their most sensitive operations, the White House needed politically astute outsiders to plan Thomas's confirmation campaign. Such arrangements would enable the White House to sidestep the anti-lobbying law, since it applied only to officials in the executive branch.

The most prominent outsider brought in for this battle was the political consultant Kenneth Duberstein. Donating his services to the White House, Duberstein served as the chief architect of the campaign for Thomas, just as he had managed David Souter's smooth passage onto the Court. Because he was not being paid or appointed to an official position, he was not covered by federal ethics laws. That meant he could continue to represent his private clients while moving freely through the White House, often attending daily meetings. He could also coordinate strategy with outside interest groups, even telling them which members of the Senate to target.

The forty-seven-year-old Duberstein, one of many in Washington who had parlayed a previous high-level political position into a successful consultancy, might not have been getting paid directly, but as Stephen Bell, a fellow Republican lobbyist, noted, "Commercially, for him it's a tremendous advantage." The highly visible assignment was a walking advertisement to his paying clients that he had the one thing lobbyists valued most: access. And ingratiating himself to the next Supreme Court justice wouldn't be bad for business, either. His client General Motors, for one, was scheduled to have a workers' compensation case before the high court in the fall.

In early July, Duberstein's office on K Street began humming with activities to promote Thomas, many of them created with the help of other prominent Republican lobbyists and strategists, including Charles Black, one of the masters of the art of negative campaigning, Haley Barbour, the future chairman of the Republican National Committee, and James Lake, a public relations expert who had worked for both Reagan and Bush. A motley assortment of other operatives joined in as the summer wore on. Many of them were hard-core religious conservatives who had watched in frustration as liberal interest groups, with their large direct-mail lists, had organized their own public opinion campaigns to defeat conservative nominees such as William Bradford Reynolds, who was denied confirmation to the number two post at the Justice Department, Bill Lucas, who was frustrated in his fight to become the department's civil rights chief, and of course Bork.

From the start, the Thomas fight was the natural consequence of the Bork fight, conceived by people determined never to let another nominee be "Borked." The liberal activist Tony Podesta, formerly president of People for the American Way (one of the main groups opposing Bork), later admitted that when the Thomas fight grew irredeemably nasty, liberal interest groups such as his own had chiefly themselves to blame. "The Thomas fight was the bitter fruit of the attacks made on Bork," he conceded. "We lowered the standard."

❖

Behind the scenes, the nominee played his own part in the campaign. Soon after returning to Washington from Kennebunkport, Thomas placed a strategic telephone call to John Johnson, a businessman in Chicago who was one of the richest African-Americans in the country. The idea for the call came from Thomas's former assistant and now unofficial spokesman, Armstrong Williams, who had been the subject of a favorable profile in one of Johnson's magazines. With a private fortune worth more than $200 million, Johnson was the publisher of *Ebony* and *Jet* magazines, leading publications that together attracted many millions of black readers. Williams, who had a knack for planting stories in the media, viewed *Jet* as "the Bible of the black community," even though it was the less glamorous of the two magazines. After getting Thomas's approval, Williams had called Johnson's office to set up an 8:40 A.M. conversation between the publisher and the judge.

Johnson identified powerfully with Thomas's life story. He too had begun life penniless in the Deep South and had worked his way up to the heights of the business elite. The telephone call had the desired effect, and Johnson pledged to do whatever he could to help. After he hung up with Johnson, Williams remembered later, Thomas phoned him to say "That was brilliant, man."

Soon the judge's picture was on the cover of *Jet;* inside was a glowing story complete with pictures of Thomas hugging his formerly estranged mother, Leola Williams. Such publicity — which would reach average middle- and working-class blacks — was worth far more than endorsements from civil rights leaders, Williams believed.

Indeed, Thomas's poll ratings with blacks started to climb after the favorable coverage he received from Johnson's magazine.

But no single piece of publicity, no matter how good, would create the needed support. As the campaign got under way, the White House was well aware that wooing black America would take time. With public opinion so malleable, it was essential to design a strategy that would keep the various black leaders who might oppose Thomas sitting on the fence quietly for as long as possible.

The plan was to create a "perception of indecision," as Fred McClure described it, to prevent momentum from building against Thomas as it had with Bork. "The worst thing was a perception of unanimity," McClure later said. "We didn't want to get ourselves in a situation where all these groups were coming out against him, where there was the perception that there was a groundswell of opposition."

Crucial again, as it had been in the D.C. Circuit fight, was staving off any negative reaction from the most important group, the NAACP. Promisingly, its head, Benjamin Hooks, was friendly with many Republicans, having been appointed to the Federal Communications Commission by President Nixon.

Immediately after Marshall's resignation, Clint Bolick, Thomas's unofficial aide, received a call from the veteran *Baltimore Sun* reporter Arch Parsons. Parsons said he was close to Hooks (the NAACP was based in Baltimore) and he liked Thomas. According to Bolick, Parsons offered to suspend any pretensions to journalistic objectivity and serve as an intermediary for Thomas between the White House and Hooks. Parsons later conceded that taking on this role was a conflict of interest, since he covered the Thomas nomination for the *Sun*. However, he explained, "I wanted Clarence Thomas to get a shot at a seat on the Court, I wanted him nominated."

"The idea was to convince Hooks that Clarence Thomas wasn't an enemy," said Bolick, "that he had actually been the conscience of the Reagan administration." To this end, Bolick assembled a packet of materials on Thomas's record prepared by the White House and sent it to Hooks. Later, Hooks denied that he had made any deals with the White House to keep his organization neutral. But he did speak to Parsons the day before the nomination was announced and assured him that the NAACP would, as Hooks later described it, "consider him [Thomas] fairly and without undue haste." Parsons forwarded this encouraging message to Bolick, who passed it on to the White House.

The silence of the NAACP at this early stage was crucial. "With Hooks neutralized," Bolick later observed, "we figured there would be no immediate opposition. That meant we could monopolize the media at the time people's impressions were being formed about Thomas."

Keeping Hooks on the fence would also make it impossible for Ralph Neas, the most influential civil rights lobbyist in Washington, to lay a glove on Thomas. The Leadership Conference on Civil Rights, Neas's organization, was an umbrella of different groups, including Planned Parenthood and the Urban League, but the most important by far was the NAACP. As long as the NAACP was not involved in the Thomas fight, Neas would not be involved either. Other liberal groups, labor unions, and feminist organizations had helped defeat Robert Bork, but the White House knew that it was Neas, a forty-five-year-old white Catholic lawyer, who more than anyone else had dealt the lethal blow. Neas was well liked and well connected on Capitol Hill — exactly the kind of enemy the Bush White House hoped to elude as long as possible.

Meanwhile, for those black leaders who continued to harbor deep doubts, McClure had a favorite ploy. He found it effective to suggest that the president's nominee would surely "grow" on the high court. This line offered both a subtle acknowledgment of Thomas's weaknesses and a challenge to respond generously to one of their own, a shrewd combination.

Vernon Jordan, the Democratic party's most influential African-American insider, was one of many who felt torn over the nomination. Jordan was best known as a past president of the National Urban League, but more recently he had become powerful in the corporate world. He served on the boards of a variety of blue-chip corporations and was senior partner at the politically connected Washington law firm of Akin, Gump, Strauss, Hauer & Feld. Bright, charming, and a smooth operator, Jordan was one of the few blacks welcome at Bohemian Grove, an annual gathering near San Francisco of elite corporate executives and political power brokers.

Jordan had been furious at Thomas over his denunciation of civil rights leaders as "whiners" and had told him so directly. Moreover, he idolized Thurgood Marshall, having been very close to the justice and his wife, Cissy, for many years. But even though Jordan was an active Democrat, his political judgment, good humor, and prowess on the tennis court had opened Republican doors to him too. Along with Danforth and William Coleman, he had been involved in the protracted negotiations with the White House over the civil rights bill.

With so many complex alliances, Jordan hadn't planned to get involved in Thomas's nomination. But shortly after it was announced, he got a call from the one boss he still heeded: his octogenarian mother.

"Clarence Thomas is insecure," he remembered her telling him. "Vernon Junior, you don't have an insecure bone in your body. I want you to go talk to him. He's black. Help him."

Jordan didn't know it, but according to an eyewitness, Thomas had long disparaged him in private as a "bourgeois black" who claimed the righteous mantle of the civil rights movement but who in Thomas's eyes had never known the kind of poverty and rejection he himself had suffered. Although Jordan was also raised during the Jim Crow era in Georgia, his mother had been a successful caterer to wealthy whites — providing an upbringing that Thomas viewed as soft compared with his own.

But Jordan could be an important ally in the fight ahead, and so, despite their earlier confrontation, Thomas and Jordan spent three hours together on a Saturday soon after the nomination to help break any residual tension. Thomas had a plastic bag of Monte Christo No. 2s ready for Jordan, who loved cigars.

Jordan came to the meeting in tennis whites; Thomas, wearing business attire, sat stiffly with a legal pad, taking copious notes. Jordan suggested that Thomas begin his confirmation hearings by acknowledging his gratitude to civil rights veterans such as Marshall, Roy Wilkins, and W. W. Law, the NAACP leader in Savannah who had been a close friend of Thomas's grandfather. He also told Thomas to forget Pin Point and, instead, to comport himself with the dignity of a qualified justice, spending every waking minute studying Supreme Court cases as if he were studying for the bar exam.

"Present yourself as a lawyer, not some bootstrap myth," Jordan recalled telling Thomas. "I know Duberstein is going to want to go with the Pin Point story. Don't do it."

Jordan left the meeting unsure what Thomas would do; he also wondered whether he had the caliber of mind and spirit to make a good Supreme Court justice. But Jordan, like other prominent blacks, was hesitant to oppose him — just as the White House had suspected. Borrowing the administration's line, Jordan hoped that, by being exposed to other ways of thinking, Thomas would indeed "grow."

❖

The White House, in the meantime, was busy trying to convince the so-called Big Three among the civil rights leaders — John Jacob of the Urban League, Joseph Lowery, who now led Martin Luther King Jr.'s Southern Christian Leadership Conference, and Hooks — that they would undermine their own effectiveness by opposing Thomas and that it was in their interest to continue to sit out this fight. At the time, they too were mired in the negotiations over the pending Civil Rights Act of 1991, which Bush was now threatening to veto. A year earlier, he had vetoed the similar Civil Rights Bill of 1990, which had been their top priority.

The civil rights leaders were persuaded that a campaign against Thomas would only amount to another loss and another drop in their personal prestige. They worried that their access to the White House, which had improved somewhat since the Reagan years, would evaporate. Thus, in a conference call, the three men agreed not to do anything precipitous — playing right into the White House strategy.

Of course, the White House could not stave off every potential opponent, and some groups did come out against Thomas publicly. But when they did, Duberstein always made sure to have an opposing story in the same news cycle. The Congressional Black Caucus, for instance, was one of the first groups to oppose Thomas. When the White House learned that it had scheduled a press conference, McClure and Duberstein quickly found Congressman Gary Franks, the sole black Republican member of Congress, and persuaded him to schedule his own press conference to announce his endorsement of Thomas an hour later. The back-to-back events, as Duberstein had figured, received equal media coverage, muting the sting of the caucus rejection.

Similarly, on July 30, when the Women's Legal Defense Fund, an influential feminist group, scheduled a press conference at the National Press Club to announce its opposition, a previously unheard-of ad hoc women's organization, Women for Judge Thomas, held its own press conference just across the corridor to endorse him. The group consisted mainly of female Bush administration officials, such as Labor Secretary Lynn Martin and Thomas's close friend Ricky Silberman, and their press conference was set up by Sheila Tate, a former press secretary for Bush who was now a public relations executive. Again, the two stories created the impression of evenly divided public opinion.

The interest groups that did come out squarely against Thomas early — the National Organization for Women (whose leaders publicly threatened to "Bork" Thomas), the Alliance for Justice, and People for the American Way — were mostly left-wing and white. Without more mainstream labor unions and major black organizations, such opposition looked elitist and out of touch, just as the White House wanted it.

Inevitably, however, Thomas's controversial record began to attract attention. As some members of the major civil rights groups took a close look at his writings and rulings, their consternation grew. The Lawyers' Committee for Civil Rights Under Law, another important organization in Ralph Neas's coalition, hired a prominent Washington law firm, Arnold & Porter, to scrutinize Thomas's record. Barbara Arnwine, the group's executive director, became anguished as she read the report. Shortly after the nomination, she had been among those who stood up before Neas at a Leadership Conference meeting and cautioned against opposing Thomas. "My early preference was not to oppose," Arnwine recalled. "The general feeling was, let's give him a chance, let's study the record." But by mid-July she had, and she was horrified.

Arnwine was especially perplexed to find that Thomas had not only criticized the *Brown v. Board of Education* case, which Marshall had won, he had also had harsh words for the 1968 *Green v. County School Board of New Kent County, Va.* decision. *Green* had hastened integration by invalidating freedom-of-choice school plans, which had perpetuated state segregated schools. After she finished reading the report, Arnwine called her friend Wade Henderson in the NAACP's Washington office. Following Hooks's lead, the NAACP, like the Lawyers' Committee, still had not taken a position on Thomas toward the end of July.

"I've looked at the record," Arnwine told Henderson, "and I don't think we have an option."

Henderson was silent for a moment. Then he responded, "Oh no, Barbara, I don't want to hear this."

Arnwine pressed on. "Let me read you some," she said, citing the troubling language she had found.

"I don't want to hear this," Henderson kept repeating.

"I'm sorry," Arnwine told him. "Let me read you some more."

With her group's support, Arnwine decided it was her duty to lobby against Thomas at the conventions of the major black organizations, including the Urban League and the NAACP, which would be holding its annual meeting at the end of July.

❖

As the NAACP began wavering in its stance toward the nominee, the White House continued to keep the pressure on. In the hope of staving off outright opposition, Thomas agreed to a private, secret meeting in Washington with five members of the organization's board, including Hooks and Henderson. Later, his friend Armstrong Williams said he had cautioned Thomas that the meeting was a "setup" and pleaded with him not to go. In fact, the meeting went badly. Thomas refused to give any assurances about his stand on specific civil rights issues that could come before the Court. The NAACP representatives left in obvious frustration.

Despite that setback, the White House did not give up. McClure helped design an elaborate lobbying campaign directed at each of the sixty-four members of the NAACP's board, who would be voting on the nomination at their convention.

"The Bush people were arm-twisters," recalled Rupert Richardson, one board member in Louisiana. In the weeks before the vote, Richardson said she received numerous calls from influential Louisiana Republicans imploring her not to oppose Thomas. "They made no bones about it. They said, 'I'm calling for the White House.'"

The argument used by the administration to try to sway Richardson and the other board members was that a conservative black nominee was preferable to a conservative white, which, the Bush people implied, was the only alternative. Charles Black, the longtime Republican strategist who had, with Duberstein, volunteered his lobbying services for Thomas, summarized the basic pitch this way: "We're gonna get a Republican in this seat no matter who it is. It's better to support an Afro-American because we don't know who they will put up next time."

The calls Richardson received parroted this line exactly. She remembered her callers arguing, "If we withdraw him, we won't get another black. Some black person is better than none." Richardson also recalled the rumor that if Thomas wasn't confirmed, the next nominee would be Edith Jones, a conservative white judge from Texas.

Finally, when the White House realized it was going to lose the NAACP vote anyway — it had heard that the board would almost certainly take a stand against Thomas when it met in Washington on July 31 — it plotted a daring countermove. Mark Paoletta, Boyden Gray's aide, came up with the idea of having a group of genuine "Pin Pointers" travel to Washington by bus to lobby for Thomas, ostensibly entirely on their own. Shrewdly, Paoletta timed the "spontaneous" outpouring of Pin Point's support for the day of the board meeting. It was a bold media stroke, a leaf right out of Duberstein's book. The press would have to cover the bus riders from the South. Not only would the event split the story, but the tableaux of the two gatherings would draw the kind of political contrast the White House wanted to make, showing Thomas supported by ordinary black folks rather than the elite.

Roy Allen, Thomas's boyhood friend who was now a state senator from Savannah, had been working closely with the White House, and he was entrusted with recruiting fifty people to pack the bus for the ten-hour trip. Although the group included a few relatives and friends of Thomas's, a number of the participants had never met the nominee, and quite a few of them had never set foot in Pin Point before boarding the bus. For the most part, no one covering the event in Washington caught on, although one elderly man in the group did introduce himself to reporters as "his professor." As it turned out, the man hadn't actually taught Thomas; he had taught an architect acquainted with Thomas's mother.

Though few people knew it at the time, the Pin Point bus trip was underwritten by Thomas's political allies in coordination with the White House. Clint Bolick's conservative legal organization, the Landmark Center for Civil Rights, paid most of the expenses for the bus. And an ad hoc group funded by a Christian right activist, former

Reagan White House aide Gary Bauer, helped foot the bill for the group's Arlington, Virginia, motel.

Georgia's two Democratic senators, Sam Nunn and Wyche Fowler, were "noncommittal before the trip," as Bolick recalled later. But a few days before the Pin Pointers were expected, they both offered help. After all, their constituents were coming to Washington, and neither senator wanted to be portrayed as snubbing a group from home. To Bolick's delight, Nunn arranged for the group to use a caucus room in the Capitol as a base of operations. Fowler offered to hold a breakfast for the Pin Pointers.

As hoped for, the arrival of the Georgia bus riders caused a media stir, in large part because Clarence Thomas himself — still largely sequestered from public view — made a rare public appearance to join them for breakfast. The candidate happily posed for photographs with his old friends, offering poignant remembrances of learning to "tie wire" (make fences) and strip vines of scuppernongs (wild grapes) back home as a child.

About a dozen senators drifted in to chat with the group. Strom Thurmond gave an impromptu pep talk, mentioning that "I've known Clarence since he was head of the Unemployment Commission." In the euphoria of the moment, the mistake was barely noticed. That afternoon, some of the Georgians trooped over to a nearby hotel, where the NAACP board was meeting. There they staged a noisy protest, also guaranteed to catch reporters' attention.

The only disappointment for the bus riders was that they would get no tour of the White House. Mark Paoletta had worried that if the Pin Pointers were seen inside the White House, the press would figure out that this event had White House rather than grass roots. As it was, Bolick later recalled, "The media was sensational. We were back to back with the NAACP."

❖

Even so, the NAACP's vote to oppose Thomas began to have the domino effect that McClure had feared, with labor unions now also joining the forces against the nominee. The NAACP's study of Thomas's record was being widely circulated among different interest groups. It blasted Thomas for having a "reactionary philosophical approach" to affirmative action and other issues. "While we appreciate the fact that Judge Thomas came up in the school of hard knocks and pulled himself up by his own bootstraps, we are concerned about his insensitivity to giving those who may not have any bootstraps the opportunity to pull them up," wrote the NAACP chairman, William Gibson.

The White House badly wanted another major black organization to endorse Thomas, but, with no real prospects, it resorted to an intense effort to win the support of a relatively obscure black organization, the National Bar Association. The NBA was a black version of the ABA, the nation's largest professional organization of lawyers. Before the NBA convention, on August 4, the White House recruited virtually every black lawyer in the entire Bush administration to sign up as a delegate. Then a phalanx of administration officials carrying elaborate communications equipment was dispatched to Indianapolis, where the NBA was meeting. Other supporters also appeared at the event; particularly noticeable was Johnny Butler, Thomas's former acting general counsel at the EEOC.

Barbara Arnwine always attended the NBA's convention, but it was usually pretty slow and routine, so she had planned to stay for only one night. Arriving at the convention's hotel in Indianapolis, she immediately sensed a change. A small army of Bush administration lawyers was buttonholing delegates in the lobby. Hoping to express her concerns about Thomas at the meeting of the judicial selection panel, she called for a schedule. But the lawyer who chaired the panel refused to give her a time or place. Alarmed, Arnwine called Wade Henderson of the NAACP and Elaine Jones of the NAACP Legal Defense Fund and begged them to come to Indianapolis. "This thing is wired," she told her allies. "It's funky here."

Arnwine finally found the group's president, Algenita Scott-Davis, and was given permission to address the selection panel the next day. By then, Henderson and Jones had arrived, but the three Thomas opponents had no time to lobby the delegates, who had already been wooed, and in some cases won, by the White House representatives. And unknown to the three, Thomas himself had already lobbied the leaders of the NBA at a luncheon in Washington, promising to be the featured speaker at their next convention after his first term on the Court.

By the time the judicial panel convened, there were, by Arnwine's and others' count, ten administration aides standing outside the room, talking to the members of the panel as they entered. Arnwine, Henderson, and Jones were told they could only address Thomas's qualifications, not his views on civil rights. Jones protested, asking, "When did you change the criteria?" and demanding that the old guidelines — which gave substantial weight to a nominee's civil rights record — be restored. By a razor-thin margin, the panel voted to make Thomas's civil rights views part of its evaluation.

A raucous debate ensued. "His supporters used a dozen different arguments," Arnwine recalled, enumerating them. "We don't really know Clarence." "He isn't what he appears to be," followed by a wink. "He's really good news for us." Then there were attacks on the NAACP. "White racist unions told Ben Hooks he wouldn't get any money, which is why the NAACP voted to oppose." Another argument, she recalled, was that "the Jews want the seat for themselves."

When those arguments fell dead, Arnwine and others in attendance said, Thomas's supporters went back to the old, more familiar ones. "If we don't get Clarence, we don't get anybody black." "It's not worth losing the black seat for a principle." "He'll be a role model." "He's black." "He's a brother." "Forget everything else. He's no light-skinned Negro like Thurgood Marshall. He knows what it's like to be black."

Finally, it was Arnwine's turn to speak. She struck a single theme: Thomas's record. "The key issue is whether Clarence Thomas will be favorable to civil rights enforcement," she told the panel. "How can he be when there's his hostility to *Green* [the school desegregation decision], his hostility to the Voting Rights Act, his gutting of the Uniform Guidelines, his consistent pattern of nonenforcement?"

When she finished, the Bush forces were visibly shaken. "Sister is mad because he has a white wife," one of them grumbled.

By two votes, the panel voted to oppose Thomas. But the Bush operatives weren't about to give up. They lobbied the NBA's executive committee, a much larger group, to reject the panel's report. The executive committee dodged the issue, deciding to accept the report without endorsing it. The full convention would vote on the nomination the next day.

As hundreds of delegates convened in the main meeting hall, Arnwine, Henderson, and Jones entered a motion to accept the report and oppose Thomas. As the delegates were casting their ballots, the White House lobbyists started complaining about vote fraud, claiming that some of the delegates had voted twice. Demanding secret, written ballots, they stood at the front of the room watching the delegates as they cast their ballots again. This time Arnwine and her allies won by four votes. The lobbyists then moved to invalidate the vote, demanding a two-thirds majority. By then the exhausted delegates had begun streaming out of the hall.

At this point, some of the White House supporters rushed into the press room and announced that the NBA had decided not to take a position on Thomas's nomination. This maneuver proved too much for Scott-Davis, who went before the press to announce the delegates' decision. "If called to testify, we will oppose," she declared firmly.

The White House, still not finished, put its own spin on the story, telling the press, "We got what we wanted, a split vote."

Arnwine left Indianapolis with sagging spirits. She had won a slim victory. But if it took this much effort just to hold one African-American organization, it was going to be nearly impossible to stop Clarence Thomas.

❖

Meanwhile, the covert campaign to win the support of ordinary black Americans was taking on some unusual dimensions. A new group called the African-American Freedom Alliance had raised $100,000 to fund an advertising campaign promoting Thomas, to run in black newspapers across the country. The ads effectively linked the confirmation battle to the historic struggle by blacks for civil rights. Any opposition to Thomas was equated with racism, pure and simple. One ad, for instance, pictured a black woman, a bus, and the Supreme Court, under the message "You can tell how well we're doing by where we sit."

Another new group, the Coalition for the Restoration of the Black Family & Society, launched a series of full-page newspaper ads in black publications nationwide featuring a picture of Thomas with a giant headline: "To the Back of the Bus!" After describing Thomas's roots in poverty, the copy read: "As the left strives to keep Judge Clarence Thomas from his seat on the U.S. Supreme Court, it's like forcing blacks to take a seat in the back of the bus. Fight racism.

Call your U.S. Senators and urge them to confirm Judge Clarence Thomas."

What the advertisements did not say was that both the new African-American Freedom Alliance and the Coalition for the Restoration of the Black Family & Society had actually been founded and financed by white fundamentalists working hand in hand with the Bush White House. And the real sponsors of these ads had no more use for the civil rights remedies invoked than Thomas himself did.

8

❖

Armies of
the Right

BEHIND THE AFRICAN-AMERICAN FREEDOM ALLIANCE was an
unlikely activist, Gary Bauer. Bauer was a white, conservative, fundamentalist Christian who had worked inside the Reagan White House.
He had no connection to the struggle for black civil rights; in fact, he
was a leader in the crusade to get federal funding for private, mainly
white religious schools.

For Bauer, cementing a conservative majority on the Supreme
Court was a central goal and Thomas's confirmation the surest way
to achieve it. Before taking a high-level post as domestic policy chief
for the Reagan White House, Bauer had been an aide to William
Bennett, Reagan's secretary of education and an outspoken social
conservative. In these positions, Bauer had helped make the conservative creed of "family values" a centerpiece of the Reagan administration's domestic social agenda. In this role, in 1986 he produced a
controversial report on the state of the American family, to which he
asked Thomas, then at the EEOC, to contribute. "I wanted him because I thought he knew a lot about the breakdown of the black
family," Bauer later explained. Because the report contained anti-
abortion language, recommended that unmarried mothers be denied
welfare benefits, and cited no-fault divorces and "liberal sexual attitudes" as the chief causes of the decline of the family, Thomas's association with it caused a ripple of controversy during his confirmation
hearings. Thomas distanced himself entirely from this conservative
manifesto, saying that he had not even read the final report.

But while he was publicly disavowing his link to Bauer's work, he
was privately benefiting, that same summer, from the enormous effort

that Bauer and his backers in the Religious Right were making on his behalf. By the time Thomas was nominated, Bauer headed the Family Research Council, an organization based in the Washington area that crusaded against abortion and pornography and supported conservative ideas such as school choice, which would give religious academies a financial windfall. While nominally independent, the Family Research Council had once been affiliated with another Christian Right organization, Focus on the Family, which had a large direct-mail donor base and whose leader, James Dobson, broadcast a daily radio program that reached hundreds of thousands of people. Bauer was thus well positioned to mobilize grass-roots support for Thomas in the form of a flood of letters and phone calls to senators. And he was more than happy to help. As he put it later, "I was not inclined to see another Borking."

All he lacked were marching orders, and not long after Thomas was nominated, these came from one of Bauer's best friends in the Bush White House, William Kristol. The son of Irving Kristol, the neoconservative polemicist, the younger Kristol had become a close friend of Bauer's during the Reagan administration, when both men worked for Bennett. By 1991, Kristol was an aide in the executive branch, where he was known as "Quayle's brain," not only because he was the vice president's top policy adviser, but also because he was considered to have one of the best political minds on the conservative end of the Republican spectrum.

Like Bauer, Kristol had been a big admirer of Clarence Thomas from the time they first met during the Reagan administration. He saw Thomas as an ideological soulmate and kindred political spirit, and naturally he wanted to do all he could to help him get confirmed. He had urged Quayle to support Thomas from the day of Marshall's resignation. Kristol was so close to the Thomas family that he watched the Kennebunkport nomination ceremony with Virginia Lamp Thomas at the White House.

Far more of an ideologue than Duberstein — whose soft sell, Kristol suspected, might not be effective enough if the going got rough — he wanted to pursue his own muscular approach. He believed Thomas would need hard-core supporters to pressure the senators in their home states, and the best agents for this, he believed, were the conservative activists who saw Thomas as one of their own. While Duberstein distrusted many of these true believers because they were hard to control and would link Thomas with controversy and political extremism, Kristol saw them as a group of invaluable allies who, if deployed under the right colors and with the right leader, could make the difference between victory and defeat.

But because Kristol was covered by the anti-lobbying act, he too needed a trusted friend outside the government to do his bidding. The ideal person, as he saw it, was his old friend Gary Bauer. And as luck would have it, the Kristol and Bauer families traditionally spent a week at the beach together — and this year it was scheduled for early July.

Thus, not long after Thomas's nomination, Kristol and Bauer and their families left Washington to spend a few days on the Delaware coast. Much to the annoyance of their wives, the men did little but plot political strategy for Clarence Thomas. They agreed that an early and loud show of organized support would help protect Thomas from the inevitable attacks by liberal interest groups. And the natural power base for such a campaign, they agreed, was white evangelical ministers and their flocks, many of whom Bauer and his allies could instantly summon.

This vacation week became the genesis of Kristol and Bauer's Citizens Committee to Confirm Clarence Thomas. The committee's goal was to raise money to pay for the activities that would give the appearance of an outpouring of popular support for Thomas. Conservatives had railed against the liberal interest groups that had attacked Bork, but now Kristol and Bauer took that effort as a model. They planned radio and television advertisements and considered other means of galvanizing support for the nominee in order to pressure the Senate to confirm him.

The two friends spent most of their vacation calling conservative donors to underwrite their Citizens Committee. The Wall Street financier and conservative philanthropist William Simon, who had served as treasury secretary in the Ford administration and now headed the rich and conservative Olin Foundation, agreed to serve as finance chairman, making a small contribution of his own to help get the venture going.

On his return to Washington in mid-July, Bauer announced the formation of the Citizens Committee and began devoting much of his time to answering allegations against Thomas in the media and holding strategy sessions for the many groups that agreed to join his effort.

Bauer did not mention his silent partnership with Kristol and other conservatives in the Bush White House. To do so would only have raised questions about the lobbying law and jeopardized the image of independent citizens acting on their own, which was necessary to impress members of the Senate. But Bauer continued to coordinate his activities closely with the White House. In fact, the White House aides Lee Liberman and Leigh Ann Metzger sometimes attended strategy sessions in his office.

By late August, the committee had raised $300,000, and Bauer unveiled plans for an ambitious advertising program that eventually cost more than $500,000. For the heaviest media buys, he selected four cities: Montgomery, Alabama; Raleigh, North Carolina; Atlanta, Georgia; and Baton Rouge, Louisiana. Not coincidentally, these targets meshed exactly with the White House's most intensive lobbying of critical southern Democratic senators.

The television ads produced by the Citizens Committee also bore the White House's fingerprints. They were created by the president's media man, Mike Murphy, a consultant in Washington who had worked on Bush's 1988 campaign. Murphy was still in his twenties, but he had learned the art of hardball politics at the knee of Terry Dolan, the legendary founder of the National Conservative Political Action Committee (NCPAC), the most potent right-wing organization of the late 1970s and early 1980s. Dolan had masterminded the Republican takeover of the Senate in 1980, when a slew of liberal Democratic senators — including George McGovern of South Dakota, Frank Church of Idaho, Birch Bayh of Indiana, and John Culver of Iowa — lost their seats in the Reagan landslide. NCPAC and Dolan perfected the use of direct mail and negative advertising to cripple the liberals by focusing on their stands on such divisive issues as abortion and gun control. NCPAC fell apart after Dolan's death in 1986, but Murphy was one of the young protégés who carried his political art forward.

Murphy also made no mention of his White House ties, but his television scripts hewed closely to the administration's Pin Point and southern strategies. Over a crescendo of dramatic music, an announcer presented Thomas: "Born poor in the rural South, Clarence Thomas overcame adversity, earned a Yale Law degree, and began a career of public service that led the U.S. Senate to confirm him four times as a fighter for civil rights." Excised were the bitter clashes

Thomas had had with civil rights leaders and with Democrats in Congress over issues such as affirmative action. Instead, they implored viewers to let their senators know of their support for Thomas. "Will your senator bow to the liberal special interests opposing Judge Thomas, interests that care more about protecting criminals than protecting us?"

Bauer also made clever use of the Christian Right's growing network of communications outlets. He provided frequent commentaries on a daily Christian radio program, "Family News in Focus," moderated by his former colleague, the evangelist James Dobson. While Duberstein was keeping Thomas's position on abortion purposefully under wraps, Bauer reassured Dobson's listeners: "I cannot predict in every case and on every issue how he will vote. But I believe in most cases those who believe in family, faith, and freedom are going to be very pleased with what Judge Thomas would do on the Supreme Court." In addition to Bauer's commentaries, Dobson's radio programs featured a barrage of messages supporting Thomas. In early August, for instance, Hiram Crawford, the president of the National Prayer Band Convention, blasted Thomas's opponents as the "anti-Christ forces."

❖

While Bauer was operating with the explicit blessings of the White House, he was by no means the only leader of the Religious Right mobilizing Christian support for Thomas. Behind the Coalition for the Restoration of the Black Family & Society, which sponsored advertisements in black outlets similar to those of the African-American Freedom Alliance, was the unexpected figure of Louis Sheldon. A white minister in California, Sheldon directed the Traditional Values Coalition (TVC), a group that was militantly opposed to homosexuality, abortion, and pornography.

Historically, such New Right televangelists had been associated with bigotry because the most prominent among them, Jerry Falwell, had first won national attention by reacting angrily to Jimmy Carter's 1978 denial of tax exemptions to all-white Christian academies. Until then, Falwell had been an unknown white minister in Lynchburg, Virginia. But soon he was recruited by Paul Weyrich, the New Right leader and founder of the Free Congress Foundation, to run an organization named the Moral Majority. Thus, by capitalizing on racial resentment, one of the most lucrative direct-mail fund-raising machines was sent whirring into the 1980s. Others, such as the religious broadcaster Pat Robertson, soon followed Falwell's example.

But what few outside the White House had noticed was that by 1991, a number of these televangelists had been making major inroads into black churches across the country. And none had pushed the racial barrier further than Louis Sheldon.

In building his membership, Sheldon had profited from the traditional social outlook of the black church, whose bedrock position in black community life had been seriously eroded by drugs, crime, and the increasing number of single-parent households. Pastors who had been among the strongest political figures in the black community were naturally attracted to the gospel of so-called traditional family values.

Sheldon also perceived that public opinion among blacks was sharply split over liberal causes such as abortion and homosexuality. Some portrayed abortion as a form of legal genocide perpetrated against African-Americans. Others opposed the movement for gay rights as a competing and less worthy civil rights cause that only detracted from their own, more legitimate grievances. These splits had caused increasing tension between traditional black civil rights organizations, many of which were still run by church leaders, and more liberal organizations, particularly white feminist groups, which were militantly in favor of abortion rights and favored extending federal civil rights protections to homosexuals. Lou Sheldon had been quick to exploit these divisions.

With his cherubic smile, snowy white hair, and thunderous homophobic gospel, "Reverend Lou" as he was called, was best known in California, where he had enlisted the support of black churches in campaigns to repeal local gay rights ordinances and to prevent the distribution of condoms in schools. Born in Washington, D.C., to an Orthodox Jewish mother and a Protestant father, Sheldon became a born-again Christian at age sixteen when, he said, a local wino persuaded him to go to church to get some "old-time religion."

Thurgood Marshall's retirement was timed serendipitously for Sheldon. To advertise TVC's growing strength in the black community, Sheldon had recently formed a new subsidiary, his Coalition for the Restoration of the Black Family & Society. And in late June, he had staged his first major event in Washington, bringing some two hundred black pastors to the city. Leigh Ann Metzger, the liaison between the White House and such religious groups, had sensed the political potential of this new alliance of black and white religious conservatives and invited Sheldon and his black acolytes back to the White House for a private audience with the president.

After Thomas had been nominated and it had become clear that he needed to appear popular among ordinary blacks, Metzger thought again of Lou Sheldon. The reverend's network of more than ten thousand churches and two hundred black pastors could be enlisted immediately for Thomas in the black community. Recognizing that this was the perfect opportunity for him to prove himself a major player in Washington, Sheldon was delighted to lend a hand. So were many of the black pastors he knew. As his daughter Andrea, whom he appointed to run TVC's Washington operation, explained, "Most of our pastors felt that Clarence Thomas's nomination was divine. They believed in self-help and empowerment and that God had answered their prayers by having President Bush pick someone like them."

As the reverend began collecting support for the nominee, he turned increasingly to his daughter. With her blond hair, showy jewelry, and long red fingernails, Andrea Sheldon might have seemed an unlikely organizer of black clerics, but she quickly became one of the important people behind the ostensibly grass-roots African-American campaign for Thomas. Having held a low-profile government post at the Small Business Administration during the Reagan years, she already knew her way around conservative circles in Washington. But after Thomas's nomination, doors to the top began opening. A few days after the announcement, she attended the first of what would become almost weekly strategy sessions with several of the campaign's most important activists, including Jipping of the Free Congress Foundation, Bauer of the African-American Freedom Alliance and Citizens Committee, and Metzger and Liberman from the White House, who attended when possible. Together, these insiders planned a series of events designed to demonstrate outside black support for the new nominee.

In addition to Bauer and Sheldon, an activist who joined the cause was Ralph Reed, the executive director of Pat Robertson's Christian Coalition. The Christian Coalition was a church-based political organization that Robertson started after his presidential bid failed in 1988. Reed, a native of Georgia, was a veteran of the Republican National Committee and an experienced campaigner. Like other conservatives, he saw in Thomas "an opportunity to see a pro-life, pro-family majority on the Court." Moreover, he explained later, "we felt we should get involved because he was a committed Christian."

Reed, too, was in frequent communication with the White House, often through Metzger and sometimes directly with Duberstein when he needed to know where a particular senator stood on the nomination. And in September, the Christian Coalition announced on Dobson's radio show that it would spend at least $1 million to see Thomas confirmed, in part through sponsoring a television ad campaign. Robertson's popular *700 Club* television show became a bully pulpit for guests who supported Thomas, including Bauer.

Also working feverishly and in step with the White House was Weyrich's large network of political action groups, which included anti-abortion organizations such as the Eagle Forum and Concerned Women of America as well as a number of Christian groups. Jipping and the Free Congress Foundation remained active, contributing sophisticated campaign technology. Free Congress had its own satellite television network, National Empowerment Television, and with fifty affiliates, it reached thousands of conservatives across the country. When the Senate recessed, Free Congress began bombarding its affiliates with messages backing Thomas. "When senators went home in August, we were ready," Jipping recalled later.

❖

As the confirmation hearings approached, the administration's strategy was working beautifully both inside and outside the Washington Beltway. While civil rights groups were fragmented in their opposition, the right was unified and active. "This was the most harmonious I'd ever seen conservative groups, from strong libertarians to strong religious," observed Clint Bolick. Jipping, who had angrily watched the Reagan White House bungle the Bork fight, was amazed at the Thomas campaign's effectiveness. "We were seeing it work in the raw numbers of letters and phone calls. There really was a grass-roots strategy this time. The coordination between inside the Beltway and out in the country was there. We used the same buzzwords."

Inevitably, some of the outside activists went too far. Over the Labor

Day weekend, a controversial conservative named Floyd Brown jumped into the Thomas fray, ostensibly on his own. A political consultant who, like Mike Murphy, had learned the art of attack politics from Terry Dolan, Brown had helped create the infamous Willie Horton ad in the 1988 presidential campaign. Now he grabbed the media spotlight again, this time with an inflammatory television advertisement that excoriated the Democrats on the Senate Judiciary Committee. The ad branded the senators as ethically compromised, liberal hypocrites.

Its most pointed barbs were aimed at Senator Edward M. Kennedy. The ad flashed a recent *New York Post* headline, "Teddy's Sexy Romp," which had accompanied an exposé of the notorious Palm Beach weekend during which the senator's nephew, William Kennedy Smith, had been accused of raping a woman. Chappaquiddick was also dredged up. Another target was Joe Biden; the ad reminded viewers that his presidential campaign had disintegrated amid allegations of plagiarism. While overdone, the ad hit these Democrats precisely at their weakest spots. More important, it put them on notice that the coming fight, should they dare to engage in it, would be very dirty indeed. "I'm a member of the 'hit 'em and watch 'em go down' school of politics," Brown later boasted.

Brown, a tall and boisterous self-promoter barely in his thirties, was convinced after Bork's defeat that attack politics was the only way for conservatives to reach the Court. "In the Bork fight I watched the conservative movement take a pass card and not fight," he recalled. "After the Bork battle I said, I'm going to form an organization and be ready for the next one. I felt we had to approach these nomination fights like they were political battles, to be aggressive and fight the battle on enemy turf." Even before there was another opening on the Court, he formed a group called Citizens United in preparation for the next nomination fight. If nothing else, a bruising confirmation battle would prove an enormously useful way of energizing conservative donors and invigorating his mailing list.

When Brown heard that Marshall had resigned, he got on the phone to his friend, the conservative political consultant Tony Fabrizio. "Tony, this is the battle!" Brown recalled announcing. It didn't matter that no one had been nominated yet for conservatives to support. It was, for Brown and Fabrizio, a chance to declare war on liberal

Democrats. "It's a battle between the values of Ted Kennedy versus the values of George Bush or whoever is George Bush's nominee," Brown told Fabrizio.

Soon, Citizens United began sending out nearly two million pieces of direct mail to raise money as well as calling its 112,000 members to urge them to lobby Congress on Thomas's behalf. Then Brown produced his inflammatory ad and arranged to have it unveiled during the slow Labor Day news cycle on the popular public affairs talk show *The McLaughlin Group*. Later, at a press conference called by Brown, he was surrounded by a throng of cameras, including a crew from *Entertainment Tonight*. When the expected controversy erupted, the network news shows ran clips from the ad. Then both President Bush and Thomas himself denounced it, guaranteeing even more attention. This was a game Floyd Brown knew well.

Actually, Brown and his compatriots had almost no money to spend on television. The ad was produced, at cost, by the National Republican Congressional Committee, one of the campaign arms of the Republican party. While the ad did appear on a few cable channels, the free publicity gave it far more air time than Brown could ever have hoped to buy. In its way, the advertisement was a triumph of attack politics.

"We touched a nerve," Brown said later. "All the opponents of Thomas were surprised. We dominated the news the week before the hearings began. That was our strategy. They reacted to us, which only got us more news." Brown's favorite appearance was on CNN, where he debated the Democratic National Committee chairman and later commerce secretary Ronald Brown, an opponent of Thomas who had once worked in the Senate for Kennedy. "They were spending all this time spinning their wheels, attacking Floyd Brown, defending Kennedy. We were getting all the coverage."

The coverage was so wide that the White House, with the legacy of Willie Horton in mind, was highly agitated. While Bill Kristol had advocated the use of outside groups to lead the activities supporting Thomas, they were supposed to be controlled by the White House. Bauer, meanwhile, was livid because his ads, sanctioned by the White House, were being completely upstaged by Brown's. Duberstein was fuming because he believed that Thomas had a fair shot at getting Biden's support, and he thought Brown's ad might backfire. After Bush vehemently disavowed the ad, he directed Sununu to call one of

Brown's associates and tell him and Brown to back off. But the ad continued to generate publicity. Indeed, Bush's harsh words and Sununu's call — which Brown later said was "a pro forma effort to distance the White House, much as they had done in 1988" — generated another night of network coverage for the ad. "We got $2 million worth of free exposure," asserted Brown, "even more than we did with the Willie Horton ad."

That same Labor Day weekend, Andrea Sheldon was also hard at work. Along with Thomas's friend from the EEOC, Ricky Silberman, and the political point man for Weyrich on the nomination, Tom Jipping, she had planned an opening day extravaganza to dramatize black grass-roots support for Thomas. As Jipping recalled, "We hatched the idea of a black pastors' rally. We picked the tenth [of September] and it turned out to be the first day of the hearings."

At their instigation, hundreds of black pastors traveled to Washington from all over the country for the opening day of Thomas's confirmation hearings. Inside the Russell Senate Office Building, where the hearings would be held, the pastors formed a praying, cheering human chain along the corridors leading to the historic Caucus Room, where Thomas would make his opening statement. A moving photograph of the pastors on the steps of the Supreme Court, their hands joined in prayer, ran the next day in the *New York Times*. The outpouring of support looked completely spontaneous, since the newspaper did not mention that they were affiliated with TVC or the Reverend Louis Sheldon, or that the pastors had been organized by politically connected white conservatives in Washington.

This covert campaign for black public opinion achieved the desired effect. At the start of the confirmation hearings, Thomas's standing among blacks had risen to more than 65 percent approval in most national polls. That level of support sent a stern warning to every member of the Senate, particularly the swing Democrats of the South. Opposing Thomas would be risky: with the major civil rights organizations split, it would be the black constituents at home to whom the senators would listen. And the Clarence Thomas whom the Pin Pointers and black preachers had introduced to them that summer was not some scary ideologue. He was a brother.

9

❖

The Stealth
Candidate

As the confirmation hearings approached, Thomas continued his intensive study of case law and began preparing for his appearance before the Senate. To his friends, the nominee seemed to be
relishing the prospect of a battle. Clint Bolick, who had spent the
summer rallying conservative support for Thomas, ran into his former
boss shortly before the hearings and was buoyed to hear him vow,
"I'm going to really take on the opposition! I'm going to be strong.
You're going to love my speech!"

But Duberstein and the White House had a different idea. The final
phase of its campaign was the inside-the-Beltway plan, which called
for Thomas to "take on" only one group — the U.S. Senate. And the
senators would be approached not with cudgels but with carrots.

The Senate was home turf for Duberstein. He had worked there for
many years, first as an aide to New York's moderate Republican senator Jacob Javits, and more recently as both a White House political
operative and a paid lobbyist. He had cajoled the Senate into selling
AWACs to the Saudis and helped President Reagan manage the Iran-
Contra backlash during his last months in office. Duberstein did not
want to wage holy wars; he wanted to win. "His attitude," said one
Democratic aide who dealt with him on the Thomas nomination,
"was, 'What do I have to do to sell him?' He wasn't trying to make
political points. All he wanted were his fifty-one votes. It was smart,
because that's the currency up here."

With a Senate comprising fifty-seven Democrats and forty-three
Republicans in 1991, the White House needed to hold every Republican and win over at least seven Democratic senators if Thomas was

to be confirmed. (In a deadlock, the tiebreaking vote would be cast by Vice President Quayle.) Few of the needed Democratic votes would come his way if Thomas appeared stridently partisan. And Republican moderates who might be scared off by Thomas's record at the EEOC would have to be quietly reassured as well.

Some of the most promising Democrats were the six moderate to conservative southern senators who were up for reelection in 1992, all of them heavily dependent on support from the southern Black Belt. Having lost such votes for Bork, Bush and Duberstein were determined this time to cut the deals and play the game, if necessary with every chit the White House had.

On its side, the White House had the Senate's traditional deference to a president's choice of nominee. In addition, by 1991, after more than a decade of Republican control of the White House, congressional Democrats were more vulnerable than ever to political pressure. The great partisan warriors Tip O'Neill and Jim Wright were gone. With the low-key George Mitchell as majority leader, Senate Democrats had been unable to muster the votes to overturn a single one of George Bush's vetoes, as moderate southerners often crossed the aisle to vote with their Republican brethren. The House, meanwhile, was now under the control of the muted Thomas Foley.

With no president to offer coattails or political cover and no party bosses with any real clout, the Senate Democrats had become unusually independent. Where they once had depended on the party for money, now many of them raised campaign funds with paid consultants, completely separate from the efforts of the party. As a consequence of these historic changes, Mitchell had little leverage with which to enforce discipline, even without the partisan skills of past leaders.

The Democrats not only lacked discipline; by 1991 most of them also lacked courage. Since losing the 1980 election to Ronald Reagan, liberal Democrats in particular had come to feel like an endangered species. That election had marked a national shift away from their ideology and had also proven beyond a doubt the power of right-wing attack politics. The very word "liberal" became an embarrassment. Senators formerly described as liberal began calling themselves progressive Democrats or, better yet, moderates. They lived in constant fear of being targeted with negative campaigns focusing on single divisive issues such as abortion and gun control.

By the summer of Thomas's nomination, the Democrats had regained control of the Senate, but the fear remained. NCPAC had by then fallen apart, but its attack strategy had been adopted by a host of other organizations that had sprung up in its wake, both liberal and conservative. These groups could generate torrents of mail and phone calls from angry constituents. They could also amass huge campaign coffers for opponents: as long as they operated separately from the Republican party, conservative political groups were permitted to finance campaigns against targeted Democrats, raising and spending enormous sums well outside the limits imposed by the federal election laws. Knowing this, Senate Democrats had become extremely leery of taking controversial stands.

In particular, at the time Thomas was bound for the Supreme Court, many Democrats were afraid of the issue of race. They may have had serious questions about Thomas's opposition to affirmative action. But after seeing Bush's landslide victory over Michael Dukakis in 1988, with its racist Willie Horton ad, as well as several 1990 Senate campaigns in which Republicans had obliterated their opponents by making an issue of their embrace of racial quotas, few white liberals were anxious to crusade for such controversial programs, especially against a black nominee. As Roger Craver, a top political adviser and fund-raiser for liberal Democrats, put it, despite intermittent legislative successes, liberal Democrats were by 1991 mired in the "politics of paralysis."

The party's credibility had been further damaged by several important Democratic senators who were ethically compromised. The dark side of senatorial fund-raising had been recently exposed in the so-called Keating Five scandal, which stung four Democrats (and one Republican) for taking more than a million dollars in contributions from a dishonest savings-and-loan operator. One of those snared in the scandal was Arizona's Dennis DeConcini, a conservative Democratic member of the Judiciary Committee; if any ethical issues arose during the Thomas hearings, DeConcini would hardly be in a position to judge the nominee harshly.

Other senators had been compromised by personal imbroglios, including Virginia's Chuck Robb, the head of the Democratic Senatorial Campaign Committee. Robb was fighting to survive an escapade in which he said he received a back rub from a young woman not his wife as well as allegations that he had attended wild beach parties where drugs were used. Another who could hardly be self-righteous in the face of any irregularities in Thomas's personal life was Ted Kennedy. As Floyd Brown's attack ad had so gleefully pointed out, this important member of the Judiciary Committee would soon be called to testify in the rape trial of his nephew. For the first time in his long political career, Kennedy's liberal activism was shut away behind a stony, embarrassed silence.

❖

The White House also knew that even without these special problems, all senators had vulnerabilities. They were generally obsessed by three worries: avoiding negative publicity, raising money, and appearing invincible to potential opponents back home. Soon after Thomas was nominated, Duberstein, Mackey, McClure, and the rest of the Bush lobbyists set about the business of gathering fifty-one votes by artfully playing on these and other concerns.

In Georgia, for instance, the freshman Democratic senator, Wyche Fowler, was up for reelection in the fall. He was far more liberal than his senior colleague, Sam Nunn, and even though he and the nominee had the same home state, Fowler's ideology suggested that he was unlikely to cast a positive vote. But the White House realized that with the election very much on Fowler's mind, he would be listening closely to Georgia's blacks to assess their attitude toward Thomas. Whether they identified with Thomas as a fellow native son or turned on him as an opponent of civil rights, Fowler would be hard-pressed to go the other way.

Not surprisingly, Fowler was thus high on the list of senators whom the White House targeted for courtesy calls from the nominee. The visit, which occurred soon after Thomas was nominated, was a success: despite large ideological differences, Fowler was quite swayed by Thomas in person. After meeting with Thomas and Danforth for an hour and a half, Fowler later explained, "I had a good impression of his character, the fact he was from Georgia, and the fact that he grew up poor and hard I thought would bring a perspective to a court that was mostly white and privileged."

While these were his stated reasons for supporting Thomas, the White House played other angles as well. Knowing how much the black vote would mean to Fowler's reelection, the White House arranged for sympathetic black leaders in Fowler's state to lobby for

Thomas. According to a black pastor at St. Paul's Christian Methodist Episcopal Church in Savannah, Henry Delaney, "A man named Mark Paoletta [Boyden Gray's aide] called me every day for a while. The White House really worked it. They told us to contact Fowler because Senator Fowler didn't know whether there was black support for Thomas." Such stage directions from the White House appear to have been in direct violation of the federal anti-lobbying act.

And the White House had still more leverage: it had something Fowler wanted. The senator was counting on heavy financial support from the lawyers in his state. The Georgia Bar Association, meanwhile, wanted a federal judgeship for its secretary, a lawyer from Statesboro named James Franklin. Although Franklin was a Republican, Fowler was trying hard to please the state bar, lobbying the White House to appoint him over another Republican candidate. Fowler, who ultimately voted in favor of Thomas, would later disavow any connection between his vote and other issues such as Georgia judgeships. (Franklin was nominated by the White House right after Thomas's confirmation but failed to make it through the Senate.) But two White House aides believe they secured Fowler's vote by nominating his judge. (Ironically, Fowler lost his bid for reelection the following fall, in part because feminist leaders and women withheld their financial and organizational support from him because of his support for Thomas.)

Fowler was one of the six southern Democrats up for reelection that year. Terry Sanford, a progressive from North Carolina, was another who felt the heavy hand of Thomas's Washington supporters in his campaign financing. A liberal former governor, Sanford too was an ideological opposite to Thomas, but the freshman senator was vulnerable to conservative attack, and he needed millions of dollars for his 1992 campaign.

Charles Black, a conservative political strategist in Washington who had been working informally with Duberstein, had special clout in North Carolina. Not only was Black a native, he had helped direct the enormously well financed campaigns of Senator Jesse Helms and so had come to know virtually every major fund-raiser in the region. During the summer of 1991, as Sanford was desperately trying to amass funds, Black helped to rally business leaders and Republican contributors in the state to contact the senator on behalf of Thomas. Sanford indeed cast his vote for Thomas; he also succeeded in raising an impressive $2.5 million for his reelection. But in the end Sanford, like Fowler, narrowly lost his reelection, in his case to a better-financed conservative Republican in the Helms mold.

The White House team also contacted major contributors to the coffers of Oklahoma's David Boren, a conservative Democrat whose vote they thought they could win. Even though Boren had been re-elected with 83 percent of the vote in 1990, he had spent $1.5 million to defeat a weak, underfinanced opponent. Not surprisingly, given Oklahoma's economic base, many of his most crucial contributors were leaders of the oil and gas industry, whose interests he fiercely protected.

An old oilman himself, Bush had his own close ties to many of Tulsa's energy executives. In fact, some of Boren's biggest contributors were also members of Bush's Team 100, the wealthy businessmen who gave or raised a minimum of $100,000 for the Republican party. Cross-party contributions were common among Oklahoma's energy interests, providing an obvious opportunity for the White House. And the Bush operatives did not pass it up. According to a former aide to Sununu, "We went to all of Boren's $1,000 contributors who were also Bush contributors and asked them to call Boren on behalf of Thomas. Those oil and gas guys could make the calls." Although a threat was not necessarily expressed, the message was, of course, that Boren's access to oil patch money might run a bit dry if the senator didn't vote with the president.

Because the White House couldn't direct such efforts legally, or appear to be mixing money with votes for Thomas, the arrangements for these lobbying strategies were made at the Republican National Committee in consultation with state party organizations. Among the Bush contributors who called Boren on Thomas's behalf was Edward Lawson, the Tulsa oilman whom Thomas had wooed at the end of the Reagan years in order to get closer to George Bush.

Boren, a former Rhodes Scholar and Yale graduate who was considered a thoughtful parliamentarian on Capitol Hill, eventually agreed to support Thomas. His vote was considered especially significant after Anita Hill came forward, because she was a native of his state. But later, after watching Thomas's early performance on the Court, Boren admitted that his support had been a mistake he deeply regretted.

Vice President Quayle also participated in the effort to lobby vulnerable senators. He knew that his golfing buddy Alan Dixon, a Democrat from Illinois who, like Boren, often voted with the Republicans, was running for reelection in 1992 and was worried about who would oppose him. The two strongest potential candidates, Labor Secretary Lynn Martin and James Thompson, a former governor, had both indicated that they would not run. But around the time the White House nominated Thomas, a successful Chicago businessman, Gary MacDougal, was poised to throw his hat into the ring. MacDougal had strong ties to Republican officials at both the state and national levels and was thought to be a serious contender who could raise large amounts of money. He had already hired a campaign plane, lined up a consultant, and had an endorsement speech written for him by the Republican governor, Jim Edgar.

Quayle was well aware of Dixon's concern. He also knew that Dixon's was a potential vote for Thomas. According to a White House aide, Quayle called Dixon, emphasizing that his vote for Thomas would be considered a patriotic gesture, something that the Bush White House would value greatly. And when Dixon decided to vote for Thomas, MacDougal found that many of the wealthy Republican business leaders who had pledged to serve on his finance team suddenly began disappearing, asking, for instance, to have their names kept off his campaign letterhead.

Although outsiders could never be sure that Dixon's vote pulled the plug on MacDougal's official Republican support, the suspicion of a deal remained in the air. "[Dixon] was led to believe he'd get a weak opponent," says a high-ranking GOP political aide. "It was done with a wink and a nod." In any case, lacking sufficient backing, MacDougal withdrew from the race. The Republicans went on to name a weak replacement whom Dixon seemed sure to defeat.

Quayle was not alone in pressuring Dixon. During August, the Christian Coalition, whose leaders were in touch with Duberstein, also earmarked him for special attention. Action alerts went out to its members in seven states, and television spots backing Thomas were run in twelve markets. In addition, the group sent out two hundred thousand pieces of direct mail and got a hundred thousand Christian activists to sign petitions supporting Thomas, which were delivered by hand to Dixon and other ambivalent senators by Christian Coalition leaders, who met with each senator's legislative assistant. The message was clear: Dixon or any senator who did not heed the Christian Coalition's call to support Judge Thomas would find himself facing a righteous and very angry army at the ballot box, and possibly even a primary challenge from the religious right.

Thus, when Dixon decided to vote for Thomas, it must have seemed politically prudent. Ironically, it turned out to be just the opposite. Dixon never got the chance even to face his weak Republican challenger; in an upset, he was defeated in the Democratic primary by a black woman, Carol Moseley Braun. Her reason for running — and some might suggest winning — was her anger over the Senate's treatment of Anita Hill.

This wheeling and dealing by the White House was cynical but hardly unusual: pandering to self-interest, after all, was the staple of Capitol Hill. What was out of the ordinary, however, was the number of deals cut before Thomas had even spent a day testifying as well as the fact that they were brokered for a Supreme Court nominee. Indeed, the White House sewed up so many votes in advance that when yet another Democratic senator, Louisiana's Bennett Johnston, announced at a luncheon of Senate Democrats that he too was supporting Thomas even before the Judiciary Committee had voted, Majority Leader George Mitchell finally exploded, "This has got to stop!"

❖

As the summer wore on, the political team at the White House also worked feverishly to polish the candidate himself so that in his first real public debut he would come across winningly. Thomas had to be thoroughly coached, first, to protect himself against allegations that he lacked the legal depth to be a Supreme Court justice, and second, to soften the rougher edges of his ideology. Duberstein instructed Thomas to appear as amiable, flexible, and moderate inside the Beltway as his supporters outside the Beltway had been assured by the likes of Gary Bauer that he was not. He was to recite his Pin Point story, know his law, and, if need be, disown past controversial remarks.

The idea was to attempt to reprise the stealth strategy used during the Souter hearings, tapes of which Thomas carefully studied. But Thomas's paper trail of speeches and writings made the sequel considerably more challenging. Precisely to raise his stock with influential conservatives, Thomas had given increasingly extreme speeches during his latter years at the EEOC. Now his intellectual flirtations —

with the theory of natural law, for instance — would be evident to anyone who made the effort to read the thirty-six thousand documents he and his legal advisers had turned over to the Judiciary Committee.

Characteristically pugnacious, Thomas confided to friends like Bolick and Mackey that he was uncomfortable with Duberstein's stealth approach. Perhaps, left to his own devices, he would have given the Senate and the public a more forthright and illuminating exposition of his views. But honesty was not the best policy, in the view of the White House strategists. As they kept reminding him, their job was to get him to the Supreme Court; once there, he could take on his critics and vote as he pleased.

On the volatile subject of abortion, the White House made a firm decision that Thomas must say nothing definitive. Among other concerns, any indication that the nominee might abrogate a woman's right to an abortion would risk alienating a crucial Republican moderate on the committee, Arlen Specter. A former prosecutor, Specter had led the Republican mutiny against Bork, dooming him with a sharp cross-examination that lasted two days. During 1991, he had voted with George Bush less than 40 percent of the time, marking himself as a dangerous wild card whom Duberstein's team would need to woo assiduously. The White House knew that the ardently pro-choice Specter was up for reelection in 1992 and was counting on strong support from women's groups. If Thomas were to speak out against abortion, Specter would almost certainly have to vote against him, which is why, as John Mackey, the Justice Department handler, later conceded, avoiding the abortion issue was a calculated decision. "If he had answered the abortion question, it would have cost him votes," Mackey said. "Specter was critical in the outcome. If he [Thomas] had answered, maybe Specter would not have supported him."

While the conservatism of Thomas was one concern, his lack of depth in constitutional law was another. Souter had been a constitutional scholar, and his command of the substance of the law was vast. Not so with Thomas. "With Thomas you had to make sure he substantively came through the hearings," explained a top White House aide. "Thomas hadn't been practicing law, he hadn't been dealing with the law as a judge for very long. All of a sudden the entire Constitution is fair game." Mike Luttig, a young attorney in the Justice Department, was charged with cramming Thomas on the law in a scant few weeks, conducting, in essence, a hectic one-man bar review course.

Luttig's participation was highly unusual and, to some Democratic aides on the Judiciary Committee, ethically offensive. About the same time Thomas was nominated by President Bush, Luttig was appointed to fill a vacancy on the prestigious 4th Circuit Court of Appeals in Virginia. Although he had not yet taken his judicial oath and so technically was still a Justice Department aide, it was virtually unprecedented for a confirmed judicial nominee to work on so blatantly political a matter as the Thomas confirmation. Nevertheless, Luttig was deemed indispensable by the White House. A former clerk for Scalia and Burger, he had one of the sharpest legal minds in the administration. Before being elevated to the federal bench, he oversaw the Justice Department's Office of Legal Counsel, an elite corps of conservative lawyers that one Democratic Senate Judiciary Committee aide called "the Green Berets of the law."

While Luttig conducted his tutorials, it fell to Duberstein to arrange for the "murder boards," the mock trials at which, in a close approximation to the Judiciary Committee's proceedings, Thomas would be grilled on his every speech and ruling. In secret, once before Labor Day and then throughout the week before the September 10 hearings, a select group gathered for these show sessions in Room 180 of the Old Executive Office Building, the ornate former War Department across from the White House. Duberstein chose A. B. Culvahouse, a lawyer who had served as White House counsel to Reagan, to question the nominee. Boyden Gray was on hand to do a hilarious imitation of Ted Kennedy; Kristol and Danforth attended as well.

Thomas also received the help of two Democrats, who agreed to participate in the mock trials as long as they were never publicly identified. Together, they could warn Thomas about what to expect in the way of tough questioning. The first was Terry Adamson, a former top official in the Carter administration, whose wife, Edie Halliday, worked for the Bush White House. The other was Duberstein's partner Mike Berman, a former campaign official and aide to various Democrats, including Vice President Walter Mondale; his presence at the murder boards shocked some of the Republicans in Duberstein's inner circle.

The trickiest question clearly was how to duck the issue of abortion. Duberstein hoped that Thomas might finesse this and other issues by personalizing them. He needed to come across as a human being, not a rigid ideologue. During the murder boards, Duberstein thus arranged for one of the questioners to ask Thomas about his sister's abortion. (An article in *USA Today* had briefly mentioned Emma Mae's therapeutic abortion, but no other reporters had picked up on it.) When the question came, Thomas appeared surprised but neither rigid nor judgmental. But evidently it was decided that his apparent acceptance of Emma Mae's choice could not be revealed during the hearings without risk of alienating his supporters in the religious right. So although abortion was one of the most important issues before the Court, neither the Senate nor the public would be allowed even a glimpse of Thomas's views.

In the last week of Thomas's preparation, President Bush himself popped in to wish him luck and express support. All eyes turned to the president as he watched the questioning for a few minutes and then warmly shook hands around the room. Thomas was beaming. It was going so well that Duberstein offered to cancel the last moot court session. But Thomas, an achiever to the core, said he wanted to stick to the plan. The sessions, he said, got him going.

Consequently, when his confirmation hearings opened, the nominee was well coached — many would later say overcoached. With dozens of IOUs and armies of well-organized supporters both inside and outside the Beltway, Clarence Thomas now stood ready to face the final hurdle before his life's dream.

❖

In contrast, the Democrats went into the hearings with only the most tenuous of strategies. Overseeing them was the Senate Judiciary Committee's chairman, Joseph Biden of Delaware. Young and handsome, Biden exuded the boyish, informal charm of a popular high school class president.

The chairman had spent much of the long, hot summer in moot court preparations of his own. After taking turns questioning and playing Thomas in trial runs, he and his aides had concluded that the only matters about which they could afford to question him sharply were his possibly extremist views on abortion and such arcane legal issues as natural law. But if the latter was an acceptable (if tedious) subject, Biden, a pro-choice Catholic from a traditionally anti-abortion state, was not anxious to make a huge ruckus over the former.

Biden had ample reason to raise the issue of Thomas's thin legal experience. The American Bar Association had given Thomas the tepid rating of "qualified" — with a minority voting to rate him "unqualified" — the lowest rating the group had given a Supreme Court nominee in modern times. But the chairman made a strategic decision not to go after Thomas on the issue of either his character or his competence. "The people who were working for Biden concluded that Thomas met the threshold in terms of judicial qualifications, so we made a conscious recommendation that it wasn't legitimate to go after him on those," explained Christopher Schroeder, a Duke University law professor who was hired as a consultant to work with Biden. "Sure, Thomas didn't have that much experience — but we worked for a senator who was elected when he himself was just twenty-nine."

Indeed, both personal experience and temperament gave Joe Biden little appetite for pursuing such potentially nasty lines of questioning. In December 1972, he had been about to join the Senate as its youngest member when his wife and infant daughter were killed in a car accident, the Christmas tree still in the back of their car. Biden never publicly discussed this awful loss, let alone exploited it for sympathy votes, but it was one reason he was wary of introducing personal or so-called character issues into politics. Very much a family man, he had remarried and was devoted to his two sons from his first marriage and his daughter from his second, returning home each evening by train to Wilmington.

More recently, Biden had been a presidential contender, and the experience had made him even more leery of questions of character or competence. In the midst of the Bork confirmation fight in 1987, Biden had been personally — and he felt unfairly — accused of unethical behavior by the press, which ridiculed him for plagiarizing biographical parts of a campaign speech from Neil Kinnock, a British Labour leader. The accelerating scandal — which included a frenzied search by reporters to document his alleged failure to footnote a source adequately in a law school term paper — had forced Biden to drop out of the race. Not long afterward, he had been rushed to a hospital emergency room with a life-threatening brain aneurysm. His background as a defense lawyer had already given him a tendency to sympathize with the accused, but after the 1987 blowout his aversion to delving into personal issues was visceral.

There was another reason — discussed privately among Biden and his staff — for soft-pedaling such questions, in Thomas's case in particular. No white senator, a top Biden aide later acknowledged, wanted to risk the racist image that might result if the second African-American Supreme Court nominee in history were made to look unintelligent. "We couldn't afford to make Thomas look like William Clark [Reagan's nominee for secretary of state, who had stumbled over questions of simple geography]," admitted the aide. "It was a racial thing."

In an interview, Biden himself confirmed that "some concern was expressed by black leaders about 'How smart is this guy?' But there was in fact a concern about whether or not to make the guy look stupid — what would happen if you embarrassed him?"

For the same reason, the Democrats had no stomach for questioning Thomas about affirmative action. It would have been natural to ask how he could oppose programs that had benefited him so much, but the wealthy white members of the Senate were very uncomfortable cross-examining a black man who had been raised in rural Georgia about his racial views. "How could these ultra-liberal white senators be pro-affirmative action in the face of a self-made black man saying 'We don't need these programs'?" asked one Democratic staff member. This racial dynamic, exactly as the White House had hoped, would shield Thomas's EEOC record from scrutiny.

In truth, harsh treatment was not Biden's style under any circumstances. He viewed his powerful chairmanship as a bipartisan role and prided himself on his friendly relations with the Republican committee members. A moderate Democrat, he was legendary on Capitol Hill for his need — some considered it a compulsion — to be liked by anyone and everyone. Famous for speaking until every person in the room had been won over, Biden was a gifted orator despite having grown up with a terrible stutter. (As an adolescent he had reportedly overcome his handicap by reciting speeches to himself late into the night with his mouth full of pebbles — a trick that, he had read, Demosthenes had used to improve enunciation.) An overachiever from way back and an eminently decent man, Biden remained more an emotional, kinetic politician than an intellectual one. But popularity and policy were not always compatible, and sometimes his need to win everyone's affection led him into trouble.

In fact, that is precisely what happened on the opening day of

Thomas's confirmation hearings. As Biden walked the nominee and his mother, Leola Williams, toward the hearing room, according to Williams, he misled them about his sympathies. At that point, Biden was still publicly neutral toward Thomas, but he gave assurances in words that later made Williams's blood boil. "Judge Thomas," she remembered Biden saying with his trademark, lightning flash of a brilliant smile, "don't worry about a thing. I'm in your court."

❖

Thus it was a confident Clarence Thomas who on Tuesday morning, September 10, strode into the cavernous Caucus Room in the Senate building named for another Georgia native, the strident segregationist of his youth, the late Richard B. Russell. Short, powerful, and so robust that the buttons were straining on his business suit, Thomas was in every way a perfect counterpoint to the aged Republican committee member, South Carolina's Strom Thurmond, with whom he now walked arm in arm. Thurmond, a former segregationist, had lived long enough to see a new day in the South, one in which cooperation with blacks like Thomas was not just desirable but politically essential.

Danforth, along with Virginia Lamp Thomas and the nominee's son from his first marriage, Jamal, sat directly behind the judge. So did both his mother and his sister, Emma Mae. Only his brother, Myers, was missing from the proud family tableau.

The mood among Thomas's supporters was upbeat. Going into the hearings, Danforth exulted that Thomas already "had it won." Indeed, Duberstein's insistence that the nominee visit more than sixty of Danforth's colleagues had paid off handsomely. Duberstein and Danforth thought Thomas had secured at least sixty votes, including all the Republicans except the notoriously independent and liberal Robert Packwood. Especially important was the indication that, barring disaster, Thomas could count on the support of all six Republicans on the Judiciary Committee, including Specter.

The White House had high hopes of capturing several Democratic votes on the committee as well. While Biden's intentions were hard to decipher, the White House and Danforth thought they had a good chance of winning over two other Democrats, Arizona's Dennis DeConcini and Alabama's Howell Heflin.

Despite his earlier vow to Bolick that he would come on strong,

Thomas began the hearings by sticking firmly to the Pin Point script. "My earliest memories are those of Pin Point, Georgia," he said. Wearing a dark suit, red tie, and his signature large frame glasses, Thomas spoke movingly of "a life far removed in space and time from this room, this day, this moment." At one point, the nominee had his audience near tears as he told of the days when his mother had earned only $20 a week as a maid and had to send her sons to live with their grandparents. "Imagine, if you will, two little boys with all their belongings in two grocery bags," Thomas implored.

While adhering to the bootstraps mythology that Vernon Jordan had warned him to avoid, Thomas also demonstrated that he had taken some of Jordan's advice to heart. Next he intoned the names of the civil rights leaders on whose shoulders he stood. "Justice Marshall, whose seat I've been nominated to fill, is one of those who had the courage and the intellect. He's one of the great architects of the legal battles to open doors that seemed so hopelessly and permanently sealed and to knock down barriers that seemed so insurmountable to those of us in the Pin Point, Georgias, of the world."

It was a persuasive, inspiring start. But as soon as the questions began, Thomas was on rockier ground. Biden launched into a long, windy excursion into Thomas's past statements about natural law, focusing in particular on a speech given to the Pacific Research Institute in 1987. In that talk, according to Biden's question, Thomas had endorsed the ideas of Stephen Macedo, a fairly obscure Straussian writer who was a proponent of natural law. Did the nominee still agree with Macedo? asked Biden. Thomas struggled to find an answer. Macedo hadn't been fodder for the murder boards, but Thomas had been warned to steer clear of natural law.

After saying that it had been a long time since he had read Macedo, Thomas fully retreated from his past embrace of natural law theory, saying, "I don't see a role for natural law in constitutional adjudication." He added that he had only been interested in the subject as an academic exercise. He also backed away from the infamous Heritage Foundation speech in which he had praised Lewis Lehrman's treatise against abortion, maintaining that he had only been praising Lehrman's ideas — which were grounded in natural law — as a polite gesture because he was speaking in the auditorium named for the New York conservative, who was also one of the foundation's early benefactors. Thomas also steadfastly refused Biden's invitation to state his position on abortion, going only so far as to endorse a constitutionally protected right to privacy.

By the time Biden banged his gavel for a break, to most observers Thomas looked wooden, unresponsive, and insincere. Some of his old friends, such as his elementary school and college classmate Lester Johnson, were astonished at the transformation in him. "He's so different from the Clarence Thomas who America saw," Johnson later said. "The real Clarence would have told it like it is. He would have laid it out. He's always been an opinionated bastard, always. That epitomizes him." But, Johnson noted, Thomas had told him about ten days before the hearings that he was going to "be out of pocket with this guy Duberstein. He was uncomfortable with it, but I think he and the White House concluded that America would not have liked the real Clarence, so they had to change his image."

It was a wobbly performance, but Thomas's supporters made a valiant stab at "spinning" public opinion in their favor. Duberstein and Danforth had carefully arranged with Biden's staff to be given a signal when the chairman was about to call for a break. That gave Thomas's partisans a chance to get in position for the television cameras. "From Bork the lesson learned was that if you sit in the room, you get painted by the spin doctors outside. At every break we used Danforth, or other surrogates, to go to the mikes," Mackey reflected.

The White House and Justice Department had also arranged for a "response research" team, conducting the confirmation like a presidential campaign. At any given time, at least three Justice Department lawyers from Luttig's Office of Legal Counsel were stationed in a room in Danforth's office one floor below, watching the hearings and matching the questions and answers with the record. In the nearby office of Mississippi's Senator Thad Cochran sat another phalanx of administration officials and political hands — the EEOC's Ricky Silberman; a White House spokeswoman, Judy Smith; the Office of Personnel Management's director and Thomas's friend from the Sullivan Group, Connie Newman; and the right-wing activist Tom Jipping. They were the spin squad, assigned to get views supporting Thomas instantly to the media.

The system worked well. At the first break, Danforth, having been coached by the Justice Department researchers, gave reporters the full text of Thomas's speech on natural law, showing that some lines expressing skepticism about Macedo had been omitted by Biden. One

Republican committee member, Orrin Hatch, whose job was to shore up Thomas following hostile Democratic questioning, exploited the issue of the full text when the proceedings resumed. In the opinion of some of Biden's advisers, this surprisingly swift and effective Republican counterattack made the chairman even more wary of cross-examining the nominee.

Despite the intensive effort to manage both the nominee and the response to him, the first day of the hearings went badly. But few thought Thomas's confirmation was really in danger. Even with opposition from the NAACP and other liberal organizations, there was a sense that the Democrats' hearts weren't really in this fight. Kennedy, who had been so devastating to Bork, was silent. Two other liberals, Metzenbaum and Vermont's Patrick Leahy, had not made a move.

Even from the more liberal outside interest groups, the opposition to Thomas appeared weak and perfunctory. On many of the ensuing five days of the hearings, the only opponents stalwart enough to remain through the proceedings were Ralph Neas and Joe Rauh, the aging lion of civil rights law. The two white lawyers presented a lonely picture, sitting together outside the hearing room waiting for their own chance to influence the media. Their presence only underscored the absence of leading black civil rights leaders, the men and women who had been so visible and vocal in Bork's fight.

Meanwhile, as the hearings wore on, Biden's queries were sometimes so long and convoluted that Thomas would forget what the question was. Biden had considered the Bork hearings his finest hour, a high-minded discourse that had engaged the country. Bork was defeated fairly, in Biden's view, because of his legal opinions. This time Biden's questioning seemed occasionally to be a vehicle to show off legal acumen rather than to elicit answers.

And the other Democrats on the committee virtually ignored Thomas's speeches and writings on affirmative action. Ironically, only Specter questioned the judge about his controversial views on civil rights, and the inquiries were gentle. Metzenbaum, the one Democrat who dared to tangle with Thomas, failed to get far. Many thought the senator looked petulant and mean-spirited as he badgered the nominee with question after question about abortion. Thomas ducked them all.

Finally Leahy, a skilled former prosecutor, did come close to prying some information out of Thomas. Leahy pointed out that the *Roe* decision, handed down when Thomas was in law school, had been the most fiercely debated decision of the year. Surely, Leahy insisted, it must have been widely discussed at Yale and Thomas must have participated in some of those discussions. The response seemed a blatant obfuscation. Thomas said that he did not recall ever discussing the case and that he hadn't had much time to debate cases because he was married with a child during law school and was busy working to earn his tuition. Leahy retorted that he too had been married and working during law school, but that these responsibilities had not impaired his legal curiosity and availability to discuss important Supreme Court rulings. He pressed again with his question. This time Thomas responded that he had never "debated" the *Roe* decision or publicly discussed his own position on the case. Leahy, the committee, and the public were all incredulous.

The only person who raised what many thought should have been the most salient issue of the hearings — Thomas's lack of qualifications — was a Washington lawyer who was nearly ninety years old. Erwin Griswold, a distinguished former dean of Harvard Law School and a former solicitor general who had argued many cases before the Supreme Court, bluntly told the committee that Thomas had "not yet demonstrated any clear intellectual or professional distinctions." But no one else dared speak out, although Thomas's limited experience and shaky grasp of the law had been apparent to virtually all the people in the room, including many supporters.

Even the White House team was aghast at Thomas's weak performance. "I thought [Thomas] was terrible, wooden," one of the moot court coaches conceded later. But they publicly blamed Duberstein, not the nominee. "He was so overcoached . . . that he didn't show he was a bright and interesting person. We overdid it," one partisan said.

The result was a disservice not only to Thomas but to the entire process. As an aide to Biden with extensive experience in previous confirmation battles put it later, "At the end of Souter, you knew a little more about his philosophy than before it started. But with Thomas, at the end you knew less. It showed that the process had been reduced to a game."

Nevertheless, Thomas's dull and unenlightening performance was followed by an orchestrated stampede of support. The votes that the

White House had worked all summer to secure were now ready to be counted. The Pin Point strategy may have been cynical, but it seemed about to pay off.

Thomas himself wryly reflected on the change in his tactics. Rather than "really taking on the opposition," as he had promised Bolick, he told another friend that his credo had become, "Don't get mad. Don't get even. Get confirmed."

10

A Duty
to Report

CLARENCE THOMAS WAS NOT the only one stifling his most controversial opinions that summer. In Norman, Oklahoma, when the White House announced Thomas's nomination on July 1, the news hit Anita Hill with such a jolt that her stomach turned. But in her first interview on the subject since the hearings, she was adamant that no matter what her private thoughts about Thomas were, "I had no plan in my mind to come forward — not one single thought about it."

A decade had passed since she had begun working for Thomas, and as he rose from one post to the next, surviving confirmation and reconfirmation hearings, Hill never thought once about publicly accusing him, she said later. If someone had asked her opinion as part of the democratic vetting process, she might have felt a responsibility, as she put it, "to report." But no one had ever asked.

With his nomination to the Supreme Court, though, Thomas achieved a level of prominence so great that much of the country was curious about him. As reporters researched the nominee's background, opponents scoured paper trails, and the White House corralled his elementary school teachers for public appearances, the odds that Hill could remain anonymous and unquestioned began shrinking rapidly.

A few of the friends with whom Hill had shared her secret about Thomas over the years thought of her instantly when the news of the nomination broke. Susan Hoerchner, the law school classmate who immediately called Hill, thought she detected pain in Hill's voice. But Hill said she was resigned to continuing her silence. By stressing how unfair she felt Bork's treatment had been, Hill seemed to be offering a rationale that construed her inaction as public-spirited.

In Washington, Ellen Wells, the level-headed friend to whom Hill had unburdened herself, recalled that on hearing the news about Thomas, she too instantly wondered about Hill. But Wells never called her. "I'm such a coward," she admitted later. "I figured this is a personal decision that concerns both her past and future, and I have no right to require her in any way to address it before she may be ready to. It was Anita's decision to make. I mean, it was possible no one would ever know. So I decided, 'Keep my mouth shut and my fingers off the dial — until she decides.'"

Although she had decided not to get involved, Hill continued to be privately torn. Her life had taken a permanent detour because of Thomas, leaving her to ruminate in Oklahoma while he prepared to ascend to the highest rung of power and prestige in their profession. Besides her troubling memories of Thomas's upsetting and perhaps unlawful behavior, she had reservations about the nomination for philosophical reasons. After she left the EEOC, Hill had watched Thomas harden from the independent thinker she had known into a man she regarded as a doctrinaire ideologue. When she was working for him, they had often argued about issues such as affirmative action, but Hill thought Thomas's mind was still receptive to other points of view. In the later Reagan years, she felt Thomas had ceased to have the open mind required of a judge.

Despite their increasing ideological differences — Hill had, if anything, become more liberal and more concerned with women's rights — she had kept up sporadic contacts with Thomas since leaving the capital in 1983. She had called him occasionally from 1984 to 1990, though most of the calls were placed for professional reasons, such as needing advice on how to obtain research grants. She had seen Thomas only twice — once during a visit to Washington, when she asked him for a recommendation (which Thomas agreed to provide but never did), and again in 1987, when he had come to Tulsa and she had joined him and Dean Kothe for breakfast and then given Thomas a ride to the airport.

Much would later be made of these contacts. Many people could not understand why Hill would see and stay in touch with a man who had treated her in such a humiliating way. She herself would only make the contacts seem more mysterious, first by denying them, and then by explaining that most of her attempts to reach Thomas had been at the request of other people and that none of the conversations had been memorable to her. These reasons, however, seemed to avoid the obvious fact that, regardless of her personal feelings, Hill chose to stay in touch with Thomas because it was good for her career. Thomas was one of the most powerful people — and probably the most powerful African-American — in her field. As Paul's question about the gap in her résumé proved, whether Hill liked it or not, she and Thomas were professionally linked, and it was up to her to either put a good face on it or allow it to be a festering problem. But her inability simply to acknowledge the advantages of maintaining professional links to Thomas would again make her vulnerable to anyone looking for inconsistencies. Moreover, her opaqueness evidently left Thomas with little idea how she really regarded him. Thus when she finally accused him, he was, by all accounts, genuinely stunned.

Hill would testify that she had come to regret not having filed a complaint against Thomas. "It was a very trying and difficult decision for me not to say anything further," she explained. "I can only say that when I made the decision to just withdraw from the situation and not press a claim or charge against him that I may have shirked a duty, a responsibility that I had. And to that extent I confess that I am very sorry that I did not do something or say something, but at the time that was my best judgment. Maybe it was a poor judgment, but it wasn't a dishonest and it wasn't a completely unreasonable choice that I made given the circumstances."

In fact, although Hill worked at the very agency where all sexual harassment complaints were supposed to originate and was thus unusually well acquainted with this rapidly evolving area of the law, her knowledge only discouraged her further. While the letter of the law may have been on her side, she believed it farfetched to file a complaint against the chairman of the EEOC, the man who was supposed to be the nation's chief protector against sexual harassment. Quite simply, she thought she'd never be believed and she'd be out of a job, branded as a troublemaker or, worse, a liar.

In making this choice, she was behaving like the large majority of sexual harassment victims. In 1981, the year Hill began working for Thomas, a government study of federal workers found that 42 percent of women said that they had experienced some form of sexual harassment. Various polls and studies undertaken since had found anywhere from 40 to 70 percent of women claiming to have been harassed on the job. Yet, from the early 1980s through the beginning of the next decade, one figure remained constant: fewer than 5 percent of these alleged victims filed lawsuits or lodged official complaints. The EEOC itself usually filed fewer than fifty cases a year. Most women responded to harassment as Hill had — they either suffered in silence or found new jobs.

This record also reflected how new the laws governing sexual harassment were when Hill worked for Thomas. A few feminist lawyers, such as Catharine MacKinnon, began bringing sexual harassment claims in federal court in the 1970s. But it wasn't until 1980 that the EEOC issued guidelines on the subject. And it took another six years for the Supreme Court to rule, in *Meritor Savings Bank v. Vinson,* that sexual harassment was a form of sexual discrimination covered by federal law. As a legal scholar in the civil rights field, Hill had watched closely and approvingly as the courts expanded the legal remedies. And as a settled, secure law professor, she had far more pronounced views on the issue than she had had as a novice attorney in Washington. But even in the summer of 1991, she was still ambivalent about what to do.

❖

Although Hill had first decided, as she told Hoerchner, that she would keep quiet about her experience, in the weeks after the nomination she seemed increasingly restless about her decision. Selectively — and only when asked her feelings about Thomas — Hill began letting a few other friends into the tiny circle of those who knew about what had happened.

In late July, for instance, she called her old law school friend Gary Phillips to chat, as she did every few months. One of the players on the coed basketball team Hill coached at Yale, Phillips was now a lawyer at the Federal Communications Commission in Washington. Though he suspected that she was tired of being asked about the nomination, Phillips still could not resist asking her opinion. Hill shocked him by explaining for the first time why she had left the EEOC. She did not provide details — and Phillips did not ask for any, knowing what a private person she was. He did ask what she planned to do with this information. Hill told him that her inclination was to keep it to herself.

But her mind could not have been completely made up, because she asked Phillips, who was savvy and politically connected, what he thought she should do. He had to agree that jumping into such a politically charged melee could have ruinous results for an ordinary citizen, no matter how truthful. "I felt [Washington politicians] didn't have integrity and would stop at nothing," he said later. "She didn't have proof that it happened. Did she want to do that, and put herself at their mercy?" During the phone call, Hill agreed that she didn't want to get involved in a political three-ring circus, but Phillips hung up thinking that "she was very much struggling with her decision."

Phillips, unlike Hoerchner, had not been sworn to secrecy — an oversight that in itself seemed to betray Hill's ambivalence. Moreover, his location in the heart of the nation's capital all but ensured that if he spread the story, it would find an exceptionally receptive audience. Although Phillips later said he had no desire to publicize her story, soon after talking with her he passed it on, without naming Hill, to a few of his most intimate friends, he believed over a bridge game. It remains unclear which of his friends spread the word further, but not long after Phillips's bridge game, the information became the sustenance of a Washington dinner party. And later that night, one of the guests passed the information on to two of Thomas's leading opponents, George Kassouf and Nan Aron, officials at the liberal lobbying group Alliance for Justice.

Aron, whose carefully researched left-wing critiques of the justice system served as a kind of tip sheet to liberal senators and the media, was immediately intrigued. On returning to the office the next week, she assigned some aides to compare the three pieces of information she had — that Phillips's friend had gone to Yale Law, had worked at the EEOC, and now taught in Oklahoma. In no time they zeroed in on the likely suspect: Professor Anita F. Hill.

But as a canny operator who understood the niceties of "deniability," Aron refrained from contacting Hill directly. "I turned the information over to the Senate staff," she later said. "I felt it was inappropriate for us to do anything more." In the wake of the Bork recriminations, smart interest group lobbyists kept their fingerprints invisible so that damaging information, when it surfaced, would not be discounted as politically inspired. The tip was passed on to the office of Howard Metzenbaum, the member of the Judiciary Committee believed to have the staunchest record of opposition to Thomas. And there it sat, unexplored, for weeks.

——◆——

That summer, Hill's uncertainty about how to respond if asked directly about Thomas could be detected in the few public comments she made about the nomination. If she had wanted to stay out of the controversy entirely, she could have refused to return reporters' phone calls. Instead, she agreed to talk to a few of those from the press who contacted her. In August, she told a reporter for the *Kansas City Star* both positive and negative things about Thomas. She was more critical in an interview with the *Washington Post,* where her nephew on the paper, Gary Lee, had passed her name to a reporter. Perhaps her connection with Lee made Hill more daring, because this time she chided Thomas for his public criticism of his sister and her children for their dependence on welfare. "It takes a lot of detachment to publicize a person's experience in that way" and "a certain kind of self-centeredness not to recognize some of the programs that benefited you," she said, adding, "I think he doesn't understand people, he doesn't relate to people who don't make it on their own."

By appearing in newspapers, even discreetly, she was dancing on the edge of involvement and, intentionally or not, calling attention to herself. But Hill distinguished between volunteering information and honestly answering questions put to her. To have ducked the inquiries entirely, as she saw it, would have been a dereliction of her duties to the process itself.

Knowing that Thomas was about to reach the pinnacle of the profession in which she expected to continue her own life's work, Hill was extremely circumspect in what she said, particularly to those with ties to Thomas. For instance, on the weekend of August 10, she went to Atlanta for the American Bar Association convention. There she ran into Stanley Grayson, a former classmate of Thomas's at Holy Cross who had served as New York City's deputy mayor, and Carlton Stewart, an old friend who had worked for Thomas at the EEOC. Chatting with these Thomas boosters, Hill concealed any reservations she had about the nomination. Indeed, the two men later testified that she seemed as excited as they were about Thomas's ascension to the Supreme Court. They remembered her saying how great the appointment was. She recalled her words differently, testifying that she merely agreed with the two lawyers that the nomination was "a great thing for Clarence Thomas." Typically, Hill had chosen her words with extreme care in order not to offend anyone, but in doing so had left some doubt about her real opinions.

Unknown to Grayson or Stewart, however, Hill revealed her true sentiments that same weekend to someone with whom she felt more comfortable. Although neither the Senate nor the public ever learned of it, she unburdened herself to a woman named Cathy Thompson.

Thompson, a partner in the Charlotte, North Carolina, law firm of Smith, Helms, Muliss & Moore who specialized in defending employers against claims of sexual harassment, had been a classmate and friend of Hill's at law school. She recalled Hill as being one of the few black students who had both black friends and white, like herself, someone "apolitical, moderate, sensible, and studious." Although the two women had lost touch, they were delighted to see each other and catch up over a long lunch. Thompson, who was by then head of the local bar association, had completely forgotten that Hill had worked for Thomas when she idly asked what Hill thought of the latest Supreme Court nominee.

"You know I worked for him," Thompson recalled Hill's saying, suddenly growing "real quiet." After a pause, Hill added, "You know, I have some concern about that."

Thompson asked whether the concern was political, personal, or what. "It's based," said Hill obliquely, "on my experience with him."

Perhaps because of her own practice or just because of the way Hill spoke, Thompson said she then asked, "Was it harassment?"

When Hill answered affirmatively, Thompson recalled, "I was just so shocked. I told her, 'This must be so hard for you, then.'"

"Yes," Hill responded, "it's really hard right now. I just don't know what to do."

Thompson wondered if she should suggest that Hill tell the FBI or some other authority. But Hill was so "quiet and serious," Thompson recalled, she decided instead just to let the painful subject go, trying to be "cheerful and positive."

Thompson, who defended people against such charges professionally, came away from the conversation with no doubt about Hill's veracity. "Knowing her personally, it is inconceivable that she made it up, or even that she misconstrued it at the time," commented Thompson. "She is one of the most level-headed, fair-minded people I know."

Respecting Hill's quandary, however, she kept the information to herself through the end of the summer and into the fall.

Later, during the hearings, Thomas alleged that Hill and her advisers had "concocted" the entire harassment story in an effort to "destroy me." But Thompson's independent recollection suggests that instead, as late as a month before the confirmation hearings began, far from trying to "destroy" Thomas, Hill was agonizing about whether she had a responsibility to get involved at all. As such, Thompson is another previously unknown witness who corroborates Hill.

At the end of August, as faculty members began drifting back to Norman for the fall semester, Hill confided in yet another source whom the public never knew, her colleague and best friend at the university, Professor Shirley Wiegand. Although she had freckled white skin and reddish hair, Wiegand came from a background much like Hill's. She was the daughter of a hard-working, churchgoing midwestern farm family. She was an unpretentious wife and mother with a good sense of humor, but she was far more liberal and had far more pronounced views about the importance of women's rights than Hill.

When Hill confided her concerns about Thomas to Wiegand on one of the five-mile walks the two liked to take to stay in shape, Wiegand was disgusted that a man who treated women in such a way could be destined for the Supreme Court. But as far as she could tell, Hill had no plans to speak out, though clearly she was very troubled by the entire situation.

Wiegand exerted no pressure on her friend; in her view, the decision to pursue sexual charges was a highly personal matter. But Wiegand clearly embraced activism. Every time Hill stopped by Wiegand's office, just down the corridor from her own, she was faced with a little handmade needlepoint sampler prominently displayed on the wall:

> Evil Flourishes
> When Good People
> Do Nothing

❖

Back in Washington, Howard Metzenbaum — not to mention the other senators on the Judiciary Committee — remained oblivious of the existence of Anita Hill. In July, the tip about Hill from the Alliance for Justice had been passed to Bill Corr, the counsel to a Judiciary subcommittee that Metzenbaum chaired. But as Thomas went through his moot court drills and the White House public relations plan moved smartly forward, the Hill item received scant attention from Metzenbaum's staff. Neither Corr nor anyone else was anxious to put the matter before the senator. The truth, say several of those who worked for Metzenbaum, was that his age, his gender, and his distaste for personal matters made him extremely uncomfortable with issues like sexual harassment.

Metzenbaum, an irascible liberal Democrat in his mid-seventies who had made a fortune in the parking lot business, was an ardent and feisty advocate for the poor, the elderly, and the mistreated. Later, the Republicans would accuse him of opposing Thomas so zealously that he and his staff leaked Hill's allegation to the press. But the true story was quite a bit less sensational. It was also more revealing of the strongest political urge on both sides of the aisle on Capitol Hill: self-preservation.

In August, the pressure to inform Metzenbaum about Hill rose a little higher when his staff received new information about Thomas from another liberal interest group, People for the American Way. People For, as the group was informally known, had played a central and controversial role in sinking Bork. Founded by the liberal television producer Norman Lear, it had assigned four aides to scrutinize Thomas's record. Soon after filing a massive Freedom of Information Act request to get hold of every piece of paper Thomas had left behind at the EEOC, Lear's aides thought they had stumbled across damning material in Thomas's travel records, including four trips to Boston and several to California and Hawaii, all of which appeared to be more personal than business. One trip to Boston, in particular, appeared to relate more to Thomas's interest in a Holy Cross event than to EEOC matters. Apparently the only official business Thomas conducted was to summon a top EEOC official in Boston, Thomas Saltonstall, to his hotel room, where he was asked to sit quietly while Thomas and his mentor Thomas Sowell ate a shrimp dinner from room service. Saltonstall was apparently called merely to provide an EEOC front; Thomas didn't even ask him about agency matters.

Saltonstall was willing to testify about this odd interpretation of official business, but only if he was compelled to by subpoena. When this information was given to Biden, however, the chairman passed. He was not about to try to stop a Supreme Court nominee by throwing an unauthorized shrimp dinner at him.

Nonetheless, in an accident of fate, these travel records also led Metzenbaum's aides unexpectedly back to Anita Hill. In much the same way that Nan Aron had quickly passed on her tip about Anita Hill, People For had deposited its massive cache of Thomas's travel records with Bonnie Goldstein, the chief investigator for Metzenbaum on the Labor Committee. Although it was the Judiciary Committee that would weigh Thomas's confirmation to the Supreme Court, the Labor Committee had jousted with Thomas for years over EEOC matters, and the aides involved with Metzenbaum's work on this committee were, if anything, even more zealous in their opposition to Thomas. Some of them had kept in close contact with the liberal interest groups intent on stopping Thomas's confirmation in any way they could.

In August, Goldstein got together with her counterpart in Kennedy's office to compare notes on the hundreds of pages of Thomas's documents. Kennedy was also a member of the Labor Committee, and his chief investigator there — a dogged, soft-spoken woman named Ricki Seidman, who had once been an investigator for People For — had also been poring over Thomas's travel records. Seidman and Goldstein were part of a secretive but powerful coterie of congressional aides who were trained investigators, hired to ferret out the kinds of hidden abuses — whether bank fraud or exploitation of migrant workers — that the nation's lawmakers were entrusted with correcting. Indeed, they had both worked as private investigators, and in this universe they were experts, far more seasoned than the relatively inexperienced investigators working for Biden.

That August day, Seidman was intrigued in particular by the unusual number of trips Thomas had taken to Oklahoma. She wondered whether Goldstein had any information that might explain them. Goldstein didn't know much about the trips (most of which had more to do with Dean Kothe than anything else, as it turned out), but she told Seidman that Metzenbaum's office had received a strange tip earlier in the summer from the Alliance for Justice. It seemed there was a law professor in Oklahoma who had worked for Thomas at the EEOC and who may have been sexually harassed by him. Perhaps, Goldstein thought, there was some connection.

Seidman, unlike the others who had been handed this information, was instantly alert to its explosive potential. She had worked closely with Nan Aron and George Kassouf on earlier judicial nomination fights, so she immediately called Kassouf and asked him about the law professor's allegation. Kassouf didn't know very much and explained that his only information had come from the dinner party the previous month.

Seidman's interest, however, was enough to light a fire under Metzenbaum's staff. Anita Hill was now seen as someone the committee ought to contact, and her name was passed to Gail Laster, a young black Yale Law School graduate who was working for Metzenbaum as counsel to a Labor subcommittee he chaired. Laster had worked in the public defender's office, where she had handled some wrenching trials, so her training as well as her racial sensitivity made her acutely aware of the danger she could be exposing Hill to. Sexual harassment was an emotional and divisive topic by itself, but such a charge leveled by a black woman against a black man, Laster knew, could ignite an especially bitter backlash. Beware, she warned those looking for pay dirt on Thomas, of getting what you think you want out of this investigation.

Laster began cautiously by calling two other women who had worked for Thomas at Education and the EEOC. (Their names and numbers, like Hill's, came from the Alliance for Justice.) They gave her very little to pursue. Then she called Hill, who was out. Laster left a message saying she was from Senator Metzenbaum's office in Washington and wanted to know about Clarence Thomas. A connection had been made; the official entanglement of Anita Hill had begun. It was Thursday, September 5, only five days before the confirmation hearings were to begin.

In making her first contact with the Senate, Hill proceeded cautiously. She returned Laster's call, but when asked how Thomas treated female employees, she sounded evasive, volunteering nothing unusual. Laster knew not to ask a direct question that could close off further inquiry. Instead, she just mentioned that there were "rumors" that Thomas had harassed women sexually.

"I'd follow up those rumors," Hill said stiffly.

Could Hill provide the names of any victims? Laster asked.

"I'll think about it" came the response.

Laster's artful phrasing — using "rumors," the plural — left Hill with the wrong impression: that the Senate knew of harassment cases other than her own. This misunderstanding proved crucial in emboldening her to go further.

Laster reported back to James Brudney, her supervisor on the Labor Committee. Later, Thomas's supporters would insinuate that Brudney was a close and possibly romantic friend of Hill's from Yale (which he had attended a year ahead of her) and that together they conspired to damage Thomas. But according to an eyewitness, on learning about Hill, Brudney did not seem to recognize her name. Instead, he casually told Laster to pursue the matter as she saw fit.

Meanwhile, Seidman had gotten approval from a superior on Kennedy's staff and contacted Hill herself, not realizing that Laster already had. Seidman's approach, too, was indirect, simply referring to an allegation that Thomas had harassed women at the EEOC. Hill quickly told her that Laster had called about this subject the day before and that she would neither "confirm nor deny" the allegation. But Hill did not close the door entirely: she agreed to talk to Seidman again.

The calls from Laster and Seidman presented, in Hill's view, a responsibility. The government — the very committee charged with evaluating Thomas's qualifications, Hill wrongly assumed, since Laster, Brudney, and Seidman all worked for the Labor, not the Judiciary, Committee — was now approaching her specifically about Thomas's harassment of women. She wanted to proceed cautiously and confidentially to protect both herself and Thomas from the public three-ring circus Gary Phillips had spoken of. But she also felt, again, as she would later describe it, "a duty to report."

"There is this question, why did you wait?" Hill later said about her role in the hearings. "Implicit in that is that I was sitting around . . . The point is that I knew this information . . . When general questions were asked, I didn't offer any information. I didn't wait. But when I was asked specifically about it, I answered. If I hadn't been asked, none of this would have happened."

By answering truthfully, however, Hill didn't realize she was losing control of her fate. Although she had worked at a politically connected law firm and held jobs in the Reagan administration, she was naive about the ways of Washington. By letting her guard down and answering the questions of two Senate aides, she had entered the political process. And given the stakes in this particular battle, with a pivotal seat on the Supreme Court hanging in the balance, the question was no longer whether the public would learn about her secret but when.

❖

Seidman was in an even more precarious position than Metzenbaum's aides. Her boss, Senator Kennedy, could scarcely afford to pursue any delicate sexual matter. Shortly before Seidman's first call to Hill, Floyd Brown's mudslinging television ad had aired, apparently proving more effective than its producer's wildest dreams. Confidants later explained that Kennedy was so chagrined by this and the other forms of negative publicity attending his nephew's rape trial that he feared his involvement on Hill's behalf could only be hurtful. Had Kennedy, with his tenacious staff and his solid standing in the African-American community, played his customary aggressive role, the outcome of the confirmation hearings might have been different. At the very least, it seems likely that Hill's allegation would have been taken seriously far sooner, allowing for deeper and broader investigation. But as it was, the ordinarily outspoken liberal conscience of the Senate was paralyzed by embarrassment.

So Seidman was forced to pass the ball. She urged Laster's supervisor, Jim Brudney, to take over. Hill had mentioned that she knew Brudney from law school, so Seidman thought Hill might be comfortable confiding in him. But Brudney had only the vaguest recollection of Hill. Aides had to hurriedly come up with a picture or physical description of her to help jog his memory. That done, Brudney was willing to approach her himself.

First, as promised, Seidman called Hill one last time, on September 9. To her surprise, she learned that over the weekend Hill had decided on her own to answer questions about Thomas's harassment of her. But again Hill sent mixed signals, saying she was not sure how far she wanted the information to go. Hill emphasized her unwillingness to give up her privacy, and Seidman offered some assurances — none of which could really be guaranteed — that her confidentiality would be maintained.

Hill then described a very general pattern of harassment by Thomas, including "requests for dates and sexual comments." She also mentioned that she had a corroborator, though she did not divulge Susan Hoerchner's name. Seidman suggested she might be more comfortable talking to someone she knew and gave her Brudney's name. Hill agreed to talk with him.

The next morning, Tuesday, September 10, the same day the hearings began, Brudney placed the phone call that would unhinge the carefully orchestrated confirmation proceedings. His notes of this conversation remain the single best snapshot of Hill's unvarnished and unrehearsed thoughts as she wavered on the brink of exposure.

Already Hill sensed some of the risks. She stressed to Brudney that she never would have come forward at all if it "hadn't been brought up to me specifically by Ricki [Seidman] and Gail [Laster]." And although she felt a responsibility to answer their questions, she confided in Brudney that she "feared" that unless other women came forward with similar accounts, her description of Thomas's outlandish behavior would be dismissed as "an isolated incident by someone who had recently been divorced." She had spent the weekend, she told Brudney, thinking "about whether [her] allegation would be helpful in [the confirmation] process" at all and had decided that it would, but probably only "if others involved experienced the same things." If she was the "only" woman ready to speak out, she feared that all of the "focus [would] be on her." In that case, Hill told Brudney, she wanted to cooperate only "in a private setting."

Hill was sophisticated enough to know that if it were only her word against Thomas's, the situation could blow up in her face. Her hope, as these notes suggest, was that her account was part of a broader investigation into Thomas's behavior — as Laster and Seidman's vague questions about "rumors" had led her to believe.

Having expressed her concerns, Hill described a troubling chain of events to Brudney. Some details were downright bizarre. After Hill related Thomas's comment about the Coke can, the former Supreme Court clerk carefully jotted down "PUBE REMARK." Later, Republican senators would question Hill's veracity by pointing out that Hill had failed to tell the FBI about the Coke can remark and other alleged "embellishments" that took them by surprise in her public testimony. Some would even imply darkly that feminist advisers had tempted Hill to concoct such details for partisan effect. But it is interesting how closely her later testimony matched the notes of her original conversation with Brudney.

Impressed with Hill's apparent credibility, Brudney relayed the gist of his conversation to his superiors on Metzenbaum's staff. Once the senator's staff was able to place the harassment allegation in the mouth of a highly believable law professor — a Yale Law School graduate, to boot — they decided that Metzenbaum himself finally had to be informed. And so, later in the day of Brudney's call, Metzenbaum's aides found the senator in his hideaway office in the Russell building.

Metzenbaum's reaction to the news that a woman whom Thomas had employed ten years earlier was about to accuse him of talking pruriently and pressuring her for dates said much about the culture of the Senate. Later, Metzenbaum would say that he instantly recognized the explosive nature of Hill's charge and felt it was too volatile for only one senator to handle, particularly one like himself, known to oppose Thomas. But according to a veteran Capitol Hill reporter with whom Metzenbaum spoke candidly soon after Hill's allegation emerged, his spontaneous reaction was somewhat different. "If that's sexual harassment," the notes of *Time* magazine's Hays Gorey show the senator said, "half the senators on Capitol Hill could be accused."

Metzenbaum seemed to want to keep a safe distance from this matter. He didn't even ask the identity of the accuser. The fact that his aides Laster and Brudney had initiated contact with her made him nervous. It really wasn't the responsibility of his office, or of these Labor Committee aides, to pursue such an allegation. The Judiciary Committee was handling the nomination. Metzenbaum ordered his staff to notify Biden's office immediately, thereby placing the hot potato in the chairman's lap. Biden, he reasoned, could deploy the Judiciary Committee's investigators and send them out to Oklahoma. But his own aides, who felt that their investigative abilities were far superior to Biden's, were told in no uncertain terms to back off.

❖

The following day, in the anteroom behind the ornate Caucus Room, Brudney cornered Harriet Grant, the straitlaced chief counsel to Biden's nominations unit. He told her that there was a woman he wanted her to speak to. He didn't want to go into any details then and there, but it had to do with Clarence Thomas and sexual harassment.

Grant was skeptical. She barely knew Brudney and was not accustomed to seeing the Labor Committee aide in her Judiciary hearing room. As far as she knew, she was now the only person in the country other than Brudney who knew of this allegation. The charge was, as she saw it, a terrible responsibility, a secret so dangerous that it could ruin the nominee no matter what its merits. And its last-minute timing made it even more suspect. If it leaked out or was mishandled, it would be her fault. Impeccably correct about process and prudent to the bone, Grant told Brudney that if this woman had something to say, she would have to contact the Judiciary Committee herself rather than the other way around.

It was a discouraging and unusual requirement, one not used by past chairmen, many of whom had been far more aggressive investigators. But Biden preferred to give the benefit of the doubt to the nominees. After all, the nominations unit heard many bizarre and often false allegations against judicial nominees and, especially in this case, did not want to appear to be in any way unfair. This charge thus presented a serious and unwanted problem. Grant dutifully informed her supervisor, Biden's staff director, Jeff Peck, and the two of them decided to keep it to themselves unless circumstances changed.

When Brudney called Hill to say that she would have to initiate contact with the Judiciary Committee if she wanted her allegation to be considered, she was confused, for she thought she was already dealing with the Judiciary Committee. And she hadn't contacted Laster and the others — they had pursued her. Why was Brudney now telling her to take the initiative? "From her perspective, dealing with all these different people and being handed from one person to another must have been like having a bad experience with a telephone company complaint," a Biden aide later observed.

Nevertheless, two days later, on September 12, as Thomas was being questioned by the committee about his views on abortion, Hill went ahead and called Grant, outlining her allegation and informing her that she had a corroborating witness, whom she did not name. Hill seemed articulate, sane, and candid to Grant. But Grant was still leery. She lectured Hill quite sternly about committee practices and procedures, warning her categorically that if she wanted to remain anonymous, there was nothing the committee could do with her information. The pivotal issue, said Grant, was that the committee would have to confront Thomas with the nature and source of the harassment charge — using Hill's name.

It was the first time anyone had described this scenario to Hill, and it took her aback. She had thought she was merely answering questions and adding her piece of information to a large collection of data. Instead, this was shaping up into a one-on-one confrontation with a former mentor, one almost certainly bound for the Supreme Court. Although Grant portrayed this so-called confrontation clause as accepted practice in such investigations, in fact it was Biden's practice, not the Senate's. Elsewhere, sources were able to provide anonymous tips that aides could investigate on their own without further involving the source. But this choice was not offered to Hill.

Clearly rattled, Hill told Grant she would consider her options. Hill and others said later that she had never opposed having her name attached to the charge if it was to be circulated only inside the committee. But what did worry her was the possibility that she might become the star of a public spectacle — particularly if she were the only accuser. She tried to learn from Grant whether the committee had found any other witnesses, and Grant indicated that Hill had made the only such complaint. As the call ended, Hill sounded discouraged to Grant but said she would try to have her corroborator call the committee. Grant concluded that all Hill wanted was to get the story off her chest. Probably it was, as Grant told other members of the staff, just a "cathartic" exercise for this woman.

During a break in the hearings, Grant found Ron Klain, Biden's chief counsel, in the anteroom behind the hearing room, and filled him in about her conversation with Hill. Klain, a former Supreme Court clerk with well-tuned political instincts, immediately realized that they had to tell Biden. The aides cut the senator off as he was entering the hearing room from the back entrance. In response to the information they provided, Biden had two questions: Is she credible? Grant replied that she thought she was. And is she willing to let the committee confront Thomas with her allegation? Grant said she thought not. (Hill would dispute this assessment.)

Biden's critics later asserted that the chairman didn't understand the seriousness of the matter, but he said he understood it all too well. "From the beginning it was clear," he said in an interview, "that this had the potential to become a giant incendiary bomb. We were handling one of the most controversial nominees in this century, and this woman who says he harassed her won't let us use her name. I was focused on how to get the truth — but without conducting a Star Chamber."

Unless Thomas would get a chance to respond to his accuser, Biden didn't think the matter should go any further. Senate rules did not require that nominees be informed of all allegations against them, but that was how Biden preferred to operate. Again, his instincts as a former defense lawyer and a public official who had been accused of wrongdoing made him sympathetic to the nominee. Besides, he already knew Thomas; he had even offered Thomas his private support. In contrast, Biden did not know Hill, and after hearing of her allegation, he made no move to talk to her himself. Nor did he send a staff investigator to talk to her, which was another option. He later explained that, after chairing a set of hearings on rape, he had been sensitized to the need for victims to decide on their own whether to press sexual charges. "It was immoral," he concluded, "to push her in any way."

Hill had no idea that her request for confidentiality was resulting in such paralysis. Assuming that her talks with Grant would surely trigger some kind of investigation, she busied herself with her classes and with lining up her corroborator, Susan Hoerchner, to talk to Grant.

Four days later, Hoerchner did indeed call Grant. She too said she wanted to preserve her anonymity. As a state judge in California, she feared retribution from the Republican administration of Governor Pete Wilson. What Hoerchner had to say, however, did not impress Grant. Hoerchner had a terrible memory for dates, and the only specific anecdote she recalled was that Thomas had warned Hill that she would ruin his career if she ever told anyone about his behavior. The statement, as Hoerchner recalled it, took place in an elevator at the EEOC — not at a going-away dinner, as Hill had said. All in all, Grant thought that Hoerchner, who sounded vague and nervous, would make a horrible corroborating witness. With this sort of support, Hill would be ripped to shreds. She thanked Hoerchner and politely told her to call again sometime if she remembered anything else. Hill's allegation seemed to be dying: by then, Thomas was well along in his hearings, and despite some skepticism over his contention that he had never once discussed *Roe v. Wade,* he was expected to be confirmed.

Back in Oklahoma, Hill was unhappy with the sluggish response she was getting. She spoke again to Brudney several times. He was torn between Metzenbaum's desire to keep some distance from the matter and his reluctance to have Hill, whom he had sought out and who had particularly trusted him, feel abandoned. But Brudney was not even sure whether the behavior Hill had described qualified as sexual harassment. He thought that if he wrote a memo to Metzenbaum, it would clarify whether the matter was serious enough to pursue. So Brudney called one of the country's foremost legal experts on sexual harassment, Professor Susan Deller Ross of Georgetown Law School, and hypothesized some situations that fit Hill's allegation. Ross responded that even if there had been no physical touching or threats to terminate someone who didn't agree to have sex, the behavior Brudney described sounded as if it could fit the legal definition of sexual harassment.

Uncomfortable playing a secret role as Hill's unofficial adviser, Brudney got Hill's permission to have Ross talk to her directly. Given the urgency of Brudney's request, Ross had already guessed that this matter probably concerned Clarence Thomas.

The introduction of Ross into the growing circle of those who knew Hill's secret was like lighting the fuse on Biden's "giant incendiary bomb." A highly respected lawyer and a well-known feminist, Ross had testified against the confirmation of Justice Anthony Kennedy because of his lower court rulings on sexual discrimination. She was immediately aware of how much damage Hill's charge could do to Thomas's nomination.

Ross quickly phoned Hill and spoke with her several times over the next few days. For Ross to counsel Hill effectively, she needed to know the particulars of the situation. Hill described her experience in detail, and these conversations with Ross crystallized into the core of a statement Hill would provide to the committee as a way of pushing her allegation forward — a goal Ross encouraged. But although she was an expert on harassment law, she did not feel competent to advise Hill on the politics of dealing with the committee, and with Hill's permission she brought in yet another outsider, Judith Lichtman, a feminist leader who had been among those opposing Thomas all summer.

Once a declared partisan such as Lichtman was added to the group, it was safe to assume that Hill's allegation was not going to disappear. Other members of the leading liberal interest groups soon learned of the charge too. Yet they all had limited room for maneuvering. Kennedy and Metzenbaum weren't interested in taking on the issue. Leahy had a policy of not meeting with such political interest groups. And

Biden's door was even more firmly shut against them. Biden had been furious at the liberal lobbying groups when, after he had privately agreed to work with them in 1987 to defeat Bork, they had leaked the agreement to the press. He had vowed never to attend another of their meetings.

In Kennedy's office, though, several senior women on the staff were concerned that days were passing, the hearings were approaching a vote, and Hill's allegation was going nowhere. These aides were of a different generation and a different gender from the senators who were ducking the issue, and they took Hill and her charge seriously. Sexual harassment was an area of law that had evolved only in the past ten years, and the staff members were far more aware of its gravity than the senators. With Kennedy too compromised even to touch the matter, surrogates who could prod Biden would have to be found.

On September 16, Ellen Lovell, Leahy's chief of staff, was surprised to get a phone call from one of Kennedy's top aides, Ranny Cooper. In a neutral tone, Cooper conveyed the facts of Hill's allegation and asked Lovell what she thought. Lovell instantly recognized a bombshell about to drop. She couldn't decide whether Kennedy's aide was genuinely perplexed about how to proceed or was telling her about the allegation in order to get Leahy involved. But as a nonlawyer, she said, she would have to share this with Leahy's chief counsel, Ann Harkins. The two women spoke and immediately sensed, as one later put it, "total danger."

Instead of seeing the risk of getting involved, the Leahy staff members saw the risk of *not* getting involved. If this woman was credible, they reasoned, and not taken seriously, and if she then went public, the committee would look inept at best and complicit in a cover-up at worst. After learning a few more details from Brudney — Kennedy's aides had refused to brief the Leahy aides fully, on the grounds that they couldn't seem too involved — Lovell and Harkins were frankly scared. They closed the office door behind them and tried to calculate how many people already knew about Anita Hill. When they reached the fingers of two hands, they realized this story would never stay secret. They would have to act.

They called Biden's longtime chief of staff, Ted Kaufman, to ask for a full briefing. He did not seem to know what they were talking about. Soon afterward, he called back to schedule a meeting for them with

Harriet Grant. When they spoke, Grant seemed to dismiss Hill, asserting that she had merely wanted to "get it off her chest." To them, Grant seemed more than willing to let the matter drop.

Leahy's aides called Kaufman back. "You've got to at least send some investigators so that the committee can evaluate the situation," they pleaded.

But Kaufman, they recalled later, replied, "It's a closed case."

Meanwhile, by September 19, the next to last day of the confirmation hearings, Hill was exasperated. Her initial reluctance to come forward had now more or less evaporated, and she wanted the Senate committee to be aware of the information she had provided about Thomas before it voted on the nomination. In a conversation with Grant, she asked impatiently, "What do I need to do to get the attention of the full committee?" Grant again told Hill that she would have to allow Thomas to be confronted with her charge by name. Hill, who apparently had not understood the reason for the delay, now said she had no objection. The hearings were almost over, and only four senators — Metzenbaum, Biden, Kennedy, and Leahy — were even aware that she existed.

At about this point, Leahy spoke to Biden. It is unclear whether he pushed Biden into taking action or Hill's new willingness to be named changed the chairman's mind. In any case, shortly before the hearings ended, one of Biden's aides passed a Leahy aide in the hallway and said, "We've done something you'll be happy about." The aide knew exactly what this meant: Biden had finally sent the FBI to talk to Hill.

❖

The use of the FBI this time was controversial in the Judiciary Committee. The FBI's boss and chief client in any administration is ultimately the president, and in this instance the needs of the committee were different from those of the White House, which of course was sponsoring Thomas. The committee had its own staff of investigators, but Biden was afraid that using them would look partisan. Mindful of appearances, he sent the FBI to interview Hill.

Grant now called both Hill and Hoerchner and told them that if Hill's allegation was to be pursued by the committee, the FBI would have to investigate both of them. Hoerchner, especially, was horrified at the notion. Hill too thought it strange that rather than investigating her allegation, Biden wanted to send the FBI to her doorstep. Hoerchner later said, "They didn't use the word 'interview,' it was 'investigation.' That had shades of J. Edgar Hoover."

Although Brudney assured Hill that an FBI interview was part of the usual procedure with such an allegation, it took Hill three or four more days to give the FBI permission to come see her. In the meantime, on Friday, September 20, the confirmation hearings were ending. Grant, who by now had endured more abrupt starts and stops from Hill than a high school driving instructor, was feeling literally sick. Biden caught her during the final day of hearings and asked what was going on. She told him that she still hadn't heard from Hill.

"For the moment," he said, "the rest of us all feel relieved. But you are holding a bomb, and it's ticking."

Grant, who felt almost single-handedly responsible at this point, started to leave messages for Hill at her office, her home, and anywhere else she could think of. Finally, that Friday Hill called back and said she needed another day to think. On Saturday, at two in the afternoon, Grant called Hill, as they had arranged. Hill said she had made up her mind: she would not talk to the FBI. She was afraid that she would lose control of her own accusation, that it would be somehow distorted, and that with the stakes so high, the committee would get her story through a hostile filter. Grant thought, "That's it. She wants to let it rest."

But on Monday, September 23, with the vote on Thomas due at the end of the week, Hill called Grant again. To Grant's surprise, Hill had devised a comfortable way to go forward, having consulted with her new feminist advisers and Brudney. She had decided to prepare a written statement summarizing the information she had given orally to an array of Senate aides. She wanted to send the committee members this statement, written in her own words, so that her charges would not be garbled or slanted by the FBI or anyone else.

Grant was amazed; she had not realized that getting Hill to specify her allegation under her own name would be that simple. She had not understood that Hill's misgivings had centered less on her fear of going forward than on her fear of being misconstrued. Grant promised that she would personally stand right next to the fax machine and catch Hill's statement as soon as it arrived.

A few minutes later, Grant, Peck, and Klain — Biden's most trusted aides — grabbed the paper as it came inching through the Judiciary

Committee's machine. Ross, the legal harassment expert, had emphasized the need for specificity, and Hill's four-page, typewritten statement did not fall short.

The first page of this "Statement of Anita F. Hill," which was signed
and dated, summarized her résumé and the fact that Thomas had
pressured her to date him. On the second page, Hill described how
these requests evolved into "vivid" discussions of Thomas's sexual
interests, including descriptions of pornographic films with "women
having sex with animals and films involving group sex or rape scenes"
and depictions of "individuals with large penises or breasts involved
in various sex acts." The last part of the statement described how
Thomas had made a comment at her farewell dinner that she would
"always remember" — that if she ever told anyone about his behavior
"it could ruin my career."

Biden's aides, as one of them later recalled, had a single, unanimous
reaction: "Holy shit!" Suddenly the aides were faced with the graphic
details. With these four pieces of paper, Hill's complaint was no longer
abstract. The gravity of the situation was clear.

Klain took the statement to Biden. Peck informed the White House
and the FBI. And Grant took a copy to her Republican counterpart
on Strom Thurmond's staff, for the first time formally notifying the
opposition. As Thurmond's aide, a polite southerner, read the statement from one page to the next, her eyes widened dramatically.

Grant asked her how she thought the nominee would respond. In
a drawl worthy of her boss, the Republican aide answered without a
second's hesitation: "Cat-egorical de-ni-al."

11

❖

The Leak

ONCE ANITA HILL surfaced, the Republicans immediately saw their mission clearly: to protect and defend Clarence Thomas. The ranking Republican on the Judiciary Committee, Strom Thurmond, was not likely to be much bothered by Hill's allegations in the first place. At nearly ninety years of age, he was notorious among female aides and reporters on Capitol Hill for his unabashed flirtations, which frequently included unsought pats and squeezes. It was a running joke that it was not safe for women to get into the Senators Only elevator if Thurmond was on board. He may have been a reformed segregationist, but he remained an unrepentant and unapologetic son of the Old South in his attitudes toward "lovely ladies," as he still called them.

Thurmond's staff, even more than most, had come to operate almost independently of the increasingly cranky and detached senator. And so when the matter of Anita Hill arose, Thurmond wasn't told all the details. He was made generally aware during that last week in September that a charge of some sort had been leveled against Thomas by an accuser who did not want to be publicly identified. Under such circumstances, his staff knew, he would want the matter investigated quietly. On many other judicial nominations, anonymous charges had been investigated and left buried. That would suit the Republicans in this case just fine.

Thurmond's formidable top aides, Robert "Duke" Short, the chief of staff and a trained law enforcement investigator from South Carolina, and the chief counsel, Terry Wooten, decided to keep Hill's statement to themselves. There was a Judiciary Committee rule that whenever the FBI was sent in to investigate a charge, all fourteen committee members had to be informed within twenty-four hours. But this time, mysteriously, the rule was ignored.

As for the Democrats, Biden decided that he would talk to them himself, probably when the FBI reported back. But he left the Republicans' briefings up to Thurmond, and Thurmond and his staff apparently felt no obligation to alert their colleagues. Arlen Specter only learned about Hill that week because he happened to speak with an informed Democratic member and supporter of Thomas, Dennis DeConcini, in a Senate corridor. Similarly Alan Simpson, the tall, lanky Republican from Wyoming, was surprised to learn of Hill's charges when he broke into an animated conversation his Democratic colleagues were having. Orrin Hatch also first learned of the allegations secondhand, seeing neither Hill's statement nor the FBI report. And two of the Republican senators on the committee, Iowa's Charles Grassley and Colorado's Hank Brown, went ahead and voted to confirm Thomas without having the slightest idea that Hill or her charge existed. Later, when he found out he had been left in the dark, Brown was furious.

Thurmond's staff reasoned that the more people who were told about Hill's statement, the more likely it was that her charge would leak out and damage Thomas. And damage control was clearly the Republicans' aim. "Washington is the rumor mill of the world," observed Terry Wooten. "It didn't look like it was going to develop into a big deal. There was an effort to control the damage."

Wooten may have considered Hill's charge no "big deal," but the Bush administration — which had believed that it was just days away from securing the Supreme Court seat for Thomas — had a different view. Biden's aides had immediately dispatched copies of Hill's statement that Monday to both Fred McClure's congressional affairs office and the Justice Department. McClure, the administration's point man on the nomination, was in San Francisco giving a luncheon speech, and his staff frantically began trying to reach him.

McClure was en route to the San Francisco airport in a limousine when the radio dispatcher suddenly asked, "Do you have a Mr. McClure in your limo? Have him call the office. It's an emergency." Grabbing his cellular phone, McClure had a cryptic conversation with his deputy, who described the general outline of the day's events. "It scared the living daylights out of me because I knew what it could possibly do," recalled McClure, who arrived back in Washington after midnight on Tuesday morning and headed straight for the White House.

By then, Hill had been contacted by the FBI. When she arrived home on Monday evening after a full day of teaching, she found a message on her answering machine that the Oklahoma City branch office of the FBI wanted to talk to her as soon as possible. About six-thirty, two agents, John B. Luton and Jolene Smith Jameson, arrived at her home on South Berry Street. The agents told Hill that if she found the questions too embarrassing, she could speak alone with the female agent. That proved unnecessary, and Hill answered all the questions methodically. The agents left her with the impression, Hill later said, that they would probably contact her again with follow-up questions. Susan Hoerchner was interviewed at her home in California later that same night.

After reviewing Hill's statement, the White House, like Thurmond's office, tried to keep a tight lid on the Anita Hill matter. Besides McClure and his deputy, only President Bush, Chief of Staff Sununu, the White House counsel Boyden Gray and his deputy Lee Liberman, and one or two aides were told of the problem. (Duberstein and Danforth had heard about the statement from Biden's staff.)

For the next few days, the Republicans were paralyzed by anxiety, waiting for the FBI to complete its investigation and especially its crucial interview with Thomas. It was excruciatingly difficult for Danforth: in order not to taint the FBI investigation, he could not even alert his friend about Hill's charge, although a Democratic senator said later that he would be shocked if Thomas had not been tipped off. For the moment, the Republicans could do little more than wait and wonder how Thomas would respond.

At nine forty-five in the morning on Wednesday, September 25, two days after Hill's statement had been faxed, Lee Liberman called Thomas to inform him that a new, unspecified charge had surfaced and that the FBI would need to interview him. Thomas later said his reaction was "panic." But he set up an interview with the FBI at his house for that afternoon. More than an hour after the appointed time, Thomas called Liberman back. He was literally sick with anxiety, he said. The FBI still hadn't arrived.

When the agents — stuck in terrible traffic, it turned out — finally got to his house in suburban Virginia and told him the details of the allegation, Thomas, according to his Senate testimony, was "stunned," "pained," and "confused." When he found out the source of the charge, his first words were "Anita? You can't — you've got to be kidding. This can't be true."

As Thurmond's aide had predicted, Thomas categorically denied all of Hill's accusations. He had never once asked her out on a date, he told the agents. He had had no relationship with her outside work. And certainly, he said, he had never discussed pornographic materials with her. Her story was, in short, a monstrous, despicable lie.

In one of a series of agonized telephone conversations after the FBI interview, Thomas told Danforth that he was devastated by Hill's allegations. He thought of Anita Hill as a protégé and friend. He couldn't begin to imagine what had possessed her to make these baseless charges. If he had earlier shown a propensity to portray himself as the hapless victim of unfair treatment, now, more than ever before, Thomas was consumed with outrage.

Danforth believed him unequivocally. "These charges did not comport with the Clarence Thomas I had known all these years," he said in a later interview. He viewed Hill's story as a vicious extension of all the other mud that had been hurled at Thomas throughout the summer, no different from the other "crap," as he put it, that he had dealt with, from the allegations of wife-beating to the charges that Thomas's praise for Louis Farrakhan made him an anti-Semite. On his friend's word alone, Danforth accepted Thomas's assertion that this was just more of the same.

It was perhaps understandable that Danforth would take Thomas's word on faith. But Danforth was so certain of his own rectitude and so sure of his judgment of his protégé — who was, after all, a reflection to some extent on himself — that he never stopped to wonder whether there might be some truth in Hill's story. He made no effort to question her or otherwise to assess the facts she alleged. In fact, he later admitted that he assured Thomas that "whether or not the charge was true," he would "support him to the end." As these comments reflect, Danforth's mind was made up before the hearings began. From the time that Hill surfaced, his "mission" — as those around him described his zealous pursuit of the goal — was to protect Thomas from being smeared, even if, as it turned out, it meant that Hill would undergo similar or worse treatment.

The White House, meanwhile, was immensely relieved by the re-

sults of the FBI interview. Anything less than complete and total denial, one senior White House official later admitted, would have been
a disaster; as he said, "The force of Thomas's conviction is what saved
it. If he'd given an inch, he would have been dead."

The Democrats, however, were in shock over Thomas's categorical
denial. Biden and his staff were, according to one of his top aides,
"blown away" by the FBI report, which was completed right after the
interview with Thomas. They had expected Thomas to deny aspects
of Hill's story but not the whole thing. After seeing the report, the
Democrats were faced with a terrible situation; they had an unknown
accuser making explosive allegations and a nearly confirmed nominee
to the Supreme Court unequivocally denying them. Clearly, one of
them was lying, and lying to the FBI was a federal offense. Suddenly
the stakes were very high and very nasty. For Biden, there would be
no politic, painless way out of this jam — except, perhaps, by avoiding any real attempt to deal with it.

If Biden thought that Hill's charge raised serious, potentially disqualifying questions about Thomas's character and conduct, as he
later asserted, he did not act accordingly. The committee was scheduled to vote in just two days, and neither he nor any other senator
had spoken to Hill in an effort to draw an independent judgment
about her credibility. Metzenbaum might have been expected to be
more aggressive, but when the FBI report appeared and mentioned the
contacts between Hill and his aides, any hope that he would support
her cause also evaporated. Instead, worried that it might seem as if he
were somehow behind Hill's assault, Metzenbaum again warned his
staff to stay out of the matter. No one, it seemed, saw any advantage
in getting too close.

❖

Having met all of Harriet Grant's demands and submitted to the FBI
interview, Hill now assumed that her statement would be circulated
to all the members of the Judiciary Committee before they voted. As
she understood it, she had fulfilled every requirement set by Biden.

So on that same Wednesday, she faxed a second copy of her statement, this time with the typographical errors corrected and thus suitable for distribution. But when she asked Grant when the panelists
would read it, Grant was noncommittal. Her alarm growing, Hill

asked whether Grant planned to distribute copies at all. To her surprise, Grant said it wasn't her decision to make. Instead, Grant assured her — incorrectly, as it turned out — that all the other senators would see the FBI report, or at least summaries of the interviews.

Hill, who had taken pains to find exactly the right words to express her allegation, was now beside herself. While she had originally been uncertain about how far she wanted to take her charge, once she had agreed to tell her story, she expected that at least the members of the Judiciary Committee would hear it. But nearly three weeks had passed since her first conversation with Laster and Seidman, and only Biden and a few other senators knew of her allegation against Thomas. Fewer still had seen her detailed description of it. Meanwhile, the committee vote was less than forty-eight hours away.

With nowhere to turn and no one representing her interests in the Senate, on Thursday, September 26, the day before the committee vote, Hill tracked down an old friend who in turn contacted an aide to Paul Simon, the liberal Democrat from Illinois, who was a member of the Judiciary Committee. In some ways, bringing Simon in at this point was like to a desperate Hail Mary pass in football, since virtually every sympathetic Democratic senator by now had been asked to charge forward with Hill's story, though none seemed anxious to run with it.

Simon told Biden that he wanted to see Hill's statement, but one of Biden's aides brought him the FBI report instead. A former newspaper editor, Simon apparently had some of the curiosity and gumption his peers lacked, because at this point he decided to call Hill. As he later put it, "I wanted to find out if she was a flake."

What he heard was impressive. Hill seemed dignified and serious. Moreover, he was amazed to hear that she was so perturbed that her allegations hadn't reached the Judiciary Committee members that she was thinking of sending her statement to all hundred members of the Senate. When Simon warned her that there was no way her anonymity would be preserved under such circumstances, Hill seemed to hesitate. But Simon was struck by her determination; he later said she "clearly wanted this information out."

In Leahy's office, concern was also building on that Thursday. Some Democrats still knew nothing. Biden seemed content to brief the members *ad seriatim* as he encountered them. But with only twenty-four hours remaining before the committee vote, Biden, Leahy knew, had yet to inform the panel's most influential Democratic member, Howell Heflin. Heflin, whose position on Thomas was not known, had indicated that he was planning to deliver a floor speech announcing his vote that day. Because Heflin was a conservative southerner whose opposition had done much to turn the tide against Bork, his vote was considered crucial, highly persuasive to other Democrats on the committee and in the Senate at large.

Leahy urged Biden to talk with Heflin before he took a public stand. Biden did so, but it turned out that Heflin, to the surprise of many, had already decided to vote against Thomas because he was troubled by his "confirmation conversion" — Thomas's effort to back away from his conservative record.

Any of these senators — as well as George Mitchell, the Senate majority leader, and the Senate minority leader, Robert Dole, both of whom Biden had dutifully briefed about Hill — could have moved to put off the committee vote for a week in order to investigate further. But no one did. Instead, the Senate leaders apparently concurred in Biden's assessment that the sexual harassment charge against Thomas should be handled privately by the Judiciary Committee; if it died quietly, so be it. No thought was given to sharing Hill's allegations with the rest of the Senate before it too voted on Thomas's confirmation.

On Friday morning, September 27, the day of the committee vote, the liberal constitutional scholar Laurence Tribe, one of Harvard Law School's most prominent professors and a longtime adviser to Biden, surprised the chairman by calling to underscore the seriousness of Hill's allegations. (Tribe had heard about Hill from a young African-American colleague, Professor Charles Ogletree, who had been pressed into action by one of Hill's friends.) Tribe's call finally persuaded Biden to distribute copies of Hill's statement — in sealed envelopes marked "Senators' Eyes Only" — to all the Democrats on the committee. If Tribe, an outsider to the entire process, knew of Hill, Biden could no longer rest assured that her story wouldn't leak. And if her charge did get out, and the public learned that the committee members had voted without even bothering to read what she had to say, the chairman might suffer huge embarrassment.

As the committee members filed into the Senate Caucus Room later that morning, reporters were buzzing about the upcoming vote. Biden had appeared on the Senate floor earlier to announce his vote: after much agonizing, he had decided to oppose the nominee because of his judicial philosophy. Hating to disappoint, he explained that "every instinct in me wanted to support Clarence Thomas." He went out of his way to suggest that any charges of improper conduct — he made no mention of Hill or her allegations, of course — were not worthy of debate. "For this senator," he said, "there is no question with respect to the nominee's character." To those watching, Biden's defensive speech was as inexplicable as it was odd.

Then, before the final debate leading up to the vote, several reporters noticed that many of the Democratic senators were scrutinizing a document while they waited. And when the vote finally came, the result was a surprise: the committee members, a majority of whom had been expected to recommend Thomas, split evenly, 7–7. A tie meant sending the nomination on to the Senate with no recommendation at all, a sign that Thomas's confirmation was suddenly not the sure bet everybody thought.

Alarmed that the unexpected tie vote would pique the curiosity of reporters and perhaps push Hill's story into the public domain, Danforth and Duberstein pressed for an immediate floor vote on the nomination. Ordinarily, the process would move at a more leisurely pace, but the Republicans lobbied to have the final vote of the full Senate that very weekend. When Metzenbaum protested, the Senate leaders worked out a compromise: the vote was scheduled for Tuesday, October 8, ten days hence.

No one who was aware of Hill's allegations knew whether they would leak to the public during this hiatus. But given the way the Senate operated, even if the charges did get out, there would not be enough time to get beyond the "he said, she said" stalemate that had so paralyzed the Judiciary Committee.

———❖———

As the Republicans had feared, the press was indeed curious about the unexpected tie vote. In particular, Nina Totenberg, the legal affairs correspondent for National Public Radio (NPR), sensed that something was wrong. Alerted by Biden's odd speech, "I started kicking the tires, and they started popping," she recalled. "If I'd had anything else to do that week, nothing would have happened." As it was, she began calling on her many sources, including those inside the liberal interest groups and senatorial staffs; at least one of them was certain to know of any new problems in the confirmation proceedings.

Totenberg, an intrepid newshound with a leonine mane of strawberry blond hair and a regal manner to match, had already brought down one Supreme Court nominee: it was her NPR broadcast about Douglas Ginsburg's use of marijuana that had forced the judge to withdraw his name. Totenberg was known as Washington's most aggressive Supreme Court reporter, a true insider in the most secret branch of the government. At high-level judicial conferences, Totenberg — whose husband was a former senator — would go off to dine with the justices, leaving her jealous competitors behind.

After just a few calls, Totenberg discovered that the FBI had recently investigated a new charge against Thomas, something serious. Then she learned that it had to do with a tip she herself had received much earlier in the summer, though it was little more than a rumor about Thomas and sexual harassment. At the time, she had been unable to get anywhere with the story; now she intensified her efforts.

Totenberg wasn't alone in picking up the scent of trouble. *Newsday*'s Timothy Phelps, who had broken several tough stories about Thomas, also figured out that the 7–7 committee vote and Biden's peculiar speech signaled problems. The day after the vote, he revealed that the FBI had reopened its background investigation and that there was a new allegation involving personal misconduct.

As the reporters scouted for information, the circle of those who knew about the charge, which Hill had carefully kept so small for so long, was widening. That weekend, her allegations were discussed during at least two Washington dinners attended by several Democratic party activists — including one attended by a lobbyist for the National Abortion Rights Action League, which was virulently opposed to Thomas. One young, well-connected Democratic operative, Tom Donilon, managed to make appearances at both dinner parties, leaving friendly Biden aides who knew his popularity with the press on tenterhooks about how much longer the secret could keep. And by the end of the weekend, several of the most powerful liberal activists — including Ralph Neas of the Leadership Conference on Civil Rights, Kate Michelman of the National Organization for Women, Anthony Podesta, a former director of People for the American Way, and Wade Henderson of the NAACP — were also aware to varying degrees of Hill's allegations and waiting anxiously to see what would happen.

That Saturday, Judith Lichtman, the feminist head of the Women's Legal Defense Fund, who had been brought in by Susan Deller Ross to advise Hill, was so frustrated by the Judiciary Committee's inaction that she told Ross she wanted to take Hill's charge to sympathetic senators outside the committee. Ross warned her not to, since Hill did not want the issue made public. But Lichtman was not content just to give up. Earlier in the week, she had told a Metzenbaum aide, according to his notes, that she personally planned to "go after" a copy of Hill's "affidavit." (It remains unclear whether she ever got a copy of the statement. After the allegation leaked, Lichtman said she never had one; she also contradicted the Metzenbaum aide's notes.)

Astonishingly, though, by the end of the weekend the story had still not appeared in the press. In fact, the lid stayed on all through the first week in October. The White House and some of Danforth's aides fully expected to see it break every day. Armstrong Williams heard a rumor that "another bomb was going to be dropped" on Thomas soon after the committee's vote. In retrospect, the surprising thing is not that Hill's allegation reached the press but that it took such a long time to do so.

By midweek, Totenberg had narrowed the harassment story down to Hill, whom she called for comment. Hill refused to cooperate. Though frustrated by the official inaction, she was anxious to avoid a public spectacle and thus eager to keep the mess out of the newspapers. But she was alarmed, she told Brudney during that week, that Totenberg already seemed to know so much about her statement.

Phelps, meanwhile, was also digging deeper into the story. Earlier in the summer, he too had learned — either from one of the interest groups or from a sympathetic Senate source — that a law professor named Anita Hill in Oklahoma thought Thomas had sexually harassed her. At the time, Phelps had been sworn by his source not to ask Hill about it directly. But in the week after the committee's vote, Phelps met with Senator Simon about another story concerning Thomas. Guessing that Hill's allegations might be behind the FBI's resurgent investigation, Phelps asked Simon if he thought there was any chance the nomination would be stopped.

"Not unless someone with important information decides to go public," Simon replied.

"You mean the law professor from Oklahoma?" Phelps said, bluffing. Simon's amazed reaction — "How do you know about *that?*" he asked — gave Phelps the momentum he needed. With Simon indirectly confirming that Hill was the source of new allegations, Phelps felt released from his promise, and he too began trying to get in touch with her.

By Friday, October 4, with the full Senate scheduled to vote on the following Tuesday, Totenberg had either been read portions of Hill's statement or had obtained an unsigned or draft copy of it. In either case, she was too uncertain of the authenticity of her information to go on the air with it. Phelps, meanwhile, had been leaked nothing, but he was piecing together the general outlines of the story.

Back in Oklahoma, Hill was nonplussed. She had no idea where the leaks were coming from, yet every hour her identity seemed closer to being made public. And the reporters were playing hardball. Toward the end of the week, Totenberg warned her that she might go ahead with the story whether or not Hill cooperated.

In an attempt to get some control of the situation, Hill told both Totenberg and Phelps — who by then were calling incessantly — that she would comment only if and when they obtained copies of her statement to the Senate. Charles Ogletree, the Harvard law professor, had warned her not to be bluffed into being the source for her own story, and she thought that by setting these limits she would get some measure of protection. It also would ensure that if the story broke, her own words — expressed so precisely in her statement — would be accurately represented.

Phelps and Totenberg were racing against both time and each other. Each knew about the other, and each was relying on some of the same sources: the Judiciary Committee members, their staffs, and the various activists in the liberal interest groups. Although later there would be intense curiosity about who leaked Hill's statement, it is unlikely that any one person was responsible. In all probability, the leak was really several leaks that came from a combination of people, all of whom, to varying degrees, had firsthand knowledge of her story.

Later, the Republican senators would protest vehemently that the FBI report itself had been leaked, in violation of federal law. This charge created a major diversion throughout the hearings and ultimately led to a federal investigation. But the investigation proved that it was a false issue: no FBI reports on the matter ever did leak, and no FBI documents were ever the basis of any news report. The only portions of any FBI documents to be publicized were brief sections from Hill's confidential file read out loud during the hearings by one of the Republicans, Orrin Hatch, and bits of purported confidential FBI interviews later published by David Brock. Thus, the publication of Hill's story may have done a disservice to her and to Thomas, but it was not even remotely a crime. It was just business as usual in the Capitol.

By Saturday, October 5, even without documents, Phelps had enough information to go with a story about Hill. But because he had not met her requirement that he have an actual copy of her statement, he was unable to get her to comment or otherwise cooperate. Hill, meanwhile, had the distinct impression that Phelps had a source who had seen her statement.

Paul Simon, who talked with Phelps that week, had seen both Hill's statement and the FBI report, and he almost certainly helped Phelps get enough information to go to press. Since Totenberg had also been in touch with the senator and had left him with the impression that she actually had a copy of Hill's statement, Simon may have believed that the story was about to become public and concluded that he was not the primary source.

In fact, that Saturday afternoon Totenberg was frantically trying to get hold of a copy of the statement in order to persuade Hill to cooperate in an interview. She reached Ricki Seidman, in Kennedy's office, but Seidman said that only senators had seen the statement. Seidman then called Brudney, who was doing research in the Library of Congress. Brudney had not told Seidman that he had a copy of Hill's statement — an unsigned early draft that he had convinced Hill to fax to him. In fact, he had both the statement and the notes of his first conversation with Hill with him in his briefcase for safekeeping. Now he related some of the information to Seidman from the statement and notes without revealing the source.

Not long afterward, at 2:26 that afternoon, Totenberg again spoke with Hill, and this time she read from a document that sounded like the statement. Now that Totenberg had met her condition, Hill finally agreed to cooperate.

Totenberg placed several calls immediately after taping Hill's first public interview. First she telephoned Seidman, to say she had the story and that it would run the next day. Then she called Lichtman with the same news. A little while later, Brudney, who had evidently spoken to either Seidman or Lichtman, told his supervisor that Totenberg had the story. With this inner circle informed, at 5:30 P.M. Totenberg called the White House for comment.

❖

In the meantime, Hill alerted the dean at the law school and her family out on the farm in Lone Tree that she was about to make some news. She also made a call that day that shows just how baffled she was about the leaks and how painful her push into the limelight was. She called Michael Middleton, the Missouri law professor who had been one of Thomas's top aides when she was at the EEOC. Middleton had been friendly with both of them and was considered reliable and straightforward by his colleagues. She thought that perhaps Thomas had confided in Middleton about her charges and that Middleton had either been involved in the leak or at least might know something more.

But to Middleton "it was a call out of the blue." He told Hill he had heard nothing. He could tell that Hill, whom he liked and respected, was deeply upset by the whole affair; his response, he said later, was to tell her how sorry he was to hear that she was about to get into such a terrible confrontation. Although he did not come right out and say so, he believed that she could not possibly prevail against Thomas, whom he liked but regarded as one of the toughest and slickest operators he had ever seen. "Anyone with that kind of brass," as Middleton later put it, "is not going to be killed by a young lady saying something happened in a room between them ten years ago."

During their phone conversation, Hill sounded resigned, telling Middleton, "Now that it's out there, if the committee asks, I have to tell the truth. I can't deny it."

Trying to cheer her up, Middleton said somewhat halfheartedly, "You're a winner, no matter what. Always were, always will be."

❖

That Saturday night, Thomas was at home with his wife. At seventhirty he received a phone call that he later said changed his whole life. "I was told this was going to be in the press," he recalled during the hearings. "I died. The person you knew, whether you voted for me or against me, died."

A short time later, the White House was forced to issue a public statement denying Hill's allegations. At 8:45 P.M. Phelps's story was going out over the *Los Angeles Times–Washington Post* news service; Totenberg would be broadcasting the next morning.

At almost midnight Lee Liberman called John Mackey, the Justice Department aide who had helped Thomas get through earlier confirmation fights. Only the day before, Mackey had told Liberman that he thought they could count on more than sixty votes to confirm Thomas "unless an atom bomb hit." At the time, he knew nothing of Hill's allegations, although he had heard rumors of some new trouble brewing.

At that hour he was half asleep, watching a sports event on television. Liberman's call jolted him awake. "Mackey," she said, "the bomb has gone off."

12

❖

Naive,
Not Stupid

AS THE PRESSES at *Newsday*'s Long Island plant rolled the name of Anita Hill into the public consciousness, in Oklahoma Hill fretted over how her family would handle her new notoriety. Except for her nephew Gary, the *Washington Post* reporter, her relatives had mainly been exposed to the press by placing marriage and death notices in the local paper.

"My parents are older, and they lead a somewhat sheltered life," she explained later. "They have their own world." Preparing them for the possibility that a story of a sexual nature concerning herself and Clarence Thomas might soon be published was terribly difficult. When she told her father the gist of Thomas's behavior — a secret she had been too "embarrassed" ever to tell her parents about before — "he was," she recalled, "as angry as I remember seeing him in a long time." To her parents, she was still the baby, Faye.

Initially Hill was not at all sure how big the Phelps and Totenberg stories would be. Given the dilatory way in which the Senate had treated her, she imagined that "a few reporters would care, and that would be it," according to a friend who spoke with her just before the story broke. "It seemed fairly simple. We weren't even sure she'd be called to testify. No one anticipated striking a nerve."

When Hill notified the law school's dean, David Swank, about the story, he took her news with equanimity, although in the coming days other members of the administration would make it clear that they wished she hadn't gotten involved. But no one who knew her well thought Hill had any political axes to grind or had ever sought out

· 258 ·

trouble, so now they supported her for doing what looked like an unpleasant civic duty.

Although Hill had volunteered at a women's social service center in Norman and worked in a program that provided transportation to the elderly and handicapped, she was not generally seen as politically active at the law school. Probably the most visible stand she had taken was to help draft a law school policy against hate speech after racist epithets had been scrawled on the school's sidewalks. Hill was also an adviser to the law school's black student association and had opposed racial discrimination by some of the white fraternities. But compared with many other faculty members, she was mild and moderate. Teree Foster, who befriended Hill at the law school but subsequently left Norman to become the dean of West Virginia University's College of Law, said that "my acquaintance with her had persuaded me that she is largely apolitical . . . If you tortured me, I couldn't tell you what her politics were."

If anything, Hill was uncomfortable with people she regarded as politically extreme. After all, as Joel Paul recounted, she had turned down his offer to consider the teaching post at American University because she thought the school was "a bit too progressive for her." In short, Hill was a most unlikely star for the great political drama that was about to unfold. And only by understanding how little prepared she was to find herself at the center of a twentieth-century culture war can the hapless nature of her national debut be fully comprehended.

❖

On Saturday night, October 5, Hill went out to dinner with two other law professors from Oklahoma, including her best friend, Shirley Wiegand. Her social life now centered around her bonds with a few other members of the law school faculty and their spouses, who got together regularly for dinners at various restaurants and watering holes. The group called itself the Bar Review. That evening, Hill seemed calm and collected as usual, wondering almost academically whether anyone would care about her charge.

It did not take long, however, for Hill to realize that she had badly underestimated the public interest. At about the time she was arriving home from dinner, the *Newsday* story was being transmitted to more than three hundred newspapers across the country, in plenty of time to make the papers' Sunday editions. Before long, the telephone began to ring. It rang all night long, making sleep nearly impossible. She stopped picking it up, but soon her answering machine was swamped with urgent messages from the press.

At dawn on Sunday she rose to find people waiting — reporters, she presumed — near her doorstep. The quiet ambience of suburban South Berry Street, she realized, was about to end. "I had no idea there would be television cameras camped out in my neighbor's yard. I had no idea there would be such an eager reaction to the story," she later said. "The Gary Hart situation did not receive this much attention. Gary Hart was a presidential candidate."

It dawned on her with growing horror that she would soon be unable to escape the cameramen and television trucks. Mounted satellite dishes now surrounded her house and overflowed her front yard into the streets, blocking traffic. Hill called Shirley Wiegand and made plans to retreat to her house. By the time Hill got there, Wiegand had bought two copies of the *New York Times,* pulled the curtains closed against newsmen, and turned the radio on so that they could hear Totenberg's broadcast. Soon, as satellite trucks from local radio stations began to circle Wiegand's house too, the women realized that Hill would have to find an even more remote refuge.

Wiegand suggested that Hill check into the Marriott Hotel on the town's outskirts under an assumed name to avoid the horde of reporters coming to Norman. As it happened, Hill ended up in a room just two doors away from *Newsday*'s Phelps, who had flown to Oklahoma in the hope of getting an interview but arrived too late to find her. (He had no idea she was staying nearby.) Meanwhile, Hill's hotel pseudonym became fodder for one of the many tabloids that immediately began scouring her life for scandal: knowing that Hill had been in the room but not recognizing the name under which it had been reserved, the paper concluded that Hill had spent the night at the hotel with an unknown female in a lesbian tryst.

Given the feverish reaction, Hill now believed that, far from being ignored, she might be called to Washington to testify. Since she had never wanted to tell her story to the news media, she declined further press interviews. Except for Wiegand, no advisers helped Hill deal with her newfound celebrity. In part to prevent the media from bothering her family and friends, Hill and Wiegand fashioned a crude press release that was delivered by a law student to the reporters camped out on Hill's front lawn.

"My interest," it said, "has been in fulfilling my responsibilities to the political process as I see them: That is to provide the Senate with information about a nominee. Allegations that my efforts are an attempt to disparage the character of Clarence Thomas are completely untrue." That done, she and Wiegand slipped past the press and went for one of their regular five-mile Sunday walks.

But any hope for a regular life was gone. On Monday, Hill tried to stick to her teaching schedule but found she needed the campus police to escort her through the media thicket. "The press was horrible — just everywhere," said a friend. "You couldn't get anything done."

It wasn't just the media. Hill's allegation had set off multiple explosions of anger. Working women of all ages and with all kinds of jobs identified strongly with the issue of sexual harassment and were furious with the Senate for stifling Hill's allegation. The story also ignited racial fury, enraging many blacks; although some sympathized with Hill, others blamed her for turning on a respected member of the race. Historically, many black men felt that black women had succeeded at their expense and so owed them special deference. Hill's willingness to sully the reputation of a prominent black man tapped directly into this anger.

Several callers left obscene messages on Hill's answering machine. A male civil rights leader called her to argue that Thomas's behavior was normal for a black man. Sisters should stand by their brothers, many said. As one writer explained it later, "Hill confronted and ultimately breached a series of taboos in the black community that have survived both slavery and the post-segregation life she and Clarence Thomas share. Anita Hill put her private business in the street, and she downgraded a black man to a room filled with white men who might alter his fate — surely a large enough betrayal for her to be read out of the race."

Inciting still more anger, Thomas's defenders in Washington lashed out at Hill with a ferocity that, in her most fearful conversations with friends, she had not envisioned. They suggested, among other things, that Hill had had an unrequited crush on Thomas and was part of a partisan plot.

With her character and motives now under assault, Hill decided to hold a press conference at the law school. On Monday afternoon, she entered one of the classrooms to confront a throng of reporters. Also present were dozens of colleagues and students, who greeted her with a standing ovation. Dean Swank, standing behind her, read a statement of support. CNN carried the press conference live, and the room was extremely hot because of the crowd and the television lights. But in the midst of it all Hill sat calmly, holding a cup of coffee. Her hair was neat, her blazer pressed, and her matching earrings and necklace in place. She spoke in a cautious, measured tone, looking about as wild-eyed as a Sunday school teacher.

She began by thanking her colleagues and students for their support. Then she proceeded to take on those in Washington who were suggesting that "this is somehow a political ploy that I'm involved in. Nothing," she said, "could be further from truth. I cannot even understand how someone could attempt to support such a claim." To those who accused her of last-minute political sabotage, she pointed out that she had not gone to the Senate or the press with this information — they had come to her. And the timing of its release, she pointed out, "has never been with me."

Hill also criticized the Judiciary Committee for its halfhearted handling of her case, stressing that she had "hoped and trusted" that her allegation would be distributed by Biden to every member of the committee before its vote on Thomas. If there had been delays in informing the senators, she said, they were the committee's, not hers.

She finished her opening remarks by asserting that the attacks on her were just "an attempt to not deal with the issue itself." Continuing, she said, "It is an unpleasant issue. It's an ugly issue, and people don't want to deal with it generally and in particular in this case. But I resent the idea that people would blame the messenger for the message rather than looking at the content of the message itself and taking a careful look at it, and fully investigating it. And I would hope that the official process would continue."

When reporters asked if she felt her charges should disqualify Thomas from the Supreme Court, Hill carefully avoided a direct answer, noting that it was the Senate's responsibility to decide, not hers. But she made it clear that she took the matter very seriously. As she put it, "I believe this conduct reflects his sense of how to carry out his job." While running the EEOC, she said, Thomas had conducted himself as if he were above the very laws he was entrusted with enforcing. By implication this called into question his fitness for the high court.

In Washington, the impact of Hill's press conference was seismic. Instead of the political zealot whom Danforth had accused of launching "an eleventh-hour attack more typical of a political campaign than a Supreme Court confirmation," many senators, even Thomas's supporters, saw Hill as a potentially lethal threat, given her reasonable demeanor.

"Oh boy, this is trouble" was the first reaction of Alan Simpson, the Wyoming Republican who was staunchly behind Thomas.

Getting ready to return to Washington from his home in Nebraska, James Exon, a conservative Democrat who had announced his support for Thomas on the floor of the Senate a few days earlier, was caught at the door by his wife, who told him to come back inside to watch the press conference. He too was caught off guard by the articulate Oklahoma law professor.

Even the stalwart Sam Nunn, whose vote Thomas had gone to such lengths to win, soon fled for cover. When asked on the *Today* show whether he still supported Thomas, the Georgia Democrat responded, "I can't say at this moment. I have to take a look at it [Hill's story] in detail."

Most important, perhaps, the news media, in the short time that it took Hill to deliver her statement and answer a few questions, collectively decided that Hill was someone to be taken seriously — which meant that the story was only going to get bigger. "This woman comes across as credible!" Tim Russert, NBC's Washington bureau chief and an influential opinion-maker in the capital, exclaimed to a colleague.

❖

The press conference had other unintended consequences. When she was first questioned by congressional aides and the FBI, Hill had only remembered telling one friend, Susan Hoerchner, about Thomas. But now a handful of other potential corroborating witnesses, whom she had evidently forgotten about, came forward to volunteer their help.

In Washington her old friend Ellen Wells went into action after receiving a phone call from her sister, who said excitedly, "David Brinkley is talking about Anita!"

Having refrained from contacting Hill all summer, Wells now took a modest step by writing a note to Hill that said: "Don't worry — I remember what you told me — I know you're telling the truth." As she mailed it, she thought, "God, I hope she gets that card."

Wells recalled that later in the week, when she had received no reply and the controversy seemed to be getting uglier, she took herself in hand and thought, "Ellen, you're going to have to be a little bit more forceful." So she actually called Hill at the law school, leaving a message offering to testify if Hill needed her. Wiegand — who was still Hill's only adviser in Norman — called back, asking what she knew. Wells described her agonized conversation with Hill about Thomas almost ten years earlier, the one in which the two women had tried to figure out how Hill could stop Thomas's behavior but still keep her job. The only idea they had come up with was for Hill to change her perfume.

Although Wells was willing to testify, she prayed all week that it wouldn't be necessary. "People were afraid," she said later. "I mean, this was the second black man in history anointed by the president of the United States to sit on its highest court. How do you buck those odds?" As the specter of testifying loomed, she felt "physically ill — nauseous all week," she remembered. Wells informed her boss at the American Public Welfare Association that she might be called; he was supportive, knowing her to be, as she put it, "a truthful person."

In New York, John Carr, the lawyer in whom Hill had been interested eight years earlier and who was now a junior partner in the prestigious Wall Street firm of Simpson Thatcher & Bartlett, also saw Hill's press conference on television. He knew about Thomas's nomination, of course, but "it was only then," after seeing Hill, he said later, "that I remembered the whole thing." Instantly Carr recalled how Hill had cried over the phone because she was so upset by Thomas's sexual behavior toward her. Carr sent off a letter saying, "If it's any comfort, I remember you saying that to me." Soon he received a call from one of Hill's friends asking if he was willing to testify. After clearing it with his law partners, he said yes.

Hill had not thought about Carr in years, and when she heard he would be present at the hearings, she indulged in a moment of amusement with a friend. This was going to be a nightmare, she said with a giggle. Now all of the men whom she had been dating at the same time were suddenly going to learn about the others.

If several friends were quick to volunteer help, others were more conflicted about their roles. Fred Cooke, the lawyer who had seen

Thomas in the video store in Washington, initially planned to keep quiet, but it was getting much harder. Some of the friends who had heard from him about Thomas's interest in *Bad Mama Jama* began to urge him to speak up. And Kaye Savage, who had seen all the sexually explicit magazines and centerfolds in Thomas's apartment, began to think seriously about contacting the committee. But she too hesitated, afraid that involving herself would be akin to committing professional and social suicide.

Joel Paul, in whom Hill had confided in 1987, had learned of her public accusation in the newspaper on Monday morning. Although some-one had told him the night before that a woman had accused Thomas of sexual harassment, it hadn't meant much to Paul until he read her name. "My God — it's Anita!" he later remembered exclaiming.

A friend whom Paul had told about the earlier statement Hill had made to him urged Paul to call the media immediately, arguing that he had material facts that he had a responsibility to bring forward. But Paul was reluctant. "That's ridiculous," he argued. "Everyone will believe Anita. She's the most believable person in the world. Just watch — Thomas will withdraw by the end of the day."

As it turned out, Paul's hope of avoiding the media didn't fare much better than his prediction regarding Thomas. Without consulting him further, his friend leaked Paul's name to several Washington reporters, and within hours Paul was under a virtual siege. He gave several interviews and thus became the first of Hill's corroborators to go public.

By one in the morning on Tuesday, he began to experience the consequences. He had finally turned out the lights and fallen asleep when the phone rang. It was Harriet Grant, one of the Senate Judiciary Committee investigators. She wanted to depose Paul on the spot. "Can't it wait until tomorrow?" he asked. "No," she replied. "It's a national emergency."

So, while lying in bed, Paul was put on a speaker phone, and the committee's lawyers took turns questioning him. By the time it was over, Paul realized he was risking great personal exposure. He was up for tenure that year at the law school, an achievement that would cement his whole career in place. But he had a private life that he would rather have kept that way. And now his name and deposition would doubtless be circulated to every member of the Judiciary Com-mittee, including those who viewed this confirmation as war.

"I'm afraid," Paul told his lawyer the next morning, "that if Thomas's supporters want to damage my credibility, they'll try to 'out' me."

A homosexual, Paul was open about his sexuality to his friends and family and in the past had championed a number of gay rights issues, including the effort to admit gays to the military. In 1984, when he supported the presidential candidacy of Gary Hart, he had attended the Democratic National Convention as a gay delegate. And before that he had headed a gay bar association in San Francisco, called Bay Area Lawyers for Individual Freedom. Anyone who wanted to learn about his past would have no trouble digging up plenty of information.

It wasn't as though Paul was ashamed of his identity. It was just that he was at a particularly delicate point in his career. He had gone out of his way to be perceived as an expert in international law, not as a political activist of any stripe. Moreover, his father, who was eighty-three, had found it difficult to accept Paul's homosexuality, and any mention of it in public hearings, Paul feared, would be deeply painful.

Soon Paul had even more reason to worry. A friend of his lawyer's who was close to Republicans on the Judiciary Committee called with a warning. He said the Republicans behind the campaign to confirm Thomas had compiled briefing books, which he described as being two inches thick, filled with detailed information on the backgrounds of Hill's potential witnesses, including Joel Paul.

Already, even before Paul had testified, his worst fears seemed to have been realized. While he was publicly known from a few brief news interviews he'd given — none of which made his homosexuality in any way apparent — he nonetheless started to receive a series of unnervingly personal phone calls at home from anonymous callers who referred to his sexual orientation. "I saw you on television," said one male caller. "You're very cute. I'd like to go out with you — and slit your throat." "I hope you die of AIDS," said another, as he and others in the background burst into laughter.

Then, before Paul was scheduled to testify, Fred Jacobs, the dean of faculties at American University and a man important in tenure decisions, received a phone call from someone who identified himself as a reporter for the *Washington Post*. "Did you know," the caller asked the dean, "that you have a militant homosexual teaching on your staff? Have you thought about how embarrassing that could be for the university?"

Since Jacobs didn't recognize the reporter's byline and thought the tone of the questioning suspicious, he asked if he might call the reporter back at his office. Oddly, the putative reporter said he wouldn't be in the office that day. Odder still, when Jacobs called the *Washington Post* to check the name, no one had ever heard of the reporter.

Meanwhile, Brad Mims, the friend who had been close to Hill during the period she described, watched with a growing sense of discomfort as her detractors accused her of belatedly concocting her charges for political and personal reasons. Mims now worked in the political office of the Smithsonian Institution; he loved lobbying Congress to keep the museum's funds flowing. Getting involved in this confirmation fight at a time when the federal government, his employer, was led by the Republican party was about the last thing he needed.

As the headlines grew bigger and the acrimony built, Mims admitted to himself, "I know this stuff. I should be there." One of the few friends in whom he had confided called him every few hours and implored him to speak up. But Mims had been in Washington long enough to see fights like this before and believed there would be no winners. In the political climate of Washington in the fall of 1991, Good Samaritans, he believed, were suckers. No one, no matter how true his story, was going to be safe in this contest. So he kept quiet.

◆

Meanwhile, the Democrats on the Judiciary Committee who had given Hill such a runaround went into a defensive crouch. The Senate aides who had helped Hill to come forward were also keeping a safe distance. After Hill's press conference, the Senate switchboards were flooded with furious calls demanding a delay in the vote, many of them instigated by various liberal political organizations, which had the same capacity to marshal their members that the Christian Right had shown earlier in the summer. Biden was a particular focus of anger; despite Hill's emergence and her call for further investigation, he was still insisting that the confirmation vote proceed as scheduled, at six o'clock the next evening.

"I see no reasons why the additional public disclosure of the allegations — but no new information about the charges themselves —

should change this decision," Biden declared. In an interview, he later said that he had personally believed Hill. But according to Thomas and his wife, Biden had called them after seeing the FBI report on Hill's charge and told them that he believed there was "no merit" to the allegation. He had also, according to an account the Thomases gave Danforth, promised that if the news of Hill's charge ever leaked out, he would be Thomas's "most adamant and vigorous defender."

If Biden did believe Hill, as he later claimed, he apparently did not see sexual harassment as a disqualifying offense. Even after Hill surfaced, he neither pushed for an investigation to determine if the harassment had in fact taken place nor shared what information was already known with his colleagues before the vote.

This decision suggests that Biden was seriously out of touch, not only with the mounting anger among women in the country, but also with his colleagues, many of whom were upset that he had planned to leave them ignorant of Hill's harassment charge. Richard Shelby, a conservative Democrat from Alabama, privately told Biden that he had let his Democratic colleagues down by bottling up Hill's story. The currents of anger against Biden were so strong that Mitchell took to the Senate floor to defend his colleague's "exemplary leadership."

Biden and Mitchell continued to maintain that the charge was not serious enough to postpone the vote. It would take the unanimous consent of the Senate, Mitchell told reporters, to force a delay. To change course at this point would mean acknowledging that the senators had misjudged the gravity of the situation, an admission they were rather unaccustomed to making.

Incensed by this response, a small group of white and black political leaders, all of them women, visited Mitchell privately to try to convince him that it was in the Democratic party's interest to delay the vote. But Patricia King, a member of the delegation who taught law at Georgetown University, recalled that Mitchell just kept citing Senate protocol and saying, "My hands are tied. I can't do anything."

"That's nonsense," the women argued. "You're the Senate majority leader." King later said, "It seemed so shortsighted . . . I warned him that if this woman turns out to have been harassed, the Democrats are going to be responsible for putting Clarence Thomas on the Supreme Court."

But Mitchell stood fast. "No," she recalled his saying, "it was George

Bush who put him on the Court." Like Biden, he seemed to believe that the best way to handle the problem was to behave as if it weren't his.

A small, extremely vocal group of female congressional lawmakers began to turn the debate, arguing that the Senate's credibility was now on the line. Barbara Mikulski, an ardent feminist and the sole female Democratic senator, thundered, "What disturbs me as much as the allegations themselves is that the Senate appears not to take the charge of sexual harassment seriously."

Her message began to worry her male colleagues, many of whom had been deluged with angry phone calls. Surprisingly, one of the first to get the message was Arlen Specter, a Republican supporter of Thomas who knew of Hill's charges early and initially dismissed them. Specter, who drew much of his financial support from women who appreciated his pro-choice record, appeared on the *Today* show on Tuesday morning and urged a delay.

Later that day, New York's maverick Democratic senator, Daniel Patrick Moynihan, nearly halted the vote himself in an unusual display of parliamentary sabotage. Moynihan, who had decided to support Thomas but was now troubled by Hill's charge, moved to plunge the entire Senate into recess for a week. Learning of the ploy, Mitchell rushed to the Senate floor to suppress it. Later, he privately reminded his rebellious colleague that it was the majority leader, not the senator from New York, who decided the body's schedule.

The ritual Democratic luncheon that Tuesday was fractious too. More and more senators were calling for a delay. In the middle of lunch there was a loud knock on the door. A group of female House members — led by Colorado's Patricia Schroeder and the District of Columbia's delegate, Eleanor Holmes Norton (Thomas's predecessor at the EEOC) — demanded entrance. Mitchell barred the door, agreeing to meet with the women after lunch in his office. He said that if they wanted a delay, they should lobby the Democratic senators who had already announced their support for Thomas. If their votes could be turned, the minority leader, Dole, might be convinced to call off the vote. Mitchell, as this new position suggested, seemed to be re-evaluating his strategy.

Throughout the afternoon there were continuous meetings among Dole, Danforth, Mitchell, and Biden in different Capitol locations. Finally, in a conference room overlooking the Mall, Mitchell gave

Dole and Danforth a list of ten Democratic senators who had come out in favor of Thomas but would switch sides if they were forced to vote that night. Although there was a possibility that Mitchell was bluffing, without fifty sure votes in his pocket, Dole informed the White House that he wasn't about to take a chance. Danforth called Thomas to say it looked as if they'd have to delay the vote.

The nominee was deeply upset about the postponement. Later, Danforth said that he convinced Thomas that without the delay he would lose. Thomas was not about to give up. He had worked for ten years to get on the high court, and although some might have contemplated withdrawing under such trying circumstances, he apparently never openly considered it. Instead, Thomas said the delay would give him a chance to "clear my name." He told Danforth, "They've taken away from me what I have worked forty-three years to create. They have taken away from me what I have taken forty-three years to build — my reputation." Danforth repeated these dramatic words in an angry speech on the Senate floor Tuesday night, portraying Thomas as the victim of an unfair, politically poisoned confirmation process.

Since the White House lacked the votes to confirm Thomas, the Democrats presumably had the power to determine the next step. But Biden chose this moment to be especially accommodating toward the Republicans. The leaders of both parties agreed that the gravity of Hill's charge required a new round of hearings; the more difficult question was when to hold them. Some Democratic senators, such as Patrick Leahy, believed it would take weeks to conduct a thorough investigation. But the Republicans wanted to get the new hearings over with immediately. "The idea," Danforth later conceded, "was to have them begin as quickly as possible and to last as briefly as possible."

Appealing to Biden's constant desire to seem evenhanded, Danforth and Dole argued that fairness dictated speed. Biden initially wanted an interval of two weeks, but now he agreed to constraints that all but sealed Hill's fate. The new hearings would begin that Friday, October 11. Further — and this was even more important to the Republicans — the full Senate would vote on the nomination the following Tuesday, regardless of what happened.

There would thus be only two days to investigate Hill's charge, find and interview other witnesses, and prepare for the new hearings, which would run through the weekend if necessary. If time ran out before important allegations were explored or witnesses heard, nothing could be done. "The schedule," commented another Democratic senator, "was insanity."

Biden also acceded to two other Republican demands. First, even if new evidence came to light during the hearings, the Judiciary Committee itself would not take another vote on the question of whether Thomas should be confirmed. Second, without any idea of what he was bargaining away, Biden agreed to Danforth's demand that the scope of the hearings exclude general questions about Thomas's sexual conduct, such as whether he had a history of interest in pornography. Biden did not know it, but Thomas had confessed to Danforth that in his earlier years he had attended a few blue movies, although he insisted that he had never talked about them to Hill.

Metzenbaum, Biden's fellow Judiciary Committee member, later commented, "Joe bent over too far to accommodate the Republicans, who were going to get Thomas on the Court come hell or high water." Or, as an adviser to Senator Kennedy put it, less decorously, "Biden agreed to the terms of the people who were out to disembowel Hill."

Biden did balk at one of Danforth's demands: that the hearing be confined to Anita Hill's allegation. Biden argued — successfully — that if other women came forward to accuse Thomas in the allotted time frame, then the committee must be able to question them. The Democrats wondered why, if Danforth was so convinced of Thomas's innocence, he was so concerned about other women.

Late that Tuesday night, Biden actually spoke with Hill for the first time — he called to tell her about the new set of hearings. Aides said that he was wounded by Hill's public criticisms of the committee's handling of her case. He had sincerely believed that he had been chivalrously respecting her wish for confidentiality and that any delays had resulted from this impulse. There appears to have been a genuine misunderstanding between the two, perhaps owing to the rapidly changing situation and the difficulty of working through so many intermediaries. And Hill, always so cautious, could be hard to interpret.

Although their discussion on the phone that night was cordial, it was beginning to dawn on Hill that the Democrats did not view themselves as her advocates. In fact, Biden's chief advice to Hill was to find herself a good lawyer. The message was clear: in a city that runs on political patronage, she had none. Three days before the hearings were to open, Thomas had the full weight of the White House and the Senate Republicans behind him. But Hill was about to travel to Washington as an outsider with no connections, an ordinary citizen with strengths and weaknesses, pressured against her own instincts into challenging the most powerful institutions in American society largely by herself.

On Tuesday night, Hill got the first warning of what this might mean. Speaking on the Senate floor, Alan Simpson said, "It is a cruel thing we are witnessing." He all but promised that "Anita Hill will be sucked right into . . . the very thing she wanted to avoid most. She will be injured and destroyed and belittled and hounded and harassed — real harassment — different than the sexual kind."

Hill hurriedly prepared to go to Washington the next morning. The Judiciary Committee would pay her way, and Shirley Wiegand had agreed to accompany her. But a tangle of other logistics needed sorting out. Hill's parents and many of her twelve siblings wanted to show their support by going to Washington. As it happened, the following week was her mother's eightieth birthday, and the family had planned to celebrate that weekend. Now the party would move to the capital. Among other problems, Hill's father had never been on an airplane before.

On Wednesday morning, Hill accepted for the first time that she would indeed require her own lawyer. She had thought testifying would be simple: she would answer a few questions and then go home. According to Wiegand, Hill hadn't even thought the hearings would be televised. Why would she need a lawyer, she had wondered, if she wasn't accused of anything? It wasn't a trial. As far as she knew, it wouldn't even be adversarial.

"It never occurred to us," said Wiegand, "that people wouldn't believe her. The worst that could happen, we figured, was that they wouldn't care."

A number of lawyers and political consultants had volunteered their services to Hill. But many of them — particularly those from the various women's groups — seemed to have their own agendas, and given the charged atmosphere, Hill didn't want anyone else's political baggage. Her first choice for legal counsel was Charles Ogletree, the Harvard professor who had advised her earlier on how to handle the calls from Totenberg and Phelps. A highly regarded public defender, he ran the university's clinical law program. And he was considered so generous and hard-working that when a worthy cause came his way, he was almost incapable of saying no. But this time Ogletree wasn't eager for the attention.

Several associates thought he was uncomfortable taking such a public role against Thomas, although later Ogletree disputed this view. Accusing a fellow black attorney bound for the Supreme Court of sexual misconduct was sure to trigger a huge racial and sexual backlash. Ogletree supported women's rights, but he was a lawyer, not a politician, and he wasn't that pleased about the way some of the doctrinaire feminists were taking advantage of Hill's cause. Another consideration was that he would soon be up for tenure at Harvard. Stepping into the middle of a losing political war might not help his chances, particularly since the law school faculty itself was bitterly divided along ideological lines.

Furthermore, the thirty-nine-year-old lawyer had been quietly active in the NAACP's campaign against the nominee, but now the NAACP had let it be known that it would sit out the second phase of the hearings. Ogletree wanted to respect that decision. Many in the civil rights community thought that since Thomas's confirmation seemed inevitable, it was time to heal wounds. For instance, members of the Black Congressional Caucus who had opposed Thomas in the first round of hearings simply vanished at this point. Even female civil rights leaders, such as Dorothy Height, the head of the National Council of Negro Women, were noticeably ambivalent.

But Ogletree, whose parents had picked cotton in the central California farmlands and whose sister, a police officer, had been brutally murdered, was a fighter. He had overcome tremendous odds to attend Stanford and Harvard Law. He had mourned his sister's unsolved death by adding to his heavy caseload of defender's work. And despite his reservations about jumping into this brawl, it bothered him to see Hill heading into such an imbroglio without proper protection. Finally, after warning Hill that he didn't want to play "too active a role," he agreed to help, but only enough to ensure that she was well prepared for her Senate appearance.

As the hearings approached, Hill began to get help from other quarters too. Susan Deller Ross, the sexual harassment expert at Georgetown brought in by Brudney, continued to advise Hill. Joining her was a haphazardly assembled team of other volunteers, including Judith Resnik, a prominent women's rights lawyer in Los Angeles; Professor Emma Coleman Jordan from Georgetown; John Frank, a well-known constitutional litigator; and Frank's law partner, Janet Napolitano, who flew in from Arizona to join Hill. Of this group, only Frank had any experience in nomination fights. Hill also tried to keep a few old friends involved, including her former Washington roommate and Yale classmate, Sonia Jarvis.

This group began to gather on Wednesday — two days before the new hearings — in some extra office space offered by a few of Hill's former colleagues from Wald, Harkrader at their new firm, Pepper, Hamilton & Scheetz. Late that afternoon, after a three-hour conference call from Oklahoma with many of her new allies, Hill and Wiegand caught a plane to Washington.

Even before arriving, they sensed that they were out of their league. "I feel like we're a couple of stupid farm girls," Wiegand recalled saying to Hill as they flew over the Potomac River into the capital.

"Naive," Hill said, correcting her. "Not stupid."

Hill was especially naive in her assumptions about how Thomas would respond. Wiegand remembered that they had heard press reports that week — incorrect, as it turned out — that Thomas had admitted to the FBI that he had asked Hill for a date. So Hill expected Thomas to agree with her on at least some of the facts. "The possibility never occurred to us," Wiegand admitted later, "that Thomas would just lie."

Another issue the two women misjudged was the extent to which the hearings would be a political free-for-all, with none of the safeguards and procedural rules used in court to ensure a fair trial. Although Hill had lawyers, the senators would be running the show. And while the Republicans clearly saw their mission as defending Thomas from what they considered slander, the Democrats believed they were impartial fact-finders, not Hill's advocates. As Wiegand saw it, the imbalance meant that "no one was there to protect [Hill] from abuse. It was just a farce."

By the time Hill arrived in Washington, her camp was already divided. Ogletree — who joined discussions by telephone since he couldn't fly in until Thursday afternoon — took a lawyerly approach. He viewed the hearings primarily as a legal proceeding, not a political campaign. "To me," as he later put it, "the most important thing was loyalty to the client, not the cause. [Hill] saw herself as a witness who wanted to clear her conscience. She didn't have an interest in broadening the issue. It wasn't her objective to take on the White House or the committee."

But several members of Hill's team disagreed, particularly the feminists, who realized that Hill's case was as much about politics as legal skill. They knew, just as the White House did, that Supreme Court nominations were no longer intellectual debates or cozy, inside-the-club deliberations — they were national political campaigns.

This group of Hill allies, which was repeatedly at odds with Ogletree and others, believed it essential for Hill to direct her case less at the Senate than at American public opinion. To do this, she would need seasoned political and public relations help. Washington had become such a prism of manipulated images that it was almost impossible, they argued, for an outsider to get the truth across without distortion. Winning this point, the group helped line up two experienced political volunteers, Wendy Sherman, who had helped run Emily's List, the leading Democratic women's political fund-raising group, and Louise Hilsen, another Democrat, who had once handled press relations for a congressman. Sherman would work out the public relations strategy; Hilsen would be Hill's contact with the media. If she couldn't begin to tap the sort of expertise available to Thomas from the White House, Justice Department, Senate, and consultants like Duberstein, at least Hill wouldn't be entering the arena unassisted.

On Thursday morning, the two camps gathered on two secure floors at Pepper, Hamilton's offices near Dupont Circle. Hill settled into a corner conference room on the fifth floor, taking one of the ten chairs surrounding a rectangular conference table. Ogletree had not yet arrived, so the most seasoned attorney, John Frank, assigned himself the task of helping Hill compose her opening statement. Janet Napolitano, working with the political advisers on a different floor, helped prepare Hill's corroborating witnesses.

Hill's team had agreed to take any major disagreements to Hill herself, and on Thursday afternoon the policy got its first real test. Frank had arranged for two of his oldest friends — the eminent Democratic lawyers Lloyd Cutler, who had been President Carter's White House counsel, and Warner Gardner — to help prepare Hill for the hearings by holding a moot court session in which the older lawyers pretended to be senators and fired questions at her. Frank also hoped that Cutler and Gardner might agree to appear at Hill's side during the hearings, signifying to the Judiciary Committee and official Washington that the young law professor from Oklahoma had powerful support from the Washington establishment.

As Hill took a break from her moot court practice over a sandwich behind closed doors, Frank gave the white-haired, gravel-voiced Cutler the draft of Hill's opening statement. The septuagenarian attorney was immediately taken aback — as much of the country would be — by the shocking nature of Hill's language. He was disturbed in particular by the graphic references to Thomas's concern with penis and breast size, pornography, and pubic hair. These unsavory words, Cutler warned, could be needlessly offensive in the decorous atmosphere of the Senate. And since some of these particulars were not in Hill's original statement to the FBI, Hill might open herself up to allegations that she had embellished her story for greater effect. (His fear proved correct, although this charge would have been easy to refute had anyone produced a copy of the notes from her first conversation with James Brudney, in which she had cited almost all of these details. But no one did.)

Susan Deller Ross took issue with Cutler. She argued passionately that the more precise Hill could be in her details and language, the better. In order to empathize with harassment victims, Ross had found, juries needed to be able to imagine exactly how it might feel to be on the receiving end of such behavior. If such language had made Hill cringe, so too should the Senate and the public cringe. In particular, the two lawyers came to a standoff over the word "penis."

"There was a difference of view as to whether the testimony should be explicit or whether benign euphemisms should be used," Frank later conceded. "The senior attorneys felt the decorum of the Senate favored delicacy."

Unable to broker a compromise, Frank asked Hill for her opinion. She sided with Ross, believing that she should repeat Thomas's words exactly as she remembered them. Come Friday, Cutler was noticeably absent from Hill's team.

When Ogletree finally appeared, he immediately won Hill's confidence by asking her several difficult questions. He told her, for example, that the Judiciary Committee had an affidavit challenging the veracity of her statement; what was her response? Hill replied that she didn't care what this other affidavit said; it wasn't true. Ogletree reassured her, saying that this was precisely the kind of strong, clear answer she should give. (There was, to the relief of the other attorneys present, no such affidavit. Ogletree had invented it to test Hill's fortitude.)

At one point Ogletree met with a secret visitor, Jeff Robinson, a black lawyer who worked for Arlen Specter and had previously worked for Biden. Hill's lawyers knew that Specter had been selected to be the lead questioner, and they wanted to know what to expect. Robinson told them Specter would be tough and adversarial. "Expect extremely close questioning," he told his friends. Robinson, however, inadvertently led them astray when he said that they could expect the senator to question Thomas equally aggressively.

Another warning came from Ron Allen, a New York lawyer and Yale classmate whom Susan Hoerchner had selected to represent her. Allen also quizzed a friend in Specter's office.

"What's the deal?" Allen asked Thomas Dadou.

"The deal is, this could get ugly," Specter's aide replied. "The Republicans see this as war."

❖

If it was war, the first wounds for the Democrats were self-inflicted. On Thursday night, Hill retired to her suite at the Capitol Hill Hotel, where she was in seclusion after joining her family for dinner. She went to sleep thinking that she would be the first witness the following morning. Her advisers thought it important for her to be the first to state her case in her own words rather than to begin on the defensive. They had argued the point with Biden's office and believed they had a firm deal that Hill would indeed lead off.

But shortly after midnight, Wendy Sherman called Louise Hilsen with bad news. Biden's office had called to say that Thomas, not Hill, would be testifying first. He would also have the privilege of testifying a second time, after she had finished. This, the two media experts realized, would probably allow Thomas to rebut Hill and deliver the last word live on prime-time television, when the audience was largest.

"We had a deal that she would testify first," said Susan Deller Ross later. "Then I heard from one of the other lawyers that the Republicans told Biden it would be racist to have Thomas go last. Biden was either currying favor, or he got rolled by the Republicans."

In fact, it was the White House's shrewd consultant, Duberstein, who had pulled off this coup. Not only had he convinced Biden that Thomas must speak first, he had also threatened that if Thomas were not given the chance to answer Hill's charge that same day, he would personally stage a press conference starring Thomas in front of the locked hearing room doors — and there the nominee would claim that the Senate had denied him the chance to defend himself. Clearly Duberstein knew how to get the chairman's attention.

Hill worried that her team was already being outgunned. At six in the morning on Friday, still without a lead counsel, she called Ogletree in his room at the Marriott and implored him one last time to take the top job. He finally relented after several of the other lawyers appeared at his hotel with the same request. It was to some extent a bittersweet victory. Hill could hardly feel triumphant; she now had a lead counsel reluctant to be playing the part and a Judiciary Committee chairman uneasy about airing her case.

Even with Ogletree in place, a host of other issues had the team in disarray. At breakfast in the hotel coffee shop, John Frank and Ogletree fought over Warner Gardner's position. Frank, believing that the legal team lacked luster, threatened to walk out if Gardner wasn't assigned a role. (Gardner did sit with the rest of the legal advisers but mainly busied himself making diary notations.)

Meanwhile, Hilsen and Sherman were fielding more than two hundred phone calls from reporters asking about Hill's legal representation, but they were unable to reach Ogletree in order to get answers. They felt frozen out by Ogletree and some of the other lawyers; they hadn't even been informed of a strategy session set for 8:00 A.M. at the Marriott. But one of them had overheard something about the meeting as well as Ogletree's room number. They stormed over to the hotel and got another guest to help them gain entry to the secure floor where he was staying.

When Hilsen and Sherman knocked on the door, Ogletree was in his undershirt, talking on the phone and ironing his dress shirt. At this point he had no office in the capital, no coordination between the various members of Hill's defense, and no plan for how to get Hill — who was under virtual siege by the media — to the hearings. He also seemed entirely unaware that a frenzy of attention awaited them in the Russell Office Building, where the hearings would get under way in less than two hours.

As they left the hotel, the two consultants glimpsed Ogletree trying to flag down a taxi, scrambling to meet Hill at her hotel in order to give her some last-minute advice about her appointment with history.

13

❖

High-Tech
Lynching

As soon as Hill's allegation was printed, Thomas and his most trusted associates realized that denial alone would not be enough to refute her story. From the moment she surfaced, they moved beyond defense to mount a brilliant offense, proceeding as if the only sure way to rescue Thomas's credibility was to destroy Hill's. Hill's story would have to be cast as the word of one suspect woman against the collective judgment of the Senate, the White House, and everyone else who had ever known Thomas. Her veracity, her motives, her private life, and even her sanity would come under assault. It would require an intense effort, but Hill's apparently pristine character would have to be completely transformed.

A high-level scavenger hunt for information that could damage Hill's credibility began almost immediately after her name erupted in the news on Sunday, October 6. As Hill and Wiegand were taking their long walk in Oklahoma, Danforth and Thomas, in a number of telephone conversations, were racking their brains about how to discredit her. At one point, Thomas mentioned that he and Hill had been on what he had assumed were such friendly terms that she had recently invited him to speak to her law school. Danforth was intrigued. "I thought, that's really curious that she called him," he later said. Why would anyone so honor a former harasser? And who would believe her if they knew this?

As it happened, Hill had opposed the choice of Thomas as a speaker at her law school. She had agreed to extend the invitation only as a favor after she was outvoted by the school's Enrichment Committee, a fact that could be verified by law school officials. But neither Danforth nor Thomas checked with the school or with Hill before publicizing the misleading information. Instead, Danforth later acknowledged, he believed that if he could document the invitation, it would advance a central thrust of the attack on Hill's credibility — to show that the professor had not acted like a woman who had been sexually harassed.

As soon as Thomas mentioned the invitation, Danforth later recalled, "I tunneled in on that." Danforth said he was even more convinced that this line of inquiry would undermine Hill when Thomas added that the invitation to speak wasn't the only friendly call; he believed he had received a number of them from Hill over the years. Moreover, there might even be some official record of them in the phone logs that Diane Holt, Thomas's longtime secretary, had kept for him at the EEOC.

The hunt for these phone logs took up much of Monday, with Duberstein joining in. Danforth reached Holt, but she no longer had the logs. She remembered packing them up in boxes after Thomas's confirmation to the appeals court. She guessed they were probably in storage somewhere at the court.

A frantic search ensued, with Thomas's clerks serving as scavengers. Finally, the logs were unearthed in Thomas's own garage. A painstaking review of the records revealed that there had been eleven phone messages from Hill since her departure from the EEOC in 1983, including an array of friendly greetings, such as "Just called to say hello." A message that particularly intrigued Danforth had been left during a visit to Washington, when she had included her hotel room number. In the campaign to show that Hill was lying about her feelings toward Thomas, these phone calls, Danforth later said he believed, would prove to be "the jackpot."

Duberstein mulled over how to leak them to the media. Wanting to leave no fingerprints, he offered to give the logs to the *Washington Post*, as long as the paper agreed not to mention their source. But the newspaper refused. Instead, selected entries were passed on to Alan Simpson, without an explanation of how they had been found. Simpson, in turn, prominently mentioned the calls from Hill on television that night on *Nightline*. In addition, Danforth released the logs to the press at a news conference on Tuesday.

During the hearings, Simpson would use these calls to insinuate that, rather than having been harassed by Thomas, Hill had actually pursued him. "We have eleven phone calls initiated by her from 1984 through the date of Clarence Thomas's marriage to Ginni Lamp, and then it all ended . . . What does that say about her behavior?" Simpson asked. His suggestion that the calls reflected a romantic interest that was crushed by Thomas's remarriage in 1987 hung ominously in the air.

In sketching this story of unrequited love, however, Simpson did not mention that Diane Holt, the person who made the notes in the phone logs, stopped working for Thomas almost immediately after his marriage. So there was no record of calls from Hill — or anyone else, for that matter — to Thomas much after that date. Eventually, Senator Leahy succeeded in eliciting this information. But as the misleading use of the logs showed, as soon as Hill's charge was leaked, fairness and accuracy regarding her were the least of Thomas and his defenders' concerns.

Five days after finding the phone logs in his garage, Thomas would radiate fury as he sat at the Senate witness table at the opening of the hearings, offering a picture of political persecution. "I have endured this ordeal for one hundred and three days," he said, decrying the search for scandalous details about his life. "Reporters sneaking into my garage to examine books that I read . . . This is not American. This is Kafkaesque. It has got to stop!" But the only person who had in fact discovered a trove of tantalizing information in his suburban garage was the judge himself.

❖

While Danforth hunted for more information that could discredit Hill in the harried days leading up to the hearings, the White House counsel's office became a virtual war room overseeing a parallel effort. The propriety of the White House counsel — the lawyer to the institution of the presidency — engaging in a campaign against a private citizen was not addressed. Boyden Gray was one of Thomas's fiercest advocates, and he plunged right in. With him came the considerable weight of the White House, which is exempt from the Privacy Act and thus has access to all government employment, tax, FBI, and other federal records whenever it can claim that national interests are at stake.

Biden's aides soon learned this when, after securing Hill's waiver —

as the Privacy Act requires — they subpoenaed her government employment file from the Office of Personnel Management. At the time, OPM was headed by Thomas's friend Connie Newman. As Biden's staff waited, days passed, and still the records didn't appear. A senior aide, furious, yelled at an OPM bureaucrat to "Get the fucking file! What's the deal?" The deal, the aide was finally told, was that Hill's file had already been taken by the White House counsel's office, without Hill's permission.

Hill's employment records offered Gray no new ammunition, but soon after the news about Hill broke, he got his first promising tip from a Republican stalwart, Judith Hope. She had been a partner at Wald, Harkrader when Hill had been an associate, and she thought — incorrectly, as the records show — that Hill had been in professional trouble, perhaps even fired from her job there. Hope knew her memory was vague; she didn't trust it enough to either testify or swear out an affidavit. But the possibility that Hill could be shown in an unfavorable light got the president's lawyer on the phone, searching for more damaging information.

Gray even called a fellow member of the exclusive Metropolitan Club, Tom Truitt. Truitt had once practiced at the Wald firm, and Gray thought perhaps he could confirm and add to Hope's account. "I'd known Boyden for years," Truitt recalled. "He wanted to know if there was anything I could contribute to debunk Anita Hill." But all Truitt remembered was that Hill was "pretty bright" but "mousy." He certainly didn't think she'd been fired.

While Gray tracked the Wald lead, his deputy Lee Liberman called friends from Yale Law School who might have derogatory information on Hill. But here too the lawyers came up empty-handed.

The White House counsel's office had better luck following another line of attack, an effort to convince other black women who had worked for Thomas to counter her charges publicly. Of immediate help was Phyllis Berry, the loyal friend who had worked for Thomas at the EEOC and helped mount his campaign to secure a seat on the D.C. Circuit.

As soon as the news of Hill broke, Gray's deputy Mark Paoletta arranged for Berry to speak to the nation's most influential newspaper, the *New York Times*. Berry, who had not held a full-time job since she and Thomas had parted ways in 1987, was delighted to help again. She thrust herself into the limelight by voicing her opinion to the *Times* — unencumbered by any evidence — that Hill was motivated by "hurt feelings" over Thomas's lack of romantic interest in her.

Under oath a week later, Berry conceded that she and Hill had never been close and that she only knew Hill "professionally." Moreover, she acknowledged that Hill had never mentioned having any romantic feelings for Thomas. Any "impression" that Hill had "a crush" on Thomas was based on Berry's belief that Hill had wanted easy access to the chairman's office during the day. Yet Berry admitted at one point: "I don't remember them having anything at any time that was more than professional, cordial, and friendly." Nor, as it turned out, could anyone else in the long list of witnesses for Thomas recall that Hill had ever exhibited anything other than a professional interest in him. In fact, another of Thomas's witnesses from his EEOC days, Nancy Fitch, admitted that "I never got any sense from [Hill] that she had any romantic interest in him at all."

The correction came rather late in the process, though. In the days before the hearings, as the public formed its first impressions of Hill, Berry's "scorned woman" theory provided a crucial element that was otherwise missing: a motive. Later that week, Armstrong Williams, an equally loyal member of Thomas's circle, pitched in too, pronouncing Hill virtually mentally unstable with respect to Thomas. As he put it in an interview with the *Wall Street Journal* for a story that ran the day the hearings opened, "There is a thin line between her sanity and insanity." Later, in another interview, he said, referring to Hill, "Sister has emotional problems."

By midweek, Paoletta was also the recipient of another helpful piece of information potentially questioning Hill's sanity. It came from a businessman and lawyer in Austin, Texas, named John Doggett. Doggett had befriended Thomas at Yale; later, while working as a business consultant in Washington, he had socialized occasionally with the EEOC chairman, through whom he had met Hill.

Doggett had switched his party registration from Democrat to Republican after the 1988 election, and his wife was a GOP activist. When he read about Hill's charge in Monday's *New York Times,* he said later, he exclaimed to his wife, "Anita's crazy." This diagnosis was based on his opinion that years earlier, Hill had chastised him unnecessarily for breaking a dinner date, ostensibly lecturing him about not leading women on. Doggett claimed that Hill's annoyance proved that she had "fantasized" about having a relationship with him.

With the help of his wife's Republican friends in Washington, Doggett found his way to Paoletta, who called him back on Wednesday. By Thursday, at Paoletta's urging, Doggett had faxed an affidavit to the Republicans on the Judiciary Committee attesting to Hill's putative pattern of imaginary romances. Doggett himself was unsure how persuasive this information was and whether he would be called to Washington to testify for his old law school friend. "I figured, if they needed me, things must be in pretty bad shape," he later admitted.

Thus, before Hill could reach the microphones, Thomas's allies had portrayed her as a liar driven by an unseemly motive. In a caricature of the "she asked for it" school of sexual criminal defense, Hill, instead of having been harassed by her former boss, was described as having lusted after him with such fervor that her sanity — not to mention her credibility — was in doubt.

Early that week, with no lawyers or public relations advisers of her own yet, Hill tried to counter some of these attacks. At her initial press conference in Oklahoma, she responded angrily to a reporter who told her of Berry's theory, saying Berry "doesn't know me." Within twenty-four hours, Berry pounced on Hill's imprecision to suggest that again Hill was a liar, since the two had worked in the same office, so of course they knew each other. Later, Hill explained that she meant that Berry did not know her well enough to be familiar with her romantic interests, as Berry would concede.

Berry's statements were merely the opening shots in a concerted, weeklong assault on Hill's mental health. Especially damaging were the comments made by Hill's former employer and Thomas's great admirer, Charles Kothe. Kothe contributed his own diagnosis early that week when he told reporters that "I find the references to the alleged sexual harassment not only unbelievable but preposterous. I am convinced that such are the product of fantasy." Neither of the news accounts carrying this statement, nor the Republicans who picked up the fantasy line and used it to portray Hill as delusional, mentioned that Kothe was an ardent political supporter of Thomas and had been on his payroll for a number of years, literally working out of his office on such special projects as "The Success Story of Clarence Thomas." Nor did the public have any sense of Kothe's instant regret at having used the word "fantasy." Only when he tes-

tified almost a week later, at the close of the hearings, did Kothe say,
"I think perhaps my selection of words there was probably unfortunate. I have never seen Anita Hill in a situation when she wasn't a
decent person."

While Thomas's associates were promoting the theory that Hill had
been romantically spurned, they were also putting forth a separate
theory: that she had been professionally spurned. While the former
theory disparaged her personal life, the latter denigrated her professional life. Both supposed that she was so hurt by Thomas's slights
that she had fabricated her tale of sexual harassment in order to exact
some monstrous revenge.

Armstrong Williams, who said that he spoke with Thomas many
times as the hearings approached, was instrumental here too. Early
on the morning of Friday, October 11 — as Hill was still trying to
convince Ogletree to be her lead counsel — Williams granted an interview to members of the Judiciary Committee staff. By this time he
was a public relations executive, and he had high hopes of testifying
on behalf of his most influential connection, Judge Thomas.

What he told the committee staff, according to a transcript of the
interview that was never publicly released, was that he had worked
with Hill at the EEOC for approximately seven months and that he
was certain that she was lying about the alleged episode of harassment.
Her motive, Williams said, was anger at Thomas's choice of another
woman to become head of the agency's Office of Legal Counsel.

Williams supplied elaborate details. He explained that Thomas had
had "grave problems" with the legal counsel's performance. Although
Hill was remarkably young for such a "coveted position," as Williams
told it, she had confided in him that she "felt she could go down and
do a good job of running that division." Williams recalled being taken
aback that Hill was so "ambitious." When instead Thomas tapped an
older and more experienced lawyer, Allyson Duncan, for the post,
Williams said that Hill had said "she was upset. She felt it was unfair.
She felt she did not belong at the Commission any more . . . that the
Chairman just did not take her serious [sic] enough." The blow was
so grave, Williams stated, that he believed Hill "had emotional problems . . . she would ramble about things that just didn't make sense
. . . she was depressed a lot, very depressed . . . devastated."

Williams could not determine the exact date when this ostensibly crushing moment occurred in Hill's career. But he recalled with some prompting that the woman whose job Hill had wanted was named Constance Dupree. Here his theory foundered. Dupree was not replaced as head of the Office of Legal Counsel by Allyson Duncan until January 1985, fully a year and a half after Hill had left the EEOC. When the Republicans on the Judiciary Committee discovered this gaffe, they decided not to call Williams as a witness for Thomas, although the Democrats toyed with the idea of calling him simply in order to discredit him.

But this theory of thwarted ambition was not abandoned during the hearings. Instead, Thomas and several other former associates testified that Hill had wanted another job that Allyson Duncan got — this one during Hill's tenure — as Thomas's chief of staff. Thomas testified that Hill had "aspired to that position and, of course, was not successful . . . That could have been a basis for her being angry with me."

Yet when asked about this specifically, none of Hill's colleagues at the agency — who were testifying for Thomas — could recall Hill's saying that she had wanted that job either. According to Hill, she never did. As the record shows, she had started talking about finding work outside the EEOC beginning in January of 1983, which was before Duncan even became Thomas's chief of staff. Moreover, an impartial witness supports Hill's stance. Al Golub, who was Thomas's deputy at the time and who took no side in the confirmation controversy, said, "It is my recollection that Anita Hill never expressed any interest in the chief of staff job."

Such far-flung attacks on Hill reflected the fact that as the hearings got under way, even many of Thomas's supporters feared that his confirmation was all but hopeless. When Bill Kristol entered the White House mess early Friday morning to order breakfast, there were already a number of people in the room. Kristol wanted to lay a bet, but he couldn't find anyone else who thought Thomas would survive the day. He took five-to-one odds that Thomas would still be confirmed.

❖

Before the hearings, Danforth repeatedly described Thomas's spirit as "very fragile"; in conversations with other senators, he reported that the nominee was close to tears, so emotionally stripped that he was sometimes crouched in a fetal position. When Danforth had first broached the subject of a delay in order to allow time for further investigation, he said, Thomas had told him that he "just couldn't take it." Indeed, Virginia Lamp Thomas told Danforth that her husband had been so distraught about the reopening of the hearings that he had gotten out of bed on Wednesday night and lain writhing on the floor in agony until nearly dawn. He had acted, according to her description, "like something was inside him physically. Like there was this battle going on inside him . . . What it felt like is that Clarence still had some sin in his life and he had to get that out in order to open to the Holy Spirit." And on Thursday morning, when Mike Luttig — who remained in place as Thomas's legal tutor — tried to go through the details of Hill's charge with him, Thomas nearly collapsed. The nominee, according to Luttig, was "crying and hyperventilating . . . just wailing" that "these people have destroyed my life."

But while Thomas's anguish was by all accounts enormous, it was matched by a ferocious determination to launch an all-out, last-ditch campaign to win. In truth, only at this imperiled point did Thomas really take charge. If earlier he had pliantly followed the instructions of the capital's best handlers, in these difficult days leading up to the hearings he threw them off and took over his own fight. "It was Clarence Thomas," said one of his advisers, "who decided the strategy on Anita Hill."

The result was a marked change in the tone and tactics of the fight. While there had been an effort to soften his rough edges before, now Thomas showed his genuine nature, revealing a combativeness that finally rang true to his old friends and relatives. As his mother, Leola Williams, later noted, "That stout man with glasses, Duberstein, made Clarence keep his mouth shut. That wasn't Clarence. He would have popped them in the mouth, just like I would. He gets mad. Really mad. It was [when] he said you can take your job and shove it — that was the Clarence I know."

On Friday morning, as Thomas prepared to make his first public appearance since Hill's allegation surfaced, the normally sepulchral Russell Office Building was a circus. The hall leading to the Caucus Room was nearly impassable. Hundreds of black women wearing red and white T-shirts emblazoned "Taking a Stand for Righteousness and for Thomas" were clapping their hands and chanting, "Thomas!

Thomas!" At dawn, these women had clambered aboard buses in front of Harvest Church in Mount Rainier, Maryland, which had one of the largest black congregations affiliated with the Reverend Lou Sheldon's Traditional Values Coalition.

Outside the hearing room, Jean Thompson, co-pastor of the church, proclaimed to reporters: "Being here today is as important as it was in Harriet Tubman's day." Phyllis Schlafly stood nearby, a "Pro-Woman/Pro-Thomas" sticker on her print blouse. Duberstein and others knew that it was essential to show that even in the face of Anita Hill's charges, Thomas still retained loyal support, particularly among average blacks and conservative activists who might have been expected to be upset by any allegation associating Thomas with pornography.

The blindingly bright television lights flooded on as the candidate himself appeared, wearing a dark suit and a steely expression. Beside him, making the climb up the grand marble staircase to the Caucus Room, were Senator Danforth and Virginia Lamp Thomas. The crush of onlookers converged so quickly toward the nominee that a phalanx of Capitol Hill police was needed to help clear a passage. Thomas acknowledged the chants and applause of his supporters with the slightest nod. His wife would later call the women from Maryland her "angels."

Thomas took his place at the green felt-covered witness table alone. Biden, facing him, sat at the center of the long committee table, the Republican committee members on his right, the Democrats on his left. At 10:01 A.M., the chairman banged the gavel. In a short opening statement, Biden seemed anxious to reassure the embattled nominee. "In this setting, it will be easy and perhaps understandable for witnesses to fear unfair treatment," he said, "but it is my job, as chairman, to ensure as best as I possibly can fair treatment . . . the primary responsibility of this committee is fairness."

As Biden spoke, Thomas silently read and reread the words he had scribbled on the brown file folder that held his own statement. "In the name of Christ. In the name of Christ," he repeatedly read, as he later told Danforth. Before entering the hearing room, Thomas, his wife, and Danforth and his wife had clasped hands behind the closed doors of Danforth's private bathroom and listened to a tape the senator had brought in of the Mormon Tabernacle Choir singing, "Onward, Christian Soldiers."

Soon it was Thomas's turn. He opened his formal statement by pointing out that he had shared his speech only with his wife and Danforth — "no handlers, no advisers," he said. Under the hot lights, he looked ready to explode as he glared through the swarm of television cameras focused on him and out at the nation beyond. The humble tone he had struck during the first set of hearings was gone, now replaced by defiance as he angrily declared that a seat on the Supreme Court was "not worth it."

He sounded perilously close to withdrawing, and many of the reporters sitting at the seven banks of long tables inside the hearing room wondered whether they'd soon be writing about the search for a new nominee. Thomas complained that he had lost more than ten pounds and had been plagued by insomnia since Hill had made her accusations. His mother was so sickened that she had become bedridden. In an odd soliloquy, he even seemed to be on the verge of making an apology, however oblique, to Anita Hill, who was watching the proceedings from her hotel suite, a few blocks away.

"I cannot imagine anything that I said or did to Anita Hill that could have been mistaken for sexual harassment," Thomas stated. "But with that said, if there is anything that I have said that has been misconstrued by Anita Hill, or anyone else, to be sexual harassment, then I can say that I am so very sorry and I wish I had known. If I did know I would have stopped immediately and I would not, as I have done over the past two weeks, had to tear away at myself trying to think of what I could have possibly done. But I have not said or done the things that Anita Hill has alleged."

The public had no idea, but this brief, conciliatory disclaimer was the last trace of Duberstein's influence. In Duberstein's judgment, it seemed possible that the charge had resulted from a misunderstanding between the two and that Hill had simply misconstrued Thomas's behavior. Fearful that she might testify to that effect, Duberstein pushed Thomas to avoid stating his denial so strongly that it eliminated the possibility of any middle ground.

But this language did not jibe with his adamant denials, and Thomas soon regained his harsh tone. He angrily warned Biden that he would not tolerate any questions that intruded on "what goes on in the most intimate parts of my private life or the sanctity of my bedroom." Then, without explaining why such inquiries would be so ruinous, he closed with a ringing refusal to "provide the rope for my own lynching."

Thomas had effectively walled himself off from embarrassing questions about his private life. Anita Hill would not be so lucky.

❖

Biden had planned to proceed with the questioning of Thomas, but the lawyers for Hill had refused to let the committee release her sworn statement as a basis for that questioning. Susan Deller Ross, for one, thought it was dangerous to let Biden characterize the allegation rather than having the Senate and public hear it in Hill's own words. So, after a heated debate with Orrin Hatch, Biden decided to excuse Thomas less than an hour after he had begun. Then the chairman called Hill to the witness stand.

The unexpected change in the schedule meant that Hill had to be quickly transported from her hotel to the Russell building and hustled into the hearing room by Capitol guards, leaving no time to seat her large entourage, which included her mother and father, numerous siblings, and several close friends who had flown to Washington. Wearing a tailored light turquoise suit, Hill took Thomas's place at the felt-covered table while Thomas repaired to Danforth's office.

She began her statement formally, reviewing her résumé. But within minutes Hill was testifying about Thomas's unwanted discussions about sex and pornography. There was an almost audible gasp in the hearing room when Hill arrived at the point when she described "one of the oddest episodes I remember." This was "an occasion in which Thomas was drinking a Coke in his office. He got up from the table at which we were working, went over to his desk to get the Coke, looked at the can, and said, 'Who has put public hair on my Coke?'"

For the next seven hours, except for a short break for lunch, Hill maintained an almost surreal calm as she answered a torrent of questions. In a disembodied tone, she described the series of tormenting conversations she had had with Thomas, then her boss, during the early 1980s. There were the pornographic films starring Long Dong Silver and women with huge breasts, the vivid descriptions of his own physical endowments, and the boasts about the pleasure he had given women through oral sex.

By the time Biden called the lunch recess, rumors that the president wanted to pull the nomination were flying. A few television reporters had gone on the air saying as much, citing anonymous White

House sources. Hearing these reports, Duberstein called Sununu and screamed, "You and your people are putting in more daggers [into Thomas] than the Senate! If you want to pull the plug, you better let me know first!" In this spiraling atmosphere of doubt, Sununu was forced to call Bush to be sure of his intentions. The president, who was trying to keep above the fray while his deputies went after Hill, told the chief of staff that he intended to stick by Thomas.

❖

While many Americans interrupted their normal work routine to watch the proceedings, for some the hearings were work. In Oklahoma, the two FBI agents who had interviewed Hill had been ordered by the Republicans in Washington to watch her testimony. As Luton and Jameson viewed her performance, they were supposed to note any discrepancies between her answers to the committee and her initial interview with them in an affidavit.

This use of the FBI was highly unusual. A veteran of the FBI and the head of one of its field offices later said, "It is extraordinary, maybe unprecedented, to have a statement from the agents." But as Bill Baker, the FBI's top spokesman at the time, later admitted, the agency was under mounting pressure. Hill's Senate testimony had included lurid and damaging details of Thomas's behavior — such as his comment about the pubic hair on the Coke can — which the agents had failed to elicit from her in their interview. They could either admit that they had done an inadequate job or suggest that Hill had fabricated the new details expressly for the hearings. "The FBI realized it was sitting on a time bomb," Baker said. "It was like the old cartoon of the Boss Tweed ring, with everyone pointing the blame at everyone else."

By the time Hill had completed her opening statement, both agents had sworn out affidavits — which the Republicans soon released to the media — suggesting that Hill had embellished her testimony, delivering a clear blow to Hill's credibility. Special Agent Jameson, for instance, swore that in the FBI interview, "Hill never mentioned or referred to a person named 'Long Dong Silver,' or any incident involving a Coke can." The public did not know that Hill's testimony — including such details as the Coke can story — followed almost word for word the account she had first given to James Brudney a month earlier, contemporaneous notes of which existed but were never released.

The two agents also later swore that Hill had changed her account of the last words Thomas had uttered to her, about what would happen if she ever told anyone of his behavior. The agents held fast to their version, which was that she said that he had threatened to ruin *her* career. They even swore out independent affidavits on the subject. But their competence, not Hill's consistency, again seems questionable; Hill, after all, had described Thomas as saying that if she talked, it could ruin *his* career, not just to the Senate but to Hoerchner, to Brudney, and in her original statement to the Judiciary Committee — a copy of which the agents had when they interviewed her. Again, the public had no way of knowing it, but the only account of Hill's words that showed any "discrepancies" was the FBI's.

"I don't know why the FBI thought they knew better than I did what I told them," Hill later said. "It strikes me as odd."

❖

Despite such attacks, Hill's daylong testimony posed serious problems for Thomas. Hill seemed believable and sincere, even to Thomas's most ardent supporters.

It fell mostly to Arlen Specter, whom the Republicans had shrewdly chosen as their lead questioner, to undermine her credibility. A former prosecutor, Specter took great pride in his legal skills. But the White House considered him the committee's Republican wild card, in part because as an independent moderate, he had opposed Robert Bork. Specter had also told a number of other lawyers over the summer that he thought Thomas was a poor nominee for the Supreme Court, and he had mocked Bush's assertions that Thomas was the "best-qualified" person for the job and that race had had "nothing" to do with the appointment. But by offering him a starring role, Danforth and Hatch gambled that they could invest Specter's considerable ego in their cause. As Biden later observed, "As soon as [Specter] saw himself as the star prosecutor, he couldn't resist. They knew his personality better than he did."

Politics — never far from this nomination fight — was working for the White House too. Specter's reelection fight was intensifying: he was facing a serious challenge in the primary from the party's far right wing, and if he could win conservative support with his role in these hearings, it might prove useful at home. Underscoring the threat, the weeks before Thomas's first set of hearings had put the literal "fear of God" into Specter. The Christian Coalition had sent an "action alert" to its members in Pennsylvania which pointedly included the senator's schedule of town meetings. Throngs of Christian Right activists had gathered at each meeting, demanding that Specter support Thomas. The last thing Specter needed was to enrage these Christian activists with another renegade vote on a Supreme Court nomination. He had even heard that there was speculation at the Republican National Committee that the White House might support his challenger because Specter had been so tepid in his support for Bush in the Senate. Specter consequently had many reasons to take up the cause of Clarence Thomas — the more visibly the better.

While many would later describe his questioning of Hill as prosecutorial, Specter was really playing the role of defense attorney. He began with an attempt to disarm Hill, stating, "I do not regard this as an adversary proceeding." But he then launched a systematic effort to point out inconsistencies in her testimony. Being able to establish a pattern of factual inconsistencies would chip away at her credibility — the key to Thomas's defense strategy.

Specter pressed Hill about her earlier remark that Phyllis Berry didn't know her. He picked over the supposed embellishments in her testimony that were missing from her FBI interview. He grilled her about her conversations with Thomas's friends at the American Bar Association meeting earlier that summer.

But he waited until Hill had completed her testimony and left the premises — and so was unable to defend herself — to accuse her of perjury, a federal crime. He was referring to a correction she had made in her testimony earlier that day concerning whether she had ever discussed the possibility that her public accusations might influence Thomas to drop out. Hill's statements on the subject were confusing, but so was the question, which centered on a news account quoting a friend of hers about a conversation they had allegedly had.

This overreaching by Specter surprised many of his admirers. "Perjury is an inflammatory term," said a former aide of Specter's who remained close to the senator. "To perjure yourself, you have to complete your testimony without correcting your testimony. Witnesses often change their testimony and recollection as they testify," just as Hill had. To do so was not considered a deliberate falsehood or even marginally criminal, but as one of Danforth's aides said, "Perjury is one of those great Perry Mason words. It was very effective on television." And it fairly shouted that Hill was a liar.

❖

In case "fantasizer," "spurned woman," "incompetent professional," and "perjurer" were not enough to ruin Hill's credibility, Hank Brown of Colorado, a new Republican member of the committee, attempted to establish yet another motive: politics.

The Justice Department aide John Mackey worked out a question with Brown designed to establish that Hill had disagreed with Thomas about abortion. (The Justice Department and the White House had together decided to enlist Brown because he was pro-choice, so he might get Hill to answer.) The question was intended to force Hill to reveal her radical, pro-choice feminism; the point that the Justice Department, the White House, and Brown hoped to convey was that Hill was finally attacking Thomas after years of silence because he was now in a position to threaten the *Roe* ruling. As an aide to Brown later put it, "We had to destroy the argument that she had no motive."

The strategy had risks. If Hill answered that she and Thomas had disagreed over *Roe,* it would be hard for Thomas to continue to claim that he had never discussed the topic. But the Republicans could deal with that later; more important now was the destruction of Hill.

That Friday, Brown did succeed in posing a general question about whether there were areas of serious philosophical disagreement between the two of them when Hill worked for Thomas. When she responded that they had disagreed on certain issues and had discussed them, Brown interjected, "Would that be the case with regard to, say, abortion or *Roe v. Wade?*" The Caucus Room was utterly silent as Hill leaned forward to answer; then she paused and looked quizzically at Biden. The hearings, he had said repeatedly, were to stay within the narrow scope of Thomas's alleged sexual harassment, and the abortion question was clearly outside this boundary. Biden ruled the question out of order, but the inference that some disagreement had occurred between them was left hanging in the air.

Since neither Thomas's nor Hill's views on abortion have ever been made fully clear, it is difficult to assess whether they truly differed on the subject or ever discussed it. But what is clear is that Hill did not lie in wait to attack Thomas, as the theory presumed; she was a conscript at the hearings, not a volunteer. Moreover, despite the Republicans' effort to portray Hill as a pro-choice zealot, she apparently is not. Although she has consistently refused to discuss her views, in 1993 she greatly disappointed the organizers of the massive abortion rights march in Washington by declining to attend.

❖

In the late afternoon on Friday, as Hill's testimony continued, new rumors began circulating at the White House. As Bush got ready to board a helicopter for Camp David, he was given some papers by an aide to Boyden Gray. The reporters who saw Bush perusing the papers immediately assumed the folder must contain the list of replacement candidates Bush would turn to if Thomas was forced to withdraw. They were wrong; the papers that so engrossed the president were the affidavit submitted by Thomas's friend John Doggett.

The affidavit was distributed by the Republicans that Friday to the president, the press, and the public before Hill, her lawyers, or the Democrats had a chance to see it and before the Senate lawyers had ever interviewed Doggett. In fact, Hill was initially questioned about it without knowing what her accuser had said. (Given the opportunity, she denied the story about their encounter.) In all likelihood, ambush was the preferred strategy because under any other conditions, Doggett's affidavit would have been ruled inadmissible. It was wild conjecture from a dubious source about a subject that was ostensibly outside the purview of the hearings: Hill's private life.

Nonetheless, because his words had already been circulated so widely, the Republicans managed to slip into the hearings Doggett's contention that the mixup over the long-ago dinner date with Hill suggested mental illness on her part. When Specter questioned Hill about Doggett, the television cameras panned to her face and caught it frozen in fearful confusion.

"Professor Hill," Specter demanded, "do you know a man named John Doggett?"

"Pardon me?" Hill asked.

Specter repeated the question, and Hill again appeared puzzled. Finally, she offered that she had met him, but when asked what the nature of their relationship was, she said in bewilderment, "I don't recall. I do not recall. We were friends, but I don't — it wasn't anything — I just don't know."

After a break, when Hill finally learned what Doggett had said about her, she stammered, "I have only a very limited memory of him." And she added that "I did not at any time have any fantasy about a romance with him."

Much later, when Doggett was cross-examined, his story and credibility as a witness imploded in a comical display of blinding egotism. After reciting the many high points in his résumé, he agreed that women found him "irresistible" and started talking, inexplicably, about some woman telling him the night before to "put your penis back in your pants." But this bizarre performance did not occur until midnight on Sunday, more than two days after his description of Hill as an "unstable" fantasizer had been read out loud on national television.

Specter, who had been Doggett's most ardent proponent, continued to insist that calling him was a brilliant stroke. But most of the other Republicans considered him a disaster. In fact, they had only narrowly succeeded in suppressing from public view the allegations of two women who had encountered or worked with Doggett and had provided Senate investigators with information about what they viewed as his offensive behavior. One of them submitted a deposition saying that Doggett had pressed unwanted sexual attentions on her at work, which he denied. Senator Metzenbaum wanted to call these women as witnesses or, at the very least, question Doggett about their accusations — which he began to do, at which point Doggett exploded in anger.

Having failed to rule out Doggett's testimony, Biden instead ruled that his would-be detractors were off-limits, thereby making it impossible for the public to understand fully the kind of viewpoint Doggett might have on the subject of sexual harassment. But as one of Biden's aides said later, "Oh my God, the calls we got on Doggett! A number of women wanted to testify against him, but we just couldn't get into every witness's track record — it would have regressed to infinity."

In one sense, however, Doggett's affidavit was a huge success. Early on, just as Hill was beginning to state her case, it suggested a pattern of psychological instability on her part when there was no evidence that one existed.

Notwithstanding such attacks, Hill ended her testimony that Friday at 7:40 P.M. feeling relatively sanguine, according to a friend. But while her speaking part was over, the characterization of her had only begun. Thomas returned Friday night, and this time he spoke with even greater ferocity.

The stakes could not have been higher. The White House realized that the prime-time audience would be much larger than the one that heard Anita Hill during the day; the Republicans had therefore been adamant that Thomas get back on television as soon as Hill finished her testimony. Biden had a toothache and was exhausted, so he wanted to stop for the day when she was done. The other Democrats also preferred to break until Saturday morning. But Biden had promised Duberstein this last word after the consultant had thrown his well-calculated fit.

It was obvious to the White House that Thomas had sustained considerable damage from Hill's testimony, but it was unclear whether the blow had been lethal. With no national poll results available yet, the Bush operatives had no way of knowing whether the viewing public believed Hill. But many of the television commentators who filled the air between Hill's final questioning and Thomas's return appearance were all but pronouncing Thomas dead.

When Thomas appeared for his rebuttal, he had been well prepared. For much of the day he had been closeted in Danforth's office, where virtually no one else had access to him. He later explained that he had refused to watch Hill's testimony, preferring instead to be briefed on it by his wife and Danforth. He had wanted to stay in this peculiar seclusion until it was time to go back before the camera.

But Thomas's great admirer on the committee, Orrin Hatch, believed that to save the nominee, the Republicans had to coordinate their efforts with him, even if such partisan prompting was unusual. So Hatch had simply barged past Danforth's staff and entered the senator's office.

He found Thomas pacing. "I'm not going to make it, am I, Senator?" Thomas asked. "Yes, you are," Hatch reassured him, "but it's going to be close."

Hatch knew Thomas personally and strongly identified with his Pin Point biography. Although the Utah Republican was now a millionaire known for his trim Savile Row suits, he too had grown up poor and remembered being teased for wearing bib overalls.

Hatch now had a plan: he thought Thomas was most effective when he was defiant, not defeatist. "I recalled an episode when he told off

Kennedy," Hatch later explained. "He had been at some hearing before the Labor Committee when Kennedy had pressed and pressed on something, and Clarence erupted, 'Senator, I was born in poverty. We didn't have much, but on the walls of our house we had three pictures: Martin Luther King, Jesus Christ, and John F. Kennedy. Senator, President Kennedy would not be proud of what is happening here today.' I knew if I could get Clarence to show that side of himself he would be all right."

Nothing aggravated Thomas more than racism, and so, like a picador at a bullfight, purposely goading the bull, the senator and the nominee settled on a series of questions about how Hill's characterizations of Thomas's behavior — boasting about his sexual prowess and penis size — exemplified the worst kind of racial stereotyping. "I told Thomas I was going to ask him some questions about black racial stereotypes," recalled Hatch. "He responded 'I wish you would.'"

The strategy was useful from the larger political standpoint too. Not only would it make Thomas angry, it would also anger the countless number of black viewers, whose sympathies were so critical to the nomination. In his opening statement, Thomas had already evoked the imagery of racial hatred, defiantly refusing to "supply the rope for my own lynching" by not answering questions about his private life. Now he would return to that theme. If Thomas could portray the inquiry into his sexual conduct on the job as a variation of black male sexual persecution, Hill's allegation couldn't possibly withstand the wave of anger he would unleash.

But that evening, when Hatch launched into the questions about racial stereotypes, Thomas seemed to miss the point. "When are you going to rise to the bait?" Hatch later said he thought to himself as he read back an array of Hill's descriptions of Thomas's language, asking each time if such language was a racial stereotype. Finally Thomas snapped alive when questioned about his alleged boasting about his physiognomy.

"This is something that not only supports but plays into the worst stereotypes about black men in this society. And I have no way of changing it, and no way of refuting these charges!" he thundered.

Thomas's temper had finally snapped. A short while later, he blasted the entire proceeding as a "high-tech lynching for uppity blacks." His language resonated so powerfully that Joel Paul, who was waiting in the hearing room to be called to corroborate Hill, said, "There was palpable tension in the room; it was as if someone had been shot." As a white man expecting to testify against Thomas, he said, "I suddenly noticed how many black people were in the room. Suddenly the room was divided between white and black. At that point I told my attorneys, 'I don't feel very comfortable anymore, let's find another office.'" Paul moved to another spot, but he later said that Thomas's racial strategy had a lasting impact. "I felt that if Thomas wasn't confirmed, I, and the other witnesses for Hill, would be held responsible for a great injustice."

As Paul sensed, and as the overnight polls showed, by playing the race card — the game of ethnic advantage that Thomas had built a career opposing — Thomas could win the victim sweepstakes. A professional woman's complaints about sexual mistreatment on the job had no chance against a black man's claim to being lynched simply because he dared to think independently and go against the political mainstream. Hill's standing, along with her grievances, was but a footnote against such historically heinous wrongs.

According to one of Thomas's oldest friends, Lester Johnson, Thomas knew that the white guilt of the committee would work for him. The senators were privileged, wealthy, and vulnerable. The uncle of one of them, Alabama's Heflin, had been an outspoken proponent of hanging the notoriously framed "Scottsboro boys" six decades earlier. As Johnson later put it, "Some white guys wouldn't let that be thrown at them. But Clarence knew that those white senators were weak. He's good at assessing the politics of his opposition. He knew it would be powerful — and it was."

"You hit a home run," Duberstein told Thomas after the performance. "In fact, you hit a grand slam."

At 10:34 P.M., when Biden recessed the hearings for the day, the verdict was unanimous — Thomas had come roaring back to life. As Orrin Hatch left the hearing room, National Public Radio's Nina Totenberg stopped him.

"Senator, you just saved his ass," she told Hatch.

"No, Nina," the Utah Republican responded. "He just saved his ass."

14

◆

Erotomania and
Other Maladies

BY SATURDAY MORNING, there was even closer coordination between Thomas and the Judiciary Committee's Republicans. Specter had ordered his aide Tom Dadou to comb Hill's testimony for inconsistencies. At eight-thirty that morning, the senator called Dadou to say that he was in Danforth's office — and so was Thomas. Dadou was surprised. "I thought it was odd," he later admitted, for an ostensibly nonpartisan Supreme Court nominee to be plotting with the Republican senators. But as Hatch had proven, the glue holding Thomas's confirmation together was rehearsal and coordination with his Republican defenders. Specter proceeded to scold Dadou for not coming up with any good ammunition against Hill.

But others proved more resourceful.

That morning, according to Dadou, an envelope was delivered to Specter's office from a law firm on K Street. In the envelope were citations to a 10th Circuit sexual harassment case that mentioned the pornographic movie actor Long Dong Silver. The envelope also contained an excerpt from William Peter Blatty's novel *The Exorcist,* which included a passage about a pubic hair floating in a glass of gin. Since there was no known connection between these items and Anita Hill, Dadou didn't think much of the material.

Hatch, however, was so taken with the references that he later credited his own office, not the downtown law firm, with digging them up. By his own account, as soon as he heard Hill's testimony about the pubic hair, he thought, "I've heard that quote before. I told my staff to start looking." Hatch claimed that it was one of his female aides who finally found the reference in the 1971 best-seller, and that he then dispatched a staff member to retrieve the Senate library's only copy of the book. Hatch also said that it was his staff who found the Long Dong Silver case, by running a search for the name through LEXIS, the computerized law library.

The Long Dong Silver case, as it turned out, had been decided at the district court level in Kansas in 1988. The plaintiff was a black woman alleging sexual harassment and unlawful termination; among her charges was that her supervisor had presented her with a photograph of Long Dong Silver. Kansas was in the same circuit as Oklahoma, where Hill taught law. To Hatch, the similarities were too good to be true. Without any proof, he was sure that Hill had read both *The Exorcist* and the decision and used them to invent her story. "It made it clear she was helped and manipulated in her testimony. I believe she had read the advance sheets in that [Long Dong] case," he later confirmed.

Again, Brudney's notes would have exonerated Hill of any insinuation that, as Hatch suggested, her "slick" legal team had found the pubic hair remark and "manipulated" her into adding it to her testimony. While she did not tell Brudney about Long Dong Silver specifically, his notes also clearly quote Hill as saying that Thomas had liked to talk about pornographic movies as well. But Brudney was staying as far away from the hearings as possible, in part because Hatch accused his boss, Metzenbaum, of illegally leaking FBI documents to the press.

No one ever produced any evidence that Hill had read the novel or the case; moreover, she had left the hearing room by the time the Republicans raised these points and so had no way of rebutting them. (Later, in an interview, she said she had not read either of them.) Ordinarily such speculation would be considered so prejudicial that it would never be allowed in an open court, let alone a Senate hearing. But that Saturday, the Republicans on the Judiciary Committee read portions from both *The Exorcist* and the 10th Circuit case out loud. Duberstein even told Hatch to hold up a copy of the book when questioning Thomas, on the theory that photos of the incriminating moment would run on the front page of every newspaper the following morning.

Chairman Biden, meanwhile, made no move to rule any of this speculation out of order. As this and so many other flatfooted judgment calls suggested, the Democrats on the committee were in almost total disarray, especially compared with the well-organized Republicans. The Democrats had had only one perfunctory meeting before the hearings, and it had dissolved into acrimony over accusations concerning the leak of Hill's allegation. The Republicans were claiming, falsely, that the FBI report on Hill had been unlawfully passed to the media; still worse, from the Democrats' standpoint, they were insisting that a federal prosecutor launch an investigation into this alleged leak. These accusations had the Democrats so completely on the defensive that Metzenbaum later concluded that they had been part of a conscious ploy to silence them.

Indeed, a few days after Hill's story broke, Hatch, speaking on the Senate floor, had directly accused Metzenbaum of leaking FBI documents. "Hatch publicly lied about me," Metzenbaum later protested. "I literally hadn't seen the damn FBI report at the time I was accused of leaking it. But Hatch must have thought it would intimidate me." And, he admitted, it had: "Sure, it created a problem — a hell of one. I lay this tactic directly at the feet of the White House. It was a smoke screen. I'd say when you tell a deliberate lie without a shred of evidence, it's a strategy." (Metzenbaum noted that later Hatch came to the Senate floor to apologize to him. But Metzenbaum, who subsequently announced his decision to retire from public office, swore that even though Hatch by now had "told me he loves me more often than my own wife, I won't forgive him until my dying day.")

Senator Kennedy was effectively silenced as well. He was the one member of the panel whose standing in the African-American community was so solid that he could take on Thomas with impunity, but on Friday and Saturday he sat through the hearings saying almost nothing. On Sunday, he could contain himself no longer. After conferring with a number of advisers about the wisdom of speaking up, he burst out about the unfairness of Hill's treatment. "I hope we're not going to hear a lot more about racism as we consider this nominee," he said, obviously irate. "The fact is that these points of sexual harassment are made by an Afro-American against an Afro-American. The issue isn't discrimination and racism, it's sexual harassment."

Shirley Wiegand, watching the hearings with Hill in their hotel, was taken aback by Kennedy's finding his voice; "He speaks!" she said to Hill. But Kennedy's moment of eloquence did not last long; he soon retreated into near silence again.

Senator Leahy, meanwhile, had expected a fair-minded, bipartisan, fact-finding expedition, but his aides came to realize they were in for something quite different when, at one point, they overheard Danforth screaming into the telephone at Duberstein: "This is war!" Leahy, a former prosecutor, finally started to lay some traps for Thomas. But he was hampered by the decision not to call either Thomas or Hill back for a second round of questions, which left his traps set but not sprung. He also may have been chastened by what an aide acknowledged to be "back-door threats from the White House," which let him know that if he was too hard on Thomas, he would pay dearly for it.

Biden was also on the defensive, becoming increasingly preoccupied with the criticisms of his handling of the charge. After Hill emerged, according to Duberstein, Biden had promised to issue a statement supporting Thomas's character; later, he changed his mind, afraid that Hill's supporters would be angered. Nonetheless, as the hearings approached — at a time when his staff could have been preparing material for the showdown between Thomas and Hill — he assigned his top aides to assemble a chronology showing that he had done nothing wrong. He told his staff that he believed the Democrats should assume a neutral fact-finding position in the hearings. This meant that, in contrast to the Republicans, who were literally rehearsing with Thomas, the Democrats would make no effort to coordinate with Hill or her legal team.

Cowed by Thomas's cries of racism and by the controversy over the leak, the Democrats resisted any tough questioning of Thomas during his two days of testimony. By the end of Saturday, the winds had clearly shifted in his direction. Hill's character and testimony were in tatters, while the forceful, angry denials of Thomas and his frontal attack on the unfairness of the Senate proceedings had almost completely rehabilitated him. Moreover, the White House finally had the ultimate weapon with which to intimidate the senators: overnight polls showing that the American people, by a comfortable margin, believed Clarence Thomas, not Anita Hill.

❖

By 6:30 P.M. on Saturday, as Thomas finally ended his testimony and the hearings adjourned for the day, Hill's team felt abandoned and overwhelmed. Simpson had delivered a tirade about Hill's elaborate array of "handlers," but to Hill's friend Keith Henderson, a Washington political strategist who was serving as an informal adviser, it seemed that Hill and her attorneys were being outmaneuvered on every side. Typical was their attempt to get Howell Heflin to ask whether Thomas had ever heard of Long Dong Silver. When the moment came, the gentlemanly southern judge stumbled badly, referring to the character as Long John Silver. Embarrassed and befuddled, he quickly dropped the line of questioning.

Equally lame was the Democrats' failure to fully explore the strange contradictions concerning Thomas's visits to Hill's apartment. Thomas testified that he had been a frequent casual visitor. However, Hill and her roommate were adamant that Thomas had come by only once, to set up her stereo. But Thomas said he had no recollection of this at all.

Brad Mims could have backed up Hill's account of the stereo. He recalled that Hill had asked him to help hook it up, and although he hadn't seen Thomas install it, Mims did remember that she told him afterward that Thomas had taken care of it for her. Hill's roommate, Sonia Jarvis, could also have testified about the stereo — and she had wanted to. But her testimony was considered dispensable by Hill's team, in part because she would have had to admit that Hill had never told her about the problems she was having with Thomas. The lawyers feared that Jarvis might raise more questions than she answered.

Consequently, the Democrats left these contradictions largely unexplored. Instead, they let Thomas and the Republicans deflect attention from the subject of Thomas's visits to Hill's apartment by insinuating that Jarvis was a lesbian, prone to playing basketball and wearing mannish "sweats."

By Saturday night, Hill herself was deeply dispirited. She had been portrayed as, among other things, a political zealot, a sexual fantasist, a scorned woman, possibly a closet lesbian, and a pathological liar who had lifted bizarre details from *The Exorcist* in a desperate effort to destroy Thomas. Worse, she, a black woman, was being publicly accused by Thomas of inciting his lynching.

At some points, the barrage became so overwhelming that she changed the channel on her TV to a basketball game for relief. Meanwhile, Wiegand went out to find fruit and other healthful snacks in a futile attempt to lift Hill's spirits. But when Gary Phillips, who had warned her not to come forward earlier that summer, visited her at the hotel, he found Hill completely demoralized. "Gary," she said, "you were right."

Later, Phillips was still bitter about his friend's treatment. "It is one thing to play dirty tricks in the political arena," he observed. "It is another thing when a private citizen steps forward and gets mauled. They set out to destroy her without ever stopping to consider if she was telling the truth."

❖

Hill might have been down, but she was not yet out. On Sunday, the Judiciary Committee was scheduled to hear from panels supporting both Hill and Thomas as well as from various expert witnesses. Hill's four corroborators — Susan Hoerchner, Ellen Wells, Joel Paul, and John Carr — were on the list of witnesses, and Hill's lawyers hoped to present two other panels, one consisting of old friends who could serve as character witnesses, the other a panel of experts on the issue of sexual harassment. The latter group would try to show that the ways in which Hill behaved — from her reluctance to file a complaint against Thomas to the telephone calls she had placed to him over the years — were not atypical of sexual harassment victims.

Thomas did not have any witnesses who could speak to the truth or falsehood of Hill's charges, but he did have a group of former female employees who were eager to testify that the behavior Hill described did not fit the man they knew. Danforth had put together two separate panels of these women, and he had found witnesses who could damage Hill's credibility further. They included Stanley Grayson and Carlton Stewart, the two lawyers with whom Hill had briefly chatted about Thomas's nomination at the ABA meeting, and Dean Kothe and John Doggett, both of whom were expected to elaborate on Hill's alleged history as a sexual fantasizer.

The Republicans were reaching even further afield for expert testimony. On Saturday night, the president's nephew Jamie Bush was having dinner at his mother's home in Connecticut with a politically conservative Jungian psychiatrist he had met at a Harvard reunion. The psychiatrist, Dr. Jeffrey Satinover, offered an ingenious theory of how Hill could have sounded so plausible in her testimony but still be lying: if she were suffering from something called De Clerambault's Syndrome, more popularly referred to in the diagnostic texts as erotomania, she could have imagined Thomas's sexual interest in her where none had existed. Moreover, because the syndrome's sufferers often seemed normal in most other ways, she could appear sane even if she were not.

There were a few problems with this psychological evaluation of Hill in absentia. Erotomania is extraordinarily rare. Moreover, erotomaniacs almost universally imagine that they have had sexual relations with someone when they have not. Nowhere in the diagnostic literature is there a case in which a patient imagined that someone had merely talked to them about sex — as Hill claimed Thomas had — rather than engaged in it. And most erotomaniacs, while appearing normal for a time, eventually get into trouble by obsessively calling, stalking, or in some other way acting out a fantasy with their imagined paramours. The sporadic professional contacts Hill had with Thomas, her steady and successful career, and her stable family and social life did not seem to suggest insanity.

But Satinover's theory apparently excited Jamie Bush. The psychiatrist said later that before he left the Bush household that evening, the president's nephew contacted the White House counsel's office. Boyden Gray's assistant Mark Paoletta was working around the clock on the Hill matter and was eager to hear more about a theory positing her mental illness. "He was really interested," Satinover recalled.

That night, at Paoletta's request, Satinover returned to his home in Westport and faxed further information on erotomania to the White House. Apparently this too was well received, because Satinover was asked to rush to the capital the next morning in order to testify.

By the light of day, however, the president's lawyers apparently had second thoughts about eliciting testimony from a psychiatrist who had never met Hill. The profession's own code of conduct prohibits doctors from providing diagnoses of patients they have not examined; the standard rules of courtroom evidence also outlaw such a practice. Biden himself would rule that these psychiatric opinions were inadmissible. "In a courtroom," Satinover admitted, "it would have been thrown out. As a hobbyhorse, it couldn't be ridden very far."

But the erotomaniac label still could be, and was, added to the overall portrait of Hill. Satinover spent hours on Sunday being grilled in the back room of Danforth's suite by Thomas's lawyers, including Thomas's old friend Larry Thompson, the former U.S. attorney in

Georgia. According to Satinover, they were trying to figure out ways in which the syndrome could be brought up obliquely, since they knew that any direct approach would backfire.

The perfect opportunity arose that afternoon. Hill, in what her lawyers thought would prove a surprise coup, had taken and passed a professionally administered polygraph test, which showed that she was not being deceptive. As Ogletree later explained, "I thought that the polygraph would be the most pivotal thing in the hearings, because her credibility had been the focal point."

But the Hill team had not expected the fierce counterattacks, both on the reliability of the tests in general and on Hill's mental suitability for taking one. Hill might not be a standard liar, as they had earlier implied, but, the Republicans now suggested in the open hearing room, she might be so delusional that she believed her own lies. If so, she could pass a polygraph test and still be wrong about Thomas.

After consulting with Satinover, Larry Thompson presented this line of attack in a statement that was read out loud that afternoon by Senator Simpson. "In the context of these proceedings," began Thompson's statement, "I understand on the basis of reliable scientific sources" — such as Satinover, presumably — "that if a person suffers from a delusional disorder, he or she may pass a polygraph test." In reading the statement into the record, Simpson did not mention that Thompson, whom he identified only as a former U.S. attorney in Atlanta, was a member of Thomas's defense team, not a neutral expert.

Also not mentioned was that Thompson had been secretly pushing hard to have Thomas take the same kind of test and had personally arranged to fly a polygraph operator he knew and trusted up from North Carolina. Danforth was so nervous that Thomas wouldn't pass, he suggested that if they did go ahead with it they should test Thomas in private, so that if he flunked they could keep it a secret. His concern, Danforth said, was that Thomas's anxious state would skew the findings. But even under these protected conditions, Thomas adamantly refused to take the test, explaining, according to Danforth, that "it was just further degradation, and he had nothing of his own humanity left."

A further irony was that although the theory of erotomania might be useful in explaining how Hill had passed a lie detector test, Satinover never actually believed that Hill suffered from erotomania or any other form of delusion. In a later interview, he said that he had thought Hill merely a liar, not an erotomaniac. But whatever medical qualms he might have had were overlooked by those whose wanted to undermine Hill's credibility.

Satinover was not the only expert on sexual deviance who was huddling with Thomas's wife, friends, and advisers behind Danforth's closed doors. As Hill's four witnesses were testifying that she had told each of them of her sexual harassment problems at the EEOC, Dr. Park Deitz, a psychiatrist, was attending his high school reunion in Camp Hill, Pennsylvania. One of the country's foremost experts on violent sexual disorders, Deitz was the author of "A Longitudinal Content Analysis of Sexual Violence in the Best-Selling Erotic Magazines" as well as articles on autoerotic asphyxiation. He had been a member of Edwin Meese's controversial pornography commission and had also been an expert witness in many of the nation's most notorious sexually related murder cases and in that of President Reagan's would-be assassin, John Hinckley. Now Deitz received an urgent phone message from Danforth's office.

Returning the call, Deitz remembered, he heard Larry Thompson tell him that he was needed in the Capitol to provide information to Senators Danforth, Hatch, Specter, and Simpson on psychosexual disorders that might be afflicting Hill. Deitz got on the next plane to Washington and was met by a member of the prestigious White House Fellows program, who rushed him to Danforth's suite in a gray Jeep Cherokee. In the Senate, Deitz recalled, the atmosphere was "like the Academy Awards," with reporters and the public lined up to get in, the corridors thronged with excited onlookers who applauded and shouted at the public figures as they walked past.

In his back office, Danforth sat down with Deitz and asked him to write a technical description of erotomania that they could use in describing Hill. "He was looking for psychological help in his case," Deitz said. The psychiatrist obligingly wrote a statement describing erotomania which he was willing to have read aloud at the hearings. But, according to Deitz, "I had to steer him away from mental health. It was technically unfeasible for psychiatry to play a part under the circumstances. People were throwing terms around with much unsuspected baggage. Danforth," he later said, "was sincere — but disappointed."

Danforth was more than disappointed. He was so frustrated at his inability to get Deitz to testify that he considered calling a press conference so that the psychiatrist's erotomania description could be distributed to the media. But at this point Danforth's own aides were so appalled at the senator's fervor that they protested vehemently; in fact, the legislative director in his office threatened to resign if Danforth persisted.

Before Deitz left, however, he was asked for an opinion on one additional matter. He was given a description of what he recalled as "a bizarre and unsubstantiated piece of evidence" concerning Hill — something, as he later remembered it, that had to do with pubic hair. What disorder, he was asked, might be lurking behind this new, damning evidence? "I told them," said Deitz, "that this was totally unsubstantiated, and that they couldn't put this sort of thing on."

Deitz didn't realize it, but he had just dismissed out of hand one of the most controversial secret weapons being held in reserve by the Republicans against Hill — what came to be known as the "pube" affidavit.

❖

On Saturday night, as the White House counsel's office was exploring erotomania, aides to Senators Brown and Simpson were working overtime to prove that Hill had sprinkled pubic hairs on the term papers she had returned to her former law students at Oral Roberts. The source of this and other gossip about Hill was the Fringe Riders, the group of rednecks from Oral Roberts who had so resented her presence as their professor.

When Hill's name surfaced, many of them started calling one another and rehashing their complaints. One of them, Brett Godfrey, whom a black classmate, Ken Ferguson, described as having "really stood out in his effort to show Hill that she didn't belong there," told his father that he had some salacious information about Hill. The father, a prominent attorney and conservative political activist in Wyoming, quickly notified Simpson, with whom he was acquainted through the state's political circles.

On Saturday, in the open hearing room, Simpson hinted broadly that Hill might not be as pristine as she appeared. "And what do we know about Professor Hill?" he demanded. "Not very much . . . I am getting stuff over the transom about Professor Hill. I have got letters hanging out of my pockets. I have got faxes, I have got statements from her former law professors, from people that knew her, statements from Tulsa, Oklahoma, saying, watch out for this woman!"

But as of Saturday, what Simpson also had was a problem: the senior Godfrey was glad to pass on his son's information, but he did not want his son — a young and politically ambitious attorney — sullied by it, so he would not let his name be used. This meant that Brett Godfrey would not testify or even back up his stories in a sworn affidavit. The situation was so tantalizing to the Republicans that top officials at both the Justice Department and the White House tried to intervene, begging the Godfreys to go public. But they would not.

Since the younger Godfrey now lived in Colorado, an aide from Hank Brown's office joined the lobbying effort, spending two hours on the phone with the young lawyer. Hill's former pupil asserted that Hill was a "radical feminist, anti-male, and a sixties-style activist" with unusual sexual habits, the aide recalled. Godfrey also said, according to the aide, that Hill was a contradictory person, both a prude and a tease, who was said to be a lesbian, but who was so attractive that he would not have minded dating her himself. On one occasion, he claimed, she had sauntered up to him at the bulletin board wearing a tight skirt and a fluffy angora sweater, smiled, and said out of the blue — ostensibly referring to herself — "Your favorite flavor has to be chocolate." On another occasion, he said, the professor had come up to a clutch of Fringe Riders, including himself, and inexplicably asked, "Who do you think you are, Long Dong Silver?"

Finally, Godfrey said that she had handed classwork back to some of the other Fringe Riders with a dozen or so pubic hairs enclosed in each of their plastic binders. The pubic hair motif, the reference to Long Dong Silver, and the picture of Hill as talking dirty to her students could not have been better constructed to show that it was Hill, not Thomas, who had a seriously strange behavioral problem. But with Godfrey unwilling to testify, Brown's office had to find corroboration.

Thomas had railed against what he considered the sleazy tactics of his opponents — "anybody with any dirt, anything, late night calls, calls at work, calls at home, badgering, anything, give us some dirt" — but now an international search for dirt on Hill ensued. One former Fringe Rider, reached in Canada, said he could not help because he was too busy studying for the bar exam. In St. Louis, an attorney named Jeff Londoff was startled to receive a call at home in the evening from an aide to Senator Brown. The former Fringe Rider was even more surprised when the aide started asking whether he still had the plastic binder with the pubic hairs that Professor Hill had returned nearly a decade earlier. Could he go up to his attic and look for it? the aide asked.

After a brief search, Londoff reported that none of the hairs had survived the years, making a forensic examination (which the aide wanted) impossible. But Londoff was taken aback by the direction of the questioning. He had been present when the papers were returned and was ostensibly one of the story's chief corroborators. As he remembered it, one of the other Fringe Riders, Larry Shiles, had found a couple of short curly hairs in his paper; he had cracked that either Professor Hill had graded the papers in the bathroom or else she didn't think much of his work. Shiles had asked if anyone else had hairs in their binders, and Londoff had found some too. But Londoff said that even at the time "the whole thing was just a joke. How the hell would anyone know whether it was pubic hair or not? The lady's black, you know, she's got kinky hair. Or it could have come from an assistant too."

Even so, the Senate aide was extraordinarily persistent, Londoff said, calling him ten or twelve times during the next day or so. The aide also faxed draft affidavits, attesting to the "pube" story and to Hill's alleged radicalism, for Londoff to sign. "They wanted to put as much crap down on her as they could," he said. "At one point they said she was a lesbian. At another, they said she had made advances to Brett [Godfrey]. I think they were looking for anything they could find, but the affidavit was so one-sided, I refused to sign."

With no one yet willing to put his name on the "pube" affidavit, the Republicans had one last hope: the jokester Larry Shiles himself. An older student while at Oral Roberts, Shiles had had academic and health problems and ultimately received his degree from another school. He now practiced personal injury law in Tulsa. But to the growing despair of the Republicans, Shiles was, according to his wife, away that weekend with their son in the wilds of Rifle, Colorado, hunting for elk.

Undeterred, at midnight that Saturday, Senator Brown's office succeeded in tracking Shiles down at his motel. Shiles — whom his friend Londoff described as having "had a problem with Professor Hill for a number of reasons," one of which was that "he didn't do too well in her class" — was happy to sign the "pube" affidavit. But time was of the essence. The Senate aide searched the *Martindale-Hubbell Law Directory* for the law office closest to Rifle and arranged for Shiles to make his statement legally binding with a notarized signature as early as possible on Sunday morning, preferably before the hearings reopened.

Even Shiles's good friends, including Londoff, doubted his reliability as a witness. Shiles had more than just a personal grudge against Hill; as Londoff put it, "You have to understand, Larry has a different view about black and white [people]. He's a great guy, but he's from down South, if you know what I mean . . . And Hill — well, the lady was black at an almost all-white school. There were a lot of racist cracks."

Yet, despite his antipathy toward Hill, Shiles denied Godfrey's second revelation, the story about her having spoken of Long Dong Silver. Reached in Tulsa a year after the hearings, he said, "Godfrey claims I heard her say it, but I have no memory of it whatsoever."

Neither did John Eagleton, the third and final Fringe Rider whom Godfrey named as an eyewitness to Hill's mention of Long Dong Silver. He remembered hearing Godfrey claim that Hill had stomped off angrily because a conversation with Godfrey had touched on pornography, but he admitted that despite Godfrey's recollection to the contrary, he had never actually heard Hill say such a thing himself. And as for the pubic hair story, Eagleton, who was present when the papers were returned and who thought very little of Hill, nonetheless said, "It's a crock."

Regardless, the Republicans knew that the "pube" affidavit could do horrendous damage to Hill. And even if it was never released publicly, it could be a powerful bargaining chip that would thoroughly intimidate the Democrats. Thomas's Justice Department adviser, Mike Luttig, personally believed that the law students' stories were "farfetched . . . politically motivated and probably made up." And Duberstein opposed any public use of the Shiles affidavit, arguing that it would sink the hearings to new depths of depravity.

But Danforth was so determined to use the material against Hill that he wanted to hand out copies of the law student's statement to the media, going outside the controlled environment of the hearings so that no one would have to cross-examine the source of the tales.

Later, Danforth admitted that "getting those affidavits was my obsession that afternoon. I knew that Anita Hill was going to be demolished . . . In my quest for affidavits I was showing no concern at all for fairness to Anita Hill."

Danforth's top staff member, Rob McDonald, acknowledged later that by this point the senator was consumed with concern that if Thomas's nomination foundered, he would be personally blamed. Winning was now crucial to both their careers. The message from Danforth, McDonald recalled, "was that we had to win at any cost."

❖

As for the other faxes, letters, and statements Simpson was getting "over the transom," not all of them were as spontaneous as he made them sound. Many of them had originated not in Oklahoma but in Washington — with a helping hand from one of Thomas's leading supporters.

At this point, Morton Blackwell, a particularly hard-core conservative activist whose ingenuity and money were behind one of the ad hoc black groups that supported Thomas's confirmation, became involved. He had a contact named Chris Wilson among the students at Hill's law school in Norman. Wilson had been a star pupil at Blackwell's Washington-based Leadership Institute, which taught young members of the Religious Right how to take a role in national politics. Now, although Wilson had not been in any of Hill's classes, Blackwell nevertheless advised him on how, as Wilson later put it, to go "about the business of making Anita Hill's life a living hell."

According to Wilson, it was Blackwell's idea to round up as many conservative students on campus as possible and have them send faxes to Senators Hatch and Simpson, describing any complaints they had heard about Hill. "Morton's really incredible!" Wilson later said. "We faxed hundreds — well, maybe thirty — letters to Simpson, Hatch, and Brown. I asked people to send them to [Oklahoma Senator] Boren too, because he'd be a swing vote, and since he's from her home state, it would show Hill wasn't even believed in Oklahoma. These were the faxes Simpson was talking about when he said he had them falling out of his pockets — that was us."

Wilson, who was chairman of the college Republicans and of the anti-abortion group Collegians for Life as well as the founder of the campus chapter of the Young Americans for Freedom, got in touch with other conservative activists at the school, and many of the faxes came from them. A number of the letters also came from Wilson's fraternity brothers in Kappa Alpha, a white, all-male redoubt on campus dedicated, according to the yearbook, to honoring the traditions of its "spiritual founder," General Robert E. Lee, with customs like its Plantation Ball. Not surprisingly, most of these faxes concerned what the students saw as Hill's radical feminist leanings.

Simpson made the faxes and letters sound like an outpouring of seriously disturbing truths about Hill. But almost all of them were from students who had never studied with her and so had no first-hand knowledge. Only one of the writers was willing to have his name used, and although he asserted that Hill was a wild-eyed radical in class, she had never been his teacher. As Wilson's roommate and fraternity brother said later, "Chris didn't even know her. He was trying to find people who didn't like her. But as far as I know, they only found one who had her as a teacher, a lawyer in Tulsa."

When this Tulsa lawyer (who asked not to be named) was reached, he confirmed that he had joined the effort to discredit Hill at the instigation of Wilson. Like Wilson, he was a member of Kappa Alpha, and he had been a conservative campus activist who had worked with the college Republicans and the 1984 Reagan reelection campaign. But he had always liked Hill personally, he said. Moreover, he had never heard her say anything that he considered politically partisan. His complaint was that "I just didn't think she was always prepared for class."

❖

The Republican attack wasn't limited to Hill. The four individuals willing to testify that Hill had told them earlier of the EEOC harassment were also subject to intensive research to identify any weaknesses that could be exploited. The idea that all of them had either fabricated or misunderstood their conversations with Hill was far-fetched; indeed, it would require belief in either a conspiracy or an astonishing coincidence. But by questioning each witness just a little, the Republicans could at least put a few cracks in the apparently solid buttress of support they provided.

A former student of Joel Paul's working for a Republican senator had confirmed that the Republicans indeed had thick dossiers on each of Hill's potential witnesses, and that, just as Paul had feared, his own included information on his homosexuality. But in the end the subject wasn't mentioned. Just the threat of being "outed," however, had been enough to put Paul on edge.

A more intense focal point of the Republicans' attention was Susan Hoerchner, the workers' compensation judge in California whom Hill had first named as a corroborating witness to the FBI. Before leaving for Washington, Hoerchner was alarmed to learn from a colleague at the Association of California State Attorneys that the White House had called with questions about her. Then Susan Hamilton, her supervisor, received a request for her personnel file from someone working for one of the political appointees of California's governor, the Republican Pete Wilson. "I was paged in L.A. with the request," Hamilton recalled. "I said, 'No, we can't do that.' I didn't think it was appropriate."

Alan Simpson's office then swung into action. Simpson's son, a Wyoming attorney, had called with an incorrect tip that Hoerchner herself had filed an unsubstantiated sexual harassment charge against a California judge, Donald Foster. One of Simpson's aides tracked down Foster, whose retirement the previous summer had ended the matter without any formal disciplinary proceedings. "We found the judge and got on the horn to him," recalled Stan Cannon, a Simpson aide. It turned out that Hoerchner had not been the complainant but had written a letter supporting the female judge who was. To Simpson, the distinction was not important. "The point was that Hoerchner was well versed on how to do someone in on a sex harassment charge," Cannon explained.

When Simpson confronted Hoerchner about this during her testimony, she became badly rattled. The senator kept pressing her about whether she had ever filed a sexual harassment complaint; the more he asked, the more unsure she seemed. A day earlier, Hoerchner had watched in horror as Specter accused Hill, the most truthful person Hoerchner knew, of being a perjurer. Now she worried that somehow the supporting letter she wrote might have technically qualified her as a complainant against Foster — which it didn't. But in fear and confusion, she answered Simpson's question in the most equivocal way possible. "I can't say that I didn't," she finally conceded.

The Republicans found another weakness in Hoerchner — her poor memory. Bill Kristol, Vice President Quayle's aide, noticed that she had given an obviously wrong date to the FBI for the original conversation she'd had with Hill about Thomas's harassment. In conversations with several reporters, he pointed out that on the date Hoerchner cited, in the spring of 1981, Hill was still working at Wald, Harkrader. Therefore Thomas could not possibly have been the "Clarence" to whom Hill had been referring in the conversation with Hoerchner. Either someone else was the perpetrator or Hill had made the whole thing up.

On the witness stand, Hoerchner said repeatedly that she could not recall the exact date of the conversation and later explained that she had only given the FBI her "best guess." But by the time the Republicans finished cross-examining her, Hoerchner had come across as a nervous and vague witness who failed to correct the impression that she herself had a history of concocting sexual harassment charges.

The notion that Hill had accused the wrong perpetrator was now seized on by Phyllis Berry, who testified on the first panel of Thomas's supporting witnesses following Hill's panel of Hoerchner, Wells, Paul, and Carr. Berry even offered a name of a potential substitute harasser: Hill's former supervisor Chris Roggerson, the man who had been Thomas's chief of staff early in his tenure at the EEOC. "Mr. Roggerson doesn't have such an impeccable reputation," Berry testified, leaving open the question of how Hill had confused the two men and why Thomas, who had portrayed himself as vigilant against sexual misconduct, would make such a man his chief of staff.

Hill's accusers found more support for the "wrong man" theory when it became apparent that neither Joel Paul nor John Carr could say for sure whether Hill had specifically named Thomas when she told them that her boss at the EEOC had harassed her. The fact that Carr was absolutely certain that Hill was referring to Thomas, who had been a recurring topic of conversation between them, was no deterrent.

Only Wells, among Hill's corroborators, was left relatively unscathed. But the Republicans did find a way to diminish the impact of her testimony. Always ladylike, Wells had testified that she hadn't pressed Hill for explicit details of Thomas's boorish behavior, although she knew the problem to be of a sexual nature. Thomas's defenders thus argued that without having heard the details, Wells could not fully corroborate Hill's story.

Meanwhile, even though none of Thomas's witnesses knew or had seen anything directly relevant to the allegations, their positive experiences with Thomas were presented as an equal counterweight, which greatly helped to neutralize the testimony of Hill's panel. Furthermore, where Hill's corroborators came off as erudite Ivy League lawyers, the women supporting Thomas, particularly former EEOC workers like J. C. Alvarez and Diane Holt, cast themselves as down-to-earth common folk. In fact, Alvarez, a successful business executive in Chicago, referred to herself in the third person as "John Q. Public from Middle America, not unlike a lot of people watching out there, and not unlike a lot of your constituents."

Both Alvarez's and Thomas's longtime personal secretary, Diane Holt, tried to establish how overweeningly ambitious Hill had been, in an effort to show that far from fearing Thomas, Hill had pursued him for her own uses. Holt testified that she and Hill had "discussed that this man was a rising star, and we wanted to be there with him." None of the senators pointed out that Holt's testimony directly contradicted a deposition she had given — which was never publicly released — only days before, in which she had stated that she and Hill had never had a single social or professional conversation about Thomas.

Perhaps most dispiriting to Hill, who was again watching the proceedings in her hotel room, was a brief appearance late Sunday by Linda Lambert Jackson, who served on a second panel of female Thomas supporters. Jackson had worked with Hill and Thomas in the early eighties and was the friend in whom Hill had confided her problems with Thomas on her first visit back to Washington in the fall of 1983. When Hill had told her the real reason she left the EEOC, Jackson's initial disbelief had brought Hill to tears. It was this conversation, Hill had later told Brudney, that had made her realize that she had better keep quiet about Thomas's harassment, because even friends found it difficult to believe.

Jackson, as it happened, had grown quite close to Thomas over the years. He had lived in the same building and, as she put it, "helped me pick up the pieces of my own crushed spirit after I left an abusive marriage." Hill had heard that Jackson planned to testify for Thomas, so she had not tried to call her as an additional corroborator. But when her former friend spoke, it took Hill's breath away.

"Anita . . . referred to Clarence with admiration," testified Jackson. She went on to say that Hill had never uttered a word about having been harassed by him. "It seems that she would have mentioned something if she were having problems at the office, even if she did not name a specific person. Subsequent discussions I had with Anita," she added, "also yielded no mention of anything improper on the part of Clarence Thomas."

Later, Jackson, who still worked for the EEOC during and after the hearings, refused to comment on the telephone when asked whether Hill hadn't told her of the harassment years before. She then quickly hung up.

Asked about Jackson's behavior, Hill commented wearily, "There is a reason for people to feel anxious about coming forward." Her own experience had proven this. Moreover, some of Thomas's witnesses, she pointed out, still relied on the EEOC as their sole source of income. Many were single parents. But finally she admitted, "I don't know how people can go to sleep at night having lied as some of them did. Certainly I couldn't. But in the end, they have to live with themselves."

❖

By late Sunday, many of Hill's lawyers were anxious to get back to commitments they had in various parts of the country the next morning. Midnight came and went, and yet the testimony — by now all of it favoring Thomas — continued. Although Kothe and Doggett produced far less than the Republicans had hoped, a second panel of eight women who had enjoyed working with Thomas was impressive.

Disgusted, exhausted, and intimidated by what another round of questioning might hold, Hill had turned down an opportunity to testify a second time. Since they had crucial testimony from a new witness still to come, Hill's lawyers wanted to save time and so scratched both her panel of character witnesses and the expert witnesses on sexual harassment. Later, some of the Democrats suggested that Hill's failure to return to defend herself had been a fatal miscalculation. Few realized it, but her decision was partly based on concern about possible testimony from the Fringe Riders. Without revealing how dubious their sources were, the Republicans had led the Democrats and Hill's lawyers to believe that they had new and even more damaging information on Hill.

"We had evidence that the hearings were no longer going to focus on fact," said Ogletree later, "but instead on outrageous comments about her sexuality, teaching performance, and relationships with men.

We could have stayed to rebut these, but it was clear the focus was going to be on diversion."

Before going their separate ways, Hill's team gathered to pose for a farewell photograph. Hill looked drained. But the camera caught one of her lawyers, John Frank, looking modestly hopeful. Frank was about to fly home to Arizona, but he actually believed that the tide was about to turn in their favor.

Frank realized that if the hearings ended then, with just Hill's word against that of Thomas, the committee would be left more or less where it started. But it was Frank's understanding that by the time his plane landed, the Senate would have heard from a woman whose testimony would show that Hill's experience was part of a pattern. Frank considered this second woman "absolutely the key witness showing parallel conduct."

So he was stunned when his wife picked him up at the airport in the early hours of Monday morning and told him that Biden had gaveled the hearings to a close — without ever calling Angela Wright.

15

The Other Women

ANGELA WRIGHT WAS the proverbial other shoe that, if permitted to drop, could shatter Thomas and his supporters' portrayal of Hill as an isolated and possibly deranged liar. Sensing this, Wright said later that she doubted from the start that she would ever be allowed to testify. And if she was, she said, "I knew these people were going to paint me as a two-headed hooker with alien babies."

Thus Wright had kept a wary distance from the proceedings in Washington. The only thing that surprised her about Hill's charges when they first surfaced was that they were considered important enough to interrupt the regular Sunday night television programming she was watching in her Charlotte, North Carolina, condominium on October 6.

Wright, who was then the thirty-seven-year-old assistant metro editor of the *Charlotte Observer*, had never met or heard of Hill, but she knew Thomas, having served as his director of public affairs at the EEOC from March 1984 until he fired her in April 1985. She recalled that when she heard Hill's charges, she thought to herself, "So what else is new?" Wright said that she expected that a whole chorus line of women could have pranced forward with similar statements, including herself.

Having been fired by Thomas, Wright naturally didn't remember him as her favorite boss. She was glad to have made a successful new life for herself outside Washington, and although she was outspoken by nature, she had no intention of getting involved. However, the day after Hill emerged, when Thomas's sponsors reacted to her allegation with such utter disbelief, Wright became annoyed enough to express it. From her standpoint, Thomas's allies seemed to be summarily dismissing Hill — a young black woman who could just as easily have been Wright under different circumstances — and, as she later put it, "sweeping the whole thing under the rug."

Wright, who had been auditioning for her own newspaper column by writing sample editorials just for her editors' eyes, dashed off one about Thomas. In it, she suggested that she knew from her own experience that Thomas was capable of the kind of behavior Hill had described. She detailed his inappropriate and sexist remarks about her anatomy when she worked for him, in particular his question to her about the size of her breasts. Since only a few editors would see the piece, she expected that to be the end of it.

On the Wednesday before the hearings, however, she was surprised to find that Mark Schwartz, a staff member on the Judiciary Committee, was trying to reach her. She assumed he had gotten her name by culling old EEOC employee lists. But when she returned the call, it became clear that he had heard of her trial column; someone from the newspaper — without her consent or knowledge — had evidently faxed a copy of it to the committee. After talking with her over the phone, Schwartz asked whether she would be willing to come to Washington to testify.

She declined. She was a journalist now and she wanted to cover the news, not make it. Having lived in Washington for eleven years, she had learned the hard way that she was not cut out for politics. She had had a happy, productive life since leaving five years earlier and no longer had any desire to participate in what she now considered "a circus." Besides, she regarded Thomas's nomination to the Supreme Court as "ridiculous" and his confirmation hearings "a farce." And after watching the kind of treatment Hill was getting as the second round of hearings approached, she believed that the only fate awaiting anyone who took on Thomas was tar and feathers.

But Schwartz, a young lawyer who had been working for Biden for only a few months, was not about to let such a potentially critical witness get away. Schwartz was amazed, he later said, that only two days before the hearings, he had found another woman with such similar complaints about Thomas. Wright's tone was quite different from Hill's, reflecting a feistier style. Wright described Thomas "as if he were an annoying fly," Schwartz later said, "like, 'What a pest that guy was'" — which is why she hadn't thought his behavior rated as harassment. But her descriptions of Thomas's manner were entirely familiar.

Wright recalled that Thomas acted as if his position as chairman of the EEOC gave him, as she put it, "carte blanche" over the women who worked for him. While he was her boss, she told Schwartz, Thomas had pressured her in a similarly obnoxious fashion to date him, had also paid a visit to her apartment, and had made similarly disturbing comments in the office appraising how sexually enticing various clothes made her look. Many of the phrases Wright remembered were also reminiscent of the words Hill said Thomas used, from the way she said that Thomas had commanded that she go out with him while never really asking for a date to his inappropriate comments during work about breast size — in her case, her own.

Thus far, the confrontation between Thomas and Hill seemed to pit one person's word against the other's. Any existence of a pattern was therefore seen as decisive. Under such circumstances, the probative value of a second woman was obvious. "As soon as she mentioned the boobs remark," Schwartz later said, "I thought, 'Oh shit — I better take good notes.'"

Schwartz completed his interview of Wright at about ten o'clock on Wednesday night. The hearings would open in just thirty-six hours. He rushed from his cubbyhole in the Russell Office Building over to Biden's inner chamber with the news. Schwartz said that when he briefed the chairman, who was meeting with a few other top aides, Biden "was very cool about it. He was not excited at any time, he was just very steady. He was already fifty steps ahead of everyone else and could see where it was leading. There was a sense of nausea, or something big. Instantly, everyone knew it was serious."

Learning that Wright would not testify voluntarily, Biden moved quickly to have one of his most able assistants, Cynthia Hogan, depose her by phone the next day. If the deposition seemed pertinent, then they could subpoena Wright.

No one understood the serious threat Angela Wright posed better than the Republicans. According to Schwartz, when Duberstein was notified the next afternoon of the new allegations against Thomas and told that Wright had been formally deposed and was now about to be officially subpoenaed to appear as a witness, "They were ballistic." Duberstein was "screaming, 'You can't do this! What are you doing?'" With the hearings set to open the following morning, Schwartz said, "there was complete shock and furiousness."

The mathematics of the situation was clear: one woman plus one more equaled the probable end of the nomination. As Thurmond's aide Terry Wooten later observed, "Any time you had a second allegation, it was going to be a big problem." "With only one accuser," agreed the White House communications director, David Demarest, "and everyone else saying something contrary, the public is doubtful. But with two accusers, no matter what the second's credibility, the public really listens."

Having only a rudimentary understanding of sexual harassment, the Republicans defending Thomas had been insisting that in order for Hill's charges to be believable, there would have to be other such victims. This premise was not necessarily accepted by the experts, but it did raise the standard in a way that they thought would protect Thomas.

But now that this threshold was in peril of being crossed, most of Thomas's supporters sensed that no matter who she was or what her credibility, it would be a disaster if Wright ever testified — even if in her eyes Thomas's behavior had not constituted harassment. So by Thursday night, the evening of the day Duberstein had learned of her existence, Thomas's supporters had already begun mobilizing to ensure that she never would.

By the time Wright got home from work that evening, news of her existence had already leaked to the media and pandemonium had broken out. The phone started ringing incessantly, then the doorbell. She stayed quietly in her study. She noticed that two strange white men were standing at her front door; she tried to pack an overnight bag so that she could flee to a friend's house. It was only when she managed to escape with her dog, Ginger, that she realized the two men weren't reporters, as she had thought, but federal marshals. They handed her a subpoena from the Judiciary Committee requiring her to fly to Washington the next day. Wright took the subpoena, grabbed Ginger, and fled to her boss's house. There, she promptly threw up.

Back in Washington, the Republicans were already poring over her government employment records. Wright's files, like Hill's previously, had been immediately obtained by the White House without Wright's permission, which under normal circumstances is a violation of the Privacy Act.

Her files contained ample ammunition for anyone trying to embarrass her or, more important, bluff the Democrats into backing away from her. In her twenties, before working for Thomas at the EEOC, Wright had been fired for losing her temper by Charlie Rose, a Democratic congressman. She had been on the verge of being fired a second time, from a job with USAID, when she quit after accusing her boss there of racism in an incendiary letter. And of course in 1985 Thomas too had fired her, pinning the termination notice to her office chair.

Armstrong Williams claimed that Wright had been so grateful for Thomas's positive job recommendation in 1989 that she had sworn to him that she was "going to be good" — and make no trouble for Thomas. But the moment that it was clear to Thomas's allies that Wright was not going to be "good," her days of glowing professional reviews were over. Even before she arrived in Washington, as news about her began to leak to the media, Thomas's defenders had engineered a negative campaign aimed at portraying her to the press as incompetent, mendacious, and, above all, vengeful. "Watch out," Duberstein warned Biden's chief counsel, Jeff Peck, and others, "your Angela Wright may turn out to be Angela Wrong."

Privately, Duberstein's efforts to intimidate Biden were even more blatant. If Wright turned out to be unreliable, he warned the chairman, Hill's credibility too would be ruined. And if this show of concern for Hill was not convincing enough, Duberstein, according to one aide he spoke to, also issued a simple threat: should Biden start dumping more dirt on Thomas, Duberstein warned, "the pendulum is gonna swing back" — meaning that the Republicans would do worse to Hill. Given that the Republicans had nothing of substance on Hill, the threat was hollow, but Biden had no real way of knowing that.

Hatch was even more aggressive. That Thursday night, in words that struck Wright as "totally inappropriate for anyone, let alone a U.S. senator conducting a supposedly fair and impartial hearing," Hatch publicly lashed out at her as "just another act to smear [Thomas] that's been dragged up by people who have to get him." In a smear of his own, Hatch later said that Wright "had accused all of her previous employers of sexual harassment." Wright denied she had ever accused any employer of sexual harassment, including Thomas. And there is no evidence to the contrary.

Meanwhile, Thomas's former aide Phyllis Berry again proved resourceful. In contrast to the story Thomas told the *Charlotte Observer*, Berry began spreading the word that Wright had actually been fired by Thomas for a very particular offense. As she told it, Wright had called another EEOC employee, a man whom her colleague Armstrong Williams later identified as John Seale, "a faggot." This, Berry said, had been such an intolerable slander that Thomas had been forced to fire her for offensive language on the spot.

When asked about this later, Seale, who supported Thomas's nomination, said he had no recollection of Wright's having referred to him as "a faggot." In fact, he said he could recall "no verbal slights" from her at all.

That same Thursday, Ricky Silberman, vice chairman of the EEOC and one of Thomas's most ardent supporters, offered a completely different explanation for Wright's firing. It conformed to Wright's own account: that she had been fired because of Silberman's and Thomas's general displeasure with her. Silberman told the *Los Angeles Times* that Wright was fired after a press conference went awry.

"The faggot line," according to Wright, "was made up out of thin air. I'd never say that — I'd put my hand on a stack of Bibles! I believe they sat down and cooked it up because it says all the negative things you can say — that a person is homophobic and insensitive." She acknowledged that she has a sharp tongue and can be hotheaded. But she insisted that her employment records — which the Republicans had in hand — contained no mention of this alleged cause for dismissal.

Despite the lack of documentation and Seale's corroboration, Thomas's old EEOC friends Clint Bolick and Silberman worked all night Thursday furnishing this and other choice details about Wright to the press in an emergency damage-control marathon. "We got out the message that she'd been fired, the faggot thing," Bolick later recalled. "By the time the story [about Wright] broke the next morning, these things were in the stories. Ricky worked the phones all night. We got across that she was a gay-bashing sewer-mouth. If that story had had a day to sit there," he conceded, "it could have killed Clarence Thomas."

Back in North Carolina that Thursday night, Wright got her first taste of what she was in for when she started to take some of the press calls asking her to comment on the Republicans' charges. "The first line of attack," she recalled, "was that 'Angela was a jealous, scorned woman.'" In fact, the *Los Angeles Times* quoted an anonymous source that night, suggesting falsely that Wright and Thomas had "social ties" predating her work for the EEOC; according to the unnamed source, "There were conflicting accounts about who sought to end the relationship." Hearing this, Wright remembered, "I was like, 'Get a grip! I never dated that man and I never wanted to.'"

Next came the firing, the faggot story, and her alleged vengeance against Thomas. In the political maelstrom, she said, the truth was so distorted that the Republicans were saying she had been fired from AID when she hadn't been, while the Democrats were denying that she had been fired by Congressman Rose when she had. "This is why I hate Washington," she later complained.

By Friday morning, as she boarded an early plane to the capital with her most conservative pinstriped pants suit in her bag, she was already shaken from the onslaught. Later she could laugh about it, she said, but in the hysteria of the moment she thought it possible that something might happen to her plane. She recalled being so nervous that she recited the Lord's Prayer and the Twenty-third Psalm over and over like a mantra all the way to National Airport.

❖

Wright was not the only woman who could provide testimony about a pattern in Thomas's behavior, Biden's office learned. At 1:45 P.M. on Thursday, contemporaneous staff notes show, Biden's office got a phone call from Kaye Savage.

Notes from the staff's telephone interview of Savage show that the former career civil servant in the Reagan White House who had known both Thomas and Hill socially was willing to testify, on the record. She was ready to tell the public about how she had visited Thomas's bachelor apartment in the summer of 1982, when he was Hill's boss, and found it plastered with explicit photos of nude women. Finding it, as she put it, "a little crazy," she had asked Thomas about it. His explanation of the display — that he didn't drink and didn't run around, so this was his one outlet — attested to the habitual nature of his interest in such materials as well as to the prominent role that they apparently played in his life at the time when, according to Hill, he talked repeatedly to her about pornography.

It had taken several days for Savage to summon enough courage to approach the committee. She now occupied a senior position in the government of the District of Columbia, and stepping into such a political battle would obviously pose risks. Earlier that week, she had tried unsuccessfully to reach Joel Paul when she read that he planned to corroborate Hill, just to talk things over. But her call had been intercepted by Paul's lawyer, Jamin Raskin.

Remembering Savage's call, Raskin said, "She started to tell me this incredible story, but I said, 'Don't tell me any more — get in touch with the committee.' But she was afraid. She said she didn't know how to do it. She's a single mother, and I think she was scared of getting caught in the crossfire."

He recommended that Savage call a lawyer first. Then, to make it easier, he offered the name and number of his wife, Sarah Bloom, an associate in the prestigious Washington law firm of Arnold & Porter. Savage placed the call. Bloom was willing to represent her, but before doing so — in an indication of how threatening the nomination fight was — Bloom had to clear it with the senior partners of her firm. "People wanted to see what cases we had pending in front of Clarence Thomas and what his prospects were. But," she said, "I was given the green light."

Like Raskin, Bloom thought it best for Savage to contact the committee herself. Both lawyers assumed that the committee would be immediately attentive because both believed that her account was directly relevant to the proceedings. As Raskin later put it, "It had a general relevance in that it reflected Thomas's attitudes toward women. And specifically, after Hill's testimony, it was absolutely relevant. If it could be shown that Thomas was obsessed with pornography, how could anyone claim that it was not relevant? It might not be seen as something that discredits his character, but it absolutely bolstered Anita Hill's testimony."

When she finally called the committee, Savage too was referred to Biden's aide Mark Schwartz. Once again she described her visit to Thomas's apartment. She also mentioned Thomas's comment that his sex magazines were the only things he had thought worth taking from his marriage.

The aide thanked Savage and told her that a decision needed to be made about whether to take her information up to Biden. He said someone would get back to her if they needed anything else.

Although noncommittal, Schwartz was evidently struck by the gravity of what Savage had to say. In the chaos of new leads and wild tips, he drew up a list of what information impressed him as most important, and Kaye Savage topped it. After her name, his notes show that he jotted, "The most probative and compelling information."

A Biden aide familiar with the handling of the Savage matter, however, said that Schwartz's superiors were considerably warier. To allow Savage to testify, they believed, would cross a line explicitly drawn by Biden, placing off-limits all but Thomas's behavior at work. Perhaps more to the point, they feared her testimony was so controversial that it would trigger a massive political backlash against the committee.

Savage, like Wright, had tossed a live grenade into the works. Biden was trying to separate public issues from private, but by its very nature the charge of sexual harassment blurred the distinction, posing difficult questions about the unofficial conduct of an official figure. Yet, as Biden well knew, the private consumption of mainstream pornographic material was constitutionally protected. An excursion into a Supreme Court nominee's sexual habits would without a doubt trigger enormous criticism of the committee from outraged Thomas supporters, civil libertarians, and the millions of people, young and old, who considered *Playboy* and other sexually explicit magazines an American rite of passage. It would also, in Biden's eyes, be unjustified.

But for the committee to bury such potentially substantiating information posed risks too. If evidence of its suppression was ever leaked to the public, it could backfire completely. Congressional hearings had no rules of evidence other than those the chairman decided to follow. But it was clear that to stonewall willing witnesses and hide information that supported Hill was to knowingly undercut her credibility and to distort the truth about Thomas.

On Thursday night, with Hill poised to testify as the lone voice questioning whether Thomas's behavior toward women befitted a Supreme Court justice, this dilemma landed squarely on Biden's polished antique desk. Over the next three days, while important allies of Thomas's, such as the current chairman of the EEOC, Evan Kemp, asserted that Hill's charges were preposterous since "Clarence finds pornography repulsive," Biden wrestled with his conscience. Meanwhile, Angela Wright and Kaye Savage waited to be called.

———❖———

Biden's dilemma only deepened when, as the hearings opened, word reached his staff that the well-known and well-respected Washington attorney Fred Cooke, formerly the District of Columbia's corporation counsel, had actually seen Thomas checking out a pornographic videotape in or just before 1989. The date was relatively recent, evidently not long before Thomas's appointment to the court of appeals, making it all the more difficult to dismiss tales of his earlier interest in pornography as a youthful indiscretion. Indeed, a number of such stories were reaching the committee, including some accounts from Thomas's former college and law school acquaintances.

Cooke had resolutely kept his distance from the hearings and had not brought the information to the committee's attention himself. Several friends said later that he told them that he did not want to get involved in a no-win donnybrook for black professionals. Everyone who was getting close, he believed, was walking away with mud all over them. Any public disclosure that Thomas had an interest in pornographic movies such as *Bad Mama Jama,* he argued, could only make the hearings more embarrassing for African-Americans, many of whom already feared that the proceedings were making them a national laughingstock.

Some of Cooke's friends disagreed. John Payton, Cooke's liberal Democratic successor as the D.C. corporation counsel, had thought the *Mama Jama* story funny when he first heard it, not long after the incident occurred. But after he heard the news of Hill's allegation that Thomas had spoken to her about large-breasted women and the like, Payton viewed Cooke's information as "a bombshell," potentially devastating to the nominee. But Payton was the top lawyer for a city that relied on federal funds at a time when the government was headed by Republicans. He too decided that it wasn't prudent, either politically or professionally, to get anywhere too near this debacle.

In the days before the hearings, however, the circle of people who knew of Cooke's encounter with Thomas widened — indeed, the news of *Bad Mama Jama* traveled as far as South Africa. There, Barbara Arnwine, of the Lawyers Committee for Civil Rights Under Law, and Mary Frances Berry, of the U.S. Civil Rights Commission, were taking a trip when a colleague in Washington telephoned them with the news. Arnwine and Berry in turn notified Hill's advisers, such as Christopher Edley, a Democratic party activist who had informally joined her team. Edley got as far as dragging Cooke into a conference call with Elaine Jones, the formidable leader of the NAACP Legal Defense and Education Fund. But even with the pressure of all of these black activists, Cooke still declined to play a public role, as notes taken of this conversation show. He told Edley that he would reconsider his position only if he were compelled to testify by a subpoena issued by the committee.

Thus, with committee action the only means of possibly getting Cooke to testify, the question of how to handle *Mama Jama* also landed on Biden's desk. Increasing the burden further was the related question of Thomas's video rental records. If Cooke's account was true, then Graffiti, the store involved, had pertinent evidence; it might also provide an answer to the publicly disputed question of Thomas's familiarity with Long Dong Silver. But given the Video Rental Protection Act, which civil libertarians on the Judiciary Committee such as Senator Leahy had helped to draft, a subpoena was required before such records could be released. This meant that any probe into such highly sensitive and inflammatory material would require yet another order from the chairman himself.

❖

By the time Wright reached Washington on Friday morning — preceded by news stories heralding "Another Woman" — the news media were in such a frenzy that a police escort had to be ordered to the airport hangar to extricate her. The committee had made hotel reservations for her near the Capitol, but Wright was so overwhelmed by the attention that she decided she'd feel safer staying in an obscure motel in a dreary stretch of the Arlington, Virginia, suburbs.

At the *Observer*'s urging, Wright had retained the same North Carolina law firm that represented the paper, Smith, Helms, Muliss & Moore, to advise her during the hearings. Expecting that she would be called in only a few hours, her attorneys rushed her to their Washington office and began to prepare for her appearance. Almost immediately, they asked Wright if she had talked about Thomas with anyone who might now corroborate her story. The committee's investigators had asked her the same thing the day before, and Wright had reluctantly informed them that she had talked quite a bit about her problems with Thomas to her best friend at the EEOC, the speechwriter Rose Jourdain.

Wright was reluctant to name Jourdain because the week before the hearings, Jourdain had been hospitalized for a neurological problem. She had temporarily lost the use of one of her legs, and given her condition, Wright did not think it fair to drag her into such a mess. But her lawyers urged that she at least contact Jourdain, just in case she was needed. When she did, her heart sank. Jourdain, who was still immobile in her hospital bed, had already been found by aides to the committee who had followed up Wright's tip. Realizing that her role in the hearings — a part she had never wanted to play — had already hurt a friend, Wright broke into tears.

While the committee had been in a rush to reach Jourdain, it seemed inordinately slow about calling Wright. She waited in her lawyers' offices all day Friday; her lead counsel, James G. "Gil" Middlebrooks, concluded that the Republicans were engaging in a series of delaying tactics. Among these, he believed, was their sudden insistence that Wright submit to an FBI interview before testifying. She had already been deposed by both minority and majority counsels and expected to testify under oath, so there seemed to be no need for this additional hurdle.

It wasn't until one-thirty on Saturday afternoon — by which time Thomas was in his second day of testimony and seemed close to winding up — that the FBI agents arrived to interview her. Once they were there, however, they seemed to have no idea why they had come. Neither agent, according to Wright and her attorney, had a copy of her deposition, and neither asked anything relating to the hearings. Instead, they proceeded to perform what sounded to Wright and her lawyer like a routine background check on Thomas, asking her, for instance, whether she had ever known him to abuse alcohol or drugs and whether she would trust him with top-secret documents. When she answered affirmatively to the latter question, her lawyer interjected, "But do you trust him?" and she answered, "No." The one-and-a-half-hour visit, as she recalled it, was more than a little strange: "They just sat there and scratched their heads in wonder."

"The performance of the FBI, if Wright's interview was indicative," said Middlebrooks, "was a sheer waste of taxpayers' money. It was unbelievable."

By that day, unknown to either Hill or Wright, Sukari Hardnett, another of Thomas's former assistants at the EEOC, also felt that it was her duty to speak up for Hill. Hardnett did not personally know Hill, but she did know Thomas, with whom she had had a number of political differences. And she thought the image of a prudish code of correctness at the EEOC that he and his supporters were promoting was utterly false.

Like Savage, Hardnett tried to reach Biden in order to offer her help. Although she now worked for the Washington Urban League, where her boss was an ally of Thomas's, she was nonetheless willing to come out against the nominee. Hardnett had been active in the civil rights movement, and she was outspoken and committed to doing what she thought was right. Through politically connected friends, she sent a statement to Biden's office and offered to testify. In a telephone conversation, she told an aide that Thomas's claim that he never "co-mingled" his work and social lives was demonstrably untrue. In fact, she was willing to testify that he had virtually auditioned young female employees to play the role of a potential mate. As for herself, Hardnett made clear that Thomas had never harassed her. But he had made her uncomfortable by calling her at home to discuss male-female relations and by requiring her to socialize with him over coffee each morning when she was in favor.

But Biden's aide Mark Schwartz — the recipient of this tip too — was evidently not impressed. His notes from his conversation with Hardnett show merely that he jotted down "was forced to have coffee with Thomas."

Hardnett's written statement about what she saw as the unmistakable sexual dimension to Thomas's treatment of women at the EEOC could have been read out loud into the record, as the Republicans did with any number of statements supporting Thomas. But instead, in unrebutted testimony, Thomas was portrayed by numerous former female employees as so meticulously correct that, as one put it, he "frown[ed] upon even consensual romantic relations [in the office] because he did not want one woman in the agency to even mistakenly believe that her dignity had been compromised."

In the end, Hardnett was never called to testify. But her name was invoked during the hearings anyway. Although she was not present to defend herself, her reputation was disparaged when Biden briefly asked Thomas's character witnesses from the EEOC about her. They portrayed Hardnett as an incompetent employee whom Thomas had to let go because she failed to pass the bar exam. Hardnett had, in fact, flunked the Louisiana bar exam, but this had happened before she went to work at the EEOC. Her bar standing was not a condition of employment, nor did it have any bearing on her job as Thomas's special assistant. Hardnett later said — and others have confirmed — that rather than being forced out, as Thomas's allies implied, she asked to be transferred from Thomas's supervision because she did not enjoy working for him. She could have stayed on at the EEOC, but she left of her own volition.

"It bothered me that they could say these things and get away with it without anyone bothering to investigate or set the record straight," Hardnett later commented. It also bothered her that no one ever allowed her to testify. She was one of the few people who had worked for Thomas who was not afraid to speak ill of him; he was, she said, "a very calculating" man whose "truths were trimmed with false-hoods." But, she concluded, "Clearly, they didn't want to hear from me."

Instead, Hardnett, like Wright and Savage, disappeared into the dark well of Chairman Biden's thought processes.

❖

With these pressures mounting, on Saturday Biden struck a private deal on the crucial issue of whether to air testimony concerning Thomas's personal interest in pornography. In a heated bipartisan meeting, according to aides to both Republican and Democratic committee members, Danforth — who was not a member but who was permitted to join the meeting — threatened that if one word of testimony connecting Thomas to pornography was allowed into the public hearing room, the Republicans would air the evidence they had about Hill's private life.

Lawrence Shiles, the former Fringe Rider, had not yet signed the "pube" affidavit, so at this point the Republicans were bargaining with two unsubstantiated accusations: the other was Brett Godfrey's anonymous and uncorroborated charge that Hill was simultaneously a prude, a lesbian, and a nymphomaniac, given to propositioning her male law students and sprinkling pubic hairs on their term papers.

For the Democratic side, Kaye Savage, a former official in the Reagan White House, was willing to testify about what she had observed to be Thomas's pronounced interest in pornography at the time he supervised Hill. Fred Cooke, a former public official and lawyer in Washington, might have been compelled to testify as an eyewitness to the nominee's specific interest in a pornographic video of the kind that Hill had described him talking about. Others had also contacted the committee with information about Thomas and pornography. After hearing Hill's testimony, the husband of a woman who had attended graduate school at Yale when Thomas was there called Kennedy's office to say that his wife, who was now a professor in Massachusetts, had told him for years about what a pornography enthusiast Thomas had been. Kennedy's aide Ricki Seidman called the woman, who told her that she was afraid for political reasons to play a public role in the confirmation fight. Given this, the lateness of the call, and Biden's decision that Thomas's behavior as a young man was irrelevant, Seidman did little more than jot down the woman's description of how Thomas had frequently carried sexually explicit magazines in the back pocket of his overalls and described X-rated movies he had seen during law school. As the woman put it to Seidman and in an interview later, almost everyone who knew Thomas knew he was "into pornography." Even one of Thomas's supporters, Lovida Coleman, had inadvertently mentioned in a news article that Thomas had enjoyed offering detailed descriptions of dirty movies he had seen in law school.

The meeting soon dissolved into a shouting match. According to one Republican aide, the Republicans, led by Danforth, argued that Biden had to let in either none of it or all of it.

Hill's potential witnesses presented a far greater threat to Thomas than anonymous former pupils did to Hill. But the witnesses for the two sides were equivalent in the only way that really mattered: politically. Calling any one of them posed a risk no committee member — and least of all the committee chairman — wanted to take. Anger at the handling of the hearings was already causing a national outpouring of disgust at Washington. The committee members — who, like most senators, lived in fear of public opinion — knew that the polls that weekend were showing public support for Thomas running twice as high as it was for Hill. Therefore, taking up Hill's cause seemed a completely thankless exercise. As an aide to a Democratic committee member later explained, "At that point there was only one desire, and it was shared by every member of the committee, Democratic and Republican: 'Shut this damn thing down!'"

So, without dissension from the Democrats, Biden accepted the Republicans' terms: no testimony about anyone's private life would be allowed. It was the course of least resistance. It sounded fair. And as a former target of media inquisitions who had been discomfited from the start by Hill's charge, Biden perceived it as a victory for decency itself.

Yet while Thomas portrayed himself as an exemplar of proper employment practices and walled himself off from questions about his personal life, Hill had already been forced to testify under the committee's subpoena about the most humiliating sexual conduct she had ever experienced. She had been subjected to unrebutted characterizations of her private sexual behavior as pathetic, bizarre, and insane. It was as if a trial were being terminated after the prosecution's case had been heard but before the defense was allowed to make its arguments. To become squeamish about personal matters at this point and to bury information that might have exonerated Hill was to tarnish her reputation and skew the result of the hearings.

But Hill's reputation was not foremost among the committee's worries. The Democrats in general, and Biden in particular, appear to have been far more concerned with their own reputations. As an aide to Biden who had favored calling Savage later put it, "There was concern about a political backlash if we got into these things — probably a very legitimate concern." Added another Biden aide, "The American public already hated us — what would it have thought if we allowed this stuff on?"

Looking back on the hearings, Biden was somewhat defensive about this pivotal decision. At one point, he argued heatedly that "it was no more relevant to whether Thomas was telling the truth if he had four thousand copies of *Playboy* in his home. Is *Playboy* pornography? Is it legal? Does reading it make someone a harasser?" Purposefully or not, Biden was overlooking the fact that *Playboy* was not the only pornography in question, and while Thomas's interest in pornography was not necessarily linked to harassment, it was nonetheless at the core of Hill's allegation concerning Thomas.

During another interview, Biden was more candid. "I could have brought in the pornography stuff. I could have decimated [Thomas] with that. I could have raised it with more legitimacy than what the Republicans were doing," he admitted. "But it would have been impossible at that point to further postpone the hearings for more investigation into his patterns of behavior . . . and it would have been wrong."

As Biden saw it, he had just been trying to be fair to Thomas. Moreover, he believed in the sanctity of privacy, which, he argued, extended to Supreme Court nominees. It was up to him, he concluded, to act as a statesman and, no matter how nasty the other side got, to uphold the standards of decency. But Biden once overheard his own wife suggesting that when it came to power, he was naive. And in this instance he ultimately came to realize that his sentiment had been misplaced. He had acted, he later admitted, "in fairness to Thomas, which in retrospect he didn't deserve."

❖

Late Saturday afternoon, Angela Wright was still waiting in a conference room at her lawyers' offices, perfecting her opening statement while watching the hearings. At one point, she heard Senator Simpson say that "Angela Wright will soon be with us — we think. But now we're told that Wright has what we used to call in the legal trade 'cold feet.' Now, if Angela Wright doesn't show up to tell her tale of your horrors," he said to Thomas, "what are we to determine about Angela Wright?"

Wright's lawyer looked up at her and asked, "Angela, are your feet cold?"

"No," she answered, "just tired."

According to Middlebrooks, "no one from the committee had even talked to us" before insinuating that Wright — a subpoenaed witness — was experiencing second thoughts. "Simpson just made it up," Middlebrooks commented. "It was like there were no rules."

Disgusted, Wright sat down and drafted a statement saying, in its entirety, "I have been subpoenaed to testify before the Committee. I have cooperated fully with representatives of the Committee on both sides of the aisle, and the FBI. I am ready to testify before the Committee and I do not have cold feet."

But before she could release this correction, she was amazed to hear Thomas himself, under oath, repeating Phyllis Berry's account of her dismissal.

"Did you fire her?" Simpson asked. "And if you did, what for?"

"I summarily dismissed her," Thomas testified, his voice even and firm. The reason "was a report to me from one of the members of my staff that she referred to another male member of my staff as a faggot."

"As a faggot?" Simpson repeated with horror.

"And that is inappropriate, and that is a slur," Thomas said, "and I was not going to have it."

Wright was furious. Stuck in a Washington law office, her hair pulled back in a businesslike bun, wearing a prim skirt she had borrowed from her sister because her lawyers thought her pants suit too sporty, Wright felt powerless to defend herself. "They were purposefully distorting my record and no one was speaking up for me," she later said. "I wouldn't care if what they said was true. I know I've made mistakes, I can live with that. But you can't fight the lies."

Middlebrooks figured that the Republicans were trying to make a preemptive strike against Wright to ensure that she never appeared — a tactic that ultimately proved successful. Looking at it in retrospect, he commented, "They were scared that if Angela took the stand it would be the straw that broke the camel's back, and the Democrats didn't know what they had. They thought she would be too rough-and-tumble."

Biden gaveled the hearings to a close for the day at 6:30 P.M. By that time, Wright recalled, "I had gotten over a lot of my early nervousness and by then was almost looking forward to being called in the morning. I kind of looked forward to going head to head." She was particularly angered by a statement she had heard that Hatch had made about her, in which he warned that the committee was going to "hand her her rear." "Actually," Wright later said, "I wanted to tell Mr. Hatch that the last time I looked, my rear was still behind me."

Middlebrooks confirmed her feisty mood at this point, adding that "by then, Angela was damn mad about the whole process. Hill was being attacked when she wasn't there, no one was asking Clarence

Thomas tough questions, and then there was the cold feet thing." He acknowledged that Wright "wasn't ecstatic about going on, seeing people using copies of *The Exorcist* and talking about lynchings. But she was ready and willing to go."

❖

The committee had other ideas, however. By Sunday afternoon, Hill's four witnesses had provided their testimony; meanwhile, sixteen character witnesses for Thomas were scheduled to make their tributes. Thomas's witnesses ranged from his former secretaries to his former college and law school friends, such as John Doggett. With the confirmation vote scheduled for Tuesday at 6:00 P.M. and a probable break on Monday, time was running out.

At about five on Sunday afternoon, the committee recessed and privately agreed that in the interest of saving enough time for Wright to testify, it would limit each of Thomas's final panel of witnesses to just five minutes apiece for their statements, and a total of thirty-two minutes would be allotted for questions. But when the committee reconvened and Senator Kennedy, who was standing in for Biden temporarily, made an effort to enforce the agreement, the Republicans publicly complained that it had been merely a "suggested" limit.

Clearly, the only way to prevent Wright from appearing was to stall. But all the public saw was a dispute that seemed trivial and childish.

"We made an agreement," protested Leahy.

"There is no agreement on this panel at all," disputed Thurmond. The agreement, he said, had only pertained to "the last panel."

In an effort to compromise, Kennedy suggested, "All right, let's make it seven [minutes per witness]."

"No," insisted Thurmond, a man who in earlier years held the record for single-handedly delaying civil rights legislation with his around-the-clock filibusters, "we don't want to limit them."

Biden, who was out of the hearing room when the fracas erupted, made a point of being generous when he returned, publicly offering the witnesses as much time as they wanted. They took four more hours.

Still sitting in the law office downtown, Wright was by this time beyond frustration. Worse, she now saw Biden, who had brought her to Washington against her will, questioning whether she had the nerve to come on, as if it were up to her.

"We will bring forward, if it is the decision of the witness to want to come forward, and that is not fully decided yet, Ms. Angela Wright," he said. "We are talking with Ms. Wright now . . . And after Ms. Wright there will be . . . a Ms. Rose Jourdain, who allegedly — I emphasize allegedly — can corroborate the testimony of Angela Wright."

As Biden suggested, the committee was indeed talking with Middlebrooks at that point. But not, Middlebrooks later said, because Wright was trying to back out. "I was raising hell with the Senate staff, mostly dealing with Cynthia Hogan in Biden's office, telling her it was silly to put these pro and con panels on. My position was, 'Put someone else on that this has happened to! Why are you doing this? No one is interested in these panels. This is crazy!'"

But Hogan, whom Middlebrooks later praised for her professionalism, was not in a position to do much but report back to Biden. She kept saying merely, "I'll pass your concern on to the chairman." By Sunday evening, Middlebrooks estimated that he had called Hogan and other Biden aides "probably twenty-five or twenty-six times. But we couldn't get them to listen."

❖

Meanwhile Rose Jourdain, though still taking heavy medication, was standing by to back up Wright's account. That Sunday afternoon, shortly before Jourdain was scheduled to be released from the Washington Hospital Center, Senate aides had reached her by telephone and deposed her from her hospital bed. As she spoke, Jourdain later recalled, she squeezed her grown daughter's hand because of the intense pain.

Jourdain confirmed that when she and Wright had worked for Thomas at the EEOC, Wright had complained frequently of his unwanted sexual attentions, which on occasion had reduced Wright to tears. Jourdain said that Wright had described Thomas's sexual comments in the office as "a constant" problem. She independently recalled Wright's mentioning that Thomas had inexplicably asked her "bra size." She remembered that Wright had complained that Thomas dropped by her apartment one night uninvited. Much to Wright's later embarrassment, Jourdain also recalled for the committee aides the time Wright had told her that Thomas had gone on a tangent about the sexiness of her leg hair. Summing up Thomas's reported behavior

— and suggesting the kind of direct, no-nonsense witness she would have made — Jourdain said, "I thought it was nutty — you know what I mean?"

That evening Jourdain was released from the hospital. She had not been home more than fifteen minutes when the committee called, saying that she might be needed to testify right away.

"My God," Jourdain exclaimed to her daughter, a student at Harvard Law School who had come home to care for her, "look at my hair!"

Over the next hour, while her daughter proceeded to braid her hair in a crown around her head and help with her makeup, Jourdain cut her painkillers into quarters so that she could be lucid if called. There was still the problem of shoes. Jourdain's medical condition had left her feet so swollen that none of her shoes fitted. For that matter, she couldn't walk without support. If she testified, she would have to be rolled up to the microphones in a wheelchair. Even then, she couldn't sit for more than ten minutes without significant pain. The Senate aides offered to send an ambulance or specially equipped van to fetch her, but Jourdain was afraid of being dropped or tipped out of her wheelchair and possibly paralyzed.

As she remembered it, the aides kept trying to reassure her when they called, saying, "Don't worry, we're the Senate Judiciary Committee."

As the hours went by, with Jourdain alternately swallowing painkillers and nibbling snacks to keep her energy up, the ordeal became increasingly onerous. More than once her daughter asked, "Mom, is it worth it?" But when Jourdain wavered, the two switched sides and her daughter would then argue, "Mom, you gotta do what you think is right."

At one point, Jourdain remembered, an aide phoned and warned her that she might not be called until two-thirty in the morning. "I said, 'At two-thirty in the morning, I don't know if I'll still be alive.'" She told her daughter that she suspected "they're going to make it so late, nobody will hear us."

Later still — somewhere around midnight, she recalled — she felt she could hold out no longer. "I was throwing up from the pain, they were telling me that it would be so late that it probably wouldn't be worth it, and my strength was really gone. If they had sent that van,

I would have gone," she affirmed. "But nobody from that committee was twisting my arm."

❖

In fact, hours before Jourdain had all but collapsed, her fate had already been more or less sealed. Early Sunday evening, the committee members had caucused behind closed doors on the issue of whether or not to call Wright — and concomitantly Jourdain.

As the two women waited, millions of viewers were treated to a twenty-minute colloquium on the history of American lynching, courtesy of Iowa's Senator Grassley and Thomas's witness, the EEOC's historian Nancy Fitch. According to Fitch, Thomas was typical of lynching victims because he was "uppity." Viewers also saw ten or so minutes of good-natured joshing between Biden and Simpson about whether Shakespeare or Congreve had originated the much-cited quote describing Anita Hill as having the fury of "a woman scorned." Meanwhile, Hill's team had dismissed an additional panel of character witnesses and Wright was supposedly on deck.

But in the caucus, the Republican members were unanimously opposed to calling Wright and the Democrats were frightened of her checkered employment record. (The White House had shown her personnel files to anyone interested.) Her possible vengefulness against Thomas was discussed. Her impetuousness and tendency to lose her temper were discussed. And her "sexiness," according to one aide, was also raised as a possible deterrent to her credibility.

Not once was it mentioned that Wright had a corroborating witness, nor was Jourdain's deposition distributed to the members. In fact, although Biden had mentioned her name earlier that day as an "alleged" corroborator to Wright, one of the senators, Metzenbaum, later claimed he didn't know of Jourdain's existence until months after the hearings.

The meeting resulted in an overwhelming, possibly unanimous sentiment against calling Wright. Biden returned to tell his staff that there had been a full committee vote on Wright that had come out 13–1 against calling her, with himself as her sole supporter. But two other Democratic senators, including Metzenbaum, said later that they recalled no such vote. Metzenbaum further commented, "I don't think Biden was anxious to bring Angela Wright on."

Later, Biden and several of his top staff members said that it had been Hill and her lawyers who had chiefly opposed calling Wright. Ostensibly they feared that since Wright had viewed Thomas's behavior as obnoxious but something less than harassment, her testimony would render Hill "an eggshell," as one staff member put it, thin-skinned and overly fragile. But Hill's lawyers and political advisers, among them Charles Ogletree, John Frank, and Wendy Sherman, strenuously denied this, as did Hill herself.

"We were waiting for Angela Wright's testimony, just like everyone else," Hill recalled. "Apparently something went wrong. I was as surprised as anyone that she didn't testify. Especially after a panel of women said, 'He never harassed me.' When there was someone who could testify to the same kind of behavior — it was astonishing to me that she was never called."

After the hearings, no Democrat wanted to take responsibility for what appeared in retrospect to have been a major tactical blunder. Metzenbaum claimed that he wanted to hear from Wright, although one of his top aides said that this was not so and that given the accusations about leaking, Metzenbaum preferred to see the hearings end sooner rather than later. Simon explained that he had never been adequately informed by Biden of the strength of Wright's case or told that Wright had a corroborator. And Biden suggested that he alone had wanted Wright to testify, but he was badly outnumbered by the others.

In such a blizzard of excuses, it is difficult to isolate the truth. Jourdain may have come closest when she concluded simply, "These people didn't want to hear from us." The reason, she believed, was that "Thomas's supporters didn't want another woman, especially one with some of the same looks, age, and brains, telling a similar story as Anita Hill. And then, on top of that, she's got a credible backup witness. Nobody wanted to deal with this."

❖

Late Sunday night, as John Doggett was testifying that Hill displayed a pattern of imagining nonexistent sexual interest from men, an aide from Biden's office called Middlebrooks and offered to release Wright from her subpoena — if she was willing to say that she had requested the cancellation.

Wright's response was typically blunt: "Bullshit. After I've been sitting here for three days being called names?" Middlebrooks also refused. "You are not going to make her look like she's cutting and running. She's the key second witness and we want our story aired," he recalled having said.

Next, the aide called back to propose a deal in which Biden would say that the decision to release Wright from the subpoena had been mutual, based on the severe time constraints.

Again Middlebrooks refused. "Angela Wright is not going to be crucified because you set the schedule and used the time badly," he recalled arguing.

After further discussion, a compromise was reached: Biden would release Wright from the subpoena, but her deposition was to be entered into the congressional record — unrebutted. And Biden agreed to issue a letter publicly explaining that the reason Wright did not appear was simply that the committee had run out of time.

Middlebrooks was thus surprised and dismayed when he received a copy of Biden's public letter by fax and read, in part: "Dear Ms. Wright: It is my preference that you testify . . . But, in light of the time constraints . . ."

"Biden wanted it to appear like he had wanted Angela to go on, but the clear message I got was that he did not," Middlebrooks said. "He made it clear to me through his aide that he had no interest in having her testify."

Cynthia Hogan, the aide Middlebrooks had been dealing with during most of the weekend, confirmed that Wright was "not a reluctant witness in the beginning." But she believed that over time, after seeing how Hill had been treated and after it had become clear that Wright would not be called until two or three in the morning, forcing Jourdain into a nightmarish situation, Wright lost whatever interest she had had in being heard.

Wright and Middlebrooks both agreed with this assessment. "I thought, 'Who needs this headache? Who wants to be called these horrible names?'" recalled Wright. "I mean I felt like, 'If you want this man on the Court so badly, you can have him.'"

The upshot, said Middlebrooks, was that "we thought we were getting the facts out without having to go through a caustic hearing."

But by the time Wright's and Jourdain's depositions were entered into the congressional record and made public, the deadline of virtually every major media outlet had passed and most reporters had gone home. Few reporters, or senators, or, for that matter, members of the

public ever heard what either woman had to say. While he felt he had
served the immediate interests of his client, Middlebrooks later said,
"In a larger sense, I'm sorry Angela didn't testify. She would have
made a great witness because she's a strong speaker, and she was
telling the truth. It might have made the difference."

❖

Biden brought down the closing gavel at 2:03 A.M. on Monday, October 14. There were now less than forty-eight hours until the vote.

After the hearings ended, Ogletree tried to encourage Hill. He told
her that she had accomplished what she had set out to do: to tell her
story in her own words to the United States Senate. Simply put, she
had fulfilled her "duty to report." He stressed that the results of the
confirmation vote to come were of little consequence to her; after all,
her objective had not been to defeat Clarence Thomas but to give the
Senate relevant information before the vote.

Others in Hill's camp were not as sanguine. Her friends Keith Henderson and Gary Phillips were outraged at the way Hill had been
treated by the Senate. They had watched, powerless, as her character
had been torn apart. Neither the Democrats on the committee nor
Hill's legal team, as they saw it, had lifted a finger to stop it. When
Henderson learned that Hill had decided not to go back for a second
round of testimony, he spent all night trying to compose a strong
statement for her to deliver to the press, possibly at a news conference
being planned for her return to Oklahoma.

Louise Hilsen and Wendy Sherman, the two advisers who came out
of the political world, also believed that Hill's attorneys had miscal-
culated. The lawyers had viewed the proceedings through a narrow
legal prism, the women thought, and didn't fully appreciate how deftly
the Republican senators on the committee had played their political
cards.

Polls taken over the weekend confirmed their worries about how
devastating the coordinated Republican strategy had been. They
unanimously showed that a majority of the public thought Hill was
lying. Indeed, by the end of the weekend, Hill's nephew Gary Lee, the
Washington Post reporter, said that even to a relative, the Anita Hill
portrayed by Thomas and his defenders was all but unrecognizable.
"Usually you can identify the strands of truth and see how they are
embellished," Lee said. "But what they did with her had no relation

to reality. I cover public relations, so I consider myself something of a student of these things, but I had never seen anything like this. They just cut an image from whole cloth. It was stunning."

Hill, meanwhile, made plans to leave Washington with Shirley Wiegand as soon as possible. They boarded a plane on Monday morning with Hill's parents and Louise Hilsen. Since Hill had had no "last word" in Washington, Hilsen had negotiated with the three major networks for her to be interviewed for a few minutes on that night's newscasts. There was also the prospect of an interview on the *Today* show the next morning, the day of the vote. Hill felt it necessary to run these details past Ogletree, so Hilsen called him from the telephone on the airplane.

Ogletree discouraged Hill from making any further media appearances. He felt she would seem partisan, as if she were trying to tip the outcome of the confirmation vote. Hilsen disagreed with him strenuously, but to no avail. Hill, too tired to argue by now, told Ogletree she'd keep a low profile. The television interviews were canceled and Keith Henderson's statement was set aside.

A change of planes in Dallas gave Hill her first glimpse of how furious she had made some members of the public. The electric cart she and Wiegand were riding between airport gates became engulfed by hecklers; one woman wagged a finger at Hill and yelled, "Shame! Shame!"; a man shouted, "Little wench!" and a clutch of men in business suits let out a stream of hisses.

From the airport in Norman, Hill drove to the university, where she appeared at a rally in the student union organized by her local supporters. Her brother Fred introduced her. "Words simply can't express the kind of anguish I have experienced over the past several days," she said. "I have been deeply hurt and offended by the nature of the attacks on my character. I had nothing to gain by subjecting myself to the process. In fact, I had more to gain by remaining silent. The personal attacks on me without one iota of evidence were particularly reprehensible, and I felt it necessary to come forward to address those attacks. It was suggested that I had fantasies, that I was a spurned woman, and that I had a martyr complex. I will not dignify those theories except to assure everyone that I am not imagining the conduct to which I testified."

Upholding her promise to Ogletree, she answered no questions.

Then, taking along some of the flowers and balloons that had been given to her, Hill drove home, played her answering machine, and began opening all the mail that had accumulated while she was gone.

❖

As Hill, in Oklahoma, was denouncing the attacks on her character, the assault was continuing in Washington. On Monday, Danforth released the affidavit from John Burke saying that he had encouraged Hill to leave her job at Wald, Harkrader, even though the Republicans on the Judiciary Committee had dropped the issue of introducing Hill's employment records. Donald Green, one of Burke's former partners, who had headed the firm's associate evaluation committee, had prepared a sworn statement directly contradicting Burke, but the entire Wald contretemps was more or less buried in the major news of the day: how members of the Senate were planning to vote.

The polls made the outcome all but certain. On such an explosive issue, the path of least resistance for most senators was to say that since the Hill-Thomas hearings had ended inconclusively, the nominee deserved the benefit of the doubt. There was, nonetheless, a furious last round of lobbying. The Christian Coalition and Paul Weyrich's political network went into overdrive. Meanwhile, Ralph Neas and a number of feminist leaders, including Lichtman, still hoped their side might prevail, and they tried to buttonhole every senator they could find.

The southern moderates still held the key, as they had from the start. On Tuesday morning, October 15, Danforth's press aide, Steve Hilton, got up and looked at the news wire. He saw that Alabama's junior Democratic senator, Richard Shelby, had announced his intention to vote for Thomas. So had Oklahoma's David Boren. Hilton heaved a sigh of relief. Later that day, Virginia's Chuck Robb also came out for Thomas. Then, on the Senate floor, two other critical votes tilted Thomas's way, Democrats Alan Dixon and James Exon. Finally, the Republicans' sole female senator, Nancy Kassebaum of Kansas, a moderate who might have swayed other moderates in her party, announced her support.

While there was no doubt that he would vote against Thomas, Kennedy rose on Tuesday to give an emotional speech decrying Hill's treatment. "Shame! Shame! Shame!" he cried to his colleagues. "Are

we an old boys' club, insensitive at best, or something worse? Will we
. . . tolerate any unsubstantial attack on a woman in order to rationalize a vote for this nomination?"

But Specter, in an unusual display of senatorial incivility, snapped,
"We do not need characterizations like shame in this chamber from
the senator from Massachusetts." Hatch, in an even less subtle allusion to Chappaquiddick, cracked, "Anybody who believes that — I
know a bridge up in Massachusetts that I'll be happy to sell them."
(Hatch later expunged this statement from the record and lamely
explained that he had meant to say Brooklyn instead of Massachusetts.)

The most stinging speech against Thomas was delivered by the former majority leader, West Virginia's Robert Byrd. One of the body's
great orators, Byrd was the only senator who dared to denounce
publicly how, in his view, the nominee had cynically played the race
card. "I'm very sorry the matter of race was injected here, not in an
effort to clear one's name but in the effort to shift the ground," Byrd
explained in stentorian tones. "And so, instead of making an effort to
clear his name in the minds of the committee members and in the
minds of other senators who are not on the committee, he shifted the
blame to the process and to race prejudice. I think it was preposterous.
A black woman was making the charge against a black American
male. Where is the racism? Nonsense. Nonsense."

As the hour of the vote approached, the White House anxiously
counted heads. Before the Anita Hill story exploded, Mackey had
counted more than sixty votes for Thomas. Duberstein was still hoping for a margin of ten votes. Thomas, who had spent most of the
day at home, listening to Christian praise music with his wife, chose
not to watch the live broadcast of the proceedings. His wife said that
the nominee was in the bath reading as the senators cast their last
votes.

The final count was 52–48, the most negative votes ever cast for a
successful Supreme Court nominee. When Virginia Lamp Thomas told
her husband the good news, he just "shrugged," she later recalled.
Word filtered back to the Senate that Thomas was refusing to come
out of his house to speak to the horde of reporters camped out on his
lawn. Strom Thurmond was sent to reason with the nominee. Finally
Thomas walked outside in the drizzle, with Thurmond holding an
umbrella, and made a brief statement calling for healing. Then a few

other Republicans, including Boyden Gray and Duberstein, gathered at the Thomas home for a small pizza party.

Still, with rumors swirling that reporters were about to unearth new damaging revelations about Thomas, including his video rental records, the White House was nervous. Thomas was not scheduled to become the nation's 106th justice officially until Rehnquist administered the judicial oath on November 1. But Thomas and the White House dared not wait that long.

So an ersatz, unofficial swearing-in was scheduled at the White House for Friday, October 18. The gala celebration would be held on the South Lawn, which was usually reserved for visiting heads of state. Thomas would be inducted into government service and swear to uphold the Constitution. It would look very much like a judicial swearing-in.

As it happened, Chief Justice Rehnquist's wife, Nan, died the day before the ceremony, and in deference to Rehnquist, the White House told Thomas that it would prefer to postpone the party or at least hold one that was somewhat restrained. But Thomas had already personally invited more than a hundred guests, including friends from Pin Point, loyal supporters like John Doggett, and even some bona fide stars, like the former baseball player Reggie Jackson and the actor Sylvester Stallone. The party went forward.

"Celebrate this day," President Bush told the joyous audience, which included most of Thomas's family. "See what this son of Pin Point has made of himself."

Among those who proudly watched Pin Point's favorite son that day was Thomas's own father, M. C. Thomas, who emerged just in time to participate in his son's day of glory. Thomas's mother, Leola Williams, was also present, though she was not happy to see her prodigal mate for the first time in some forty years, standing there beneath the Truman Balcony. But Thomas, who had been in contact with his father in recent years, had wanted the whole family to attend. As his mother commented later, "I really didn't like it, but for my kids I'd do anything."

But she was, if anything, even less happy about seeing Senator Biden there. While some of Hill's supporters were outraged that Biden lent his dignity to the event, Leola Williams was still furious at what she regarded as his broken promise to support her son. "I wanted to get to that Biden at the swearing-in," she later recalled, "and say, 'Senator, I hope when your son grows up to be a man, if he goes into politics, I hope and pray nobody would cut him down like a dog, the way you did my son.'"

Although Thomas took the oath of office that day and the White House suggested that he was essentially an official member of the Court, he was still vulnerable to any last-minute revelations. Once a member of the Court, his protection would be nearly absolute: he would have to be impeached to be removed from the bench. Moreover, most news organizations considered the threshold for publishing allegations about a sitting Supreme Court justice much higher than it was for a confirmed but not yet sworn-in nominee who was still arguably subject to the vetting process.

With so much at stake, the White House took no chances. At noon on October 23 — eight days after the confirmation vote and nine days ahead of schedule — Clarence Thomas was sworn in by Chief Justice Rehnquist in the first such private ceremony in fifty years. In addition to a single administrative aide, only Thomas's wife and a few loyal supporters, including Senator Danforth, were present to witness the historic event in the Supreme Court's private conference room. Not even the other justices had been invited. The official reason given for the rushed oath was that Thomas was eager to get his staff on the Court's payroll. Why the brief delay would have mattered to the employees, most of whom were already on the appeals court's payroll, was not explained.

The White House acted none too soon. That same day, three reporters for the *Washington Post,* two of them working together, burst into the newsroom almost simultaneously with information confirming that Thomas's involvement with pornography far exceeded what the public had been led to believe. They had eyewitnesses, some ready to talk on the record. Among them was Barry Maddox, the proprietor of Graffiti, who remembered Thomas as a customer in his store. Just as the editors of the *Post* were weighing this news, reports of Thomas's surprise swearing-in began crossing the news wires. As of that moment, Clarence Thomas was officially a justice on the country's highest court. It was a difficult journalistic judgment call. But to print anything now would be pointless. The story was over.

Epilogue

GEORGE BUSH WON the battle to get Clarence Thomas on the Supreme Court but, a year later, lost his own reelection. The goodwill he had hoped to gain from conservatives by nominating Thomas almost completely dissolved in the weeks after the justice's confirmation. Nervous about the mounting backlash aroused by the hearings and owing Danforth a major debt, the president went ahead and finally signed new federal civil rights legislation. His support of what conservatives castigated as a racial "quota bill," along with the earlier renunciation of his pledge not to raise taxes, was enough to launch the candidacy of Patrick Buchanan, weakening Bush badly from the right. After winning the nomination, Bush, in order to placate conservatives, gave Buchanan an opportunity to deliver a major speech at the 1992 Republican convention, and he spent the final night of the proceedings on the stage with a number of right-wing luminaries, including the Reverend Louis Sheldon.

But the strident and intolerant political message sent by the convention alienated masses of moderate voters and thus contributed to the sharp decline in the president's popularity. National opinion polls showed that women under the age of forty-five were particularly affected, allowing Bill Clinton to enjoy a ten-point lead over Bush in this critical group, which was one third of the electorate. African-Americans too were not inspired by Bush, offering him no more than 10 percent of their votes.

Meanwhile, at the Democratic convention, Anita Hill's name drew sustained applause from the delegates, and the Democrats did a creditable job of presenting themselves as "the party of inclusion" — embracing women's rights, civil rights, and gay rights. By the time the election returns were tallied that fall, four new female Democratic senators had been elected; all of them had embraced the cause of Anita Hill in their campaigns. A record number of women were also elected to the House and called themselves "the Anita Hill class."

A year after the hearings, the public's perception of who was telling the truth had undergone a sea change. While a majority of Americans still felt that Thomas should have been confirmed (apparently because they did not find Hill's ten-year-old charges disqualifying), a Wall Street Journal/NBC News poll taken in October 1992 found that 44 percent of registered voters said they believed Hill, while only 34 percent found Justice Thomas credible. (In October 1991, 47 percent had believed Thomas and only 24 percent had believed Hill.) Most of the shift occurred among women, according to a similar poll taken by Gallup.

But in 1993 Hill's reputation was bruised by the publication of *The Real Anita Hill,* by David Brock, which became a national best-seller. The book highlighted a number of inconsistencies in her testimony and was enough to convince Hill to change her mind about telling her story: although she had testified to the Senate that she had no intention of writing a book, in late 1993 she signed what was reportedly a million-dollar contract for two books, one autobiographical, the other theoretical.

Sexual harassment, in the meantime, seemed to become the issue of the hour. The Thomas-Hill hearings were followed by the Tailhook scandal, in which a group of naval aviators were charged with lewd behavior toward women at a convention. Although the court cases bogged down in a welter of conflicting accounts, the incident claimed the navy's top officer as a political casualty. Then, shortly after the 1992 election, a group of women accused Oregon's Senator Robert Packwood of a variety of harassing incidents, some dating from the early 1970s. President Clinton himself became the target of allegations of sexual harassment, a development that forced even liberals to wonder about the appropriateness of such charges. And the private sector was equally affected. The EEOC experienced a surge of harassment complaints after Thomas's confirmation hearings, registering a 50 percent increase (to nearly five thousand complaints) in the first six months of 1992 alone.

But it may have been inside the Senate itself that the hearings left their most lasting impression. Instead of abating, the anger of the women whose calls had clogged Senate switchboards before and during the hearings only intensified. The overwhelmingly male Senate heard a steady refrain from women nationwide charging that "they just don't get it." To show that they did, indeed, "get it," the senators rushed to sign a code of conduct for their office that prohibited harassment (because Congress is itself exempt from federal civil rights laws). They also passed a flurry of bills aimed at helping women — overriding President Bush's veto of family leave legislation and diverting $200 million in military spending to breast cancer research.

Yet some senators who had discounted Hill's charges continued to feel the wrath of dissatisfied voters. Charles Robb, appearing at a Democratic fund-raiser for Senate candidates shortly after he had voted to confirm Thomas, found himself surrounded by picketers demanding a boycott of Democratic contributors. Roger Craver, the leading political consultant who had long helped raise funds for the Democratic Senatorial Campaign Committee headed by Robb, resigned because of the senator's vote.

The members of the Judiciary Committee found themselves in the most difficult spot of all. Many of the Republicans were caught in a backlash of anger not just from Hill's supporters, but also from huge numbers of Americans who had found the whole spectacle so distasteful that they became disgusted with participants of all political stripes. Alan Simpson, looking extremely pained, granted an interview in his Senate hideaway a few weeks after the hearings; he conceded that he had perhaps too readily identified with Thomas as someone wrongly accused and that he had perhaps gone overboard in attacking Hill. He later issued an oblique apology for his behavior in a speech at a Wyoming political event after being jeered by students at a football game. Arlen Specter, facing a female Democratic challenger whose sole campaign issue was Anita Hill, also apologized for giving the appearance that he had unfairly victimized Hill. And John Danforth decided to quit politics altogether. The Missouri senator continued to brood about the victimization of his friend; he spent his final months in the Senate writing a personal account of the hearings, called *Resurrection.* While he argued that Thomas had been blameless, he criticized his own fervor, admitting that he had never stopped his defense of Thomas long enough to consider whether he had been fair to Hill.

The Democrats, meanwhile, had to endure the official criminal investigation into the leak of Hill's charges, in which they were the chief suspects. While the Senate's special counsel spent many months and hundreds of thousands of dollars on his investigation, in the end no one was charged with wrongdoing. Moreover, it was found that no FBI materials had been leaked. But Howard Metzenbaum, who had been publicly accused by Orrin Hatch of leaking FBI materials he had not even seen, decided to retire, hoping to turn over his Senate seat to his son-in-law. And James Brudney, his top aide and Hill's first extended point of contact on Capitol Hill, quit Washington even before the senator, leaving to teach law in Ohio shortly after the special counsel announced his findings.

Several members of the Judiciary Committee came to regret their roles in the hearings. Leahy was so overcome by stress and remorse for not having been tougher on Thomas that he thought he was having a heart attack shortly before the confirmation vote and was rushed to a hospital. Kennedy, who had been rendered almost speechless by his own transgressions, was also repentant, giving an address in Boston in which he acknowledged that his disastrous personal behavior was interfering with his political effectiveness; he vowed to reform.

Biden, perhaps alone, seemed content with his performance. In an interview, he said that "if the polls are correct, 85 percent to 86 percent of the country knew who I was and had an opinion of me. That's a highly unusual exposure rate for a senator," he pointed out. "Most voters can't name their own senator. But now everywhere I go, I get recognized." More important, he noted, the great majority of those polled felt, after watching the hearings, that he had been, as he had tried so hard to seem, "fair."

❖

If Thomas's conduct before his confirmation raised questions about his candor, his performance since has only underscored this concern. After the hearings, Thomas acknowledged that he had purposely masked aspects of his identity from Congress and the public in order to win the Senate's approval, contending that "if you are yourself, like Bob Bork, you're dead." His early record on the Court has borne this out, suggesting that his testimony was indeed misleading about matters beyond the allegations of Anita Hill.

For instance, during the hearings, Thomas testified that he saw no place for ideology on the high court. "I think," he said, "it is important for us . . . to eliminate agendas, to eliminate ideologies. And when one becomes a judge . . . that's precisely what you start doing. You start putting the speeches away. You start putting the policy statements away. You begin to decline forming opinions in areas that could come before your court because you want to be stripped down like a runner. So I have no agenda."

However, rather than setting ideology aside and distancing himself from controversial issues that might come before the Court, in his first three years Thomas has proven himself the most political of justices, standing out for his extreme conservatism even on one of this century's most conservative Courts. Perhaps this was the inevitable outgrowth of a Court nomination that was conceived in electoral politics and waged more than any before it as a full-fledged, and at times exceedingly negative, political campaign. But the result has been a blurring of the distinction between politics and law that has bothered some judicial ethics experts, including some of Thomas's fellow justices.

The first jolt to his brethren came soon after the swearing-in, when Clarence and Virginia Lamp Thomas appeared on the cover of *People* magazine. Inside were photographs of Thomas and his wife snuggling on a couch, holding hands, and reading the Holy Scripture together — an exercise in the kind of image rehabilitation more commonly associated with those seeking office than with cloistered judges. The accompanying article was a first-person story by Virginia Lamp Thomas excoriating Anita Hill and Thomas's other perceived political enemies. Unabashedly, the justice's wife embraced the interpretation of Hill as a spurned, jealous woman bent on revenge because of her unrequited crush on Thomas. The allegations, in Virginia Lamp Thomas's characterization, were nothing short of "spiritual warfare. Good versus Evil." While the hearings had been too dispiriting for at least one justice to watch and the hastily arranged swearing-in had offended the sensibilities of a number of others, the *People* cover story became an even more intense focus of disgruntlement. Justice Sandra Day O'Connor, a stickler for judicial decorum, was described by one former Supreme Court clerk as being "aghast."

The few public appearances Thomas made during the months that followed raised even more questions about his sensitivity to judicial codes of conduct. Like a victorious candidate, Thomas paid a round of thank-you calls to the conservative groups that had helped him win.

To anyone who had watched his campaign for the Court, the faces along the whistle stops were familiar.

In March 1992 he attended a private breakfast with the black pastors affiliated with Sheldon's TVC. Thomas also paid several courtesy calls to the political activist Paul Weyrich, the founding father of the New Right, whose aides, beginning with Tom Jipping, had lobbied so hard to secure Thomas's seat for him. On three occasions the justice visited Weyrich's headquarters at Free Congress Foundation, a center of anti-abortion, anti-pornography, and pro–school prayer activism on Capitol Hill; he also appeared at least twice on National Empowerment Television, the conservative leader's increasingly influential satellite television network.

In a fifteenth-anniversary tribute Thomas delivered to Weyrich's group in April 1993, he made explicitly clear how much he felt he owed the right wing. Joining a group of speakers that included the North Carolina senator Jesse Helms, the conservative talk show host Rush Limbaugh, and Oliver North (soon to be a Republican candidate for the Senate from Virginia), Thomas said, "One of the things I can say about Paul and Free Congress and all my friends over here is that in this city, when times are good, your friends know you. When times are bad, you know your friends. And I got to know these friends when times were bad. So it's with deepness and a sense of gratitude, and a sense of loyalty and friendship, that I congratulate Free Congress and all my friends here."

Although many of the justices appear publicly before legal groups and several have been keynote speakers at events organized by the conservative Federalist Society, Thomas's ties to Weyrich and other political activists who were taking sides on major issues before the Court are unparalleled. In fact, at the moment that Thomas appeared at Weyrich's anniversary gala, the Court was considering a case about religious instruction in public school facilities in which Free Congress Foundation had filed a friend-of-the-court brief.

Thomas stirred further concern in the spring of 1993 when he appeared before the Georgia Public Policy Foundation, a conservative group based in Atlanta. The group sent out invitations seeking support for a "more conservative government" and sold $40,000 worth of tickets for an awards dinner honoring Thomas. Guests were advised to make their checks payable to the group's political action committee.

In these activities, Thomas appeared to be flouting not only his promise to the Senate to "put ideologies away," but also the canons of the Code of Judicial Conduct, which states that judges should not "make speeches for a political organization" and "should not be a speaker or the guest of honor at an organization's fund-raising events." Although the Judicial Code is not binding for Supreme Court justices, it has traditionally been closely followed by the brethren.

Some of Thomas's speaking engagements also attracted critical media attention, which is frowned on by most of the Court's justices. For instance, in the fall of 1993 Thomas promised to deliver a "message from the heart" to the annual convention of Concerned Women of America, a militant anti-abortion and anti-feminist group that helped to promote his confirmation. Since CWA is directly involved in trying to overturn *Roe v. Wade,* Thomas's planned appearance provoked so much controversy that he was forced to cancel it.

Then, in June 1994, Thomas surprised even friends like Armstrong Williams by officiating at the wedding of Rush Limbaugh, which took place at Thomas's home. Limbaugh, famous for his flamboyant partisanship, had been a tireless defender of Thomas, denouncing Hill's supporters as "FemiNazis." Limbaugh had also promoted the *American Spectator,* the conservative magazine that published, in March 1992, the long article by David Brock that became the basis for his subsequent book.

———◆———

Meanwhile, Thomas's performance on the bench in his first three years has also belied his promise to cast off all ideological agendas when he joined the Court. In his confirmation hearings, Thomas suggested that as a black man he would bring a special empathy to the high court, supporting the claim with an anecdote about watching convicts being bused in for their appeals and thinking that "but for the grace of God there go I." He added, "So you feel you have the same fate, or could have ... So I walk in their shoes, and I could bring something different to the Court."

But, four months into his first term, Thomas was condemned by the *New York Times* as "The Youngest, Cruelest Justice" for dissenting from the 7–2 majority in a case involving the beating by two guards, in front of their supervisor, of a shackled prisoner who suffered a split lip, a broken dental plate, and loosened teeth. Thomas's dissenting opinion — that this treatment was not "cruel and unusual" and therefore was constitutional — was criticized by the Court's majority opinion as ignoring "the concepts of dignity, civilized standards, humanity and decency that animate the Eighth Amendment."

Thomas also proved to be a consistent defender of capital punishment, writing a separate concurring opinion in one death penalty case stressing the irrelevance of an inmate's troubled, impoverished background. He contended that such handicaps should not be considered in the course of sentencing because they might lead to arbitrary leniency, which could discriminate against black defendants. This argument drew fire from Justice John Paul Stevens, who called it "remarkable" to suggest that considering a defendant's handicaps "somehow threatens the progress we have made in eliminating racial discrimination and other arbitrary considerations." Thomas also voted that prisoners on death row had no constitutional right to have new, potentially exculpatory evidence heard by a judge. In another case, Thomas joined Scalia's scalding dissent from the majority after it ruled that jurors hearing death penalty cases must be told that life without parole is also an option.

Only on rare occasions did Thomas rule against the state. One such case involved a Nebraska farmer who, Thomas and four other justices ruled, had been entrapped by the government into ordering child pornography through the mail. A former clerk explained that after all Thomas had gone through, the justice was especially sensitive to the overreaching powers of prosecutors.

In taking these positions, Thomas often had only Justice Antonin Scalia as company. Yet while his voting record mirrored Scalia's 85 percent of the time — a level of agreement not matched by any of the other justices — Thomas did not distinguish himself in the eyes of most Court watchers as matching either Scalia's brilliance or his vigor. And while Scalia's hard-edged conservatism was accepted as a legitimate expression of his views, Thomas's equally tough-minded stands were seen as disappointing in many circles. The difference sprang in part from the fact that Scalia had never hidden his views before or after joining the Supreme Court, whereas Thomas had. But the unflattering comparisons also reflected the fact that unlike Scalia, Thomas rarely spoke from the bench and frequently seemed content to let Scalia write the dissenting opinions, to which he merely added his silent assent.

At the end of the 1993–94 Court term, for instance, Thomas joined Scalia in his dissent from a decision that upheld the right to prevent anti-abortion protesters from blocking access to abortion clinics. He and Scalia also voted together in several other major cases, including the most important abortion case heard after Thomas joined the Court, *Planned Parenthood v. Casey.* In that case, the Court declined an opportunity to overturn *Roe v. Wade.* But Scalia, with Thomas joining, wrote a separate dissenting opinion.

Thomas parted with Scalia, of course, in some cases, and on a few occasions Scalia signed Thomas's dissent, as in his controversial opinion on the beaten prisoner, *Hudson v. McMillan.* But Scalia's perceived dominance led more than a few Court watchers to criticize Thomas; the conservative legal expert Bruce Fein, for instance, said that Thomas was "basically in Scalia's pocket." Whether or not this was a fair assessment, there were few complaints from Thomas's strongest supporters. As Gary Bauer, the president of the Family Research Council, said with satisfaction, "I have not seen any decision where I have been surprised or disappointed by Justice Thomas."

Some of the African-Americans who had rallied to Thomas's cause during the confirmation process were equally pleased. But many others felt betrayed. Thomas's failure to rule sympathetically in the cases of minority and civil rights litigants surprised and angered a great number of his African-American supporters, especially those who had been promised by the White House that once on the Court, Thomas would surely "grow." In particular, Thomas's stance in a series of voting rights cases provoked outrage because they seemed to endanger the gains made in electing black public officials and to be hostile to the Voting Rights Act.

The disappointment expressed by Royce Esters, the president of the Compton, California, branch of the NAACP, was a representative response. In the summer of 1991, Ester's branch dramatically broke with the parent organization's opposition to Thomas in the belief that "because he is black we assumed he would have to be sensitive to black people." But in 1993 Esters told *Emerge Magazine,* "I, along with 57 percent of other blacks in this nation, was conned. Clarence Thomas has turned out to be the house Negro. Here is a man we thought we could have some faith in because of his humble background, but now I feel foolish."

Niara Sudarkasa, the president of Lincoln University in Pennsylvania — who testified on Thomas's behalf before the Senate Judiciary Committee and wrote a column in *Newsweek* urging other blacks to support Thomas — also pronounced herself "very disappointed . . . In no instance have I agreed with the positions he took." And Grover Hankins, a Republican supporter of Thomas who was deputy general counsel for the Department of Health and Human Services and now teaches law at Texas Southern Unversity, said he too was deeply dismayed. Thomas's opinions in a number of cases, including *Hudson,* "lacked humanity," as Hankins saw it. Although Thomas was a personal friend, he said, "I'm disappointed in his decisions so far, and as a Republican, this may not bode well for me, but I don't give a damn. Civil rights is a life-or-death issue for people of color."

Some of Thomas's white supporters expressed similar sentiments. As they watched his performance on the Court, a few of the swing senators whom the White House had so intensely lobbied conceded that they regretted having yielded to the Pin Point strategy. David Boren, for one, said in an interview, "I simply continue to be surprised that the person I talked to before the confirmation hearings, who told me about growing up poor and black, is the person who has cast these votes on the Court."

But Thomas himself remains defiant. Noting that when Justices Souter, Kennedy, and O'Connor proved to be unexpectedly centrist in their rulings, they were described by the media as "evolving" or "growing," Thomas announced to his clerks, "I ain't evolving." Nor was he planning to give his detractors the satisfaction of an early departure. While there were intermittent rumors that he might step down long before retirement age, Thomas himself vowed on the day of his confirmation, at the age of forty-three, that he intended to spend the next forty-three years of his life as a Supreme Court justice. It would take that long, he told friends, to get even.

Notes

❖

We have based this book on hundreds of interviews with as many of the principal and ancillary players in this drama as would talk to us. We spent more than two years trying to interview both Clarence Thomas and Anita Hill; in the end, Hill agreed to grant us the first lengthy interview she has given about her role in the hearings. Unfortunately, Justice Thomas declined our multiple requests for an interview.

In his absence, we talked to his mother, his sister, and dozens of his friends and associates over the years who helped us to try to fill in the blanks. We have also interviewed seven members of the Senate Judiciary Committee, some of them speaking for the first time since the hearings, as well as aides for the remaining members and numerous other White House and administration officials.

In the course of assembling these interviews into a coherent narrative, we have tried wherever possible to attribute all information that is on the record. We have also used multiple sources wherever possible for disputed or controversial allegations. Where sources disagreed, we have so noted in the text or notes.

We would like to thank everyone who has helped and encouraged us. This project has withstood a family death, a marriage, a birth, two cross-country moves, an earthquake, a fire, and a flood. We have nothing but gratitude for those who kept us going and kept going, too often without us. First and foremost are our husbands, Bill and Henry, and our families, as well as our professional family at the *Wall Street Journal,* whose support has made this project possible. Finally, our greatest thanks go to Houghton Mifflin and our extraordinary editor, John Sterling.

PROLOGUE

2 *Since then:* David Brock, *The Real Anita Hill: The Untold Story* (New York: Free Press, 1993).

4 *Like his accuser:* Justice Clarence Thomas declined repeated written requests to be interviewed for this book.
Thomas had hoped: "The Reliable Source," *Washington Post,* June 24, 1994, reported this story, overheard at a Washington restaurant. Thomas had joked that with his luck people would say, "There's Clarence Thomas with his wig, his hat, and his sunglasses . . ."
But now Thomas: Jeffrey Toobin, "The Burden of Clarence Thomas," *The New Yorker,* September 27, 1993.

5 *And so, with:* Armstrong Williams says he had to tell Thomas that Alex Haley, the coauthor of *The Autobiography of Malcolm X,* which Thomas greatly admired, had died.

6 *"outlive my critics":* Report on Thomas's speech to the Missouri Bar Association, *Kansas City Star,* October 9, 1993.
"Do I look bitter?": Claremont Institute speech, November 1993.
"Ideally": Orrin Hatch, *Leading the Charge* (Carson City, Nev.: Gold Leaf Press, 1994), p. 370.

7 *"Among members":* Stephen L. Carter, *The Confirmation Mess: Cleaning Up the Federal Appointments Process* (New York: Basic Books, 1994), p. 134.

8 *"In the hearing":* John A. Danforth, *Resurrection: The Confirmation of Clarence Thomas* (New York: Viking, 1994), p. 28.

1: THE DEAL

12 *"bloop single":* "New Clues Surface on Souter's Views," *Los Angeles Times,* September 9, 1990.

13 *"it will be a knock-down":* Sununu declined to be interviewed, but correspondence between Jipping and Sununu confirms Jipping's account. A memo from Jipping to Sununu dated June 27, 1991, states: "You will recall our conversation at Justice Souter's swearing-in last October about the next vacancy. At the time, you said the strategy was to gain a large block of support in the Senate for the first Bush nominee, then go for someone more clearly conservative the next time around. I hope and pray that is how the Administration is thinking about this nomination."

14 *"The entire conservative movement":* A second memo from Jipping to Sununu, June 27, 1991.

PAGE

14   *"Marshall would shake"*: Carl Rowan, *Dream Makers, Dream Break-
ers* (Boston: Little, Brown, 1993), p. 419.
"wild about the Constitution": "Clarence Thomas on Law, Rights and
Morality," *Wall Street Journal*, July 2, 1991.

15   *The 1990–91 Court term*: The Rehnquist Court was going to
strengthen the death penalty by reversing earlier decisions that held
that "victim impact statements," emphasizing the damage done by a
crime, could not be considered in capital cases.

17   *"watching the destruction"*: Juan Williams, "Thomas and the Isolation of the Liberal Establishment," *Washington Post*, September 9,
1981.
With this unique résumé: Using Thomas to placate the right was not
far-fetched. Looking back on her brother's candidacy, Bay Buchanan,
his campaign manager, acknowledged that the choice of Thomas had
almost mollified him enough not to run until Bush swiftly changed
course after the confirmation and signed the Civil Rights Bill. Campaign for President, a symposium at the Institute of Politics, Harvard
University, Fall 1992.

18   *"I did not ask"*: Senate Judiciary Committee, "The Nomination of
Clarence Thomas to the Supreme Court of the United States," 102d
Cong., 1st Sess. (Committee Print Draft), October 11–13, 1991, p.
231. "Hearing" will be used in subsequent references to this document.
"The first day": Interview with Michael Middleton.
So as the Reagan years: Neither Thomas, who declined to be interviewed, nor the Bush White House would elaborate on how much
time Thomas spent alone with the president.

19   *After the NAACP meeting*: "Mending Fences with Black Voters,"
Washington Post, August 8, 1988.
Such loyalty paid off: Interview with John Mackey.

20   *"Only in America"*: Thomas's acceptance speech.
"Anyone who takes him on": "A Conservative Black Picked for High
Court," *Los Angeles Times*, July 2, 1991.

21   *In many ways Thomas*: Thomas had ruled on only administrative and
procedural constitutional matters. As for not litigating jury trials, he
said in his questionnaire for the appeals court that "none" of his
appearances in court had been before juries. P. 230 of the court of
appeals nomination record.
Moreover, Bush's assertion: Bush's other top contenders were three
federal judges: Edith Jones, a woman, and two Hispanics, Emilio
Garza and Ricardo Hinojosa.

PAGE

21   *"Had Thomas been white"*: Interview with Joseph Biden.

26   *Already, one such poisonous:* Danforth, *Resurrection,* p.10.

27   *"a gift"*: Interview with John Mackey.

28   *"Think of it like"*: "Making the Case for Thomas," *Washington Post,* July 19, 1991.

29   *But Attorney General:* This account comes from a participant at the meeting.

2: THE PIN POINT REALITY

31   *"the first author"*: Richard Hofstadter, *The American Political Tradition* (New York: Random House, 1948).

32   *"a model for all"*: Nomination speech, July 1991.
     "We learned to fend": Chamber of Commerce speech, Palm Beach, Fla., May 18, 1988.

33   *"They stuck by you"*: Interview with Leola Williams.
     A little more than: Ibid.
     It was unclear: Myers Anderson's best friend, Sam Williams, believes that Leola and M. C. Thomas were never married, and one of Thomas's confidants agrees; their Pin Point neighbor Thad Harris thinks the couple was married, although not in Pin Point's church.

34   *"You know, I've"*: Interview with Tony Califa.

35   *"when I grew up"*: A symposium of black conservatives, "Black America Under the Reagan Administration," *Policy Review* 34, 1985.

37   *The hardships preceding:* "He talked bitterly about his mother leaving him," recalled a former speechwriter for the EEOC. "It was a miserable childhood."

38   *"they'd have the shit"*: Interview with Tony Califa.

39   *"Clarence told me"*: September 16, 1991.
     "We were physically": Interview with Carol Delaney.

40   *"trifling and lazy"*: "Trifling" and "lazy" are words Thomas used to describe his mother and sister, according to EEOC employee Sukari Hardnett.
     "It's a myth": Interview with Roy Allen.
     "He likes to talk": Interview with Sam Williams.
     "Everyone is emphasizing": Floyd Adams, in John Lancaster and Sharon LaFraniere, "Growing Up Black in a White World," *Washington Post,* September 8, 1991.
     To some observers: Savannah State, November 16, 1990.
     "Thomas's was a select": Interview with W. W. Law.

PAGE

40   *"I don't understand": Law Weekly,* April 25, 1988, coverage of a symposium sponsored by the Federalist Society.

42   *"we were taught":* Interview with Lester Johnson.

The result: The parochial schools Thomas attended began to integrate voluntarily during his later high school years. As a consequence, he experienced the isolation of being a black pioneer in previously white territory but not the violent upheaval of forced integration.

Thomas's later characterization: Emerge, November 1993, p. 42.

44   *"Thomas used to tell":* Interview with Sam Williams. Thomas's mother challenged the reliability of Williams's account and suggested he and her father weren't even particularly close friends. But in a draft of a speech he never delivered, Thomas described Williams as one of the formative role models in his early life, suggesting that he was indeed close to his family. And Law confirmed Williams's account. Leola "wouldn't know," said Law. "She wasn't around during those years. But Sam Williams was Myers Anderson's best friend, and what he says is the truth. In the end, Thomas and his grandfather were estranged."

"I don't like talking": Interview with W. W. Law.

But according to: Interview with Julie Martin and visual review of registration documents.

45   *"He was darker":* Interview with Sara Wright.

Later, Thomas: Juan Williams, "A Question of Fairness," *Atlantic Monthly,* February 1987.

light-skinned elite: Sharon LaFraniere, "Despite Achievement, Thomas Felt Isolated," *Washington Post,* September 9, 1991.

46   *"It made you a double":* Interview with Lester Johnson.

48   *"was that we should":* Interview with Carol Delaney.

49   *"the first thing":* Interview with Russell Frisby.

50   *The decision to abandon:* Claremont Institute speech, November 1993.

He turned to one: Lancaster and LaFraniere, *Washington Post,* September 8, 1991.

51   *"really woke me up":* In Edith Efron, "Native Son, The Stereotyping of Clarence Thomas," *Reason Magazine,* February 1992.

52   *As one classmate: U.S. News and World Report,* September 16, 1991.

"I don't fit in": Interview of Thomas in *Legal Times,* 1984.

54   *But his view of women:* Paula Giddings, *When and Where I Enter: The Impact of Black Women on Race and Sex in America* (New York: Morrow, 1984) p. 302.

54 *"Fortunately"*: The female graduate student at Yale quoted about what she saw as Thomas's chauvinism and his avid interest in pornographic materials wished to remain anonymous. She was willing to share her recollections of Thomas during his confirmation hearings and was in contact with Senator Kennedy's staff, a member of which independently confirmed her account. But after the hearings were over, she felt that the professional risks she, a New England academic, would run by speaking out overwhelmed any good that might come from it.

55 *Within only days:* Kathy Ambush was reached but declined to comment for this book.
Old-fashioned: Interview with Edward P. Jones.

57 *Henry Terry:* In an interview, Washington explained his refusal to comment by noting that Thomas's friendship continued to be important to him, but he also was not going to lie about it.

58 *"utter a profane":* Hearing, pp. 543, 21, 399.

59 *"This thing about how":* Williams, *Atlantic Monthly.*
"He had a disdain": Interview with Bobby Hill.

60 *"He thought the South":* Interview with Clarence Martin.
These goals: Only two classmates scored lower than Thomas. One of them, John Doggett, who would defend him during his confirmation hearings, tied for last place with a score of 68.

61 *The choice:* Interview with Fletcher Farrington.

3: JOINING THE CLUB

64 *"By the time":* Interview with Clarence Martin, December 1992.

67 *And in or about:* Emma Mae Martin said in an interview that she talked with Thomas about her 1974 abortion around the time that she went ahead with it. But, according to the *Savannah Morning News,* which also interviewed her, she said she had not talked to Thomas about it at the time.

68 *There was one jarring:* Ashcroft, reached after the Hill controversy had erupted and when he was raising money to run as a conservative Republican candidate for the Senate seat vacated by Danforth, declined to comment about these recollections, explaining that his memories concerning these events were vague. Given this, he said, "it's not a good idea for me to testify about how he talked."
The target: Mark Mittleman, who has an ongoing social relationship with Justice Thomas, recalled that he simply "enjoyed shocking Ashcroft with colorful stories about the life he had led growing up in

Savannah." For instance, he offered, Thomas liked to describe how his grandfather made them eat fish eyes. "He clearly knew what he was doing in telling that kind of story. It was to tease John," he said. "John was so straight. Dishing it back was not John Ashcroft's style." *"In a staff"*: LaFraniere, "Despite Achievement."

69   *None of the other*: According to a fellow black Hill staff member, Mary Helen Thompson, who was at the time working for Paul Tsongas, a Democratic congressman from Massachusetts. Interview with Jon Sawyer.

To get there: Sawyer, who lunched with Thomas a number of times, says he believed that Thomas "seemed very comfortable with Danforth's positions. He really wasn't particularly ideological. My chief impression," Sawyer said a dozen years later, "was of his ambition." Interview with Sawyer and Charlotte Grimes, *St. Louis Post-Dispatch*, July 7, 1991. But Harris says that by the time Thomas reached Washington, he was already "extremely conservative."

70   *At times Sowell*: Alex Haley and Malcolm X, *The Autobiography of Malcolm X* (New York: Ballantine Books–Random House, 1964), p. 272.

"The NAACP's agenda": Thomas Sowell, *The Economics and Politics of Race* (New York: Viking Press, 1985).

"It was like pouring": Interview with Clarence Thomas, *Reason Magazine*, November 1987.

Thomas was also: In explaining that women and men carry the burden of parenthood unequally, which affects their economic choices differently, Sowell wrote, "However parallel these roles [of men and women] might be verbally, they are vastly different in behavioral consequences. There are reasons why there are no homes for unwed fathers" (*The Economics and Politics of Race*). Like Sowell, Thomas was less apt to blame sexual discrimination for the pay differential than the choices women made. As he put it, "For whatever reason, women tend to go into job category A, and men into job category B. And women's jobs tend to pay less" (*Chicago Tribune*, January 6, 1985).

72   *The proud son*: IPAC filings show that the dinner in 1987 for Ambassador Piet Koornhof included Clarence Thomas. Filings listed in Report on J. A. Parker prepared by Fairness & Accuracy in Reporting. In 1985, as the sanction issue loomed, Parker, who by then had registered as a foreign agent representing the Embassy of South Africa in Washington, listed his lobbying company's salary from Pretoria at $360,000 plus expenses.

72 *Many blacks saw Parker:* Thomas's secretary at the Department of Education and the EEOC, Diane Holt, said in her deposition that J. A. Parker was one of the few people whose telephone calls she was directed by Thomas to pass to him without screening.

73 *"The elimination of":* This transition memo was made available to the Judiciary Committee when Thomas was nominated to the Supreme Court.

Twelve years later: Paul Taylor, "Thomas Views of Harassment Said to Evolve," *Washington Post,* October 11, 1991.

74 *"by definition we":* Arch Parsons, "Black Conservatives Grow More Visible," *Baltimore Sun,* July 11, 1991.

Williams later explained: Interview with Armstrong Williams.

75 *This public attack:* Williams said that Thomas drove all night from Washington to Savannah to tell his sister how sorry he was. But in Danforth's *Resurrection* (p. 13), the senator said that Thomas "flew to Georgia" to apologize. Interviewed for this book, Thomas's sister said she had no recollection of his coming to see her in order to apologize. She recalled instead that they talked about the subject on the phone, and rather than being apologetic, his remarks sounded like part of an ongoing dialogue the two had been having for years about his opposition to her receiving welfare. Despite such disputes, Thomas's sister admires her brother, whose official Court portrait hangs on the wall of her living room, and said she feels no anger toward him.

Again, these comments: Thomas made the statement to Williams in a *Washington Post* story of December 16, 1980, datelined San Francisco.

76 *Why Thomas singled out:* Timothy M. Phelps and Helen Winternitz, *Capitol Games* (New York: Hyperion, 1992), p. 86.

Apparently he anguished: LaFraniere, "Despite Achievement."

78 *Chief among these:* Terrel H. Bell, *The Thirteenth Man* (New York: Free Press, 1988), pp. 104–9.

79 *"Her attitude":* Ambush declined to comment on any aspect of her marriage to Thomas.

80 *"I guess I felt":* Kaye Savage's account has been pieced together from interviews with Joseph Biden, Anita Hill, Mark Schwartz, the staff member of the Senate Judiciary Committee who interviewed Savage and whose contemporaneous notes were obtained, and two lawyers whom Savage consulted at the time, Jamin Raskin and Sarah Bloom. Athough Savage declined to volunteer any information, she confirmed the accuracy of what had already been made available by these sources.

81   *It was precisely:* Hill told James Brudney, according to his notes, that she first met Thomas in early 1981 before his confirmation to the Department of Education was final.

4: TALKING WILD

85   *But if Hill:* "Have you ever heard or known Anita Hill to lie on any other occasion?" Senator Hatch asked one of Thomas's character witnesses, Nancy Fitch. "No, I haven't, Senator," she replied (Hearing, p. 335). Senator Specter asked Diane Holt, "Do you think she [Hill] is the kind of person who would come here and say that it happened if she didn't think it had happened?" And Holt replied, "I don't know. She didn't appear to be that kind of person when I knew her" (ibid., p. 359). Specter also asked J. C. Alvarez, who while saying she "didn't know her well enough personally" nonetheless "didn't see her professionally as somebody who would do that" (ibid., p. 359). Joseph Biden asked Thomas repeatedly whether he believed that Hill had "[made] up a story." But while Thomas continued to insist that the story Hill told was "concocted," it's noteworthy that he stopped short of accusing her directly of concocting it herself, suggesting instead that "my view is that others put it together and developed this" (ibid., p. 234).

88   *Deborah Leavy:* Leavy went on to be a counsel to the Senate Judiciary Committee before running the ACLU office in Philadelphia.

90   *"It was never suggested":* Hearing, p. 48.
     Hardy might have been: In her unreleased deposition, obtained independently by the authors, Diane Holt placed the date of Hardy's death as 1989 (p. 19).

93   *"relaxed and open":* Hill describes this in her written statement to the Senate Judiciary Committee, referred to in future footnotes as "Senate statement."
     "I cannot characterize": Hearing, p. 174.

94   *"She repeatedly received":* Hearing, p. 243.
     "categorically" . . . *"in the strongest":* Hearing, p. 222.

95   *"You ought to go out":* Hearing, p. 53.
     According to notes: James Brudney's notes of his telephone interview of Hill on September 10, 1991, were obtained without his knowledge or permission after copies of them had been shared with the special counsel investigating the leak of Hill's allegations to the media. They have not been previously released to the public.
     "I . . . do not commingle": Hearing, p. 350.

96   *"measured his penis"*: Brudney's notes.
      "offensive and disgusting": Hearing, p. 104.
      It is possible: Hearing, p. 157.

97   *To Hill*: Hearing, p. 71.
      Hoerchner confirmed: Hearing, p. 256.

100   *"I was really upset"*: Hearing, p. 71.
      In June 1981: Associated Press, "Reagan May Withdraw His Choice
      to Head EEOC," November 13, 1981.

101   *To the surprise of*: Interview with Harry Singleton. McEwen has re-
      fused all comment, keeping silent about anything she might know and
      even whether she supported Thomas, throughout the hearings and
      since. Others who saw the romance as on and off were Sukari Hard-
      nett, who says Thomas told her a constant problem was that Lillian
      disapproved of his politics.
      "relief and hope": Hearing, p. 221.

103   *"No one knew"*: Hearing, p. 91.

104   *"assumed that the issue"*: Brudney's notes.
      "Who has put pubic hair": Hearing, p. 43.
      "I didn't have a clue: Hearing, p. 91.

105   *Since no one actually*: Interview with Michael Middleton.

106   *Another odd recollection*: Hearing, p. 53. Actually, Heflin garbled the
      name, asking about "Long John Silver."

107   *Among the pornographic*: David Brock has written that there is no
      evidence that Thomas had any interest in pornography after his stu-
      dent days, and he quotes Thomas's aide Armstrong Williams saying
      Thomas had been deeply offended by Williams's purchase of a single
      issue of *Playboy* magazine. Thomas, according to Williams, demanded
      to know, "How can you buy that trash?" *The Real Anita Hill*, p. 273.

110   *"deeply troubled and"*: Hearing, p. 253.
      By the winter of 1982: Hearing, p. 254.

111   *"I'm so embarrassed"*: Interview with Brad Mims.

112   *"related to stress"*: Interview with Ellen Wells.
      "out of the blue": Hearing, p. 397.
      "fantasy": Hearing, p. 521. Kothe later regretted the choice of word
      in the hearings.
      Neither Kothe nor Thomas: Interview with Charles Kothe.

113   *"I can speculate"*: Hearing, p. 68.

114   *"If you were ever"*: Brudney's notes.
      "forget about the unpleasant": Ibid.

115   *This conversation with Lambert*: At the time of her initial conversa-
      tion with Brudney, Hill apparently did not remember telling Joel Paul

about her problems with Thomas — although he was one other person, after Linda Lambert Jackson, whom she later said that she spoke with about it. Lambert, who testified under the name Linda Jackson during the hearings that Hill had never mentioned any problems with Thomas to her, refused comment when she was reached about Hill's recollection.

5: THE TURKEY FARM

117 *"there is nothing"*: Williams, *Atlantic Monthly.*
     "hell on integrationists": Ibid.
     "a crutch": Ibid.
118 *"a man I have admired"*: The *Dallas Times-Herald* reported that in 1983 Thomas had prepared two speeches praising Farrakhan, both of which ended, according to the prepared texts, by quoting from Farrakhan, saying that "we the poor, we the oppressed, we the blacks, we the Hispanics, we the disinherited, we the rejected and most despised, we will overcome and then together we will be able to say in the words of Dr. Martin Luther King: Free at last, free at last, thank God Almighty we have united and made freedom a reality at last" ("Thomas Admired, Quoted Farrakhan," July 12, 1991). See also Phelps and Winternitz, *Capitol Games,* p. 66.
119 *"It often seemed"*: Heritage Foundation Lecture, "Why Black Americans Look to Conservative Policies," June 1987.
120 *"He prided himself"*: Interview with Al Golub.
121 *"Don't tell me"*: Phelps and Winternitz, *Capitol Games,* p. 99.
     "like pulling hens'": Williams, *Atlantic Monthly.*
123 *"Young man"*: Hearing, p. 386.
     An especially loyal: This title is used by Williams in his deposition.
     As Williams told it: Williams's unreleased deposition, obtained independently by the authors.
     Some of Thomas's aides: Interview with Angela Wright and confirmed by two other EEOC employees, both of whom were supporters of Thomas.
124 *Berry, a young:* Berry, who now uses her married name, Phyllis Berry-Myers, denied ever wearing such a costume. She did say she was sometimes teased for her unusual clothes, including overalls.
     "Seeing Phyllis Berry": Interview with Al Golub.
     "He used to come": Wall Street Journal, July 19, 1991.
125 *"You will be fired"*: Hearing, p. 181.
     "Clarence finds": Aaron Epstein, "Thomas Now Accused of That

Which He Policed," Knight-Ridder newspapers, October 10, 1991.

126 *But earlier, when:* Repeated efforts to contact Earl Harper for comment were unsuccessful. Having retired from the EEOC, Harper moved to Texas, where he could not be reached by either his last known telephone number or address.

According to Cruz's: The internal EEOC investigative report names each woman who made allegations against Mr. Harper, but since they made no public allegations, we have withheld their names in order to protect their privacy.

127 *"The fact that Mr. Harper":* Memorandum to John Seal, Management Director, Office of Management, from Nester Cruz, Acting Legal Counsel, November 19, 1982.

"I felt very strongly": Hearing, p. 198.

However, the record: The general counsel who informed Harper that he proposed to terminate his job was David Slate, in a memo on December 3, 1983.

"Thomas wanted someone else": Interview with Michael Middleton.

"When push came to shove": Interview with Susan Silber.

129 *"Is this all":* According to the memos, Schutt was certain that Thomas had not even read the report critical of the Philadelphia office before dismissing it, although Thomas claimed he had. When asked about the computer disk showing outside legal work, Schutt said, Thomas seemed "surprised" and "apparently didn't know it existed."

130 *"He lied about me":* Interview with Lynn Bruner.

Against this backdrop: Interview with Joel Paul.

"I did not": Hearing, p. 350.

"is the only person": Hearing, p. 154.

131 *Wright had been fending:* Later, Thomas's defenders would attempt to make it look like Wright had cooked up the racism charge in retaliation for being fired at AID — showing a taste for vengeance that they said she repeated with Thomas. But Wright resigned, rather than being fired, and her charge of racism accompanied her resignation. Her supervisor at AID, Kate Semerad, told the FBI that she had "advised Wright that she would have to fire her *if* [our italics] her job performance didn't improve. She [*sic*] advised before she could fire Wright, she received a letter of resignation from Wright claiming race discrimination" (Brock, *Real Anita Hill,* p. 261). The fact that Wright had to be subpoenaed to testify also undermines attempts to paint her as seeking revenge. She never sought any role in the hearings at all.

132 *"the Republicans were":* Interview with Angela Wright.

"consistently pressure": Wright's deposition was taken prior to both

Hill's and Thomas's testimony, but only became a sworn affidavit on the Monday after the hearings, when she and her attorney got it notarized.

"In general": Deposition of Angela Wright, p. 16.

"You ought to": Hearing, p. 53.

"he didn't seem to": Interview with Angela Wright.

133   *"I said something"*: Deposition of Angela Wright, p. 48.

"I really love": The original account came from Rose Jourdain, who mentioned it to congressional investigators. Wright said she had been too embarrassed to discuss it with investigators, but she nonetheless confirmed the incident in an interview after the hearings. Also, interview with Angela Wright.

134   *Wright's friend:* Skeptics might suggest that Jourdain colluded with Wright to lie about Thomas. But Jourdain had been hospitalized when Wright was deposed. And Wright had refused to tell investigators Jourdain's whereabouts because she didn't want her friend bothered. They nevertheless found her in the hospital. When asked, Jourdain specifically told investigators that she and Wright had not discussed Thomas's behavior in years. Jourdain, on page 23 of her deposition on October 13, told investigators that she had not heard from Wright, who had been deposed on October 10, for at least a week to ten days, and then Wright had only called to ask about her health.

"When Ms. Wright": Jourdain also independently recalled that Wright had told her that Thomas had "the nerve to show up at her house . . . unannounced." Wright had called Jourdain shortly afterward and implored the older woman to advise her, asking, "What do you do about this sort of thing?"

135   *"wait for him"*: Deposition of Angela Wright, p. 30.

136   *Looking back:* Interview with Angela Wright.

"there seemed to be": Conversation with Specter recalled by Specter as taking place on September 27; see p. 245.

A third African-American: Interview with Sukari Hardnett.

137   *Hardnett recalled:* The woman in question, Aysa McCullough, confirmed the substance of the original conversation, recalling that it touched on what men and women want and how he felt about wanting no further children. But she said she did not find it strange, for she already knew Thomas socially and considered such chitchat appropriate considering that it took place in the office late, after working hours had ended.

139   *"Clarence and I"*: Hearing, p. 383.

140   *After Reagan's reelection:* Interview with Michael Middleton.

PAGE

140 *Thomas replaced Middleton:* Zuckerman confirmation proceedings and Howard Kurtz, "EEOC Aide Saw Lower Wages as Way to Beat Discrimination," *Washington Post,* March 5, 1986.

141 *One theory that seemed:* There are many articles exploring Thomas's interest in natural law theory, including David Lauter, "Justices Often Use Natural Law Concepts; Constitution's Vagueness May Require It," *Los Angeles Times,* September 12, 1991. Lewis Lehrman outlined his belief that natural law would prohibit abortion in an article, "The Declaration of Independence and the Right to Life: One Leads Unmistakably from the Other," *American Spectator,* April 1987. Thomas praised this article in a speech two months later at the Heritage Foundation, saying, "Lewis Lehrman's recent essay in the *American Spectator* on the Declaration of Independence and the meaning of the right to life is a splendid example of applying natural law." But at his confirmation hearings, Thomas distanced himself from natural law theory.

143 *"not brought to":* Interview with Senator Howard Metzenbaum.
By September: Interview with Clint Bolick.

144 *"It's a proud moment":* Williams, *Atlantic Monthly.*
While in the capital: Laura Blumenfeld, "The Nominee's Soulmate," *Washington Post,* September 10, 1991.

145 *Lamp withdrew:* Blumenfeld, "The Nominee's Soulmate."
"If you were not": Heritage Foundation Lecture, June 1987.

6: BENCHED

147 *Hill had never taught:* Hill's birthday was July 30.

150 *"She said that it":* Susan Dunham confirmed this conversation.

152 *During their dinner:* Interview with Patrick McGuigan.

153 *Whatever else the two:* McGuigan had opposed Bush's nomination of Robert Edward Jones to the District Court in Oregon because Jones had written an expansive opinion restricting the regulation of obscenity.
"intellectual feasts": Interview with Boyden Gray, 1989.

155 *"When I heard":* Interview with a former Justice Department official who requested anonymity.
"He wasn't getting": Interview with Eddie Mahe.

156 *"You know he's":* Interview with Angela Wright.
"swore revenge": Interview with Armstrong Williams.
"Armstrong knows": Interview with Angela Wright.

157 *"Suddenly, in like":* Interview with Barbara Arnwine.

157 *"You can't know"*: Interview with George Kassouf.

158 *"I wanted you"*: Ibid.

159 *In the months*: Gary Lee, "Nominee Thomas Finds No Middle Ground," *Washington Post*, August 9, 1991.

"I think": Letter from William Coleman to President Bush, October 31, 1989.

162 *"the Bush administration"*: Interview with an eyewitness to the swearing-in who wishes to remain anonymous.

Unlike his speeches: Interviews were conducted with numerous court clerks, none of whom felt free to speak on the record.

163 *Thomas's performance*: The professor was Ronald Rotunda.

164 *"out of control"*: In a published article and in a speech to the conservative Cato Institute, Thomas had hailed North for standing up to Congress. In 1988, while still at the EEOC, Thomas had written, "As Lt. Col. Oliver North made perfectly clear last summer, it is Congress that is out of control," and he told the Cato audience that Congress had "beat an ignominious retreat before North's direct attack on it." Both the National Association of Criminal Defense Lawyers, a generally liberal group and Bruce Shapiro of Supreme Court Watch, another liberal advocacy group, were critical of Thomas's failure to withdraw in the case given his stated sympathies for North.

So in July 1990: Interview with a member of the White House counsel's office.

7: MARSHALL'S HEIR

169 *"some of the far right"*: Ruth Marcus, "What Does Bush Really Believe?," *Washington Post*, August 18, 1992.

171 *"go to the mat"*: Quayle was quoted by Danforth in an interview; also confirmed in interview with William Kristol.

"vicious as political": Interview with Senator John Danforth.

"do anything I can": Ibid.

175 *As they pored*: Data from *USA Today*, July 5, 1991.

176 *"We have to walk"*: Interview with David Demarest.

177 *"Commercially, for him"*: Jeffrey Birnbaum, "Bush's Use of Lobbyist in Nomination of Thomas Leads to Anger and Envy," *Wall Street Journal*, July 18, 1991.

178 *"The Thomas fight"*: Interview with Anthony Podesta.

179 *"perception of indecision"*: Interview with Fred McClure.

Immediately after: Dan Fesperman, "Sun Reporter Aids Thomas," *Baltimore Sun*. Parsons retired from the *Sun* in January 1992.

179   *"The idea was":* Baltimore Sun, June 2, 1992.
181   *Jordan didn't know:* Interview with an acquaintance of Thomas's.
182   *"grow":* Interview with Vernon Jordan.
185   *Roy Allen:* Sharon LaFraniere, "Hometown Wellwishers Take Bus to Breakfast with a Favorite Son," *Washington Post,* August 1, 1991.

8: ARMIES OF THE RIGHT

191   *For Bauer:* Ruth Marcus, "Thomas Refuses to State View on Abortion Issue," *Washington Post,* September 12, 1991. The 1986 Bauer Report is discussed in numerous articles, including Lee May, "Panel Asks Curbs in Unwed Mothers' Aid," *Los Angeles Times,* November 14, 1986. See also Jane Mayer, "Welfare System Causes an Array of Family Ills," *Wall Street Journal,* June 13, 1986.
192   *All he lacked:* James M. Perry and John Harwood, "Kristol, White House's 'Smartest Guy,' Is Leading Quayle Defenders Against Administration Critics," *Wall Street Journal,* July 30, 1992.
196   *With his cherubic smile:* Eric Lichtblau, "A Savvy Free Agent for God," *Los Angeles Times,* November 26, 1989.
200   *"We touched a nerve":* Brown would emerge again in the 1992 election as the champion of Gennifer Flowers, the bleached-blond lounge singer who claimed to be Governor Bill Clinton's lover for twelve years and who had taped several conversations with him. Brown used the Flowers tapes to make ads attacking Clinton. And later, although a champion of Thomas against Anita Hill, Brown helped publicize the accusations of another Arkansas woman, Paula Jones, who alleged that Clinton had sexually harassed her by allegedly making a lewd come-on.
201   *At their instigation:* Photograph, *New York Times,* September 11, 1991.

9: THE STEALTH CANDIDATE

204   *"politics of paralysis":* Interview with Roger Craver.
205   *While these were:* Because of the extremely narrow scope of the anti-lobbying act, the involvement of the White House in direct grass-roots lobbying activities to generate congressional support for Thomas may have been legal. The act prohibits such lobbying to influence members of Congress "to favor or oppose, by vote or otherwise, any legislation or appropriation by Congress." Since a nomination isn't legislation or an appropriation, some lawyers in the White House counsel's office

argued in interviews that their activities weren't covered by the act. But other White House officials say they were careful to circumscribe their activities to keep them within the anti-lobbying law.

211 *The trickiest question:* But Duberstein did figure out how the story of the abortion might nonetheless be put to use. In a completely off-the-record conversation — which meant that the information was barred from ever getting into print — he hinted at Thomas's open-mindedness concerning his sister to the *New York Times,* evidently in hopes of softening the influential liberal paper's coverage of the nominee.

212 *In the last week:* Interview with Terry Adamson.

214 *"some concern was expressed":* Interview with Senator Joseph Biden. *In truth:* Richard Ben Cramer, *What It Takes* (New York: Random House, 1992).

10: A DUTY TO REPORT

221 *Clarence Thomas was:* Susan Hoerchner said Hill told her her stomach turned (p. 267).

222 *Although she had decided:* These early reactions of Hill to the Thomas nomination are derived from comments she made to friends and relatives at the time.

230 *That August day:* Report of the Temporary Special Independent Counsel, 1992.

231 *Laster began:* The two women were Judy Winston and Allyson Duncan.

232 *Laster reported back:* Brudney declined to be interviewed. Critics of Hill would later theorize that she and Brudney together concocted her charge against Thomas. The theory rested on the word of two of Thomas's main defenders, Armstrong Williams and Diane Holt, both of whom alleged that Hill and Brudney had had a close and possibly romantic relationship while she worked at the EEOC. In his unreleased deposition, Williams told Senate investigators that while he worked with Hill in 1983, she boasted of her friendship with Brudney. "She let me know that he was on the staff of a senator," said Williams. He added in an interview with Larry King, "One of her good friends was Jim Brudney from Senator Metzenbaum's office."

But Brudney did not join Metzenbaum's staff until 1985, two years after Hill left Washington. For the entire time that Williams said Hill boasted of his Senate job, Brudney was at a private law firm.

Diane Holt did not testify about Hill's alleged closeness to Brudney, but she later told David Brock that while working at the EEOC, Hill talked about going out with Brudney and even "mentioned several times having spent the weekend at his apartment at Foggy Bottom, I think."

But Brudney never lived in the neighborhood known as Foggy Bottom. And for almost the entire time that Hill worked at the EEOC, from 1981 until 1983, he was living elsewhere in Washington with the woman he went on to marry. Both Hill and a spokesman for Brudney say they were only casual acquaintances in law school with no social relationship whatsoever afterward. Mutual friends, such as the Yale law professor Stephen Carter, confirmed this account, as did colleagues of Brudney's in Metzenbaum's office, who observed his confusion about who Hill was.

232   *"There is this question":* Interview with Anita Hill.

234   *Impressed with Hill's:* Some might be surprised that a senator's staff felt free to go this far in such a politically charged investigation on its own, without checking with the elected officeholder. But the dismantling of the seniority system and the creation of a profusion of new committees and subcommittees that sprang from the congressional reforms after Watergate gave congressional aides enormous autonomy. By 1991, officeholders were so overextended that inevitably their staffs initiated action on various issues, even controversial ones.

235   *"If that's sexual":* Interview with Hays Gorey.
         The following day: Interview with Harriet Grant and Special Counsel's Report.

236   *"From her perspective":* Interview with a Judiciary Committee staff member.

11: THE LEAK

245   *As for the Democrats:* Interview with Senator Hank Brown and interview with a staff member of Senator Brown's.

246   *"panic":* "Panic" is how Thomas told Danforth that he reacted (*Resurrection*, p. 33). In addition, Thomas is quoted as saying, "I was just sick. I felt like throwing up (p. 34).
         When the agents: There has been some confusion about the date of the FBI's interview of Thomas. During the hearing, Thomas said he was questioned on a Thursday afternoon (p. 203), but he also said he was questioned on a Wednesday afternoon (p. 182). Others recalled Wednesday, September 25, as the correct date.

247   *"whether or not":* Danforth, *Resurrection*, p. 40.

249   *Hill, who had taken:* Again, Hill sought Brudney's counsel. On that

Wednesday, Brudney told her he was preparing a memo on sexual harassment in order to clarify the legal standing of her allegations, and needed a thorough account of her charges if he was going to succeed in getting Metzenbaum to intervene on Hill's behalf to delay the vote. He suggested Hill send him a copy of her statement to the Judiciary Committee. Hill was reluctant, and agreed only after Brudney promised not to show it to anyone else. She then faxed him an undated and unsigned copy of her statement. But even with this, Brudney was unsure after researching the law whether Thomas's behavior constituted illegal behavior. At the time Hill had worked for Thomas the legal standard was far more narrow than in 1991. Instead of zealously promoting Hill's cause, Brudney's memo was thus full of caveats, and as such was never forwarded by his supervisor to Metzenbaum.

249 *With nowhere to turn:* The friend Hill contacted was her former roommate in Washington, Sonia Jarvis. Jarvis, a lawyer and Democratic activist, had some knowledge of how the political game was played. She in turn called an aide to Simon whom she knew. As it turned out, Simon had just been told that day by Ted Kennedy that there was an affidavit from a woman charging Thomas with sexual harassment. Learning of Hill's allegations, Simon found Biden in the Senate cloakroom and was given a brief description of Hill's charges, which, Biden warned, had to be kept confidential.

Simon told Biden: Interview with Senator Paul Simon.

250 *On Friday morning:* Hill's friend was Sonia Jarvis.

251 *Alarmed that the unexpected:* Mitchell and Dole attempted to set the vote for Friday, October 4, but failed to get unanimous consent when Metzenbaum protested.

253 *That Saturday:* Clearly, however, because of her advisory role, Lichtman was extremely well informed about Hill's charges. And unlike Hill, whose motive was to provide the Senate with information that she felt was relevant to Thomas's qualifications to serve on the Supreme Court, Lichtman was dedicated to killing the nomination.

By midweek: Report of the Temporary Special Independent Counsel, p. 60.

Phelps, meanwhile: Phelps and Winternitz, *Capitol Games*, p. 229. The book does not identify Simon as the senator with whom Phelps conversed, but numerous other sources make it possible to identify Simon as the senator who provided Phelps with the information necessary to pursue the Anita Hill story.

254 *Phelps and Totenberg:* Interview with Nina Totenberg. Totenberg said

she only became aware that Phelps too was chasing the Hill story toward the very end of the week.

255 *Paul Simon:* During the hearings, Simon made a point of denying that he had ever leaked Hill's statement to anyone. Since he was dealing with Phelps, and Phelps never did get the statement, this seems to support his denial. But oddly, when Phelps's and Totenberg's news accounts did run, both quoted Simon by name, saying he had not been informed of Hill's charges before the Judiciary Committee vote. This was false — but created a protective impression of ignorance on his part. Simon had not only seen the FBI report by then, he had even talked to Hill before the vote. Later, he said he had merely misspoken.

By Saturday, October 5: Phelps and Winternitz, *Capitol Games,* p. 231. "Hill did not want attention," Phelps wrote. "Hill said she would talk to me only if I could get the statement she had sent the Senate. She would confirm what was in her statement, but she refused to be the one to open the floodgates of the national media."

In fact, that Saturday: Brudney obtained his draft in order to write the harassment memo for Senator Metzenbaum.

256 *"it was a call":* Interview with Michael Middleton.

257 *"I was told":* Hearing, p. 233.

12: NAIVE, NOT STUPID

258 *"My parents are older":* Anita Hill's quotes are from *Essence Magazine,* March 1992.

260 *"The Gary Hart situation":* *Essence Magazine,* March 1992.

261 *"Hill confronted":* Rosemary Bray, "Thomas-Hill Hearing Raised Deeply Buried Issues," *New York Times Magazine,* November 17, 1991.

264 *"it was only then":* Brock suggested that Hill misled the FBI because she told them that she had not confided in her boyfriend at the time, yet she had told Carr. But Hill said she forgot she told Carr, and neither she nor Carr considered themselves boyfriend and girlfriend. Carr later said that their relationship had largely been a long-distance phone friendship, so he didn't think it odd that she seemed to have forgotten about him when trying to recall corroborating witnesses. He had more or less forgotten about her too.

"If it's any comfort": Brock would later accuse Carr of being unsure whether Hill was specifically referring to Thomas, but Carr said in an interview that although he can't say with legal certainty that Hill

named Thomas in that conversation, he knew with complete certainty that Hill was referring to Thomas, since this was one of many conversations they had had about him. And although he wasn't sure that Thomas's name was spoken per se, he specifically remembered referring to the irony that the head of the EEOC of all people would be sexually harassing an employee at work.

265   *"My God"*: Interview with Joel Paul.

268   *"no merit"*: Danforth, *Resurrection,* p. 48.

        "It seemed so shortsighted": Interview with Patricia King.

269   *Throughout the afternoon*: Interview with an aide to Senator Danforth, who requested anonymity.

271   *Biden also acceded*: Danforth, *Resurrection,* p. 84.

        Biden did balk: Danforth said later, "It was just clear that the longer this went on, the more these groups, staffers, and press, and the whole pack was just going to continue to — there would be one thing after another, just as it had been ever since July first that these people would just not stop it. Now it's Anita Hill, what's it's going to be tomorrow? This is just going to continue. This is the pack chasing the rabbit and this just has to end."

272   *On Wednesday morning*: Interview with Shirley Wiegand.

        A number of lawyers: Interview with Charles Ogletree.

273   *As the hearings*: At her press conference, she had stressed that she was not out to defeat Clarence Thomas but simply to provide relevant information to the committee. And during the hearings, she insisted that she had maintained a distance from the organized forces against Thomas, testifying that at no time did any political group or individual urge her to speak out against him. Technically, this may have been accurate, since no activist actually pushed Hill to do so. Yet Hill had been receiving advice from declared opponents of Thomas, including Judith Lichtman, the head of the Women's Legal Defense Fund. And in deciding on her lawyers, she did not turn away additional volunteer help from friends, even though some were identified with liberal causes or groups opposing Thomas.

274   *"Naive"*: Interview with Shirley Wiegand.

        By the time: "During the preceding week (before the second round of hearings), we had a couple of late-night conference calls with Charles," recalled Christopher Edley, another Harvard law professor with Democratic connections. The lobbying campaign to get Ogletree to take Hill's case involved Tribe, Susan Estrich, the law professor who had served as Michael Dukakis's campaign manager, and Kathleen Sullivan, another professor. "He didn't want to take the lead counsel role," said Edley. " We were pushing him as hard as we could."

275   *On Thursday morning:* Interview with Donald Green, John Frank, and Janet Napolitano.

276   *When Ogletree finally:* American Lawyer, December 1991.

278   *In fact, it was:* The Hill team expected two additional panels of witnesses: a set of character witnesses including her former roommate, Sonia Jarvis, and the law school's Dean Swank; and a panel of sexual harassment experts. Neither was used during the hearings.

13: HIGH-TECH LYNCHING

280   *"I thought":* Interview with Senator John Danforth.

281   *"the jackpot":* Ibid.

283   *"Get the fucking":* Interview with an aide to Biden who tried to get the OPM file.

Hill's employment records: In an interview after the hearings, Hope still insisted that she did have a recollection of Hill's having been in deep professional trouble at Wald, Harkrader. She also said she hadn't confused Hill with another black female associate who worked at the firm at the same time. In an interview, Thomas Dadou of Senator Specter's staff described Hope's memory as vague. He said he learned that Hope had information about Hill's past employment troubles from Ricky Silberman. "She told me that Judy Hope could confirm that Anita Hill got fired. I thought that might be important," Dadou said. "We pursued that. But Judy Hope said, 'I can't confirm it.'"

"I'd known Boyden": After John Burke supplied his affidavit to the committee in which he alleged that he'd told Hill to find work elsewhere, several former Wald partners found the firm's associate evaluations, which contained no indication that Hill had been dismissed. Republicans moved to subpoena the records, but Biden, in consultation with Hill's lawyers, refused. They were concerned that the Republicans would sensationalize the few negative appraisals of Hill's work and overlook the fact that the majority were positive.

284   *"I don't remember":* Hearing, p. 325.

"I never got any sense": Hearing, p. 339.

285   *"I figured":* Interview with John Doggett.

286   *Williams supplied:* Interview with Armstrong Williams.

287   *"It is my recollection":* Interview with Al Golub.

Before the hearings: Interview with Senator John Danforth.

288   *"like something was inside":* Danforth, Resurrection, p. 106.

"crying and hyperventilating": Ibid., p. 108.

288 *"That stout man":* Interview with Leola Williams.

289 *"angels": People,* November 11, 1991.
 As Biden spoke: Danforth, *Resurrection,* p. 128.

290 *"not worth it":* Hearing, p. 172.
 "the public had no idea": Danforth, *Resurrection,* p. 123.

293 *"I don't know why":* Interview with Anita Hill.
 It fell mostly: "I publicly disagreed with the president who said he was the best qualified and named others who were better qualified," Specter said in an interview after the hearings ("A Conversation with Arlen Specter, *Daily Record,* October 18, 1992). "And I also publicly disagreed with the president that race was not a factor because I think race was a factor, and a relevant factor. I believe that it is indispensable, not optional, but indispensable that there be an African-American on the Supreme Court."

297 *"Oh my God":* Interview with an aide to Biden.

298 *"I'm not going to":* Interview with Senator Orrin Hatch.

299 *"When are you going":* Ibid.

300 *According to one of:* Alabama's Senator Thomas "Cotton Tom" Heflin is quoted in James E. Goodman's *Stories of Scottsboro* (New York: Pantheon Books, 1994), warning that if the Scottsboro Boys were not hanged, it would place "wicked thoughts in the minds of the lawless Negro men."
 "You hit a home run": Danforth, *Resurrection,* p. 149.
 "Senator, you just saved": Interviews with Senator Orrin Hatch and Nina Totenberg. Totenberg recalled this encounter but said her exact words were "Senator, you saved his butt." She did not recall Hatch then saying that Thomas had saved himself.

14: EROTOMANIA AND OTHER MALADIES

301 *Hatch, however:* Danforth said that it was one of the Justice Department lawyers working for Mike Luttig who first remembered the pubic hair line from *The Exorcist.* And he says it was Thomas's successor at the EEOC, Evan Kemp, who first found the Long Dong Silver reference in an earlier sexual harassment case (*Resurrection,* p. 152).

302 *No one ever produced:* Interview with Anita Hill.

304 *Biden was also:* Duberstein's account that Biden initially said he would issue a statement supporting Thomas's character appears in Danforth, *Resurrection,* p. 53.

305 *Consequently, the Democrats:* The Republicans never directly accused Hill or Jarvis of lesbianism. But Thomas was able to use his descrip-

tion of Hill's roommate — whom he pointedly described as wearing "sweats from a basketball game or something" — to suggest that Hill was rooming with a woman who had notably mannish attributes. And Senator Simpson came close by saying, ". . . if we had 104 days to go into Ms. Hill and find out about her character, her background, her proclivities, and all the rest I would feel a lot better about this system." In fact, in the few days they did have, a stab was made at exploring these so-called proclivities. Jarvis herself heard that the Republicans had been asking questions about her personal life. And Hill and Wiegand later learned that gay bars in Norman had received anonymous phone calls asking if either of them was a frequenter, which they were not.

306 *The Republicans were reaching:* According to Danforth in *Resurrection,* Dr. Satinover, who is not named, made contact with the White House on Friday night (p. 168). But in an interview, Dr. Satinover said he believed it was Saturday night.

307 *By the light of day:* Thomas's defenders also decided against calling Dr. Satinover because they feared his ties to the Bush family would undermine his credibility (Danforth, *Resurrection,* p. 169).

308 *"In the context of":* Hearing, p. 348.
"it was just further degradation": Danforth, *Resurrection,* p. 182.

309 *Danforth was more than:* Ibid., p. 170.

310 *Before Dietz left:* Alarmed by the Republicans' use of psychiatrists, the Democrats decided that they too had better seek professional medical advice, and on the Monday after the hearings they reached a professor of psychiatry at Columbia University, Robert Spitzer. Dr. Spitzer, who edited the basic diagnostic textbook used throughout North America, ruled out any possibility that Hill could be suffering from erotomania. But he was a bit late.
When Hill's name surfaced: Reached for comment about his role a year later, Brett Godfrey wouldn't comment on the record. But a number of others involved were more forthcoming.

311 *But as of Saturday:* Hearing, p. 235.
Since the younger Godfrey: According to a Brown aide, Lee Rawls of the Justice Department and Jim Dire of the White House tried to convince the Godfreys to take a public role.

312 *After a brief search:* Interview with Larry Shiles.

313 *"far-fetched":* Danforth, *Resurrection.*

314 *Danforth's top staff:* Ibid., pp. 162, 163.
"about the business": Wilson was quoted about making Hill's life a "living hell" in *Newsweek* (February 10, 1992); at the time, he was

youth coordinator for the Patrick Buchanan campaign. Other Wilson quotes are from our interviews with him.

315 *Simpson made the faxes:* Interview with a roommate of Chris Wilson's.

317 *The notion that Hill:* In *The Real Anita Hill,* David Brock also posits the theory that Roggerson might have harassed Hill. Besides the fact that neither Berry nor Brock provides any evidence to support this theory, Hill denied emphatically that Roggerson had ever harassed her or that she had ever complained of sexual harassment by anyone other than Thomas.

318 *"Discussed that this man":* Hearing, p.327.
None of the senators: Deposition of Diane Holt-Norwood, October 10, 1991, p. 13.
Perhaps most dispiriting: Jackson's account is based on Brudney's notes, confirmed by Hill in our interview.
"Anita . . . referred": Hearing, p. 552.

319 *"There is a reason":* Interview with Anita Hill.
"We had evidence": Interview with Charles Ogletree.

15: THE OTHER WOMEN

321 *Angela Wright was:* Interview with Angela Wright.

323 *"As soon as":* Interview with Mark Schwartz.
No one understood: According to Danforth's account in *Resurrection* (p. 119), he personally saw Wright as "no threat at all" because after reading her deposition, he thought "her story seemed weak and open to attack on cross-examination," so that her appearance might actually benefit Thomas. However, there is no evidence that Danforth or any of the Republicans wanted to call Wright, and instead, according to Biden and his staff, the Republicans uniformly opposed calling her.

324 *But now that this threshold:* Later, during the hearings, Thomas himself would subscribe to the theory that a pattern was usually a prerequisite to harassment, suggesting that in his experience with such cases as chairman of the EEOC, "What we would generally find is . . . a pattern of that kind of practice . . . when you find a person who has engaged in grotesque conduct or harassing conduct, you will find more than one [victim]."
By the time Wright: Jane Shoemaker, the executive editor of the *Charlotte Observer* and Wright's boss, confirms her account.

325 *Armstrong Williams claimed:* Interview with Armstrong Williams.
Privately, Duberstein: Interview with an aide to Biden and confirmed by a source close to Duberstein.

326   *That same Thursday:* Silberman quote, *Los Angeles Times,* October
11, 1991. In a similar vein, Wright said in an interview that she
believed Silberman had been out to get her and had convinced Thomas
to fire her after a press conference ran into trouble.

328   *"She started to tell":* Interview with Jamin Raskin.
"People wanted to see": Interview with Sarah Bloom.

329   *Although noncommittal:* After they were sent on to the special counsel
investigating the leak, copies of Schwartz's notes were made available
to the authors.
"Clarence finds pornography": Letter to the committee from Evan
Kemp.

330   *In the days before:* Neither Cooke nor Jones would comment on the
record about these negotiations, but Edley and Arnwine and Payton
all described the effort to get Cooke to come forward, and Edley also
reviewed his notes from the conference call with Cooke. Reached on
two separate occasions, Cooke would neither confirm nor deny the
account on the record.

331   *Thus, with committee action:* Two Biden aides independently confirmed that word of Cooke and his story reached the committee,
although Biden said he could not recall whether he heard it himself.

333   *"did not permit even consensual":* Hearing, p. 565.

334   *"It bothered me":* Interview with Sukari Hardnett.

335   *The meeting soon dissolved:* Interview with an aide to a Republican
member of the committee.

336   *Looking back:* Interview with Senator Joseph Biden.

337   *"I could have brought":* E. J. Dionne, Jr., "On Once and Future
Supreme Court Nominations," *Washington Post,* June 19, 1992.
As Biden saw it: Cramer, *What It Takes,* p. 710.
"in fairness to Thomas": Dionne, "Once and Future Supreme Court
Nominations."

343   *"We were waiting":* Interview with Anita Hill.
"These people didn't want": Interview with Rose Jourdain.
"Dr Ms. Wright": Hearing, p. 407.

344   *The upshot:* In *Resurrection* (pp. 174–75), Danforth overlooked these
drawn-out negotiations, which have been confirmed by Wright, Middlebrooks, and several members of Biden's staff, and so misleadingly
stated only that an unnamed "Judiciary Committee staff member"
phoned Angela Wright's lawyer to determine her preference with respect to appearing. When the staff member hung up the phone he
reported to the committee, "She's not going to testify." Danforth also

PAGE

said that this call took place on Sunday afternoon, well before Wright and her lawyer recall giving up.

345 *Polls taken:* Before the hearings, a CBS News/New York Times poll showed that 47 percent of those polled thought Hill's charges were untrue, whereas 27 percent believed her. The rest were undecided. On Sunday night, the companies polled again and found that the undecideds had shifted to Thomas's side, with 58 percent now believing him and 24 percent believing Hill.

346 *A change of planes:* David Maraniss and Jim McGee, "Anita Hill Facing Anger and Finding Peace," *Washington Post,* October 20, 1991.

348 *As the hour:* See also Danforth, *Resurrection,* p. 195, for a fuller account of Thomas bathing during the vote.

349 *But she was:* That evening Leola Williams was hospitalized for heart palpitations. A year later, she was still mad at Biden and the other Democratic senators. "I know they say you should love your enemy," she said, "but I cannot love those people. That Kennedy, that Biden, that Metzenbaum, Leahy, and Heflin, they should all be thrown in the garbage."

EPILOGUE

352 *A year after the hearings:* Suzanne Garment, "Confirming Anita Hill?," *American Spectator,* January/February 1993.

353 *The members of the:* Interview with Alan Simpson.

354 *"if the polls are correct":* Dionne, "Once and Future Supreme Court Nominations."
"if you are yourself": Danforth, *Resurrection,* p. 28.

355 *However, rather than setting:* Joan Biskupic, "Thomas's Speech to Georgia Group May Have Violated Judicial Code," *Washington Post,* May 8, 1993.

356 *In March 1992:* The best account of Thomas's ties to right-wing interest groups appears in Toobin, "The Burden of Clarence Thomas."
Although many of the justices: The Court ruled unanimously in favor of the religious institution, Lamb's Chapel Church, with Thomas and Justice Antonin Scalia filing a concurring opinion that went further toward Free Congress's position, according to Timothy Phelps, Los Angeles Times/Washington Post News Service, October 17, 1993.

358 *"the concepts of dignity":* Paul M. Barrett, "Thomas Is Emerging as Strong Conservative Out to Prove Himself," *Wall Street Journal,* April 27, 1993.

359   *"basically in Scalia's pocket"*: Joan Biskupic, "Scalia, Thomas Stand
      Apart on the Right," *Washington Post,* June 24, 1994.
      "I have not seen": Ruth Marcus, "Justice Souter, Thomas Follow
      Separate Paths," *Washington Post,* July 5, 1992.
      "I, along with": Trevor W. Coleman, "Betrayed: Clarence Thomas'
      Former Supporters," *Emerge Magazine,* November 1993.

360   *"lacked humanity"*: Coleman, "Betrayed."
      "I simply continue": Joan Biskupic, "For Justice Thomas, Work Is
      Refuge," *Washington Post,* April 19, 1993.
      But Thomas himself: Barrett, "Thomas Is Emerging."

Index

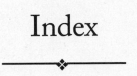

speaking invitation from Hill, 280–81; and phone calls from Hill, 281–82; White House effort, 282–83; witnesses to show Hill romantically scorned, 283–86; and Doggett, 284–85, 296–97, 306, 319, 339, 343; witnesses to show Hill professionally thwarted, 286–87; pessimism in, 287; organizing of grass-roots support, 288–89; attempt to show feminist motivation, 295–96; racial stereotype strategy, 299–300; supporting witnesses, 306, 317–19, 339, 342; effort to portray Hill as erotomaniac, 306–10; "pube" affidavit and allegation of "Long Dong Silver" remark at Oral Roberts, 310–14, 319, 334–35; student complaints against Hill instigated, 314–15; attacks on Hill's corroborating witnesses, 315–17; and Wright, 323–27, 332; post-hearing attacks on Hill, 347

AS IMBALANCED OR BIASED PROCESS: requirement that Hill initiate contact, 236; and Danforth's zeal, 247, 303–4, 309–10, 313–14; time constraints against Hill, 270–71; Republicans as partisan vs. Democrats as neutral, 271, 274, 304; use of phone logs, 282; White House exemption from Privacy Act, 282, 325, 342; Hill's but not Thomas's personal life probed, 296, 336; Doggett ruled in but detractors ruled out, 297; Democrats' disarray and failure to press Thomas, 305

SEQUEL: Hill's trip home and appearance at rally, 346–47; senators' announcements of intentions and speeches, 347–48; vote, 348; Thomas's reaction, 348–49; swearing-in ceremonies, 349–50, 355; reporters learn of Thomas's pornography interest, 350–51. *See also* Hill's allegations against Thomas

Congress, Thomas on (North case), 164
Congressional Black Caucus, 182
Conservatism: cultural, 13; as concern in hearings, 25, 210; Thomas's success as argument for, 32; judicial (Thomas), 163; and Thomas on Supreme Court, 355

Conservatives: Bush's promise to, 11–12; and Marshall's retirement, 15; Religious Right, 16–17, 191–98, 208–9, 294, 314; Bush challenged by, 17–18; Straussians in Reagan administration, 141; Thomas's appeal to, 170; and anti-Bork groups, 193; and 1992 Republican convention, 351; and Thomas after confirmation, 355–57. *See also* Black conservatives

Consultants in Washington, 25
Cooke, Frederick Douglass, Jr., 107–8, 264, 330, 335
Coombs, Mary, 89
Cooper, Ranny, 240
Cormier, Rufus, 62
Corr, Bill, 229
Council of One Hundred, 151
Craver, Roger, 204, 353
Crawford, Hiram, 195
Cribb, T. Kenneth, Jr., 78
Cruz, Nestor, 126
Culvahouse, A. B., 211
Cutler, Lloyd, 275–76

Dadou, Thomas, 277, 301
Dallas Cowboys, Thomas as fan of, 80
Danforth, John C. (Jack), 18, 62–63; Thomas quoted by, 8; and appearance offered by Thomas, 58; Thomas works for in Missouri, 63–68; and *Roe v. Wade*, 67; Thomas works for in Washington, 69; and Thomas for Circuit Court, 160; and Thomas in Ralston Purina case, 163; and Thomas as Supreme Court nominee, 170; and civil rights bill, 181; at Supreme Court "murder boards," 211; at confirmation hearings, 215, 217, 289; and Hill's allegations, 246, 247, 263, 270; and floor vote scheduling, 251, 269–70; Thomas confesses to about blue movies, 271; and attacks on Hill, 280–81; on Thomas's spirit, 287–88; and Specter's role, 293; and